Enoch Powell and
of Postcolonial Britain

Camilla Schofield

CAMBRIDGE
UNIVERSITY PRESS

CAMBRIDGE
UNIVERSITY PRESS

University Printing House, Cambridge CB2 8BS, United Kingdom

Cambridge University Press is part of the University of Cambridge.

It furthers the University's mission by disseminating knowledge in the pursuit of education, learning and research at the highest international levels of excellence.

www.cambridge.org
Information on this title: www.cambridge.org/9781107595477

© Camilla Schofield 2013

First published 2013
First paperback edition 2015

A catalogue record for this publication is available from the British Library

Library of Congress Cataloguing in Publication data
Schofield, Camilla, 1978–
Enoch Powell and the making of postcolonial Britain / Camilla Schofield.
    pages   cm
ISBN 978-1-107-00794-9 (hardback)
1. Powell, J. Enoch (John Enoch), 1912–1998.   2. Great Britain – Politics
and government – 1945–1964.   3. Great Britain – Politics and government –
1964–1979.   4. Imperialism – Government policy – Great Britain –
History – 20th century.   5. Decolonization – Great Britain –
Colonies – History – 20th century.   6. Politicians – Great Britain –
Biography.   I. Title.
DA591.P64S37 2013
941.085–dc23   2012048494

ISBN 978-1-107-00794-9 Hardback
ISBN 978-1-107-59547-7 Paperback

Enoch Powell and the Making of Postcolonial Britain

Enoch Powell's explosive rhetoric against black immigration and anti-discrimination law transformed the terrain of British race politics and cast a long shadow over British society. Using extensive archival research, Camilla Schofield offers a radical reappraisal of Powell's political career and insists that his historical significance is inseparable from the political generation he sought to represent. *Enoch Powell and the Making of Postcolonial Britain* follows Powell's trajectory from an officer in the British Raj to the centre of British politics and, finally, to his turn to Ulster Unionism. She argues that Powell and the mass movement against 'New Commonwealth' immigration that he inspired shed light on Britain's war generation, popular understandings of the welfare state and the significance of memories of war and empire in the making of postcolonial Britain. Through Powell, Schofield illuminates the complex relationship between British social democracy, racism and the politics of imperial decline in Britain.

CAMILLA SCHOFIELD is a lecturer in Imperial History at the University of East Anglia and teaches classes on collective memory, British imperialism and modern Britain.

For my dad and in memory of Bua

Skin-colour is like a uniform.
Enoch Powell, 1978

The symbols of social order – the police, the bugle calls in the barracks, military parades and waving flags – are at once and the same time inhibitory and stimulating: for they do not convey the message 'Don't dare to budge'; they cry out 'Get ready to attack.'

Frantz Fanon, 1961

Contents

Acknowledgments

The research for this book was made possible thanks to the work of archivists and librarians at the Churchill Archive, the Birmingham City Library, the Staffordshire Record Office, the Conservative Party Archive at Oxford University, the British Library and the National Archives at Kew Gardens. I owe particular thanks to Katharine Thomson for her meticulous work cataloguing Powell's massive collection of papers at the Churchill Archive. I would also like to thank Joseph and Alison Fox for founding the Fox Fellowship, which enabled me to spend countless hours with Enoch Powell's personal papers at Cambridge. I am also grateful to Yale University's Macmillan Center for providing further funding for me to pursue research at the Birmingham City Library and at the Staffordshire Record Office. There, in Powell's largely unpublicized constituency papers at the Staffordshire Record Office, I stumbled upon a treasure trove of evidence that Powell had deemed unsuitable for his official archive in Churchill College. The evidence I found there of Powell's obsession with the threat of anarchy in Britain in the 1960s and 1970s had a profound impact on the argument in this book. Thank you, also, to the School of History at the University of East Anglia for purchasing the rights to the cover image. Extracts of Powell's papers are published with the kind permission of The Trustees of the Literary Estate of the late J. Enoch Powell. I am also very grateful to Lord Howard of Rising for his helpful guidance on the uses of Powell's papers. In keeping with Enoch Powell's wishes, I have kept the names of his supporters anonymous and maintained the anonymity of private letters. Some names have, therefore, been changed.

This project began as a PhD dissertation. I would like to thank my PhD supervisor, Jay Winter, whose work on remembrance remains a constant inspiration for me, both in my research and my teaching. It was Jay Winter's final push and support to the end that made it possible for me to complete my doctorate. Thanks, also, to Karuna Mantena, Paul Gilroy, Jean-Christophe Agnew and Eamonn McGrattan for helping me through that process. Thank you, Emma Griffin, for reading drafts of chapters with such a keen eye. I also owe a deep debt of gratitude to Bill Schwarz for his comments on a draft of this book and for all his kind support over the years. My publisher and editors have also been particularly supportive and supremely patient. Special thanks to Michael Watson at Cambridge University Press, Jamie Hood and my copy-editor, Laila Grieg-Gran. All the errors and omissions that remain in this text are, of course, definitely mine.

Friends and family made writing this book possible. Thank you, Sarah Dalton Rota, Lynsey Allett, Becky Moore, Chris Woodard, Mary and Patrick Woodard, Colin Fink, Ben and Veronica Moore, Charles and Nikki Burst, Margaret Lee, Persephone Pearl, Ben Jones, Emma Griffin, Eamonn McGrattan, Paul and Marie Crosbie, Elizabeth Prochaska, Sean Rothery, F. Matthew Frederick, Matt Pace, Rudi Zygadlo, Louise Walker, and, especially, Isobel, Tom, Liz and Norman Schofield. I am incredibly lucky to have such a supportive family. I have two final, special thanks. Bua, my dog, remained with me on both sides of the Atlantic for seven years while I worked on this book. He was my best friend and my family when I was an immigrant in England. He had a huge beautiful soul, and I will not forget him. This book is dedicated to his memory. Finally, I would like to express loving gratitude to my partner David Crosbie, who put up with three years of my mess. Thank you, love.

Introduction

Row upon row they stood to sing,
A thousand at a word,
And loud arose 'God save the King'.
But as I watched and heard,
The upturned faces in the light
Of early afternoon
Reminded me of crosses white
Beneath a silent moon.

Enoch Powell, 1938[1]

The breath which condemns submission to laws this nation has not made condemns submission to scales of value which this nation had not willed. To both sorts of submission I ascribe the haunting fear, which I am sure I am not alone in feeling, that we, the British will soon have nothing left to die for.

That was not a slip of the tongue. What a man lives for is what a man dies for, because every bit of living is a bit of dying. At the beginning I refused to define patriotism; but now at the end I venture it. Patriotism is to have a nation to die for, and to be glad to die for it – all the days of one's life.

Enoch Powell, 1977[2]

Old soldier

In February 1998, close to thirty years after Powell delivered his landmark 'Rivers of Blood' speech, he lay in state at Westminster Abbey, in the Chapel of St Faith, until his funeral at St Margaret's Church. Powell, one of the most hated and most revered of British politicians, even in death, could not avoid controversy. Criticism surrounded the fact that the Church of England had accorded the honour of lying in state in such a 'shrine of British nationhood' to a politician so much

---

[1] Enoch Powell, *Collected Poems* (London: Bellew Publishing, 1990), p. 64.
[2] Enoch Powell, *Wrestling with the Angel* (London: Sheldon Press, 1977), p. 8.

equated with racism and anti-immigrant sentiment in Britain.[3] Powell was allowed to lie in state at the Abbey's Chapel of St Faith (a third-century martyr whose name is invoked by soldiers, prisoners and pilgrims) because he had been a warden of the adjoining parliamentary church of St Margaret's and a regular communicant at Westminster Abbey – not, one Abbey divine insisted, because he was a politician. Still, anti-Powell protesters gathered outside the Abbey that day.

Due to his outspoken opposition to the rights of entry of black, New Commonwealth immigrants into Britain and his insistence that Britain needed to rid itself of its commitments to a long-dead empire, Powell was, by 1998, more than just a politician. Enoch Powell was not just a single soul due the solace of the Church; he was, rather, 'a myth, bogyman.'[4] As race relations expert Mike Phillips put it, 'I shall always think of him as part of my history and as part of my identity as a Briton.'[5] Powell was a historical symbol. The continued currency and controversy of his name attest to this. Allowing such a symbol into Westminster Abbey was, according to some, a political act.[6]

Powell's funeral service was high Anglican. His coffin was draped in the Union Jack. The choir preceded the coffin with music of high Anglican austerity.[7] A reading from A. E. Housman's poem 'A Shropshire Lad,' which Powell even in his eighties could not recite without breaking into tears, was given at the funeral.[8] This iconic and sentimental poem spoke of lost innocence and is intimately tied in Britain to the massive loss of humanity of the First World War. Significantly, Powell was buried in his brigadier's uniform. As one obituary put it, he was laid to rest, not as a scholar or politician, but 'as the old soldier he really was.'[9] He asked for a full military funeral and, over fifty years after the end of his service in the Second World War, was buried alongside his former comrades in the Royal Warwickshire Regiment. As well as indicating his embrace of hierarchy and institutional authority, this endpoint in the story of Enoch Powell reveals Powell's deep nostalgia for war service and military comradeship.

[3] Paul Vallely, 'Established Values: How the Church Nearly Lost its Way over the Death of Enoch Powell,' *The Independent*, 19 February 1998.
[4] Norman Shrapnel and Mike Phillips, 'Enoch Powell: An Enigma of Awkward Passions,' *The Guardian*, 9 February 1998.
[5] Ibid.
[6] Vallely, 'Established Values.'
[7] Paul Vallely, 'Old Order Mourns Enoch Powell,' *The Independent*, 19 February 1998.
[8] Ibid.
[9] Sarah Wilson, 'Powell Laid to Rest as the Old Soldier He Really Was,' *The Scotsman*, 19 February 1998.

Powell's desire to be buried in full military attire suggests a preoccupation with the glory of war and violence – and a performance of the lost political rectitude of, as he put, 'to kill and be killed.'[10] To many, it is the fitting endpoint of a man thought to have fascist inclinations. It is the contention of this book, however, that Powell represents something quite different in British political history than Oswald Mosley and the (distinctively unsuccessful) British Fascist movement.[11] Powell's career even fits uneasily within the political parameters of the heavily Powellite National Front party. While his political views were at times racist and authoritarian, it is important to clarify that they were grounded in a distinctively English, postwar and *postcolonial* version of nationalism. Like fascism, Powell's postcolonial nationalism relied on an obsessive preoccupation with community decline and victimhood. But whereas fascism and imperialism maintain a faith in the power of the state to transform or purify society, Powell's postcolonial nationalism was touched by the lessons of empire's end. The experience of empire left an indelible mark on Powell.

Powell's nationalism grew out of an intense belief in the necessity of allegiance to the Crown – and, more generally, to 'the unique structure of power' for which the English Crown was the 'keystone (the only conceivable and indispensable keystone).'[12] Early on in Powell's life, allegiance offered political certainty in the uncertain world of empire. As he put it to his parents when writing home from India in 1943, his willingness to sacrifice himself to Britain's 'unique structure of power' represented to him, 'the nearest thing in the world to an absolute (as opposed to a relative) value: it is like the outer circle that bound my universe, so that I cannot conceive of anything beyond it.'[13] Powell's deference to institutional authority and hierarchy was, he believed, what gave meaning or value to the individual.[14] The individual alone was a nonentity – claims of superiority, inferiority or equality would, therefore, apparently fall on deaf ears – it was the hierarchical organic (national) whole that mattered. The nation was, then, in Powell's mind a collective project; it endowed everyday life and individual aspirations with meaning. 'It enables us,' as he put it in 1965, 'to daydream as we live out our lives, as the factory-girl daydreams with the aid of her

---

[10] Letter from Powell to Ellen and Albert Powell, 19 March 1939. POLL 1.1.4.
[11] For the discussion of the need in the West to move beyond conceiving of racism in terms of (Second World War era) fascism, see Paul Gilroy, *Against Race: Imagining Political Culture Beyond the Color Line* (Cambridge, MA: Harvard University Press, 2000).
[12] Powell to Ellen and Albert Powell, 9 March 1943. POLL 1.1.5.
[13] Ibid.
[14] Enoch Powell, Bill Schwarz interview, 26 April 1988.

paperback thriller.'[15] According to Powell, then, the individual finds the essential drama, romance and moral meaning of life via the nation in history, in maps, in *identification* with the collective project of the nation. Identification with the 'power and glory' of the nation was, he argued, the very basis of social deference and political order. As Powell put it, 'If we are not to be powerful and glorious ourselves it is some compensation to think we belong to something powerful and glorious ... "thou shalt get kings, though thou be none."'[16] As this book will reveal, Powell's recognition that this collective project was a fragile construction – a dream that could be lost – was born out of his experiences of the colonial world.

The peculiarities of political belonging in Britain have a long history. As Linda Colley's work has emphasized, a shared national identity of Britain was 'forged' between 1707 and 1837 in relation to the alien other, through the vehicles of war and religion.[17] Francophobia was, she argues, its foundation. Even more, it was largely through war that British people had first-hand experience of Britishness as a universal, Christian project of empire.[18] In 1970, Tom Nairn made a similar point on the character of English political dominance in Britain. 'Modern English conservatism was forged,' he notes, 'out of its 22-year war against the French Revolution and Napoleon.'[19] That war fathered what Nairn calls 'a non-popular nationalism' that 'survived on the surrogates of imperialism and foreign war.'[20] This was a conservative nationalism that did not rely on 'the genius of the people,' on a picture of a unified and essentialized culture of the people.[21] War and allegiance were, therefore, particularly significant in defining who belongs in a historically imperial, multinational and profoundly classed society. And so, Nairn claimed in 1970, for a nationalist (and unionist) like Powell: 'England needs another war.'[22] Only then would the English remember who belonged and who did not.

Though Powell spoke consistently of the British nation and later tied his career to the cause of Ulster Unionism, it was the English countryside, the English people, English history and the English Crown in

---

[15] 'Power and Glory: The Nation in the Mirror,' speech by J. Enoch Powell to Manchester Convention Dinner, 6 November 1965. POLL 4.1.2.

[16] Ibid. Here Powell is quoting the Third Witch of Shakespeare's *Macbeth*.

[17] Linda Colley, *Britons: Forging the Nation, 1707–1837* (New Haven, CT: Yale University Press, 2005).

[18] Jay Winter, *Remembering War: The Great War Between Memory and History in the Twentieth Century* (New Haven, CT: Yale University Press, 2006), p. 169.

[19] Tom Nairn, 'Enoch Powell: The New Right,' *New Left Review* (1/61, May–June 1970), p. 8.

[20] Ibid.   [21] Ibid.   [22] Ibid.

Parliament that sat at the heart of his political imagination. This slippage and acceptance of English hegemony within the British nation does not mean, however, that we can deny that Powell thought in the postwar years in terms of the Union. The Union was a collective project that could, Powell told an Ulster audience in 1978, contain diversity; it could contain 'regional dimensions' that were 'profound, historic and self-conscious.'[23] In fact, Powell argued that Parliament was 'the natural protector of all minorities' because 'it is itself made up of minorities,' which meant, he argued, that all are prevented as minorities from 'coercing or trampling upon one another beyond a certain point.'[24] The English were one among many. This is, of course, a far cry from his views on the political impact of ethnic minorities in Britain.

Despite this faith in the historical institution of Parliament, war remained, for Powell, the answer to the problem of belonging in an imperial and multinational state. For Powell, war was the ultimate and final assertion of political allegiance – the sacrifice of one's body and soul to the state. In parallel with his views on Church membership, political identity was necessarily proven in the moment of war, in action and ritual not in shared abstract principles or democratic commitments. This he explicitly juxtaposed with the presumptions of postwar internationalism and human rights.

Critically, after the empire, Powell believed that the loyalty of black Britons would always be problematic; the black Briton, according to Powell, would always carry the problem of a failure of allegiance – or deference – to the nation. Unsurprisingly, these views underpinned a profoundly gendered vision of political belonging. We see this, for instance, in 1981 when Powell moved an amendment against a provision in the new Nationality Bill which would extend the transmission of British citizenship through mothers as well as fathers. Powell argued that nationality must be transmitted only through fathers for one simple reason:

Nationality, in the last resort, is tested by fighting. A man's nation is the nation for which he will fight. His nationality is the expression of his ultimate allegiance. It is his identification with those with whom he will stand, if necessary, against the rest of the world, and to whose survival he regards the survival of his own personal identity as subordinate.[25]

---

[23] Enoch Powell, speech at Inch, Downpatrick, 6 May 1978 as cited in Paul Corthorn, 'Enoch Powell, Ulster Unionism, and the British Nation,' *Journal of British Studies*, 51: 4 (October 2012), pp. 967–997.

[24] Enoch Powell, speech at Eglinton, 25 April 1980 as cited ibid., p. 985.

[25] As cited in Graham Dawson, *Soldier Heroes: British Adventure, Empire and the Imagining of Masculinities* (London: Routledge, 1994), pp. 11–12.

In this light, it is perhaps not surprising that Powell used the language of war and invasion to comprehend black immigration and the growth of ethnic communities in Britain.

Importantly, Powell's understanding of race was Tory in character. Though racism takes many forms in Britain, in one variety of British racism, 'race' functions uniquely: as Powell noted in 1978, 'Skin-colour is like a uniform.'[26] In this single line, we begin to see the limits of David Cannadine's argument against the historical significance of racial difference both in the empire and within Britain. Cannadine insists that the British imperial world was not imagined in black and white, or British 'self' and racial 'other.' Rather, we must look to imperial elites, to their pomp and ornamental display of a complex, finely gradated and multiracial hierarchy, to find a more accurate vision of the way in which Britain's imperial community was imagined – at least until the 1950s. But race, like class, *ordered* British rule.[27] It was, in a sense, another part of the 'ornamentation' of the social order. Race was a uniform which structured the hierarchical whole. Powell's use of this term 'uniform' is significantly ambiguous: it suggests both an acceptance of the historical constructedness of racial categorization while at the same time posing it as an untranscendable boundary. The immigrant's complete assimilation is dependent on her ability to shed her skin. This impossibility, in many ways, represented for Powell the impossibility of maintaining an ahistorical, abstract space for democracy. Here, we find a Tory acceptance of an imperfect, racist world. With this, it is clear that Powell's understanding of the consequences of immigration was not merely a brand of cultural xenophobia. Remarkably, it did not matter to Powell when estimating Britain's future 'alien' population that a person might be born of a British mother or father: cultural conformity (and *classed* habits) would not suffice. Even more, Powell was unconcerned with the vast numbers of European immigrants who settled in Britain during and after the Second World War. Simply put, in Powell's mind, the black Briton's visible presence in the metropole disordered the hierarchical whole. This view of blackness as a seed of social disorder was not unique to Powell but part of a broad current of opinion, which took hold especially after the Notting Hill race riots of 1958 and borrowed much from the increasingly contentious politics of white settler

---

[26] J. Enoch Powell, *New Statesman*, 13 October 1978.
[27] David Feldman, 'Why the English Like Turbans: Multicultural Politics in British History,' in David Feldman and Jon Lawrence (eds.), *Structures and Transformations in Modern British History* (Cambridge University Press, 2011), pp. 281–302.

communities in British Africa.[28] It is not accurate, then, to simply view postwar British society as the inheritor of a singular, imperial belief in white racial superiority and social order. Rather, 'race' as a belief is not fixed but is a flexible entity that promises to make sense of the tensions and social hierarchies of a particular moment with a set of (malleable) 'truths.' The lessons of empire, and the medium of the message, changed over time: the rearguard protection of white privilege in Africa reflected back onto Britain.

Powell at various times denied that there was any meaning to the words 'race' or 'class' (what he never denied was that 'the unique structure of power' of British rule depended on both homogeneity and deference).[29] Conflict did not occur between races, he insisted, but between 'social organizations' – on political, not biological terms.[30] This is not to say that this strictly political view of race in postwar Britain is sufficient in explaining the power of Powell's impact in 1968. This view of 'race' as a political division echoes the post-Nazi arguments in favour of racial segregation in South Africa and the United States. Powell's use of the war experience in his speeches provided his supporters with a (political) logic of racial exclusion – a logic which his listeners could make immediately personal and self-evident. As the following letter to Powell makes clear, the incorrect belief that black Britons were absent from the sacrifices of the Second World War was often a backdrop on which to project blatant racism:

I never saw 1 coloured person at Dunkirk and they want to come here and run our little Island what was peaceful and now it is full of MONGREL'S [sic] ... I hope you could bring up some of these points in Parliament and better still bring back our FREE SPEECH FOR THE BRITISHER, I MEAN WHITE, AND FREEDOM WHICH WE FOUGHT FOR AT DUNKIRK ... I ONCE HEARD A NIGGER SAY TO ANOTHER NIGGER ... HAVE INTERCOURSE WITH WHITE WOMEN AND KILL ALL WHITE MEN, AND I REALLY BELIEVE IT SIR THE PATTERN IS HERE BUT NOT TO STAY I HOPE.[31]

The war, and particularly the potent myth of British self-reliance at Dunkirk, served as a means to define who belonged. As this letter

---

[28] Bill Schwarz, *The White Man's World* (*Memories of Empire*, vol. 1; Oxford University Press, 2011), p. 11.

[29] For Powell's denial of a consciousness of 'class' see J. Enoch Powell, Bill Schwarz interview, 26 April 1988. For Powell's denial of 'race' see J. Enoch Powell, 'Beyond Immigration,' *Frontier* (February 1973), cited in Rex Collings (ed.), *Reflections of a Statesman: The Writings and Speeches of Enoch Powell* (London: Bellew Publishing, 1991), pp. 152–158

[30] Enoch Powell, 'Beyond Immigration,' in *Reflections of a Statesman*, pp. 153–154.

[31] Letter to Powell sent 21 April 1968. POLL 8.1.8.

demonstrates (and it is one of a great number), remembering war was entangled in deep racism. As Paul Gilroy has underlined, memories of the Second World War continue to serve the purpose of racial exclusion.[32] In this startling letter to Enoch Powell we see the recollection of war used as an assertion of free speech, freedom and parliamentary democracy against the black immigrant – a racist 'anti-fascism.'

In a discussion of race and memory, Bill Schwarz makes clear that 'the palpably conservative or racist manifestations of ethnic belonging in the 1950s and 1960s' were 'neither simply recidivist nor in any simply sense only domestic.' Rather, they may have 'a more dynamic and complex history than they are conventionally accorded.'[33] Powell's letters from the public tie tightly together old war stories with new experiences of social uncertainty and postwar scarcity. The letters in favour of greater immigration restrictions, which are estimated to number over 110,000 in response to the 'Rivers of Blood' speech alone, are steeped in racism, yet they also highlight experiences of profound social and economic vulnerability and serve as testaments to social and political changes unrelated to immigration. Powell's letter-writers speak of student protests, labour unrest, but most of all they speak of the indignities of declining welfare provisions – filled hospital beds and unavailable council houses.[34] Charles Tilly insists that we must look to the ways in which particular rights and obligations are bundled together to 'activate' certain identities and bind participants in political action.[35] The confessional letters Powell received from the public should not merely be read as irrational or misdirected emotional outbursts.[36] Powell and his supporters framed the issue of black immigration within a set of coordinates that reveals a great deal about the moral architecture of public and private life at this time. Their emphasis on wartime sacrifices and their expressions of postwar shame and indignation disclose something of the prevailing vocabulary of 'legitimate' grievances and of the broader emotional culture of postwar Britain. 'The process of becoming modern,' Schwarz argues, 'can turn on the telling of old stories, the fabrications of memory

---

[32] Paul Gilroy, *Postcolonial Melancholia* (New York: Columbia University Press, 2004).

[33] Bill Schwarz, 'Reveries of Race: The Closing of the Imperial Moment,' in Becky Conekin, Frank Mort and Chris Waters (eds.), *Moments of Modernity: Reconstructing Britain, 1945–1964* (New York University Press, 1999), pp. 189–207 (p. 190).

[34] 'Selection of letters from public following 20 April 1968,' POLL 8.1.8.

[35] Charles Tilly, 'Political Identities in Changing Politics,' *Social Research*, 70: 2 (Summer 2003), pp. 605–620 (p. 611).

[36] For a discussion of the significance of emotion in political activism, see Jeff Goodwin, James M. Jasper, and Francesca Polletta, *Passionate Politics: Emotions and Social Movements* (London: University of Chicago Press, 2001).

serving to compensate for the dislocations of modernization.'[37] As one man wrote in 1968:

Dear Sir, I was there – [on] the Somme (where many whites from S.A. lost their lives) ... I stopped a bullet. 1967 In my old age, I was driven out of my home, by Pakistanis who coveted the house I lived in.[38]

The formation of postwar conservatism entailed, then, the 'reworking' of old forms of identity – and particularly memories of war service – to face new circumstances. Not least of these new circumstances was the closure of the colonial era and, linked to this, the increasing challenges to Britain's postwar settlement.

Powell and a political generation

Biographies usually begin with birth and end in death. In one way or another, the historical question to be answered through that window of time is why the person studied came to do the things he or she did. Psychoanalytic theory promises an answer: childhood, as well as grand-parents and parents, clear the path for the history that follows. So, too, does a highly empirical approach – wherein the particular moments of day-to-day life elicit choices and the small, understandable steps forward until death. This is the approach of Simon Heffer in his biog-raphy, *Like the Roman: The Life of Enoch Powell*.[39] Powell was a prodigy from humble beginnings – a quiet and diligent outsider, the son of a Birmingham elementary schoolmaster and a teacher of nonconform-ist stock. According to Heffer, the historical answer to the question of Enoch Powell is that Powell did what he did due to the particularities of circumstance and, to a lesser extent, due to the constraints of his immutable personality. Heffer's approach carries an inherent sympathy for the subject. We are placed always in the same moment of time as Enoch Powell, with the same blinders and – despite our knowledge of Powell's mistakes – the same overarching ideological vision. In an effort to assert ideological difference, left-wing criticism has too often repre-sented Powell as entirely alien: he is a timeless monster whose political vision is held together by a disturbing mother complex or an impassable racism.[40] For example, as Paul Foot wrote in an obituary for Powell, he

---

[37] Schwarz, 'Reveries of Race,' p. 191.
[38] Letter to Powell, 23 April 1968. POLL 8.1.8.
[39] Simon Heffer, *Like the Roman: The Life of Enoch Powell* (London: Weidenfeld & Nicolson, 1998).
[40] See Paul Foot, 'Beyond the Powell: Obituary of Enoch Powell,' *Socialist Review* no. 217 (March 1998) and Jonathan Rutherford, *Forever England: Reflections on Race, Masculinity and Empire* (London: Lawrence and Wishart, 1997).

was 'a racist to his bones ... Almost licking his lips, he looked forward to race riots ... There was no satisfying his racist appetite.'[41] Powell here is obscene. His 'passion for empire' was an ideology that continued to his death and gave him 'an incontrovertible belief that the white man was ordained by god to conquer and control the world which was populated mainly by inferior black people.'[42] There is no sense of change over time. Powell is the imperial monster that can come again: his life must be used as a warning 'to prepare for the next racist demagogue to come along, and to shut him up.'[43]

Questions regarding Powell's apparently repressed homosexuality as well as his strong childhood attachment to his mother similarly provide some with an explanation for Powell's (political) perversions. Jonathan Rutherford offers a Freudian analysis of Powell's views on racial ghettoization. In this analysis, Powell's love of India served as a replacement for his feeling of abandonment by his mother:

> Powell's twin imagery of invasive fragments and unassimilable lumps are the representations of his own infantile defence mechanisms against the dread of his mother's absence ... The black and Asian immigrants who had once constituted the anonymous, passive backdrop to Powell's idealisation of empire, and who, through his splitting and projection became the persecutory cause of the loss of his loved empire, have now come to symbolise the return of the repressed.[44]

Simon Heffer – and, in fact, perhaps all of Powell's sympathetic biographers – would probably be pleased to accept that Powell had a mother complex. With such a diagnosis, we are left prone to find undue satisfaction in uncovering the unhealthy roots of Powell's racism and leaving the argument at that.

Both efforts, to humanize and to dehumanize Powell, fail as history. Perhaps because his words in 1968 still reverberate loudly in Britain, both those who criticize and those who sympathize with Powell write his life-story as though they are revealing the backstory of a present enigma in British popular consciousness.[45] The popular mantra 'Enoch

---

[41] Foot, 'Beyond the Powell.' Strangely, this stands in contrast to Foot's assessment of Powell in 1969. At that time, Foot offered the first serious critical assessment of Enoch Powell in *The Rise of Enoch Powell*. Powell is represented as ideologically malleable and opportunistically pandering to popular fears in an effort to take the Conservative leadership. Paul Foot, *The Rise of Enoch Powell: An Examination of Enoch Powell's Attitude to Immigration and Race* (London: Cornmarket Press, 1969).

[42] Foot, 'Beyond the Powell.'   [43] Ibid.

[44] Rutherford, *Forever England*, p. 127.

[45] Patrick Cosgrave, *The Lives of Enoch Powell* (London: Bodley Head, 1989); Howard Pedraza, *Winston Churchill, Enoch Powell, and the Nation* (London: Cleveland Press, 1986); Robert Shepherd, *Enoch Powell: A Biography* (London: Hutchinson, 1996).

was right' is just one example of the way past and present are entangled in Powell. As a self-styled prophet, he is a ghost in the room, not a man with an entirely different vision of reality. Unlike Heffer, Foot or Rutherford, we must read Powell as a historical figure, as contained within a different historical moment from our own.

With such a perspective, it is possible to see Powell as part of a political generation. When speaking in 1968, he did not speak to the realities of the twenty-first century but to those who witnessed or were affected by the hardships of the interwar years, the bombing of cities at war, the newness of the culture of consumption, as well as the last gasps of British imperial power. As Powell himself put it in 1959: 'To be one of the diminishing number of those who actually witnessed the phenomenon of British India is like belonging to a dying race which cannot pass its secrets on.'[46] In other words, as evidenced by Powell's supporters, Powell enunciated a particular vision of Britain grounded in shared political time. Such a perspective opens up the possibility of viewing Powell's life and thought not as one coherent idea, but as evidence of the experience of historical change. Patrick Cosgrave's *The Lives of Enoch Powell* comes closest to historicizing Powell – yet here his life in academia, in war, in politics is separated into different 'lives' such that a singularity of experience through time is obscured.[47] Like all historical actors, Powell brought old eyes to new events. But this was a moment of profound change.

Powell's life and the nationalism that he espoused happened at a particular moment in British history. While Powell's biographers have rightly pointed to the importance of the collapse of British imperial power, and especially the loss of the British Raj, in understanding Powell's nationalism, they have failed to tie it to the co-terminal loss in legitimacy of the domestic structures of authority in Britain. New forms of representation and contestation in the media, new technologies of domestic housework, social planning and anxiety surrounding the future of family life, investigations into the experience of working-class masculinity in British literature and film, the hybridizing effects of the social and cultural movements of migration from the Caribbean, West Africa and South Asia, the infiltration of an 'Americanized' mass culture and the decline of Church membership point to a postwar society in transition on multiple fronts. In other words, the structures of social difference which had once

[46] Enoch Powell, 'Passage to England,' *Birmingham Post*, 20 August 1959. POLL 6.1.1C.
[47] Cosgrave, *The Lives of Enoch Powell*.

ordered British imperial rule were beginning to unravel. Through all this, Powell retained a profound belief in the imperatives of patriarchy and dramatically committed himself to the 'survival' of the nation, against (post) imperial international concerns and, later, against the transnational commitments of both the New Left[48] and postcolonial, diaspora communities in Britain. It is not enough to explain this intense commitment to the nation as mere evidence of how traumatic the collapse of the British Empire was for Powell[49] or as the result of Powell's seemingly courageous effort to face some hard, post-imperial realities.[50] Nor is it enough to see Powell as a consequent Little Englander: he did not oppose international military action that, he believed, would increase the 'power and glory' of the British state.[51] Rather, as Stuart Hall et al. made clear in an analysis of the 'law and order' campaigns of the 1970s, Powell, more than anything, was concerned with the break-up of the institutional and social structures of authority of a post-imperial Britain. The threat of racial 'anarchy' was used, by Powell, to shore up support for the increased power of the state.[52]

As David Cannadine asserts, the fall of British imperial hegemony saw, too, the fall of entrenched class hierarchy.[53] Though Cannadine underplays the dependency of British imperial rule on a belief in white racial superiority, still the connections he draws between the international and domestic are useful. Looking to Britain's colonies and mandates, Cannadine offers a reading of 'the ending of empire as the ending of hierarchy.'[54] The repudiation of the imperial connection for some nations – such as Ireland, the Sudan, Burma, Egypt, Iraq and the Yemen – went hand in hand with American-style republicanism

[48] Via an emphasis on international issues, social values and identity politics, the 'New Left' of the 1960s and 1970s in Britain and elsewhere challenged a vision of progressive politics wholly defined by the struggle of labour against capitalist interests.
[49] For this argument, see Andrew Roth, *Enoch Powell: Tory Tribune* (London: Macdonald and Co., 1970); Humphry Berkeley, *The Odyssey of Enoch: A Political Memoir* (London, 1997); Rutherford, *Forever England*.
[50] For this argument, see Heffer, *Like the Roman*.
[51] For instance, Powell argued forcibly in the lead-up to the Falklands War that the use of military force was necessary. He challenged the 'Iron Lady' to show Britain 'of what metal she is made.' This public challenge apparently had a 'devastating impact' on Prime Minister Margaret Thatcher and helped form her resolve to fight. Cited in Heffer, *Like the Roman*, p. 856.
[52] Stuart Hall, Chas Critcher, Tony Jefferson, John Clarke and Brian Roberts, *Policing the Crisis: Mugging, the State and Law and Order* (Basingstoke: Palgrave Macmillan, 1978).
[53] David Cannadine, *Ornamentalism: How the British Saw Their Empire* (Oxford University Press, 2001).
[54] Ibid., p. 170.

and the explicit overthrow of 'traditional' hierarchies.[55] For others who remained members of the Commonwealth and continued to recognize the Queen as the head of the Commonwealth, social hierarchies were slowly undermined as imperial connections were severed.[56] But what of Britain? As John Darwin has noted, the United Kingdom was just as much 'a successor state of the old imperial system' as other post-imperial nations; Britain similarly had to make social and political adjustments.[57] Recent work on the long shadow of the memory of empire on Britain indicates the possible depths of this readjustment.[58] As the empire waned in the 1960s, the whole culture of what Powell called Britain's 'unique structure of power' fell victim to 'satire and scepticism and scorn.'[59] Recognition of the decline in the class order is nothing new: John Goldthorpe used 'the decay of the status order' to explain industrial militancy in the 1970s, for instance.[60] But its links to imperial decline are unclear and uncertain. Cannadine insists that this 'decline of deference' and lessened respect for historical institutions has 'undoubtedly been the most significant domestic consequence of the loss of empire – though it is a large and complex subject that still awaits its historian.'[61] As the following chapters will I hope reveal, Powell represents one of the first conservative theorists of this complex history.

Postwar, postcolonial Britain

Obviously, in trying to situate Powell in the politics and culture of postwar Britain we encounter a large historiography. There is a wealth of historical literature, for instance, that has established the shifting meanings and memories of the Second World War in the postwar period.[62] Yet,

---

[55] Ibid.   [56] Ibid.

[57] Cited ibid., p. 172.

[58] Schwarz, *The White Man's World*.

[59] Cannadine, *Ornamentalism*, p. 172.

[60] John H. Goldthorpe as cited in Jon Lawrence, 'Paternalism, Class, and the British Path to Modernity,' in Simon Gunn and James Vernon (eds.), *The Peculiarities of Liberal Modernity in Imperial Britain* (Berkeley: University of California Press, 2011), pp. 147–164 (p. 163).

[61] Cannadine, *Ornamentalism*, p. 172.

[62] Angus Calder, *The Myth of the Blitz* (London: Pimlico, 1991); Monica Riera and Gavin Schaffer (eds.), *The Lasting War: Society and Identity in Britain, France and Germany after 1945* (New York: Macmillan, 2008); Geoff Eley, 'Finding the People's War: Film, British Collective Memory and World War II,' *American Historical Review*, 105 (2001), pp. 818–838; Malcolm Smith, *Britain and 1940: History, Myth and Popular Memory* (London: Routledge, 2000); Mark Connelly, *We Can Take It! Britain and the Memory of the Second World War* (Harlow: Longman, 2004); Lucy Noakes, *War and the British: Gender, Memory and National Identity* (London: I. B. Tauris, 1998); Rodney

despite Paul Gilroy's insistence that we must critically analyse the abiding myths of the Second World War in order to comprehend Britain's 'postcolonial melancholia,'[63] our understanding of the interconnected histories of post*war* and post*colonial* Britain remains in its infancy.

It would be difficult to read the letters to Enoch Powell in 1968 without recognition that individual and collective memories of the Second World War served as a significant backdrop on which to comprehend the social and political transformations of the postwar period. As Alessandro Portelli explains in his work on memory, 'War keeps coming back in narratives and memories as the most dramatic point of encounter between the personal and public, between biography and history.'[64] Still, it is perhaps surprising that the war holds such weight for these supporters twenty-three years after its end. In an analysis of postwar films, Geoff Eley explains that the Second World War and the radical potential of the 1945 general election remained in the postwar period a 'remembered horizon, [with] an indistinct but evocative popular democratic nostalgia' – providing 'the steel girding of post-war political architecture' and 'the hardwiring of post-war political imagination.'[65] Political scientist Henry Tudor's long-established account of 'political myth' is useful here. Political myths, simply put, have a protagonist and a beginning, a middle and an end.[66] What marks the myth-maker's account of the past as a myth, as well as history or memory, is a dramatic form that serves a practical political purpose.[67] It is this – the myth's beginning, middle and end – that can contain and justify the contradictions of a political order. In the case of the Second World War, myth powerfully contained, among other things, the problem of a single political community profoundly divided by social class. The historic political marginalization and poverty of industrial workers, especially in the interwar years, and the state's wartime industrial and military needs posed a contradiction that was mythically resolved in the heroic loyalty and sacrifice of the working man. 'The people' dramatically

---

Lowe, 'The Second World War, Consensus, and the Foundation of the Welfare State,' *Twentieth-Century British History* 1: 2 (1990), pp. 152–182; Joy Damousi, *The Labour of Loss: Mourning, Memory and Wartime Bereavement in Australia* (Cambridge University Press, 1999); Penny Summerfield, *Reconstructing Women's Wartime Lives: Discourse and Subjectivity in Oral Histories of the Second World War* (Manchester University Press, 1998).

[63] Gilroy, *Postcolonial Melancholia*.

[64] Alessandro Portelli, *Battle of Valle Giulia: Oral History and the Art of Dialogue*, (University of Wisconsin Press, 1997), p. ix, as cited in Anthony King, 'The Afghan War and the Making of "Postmodern" Memory: Commemoration and the Dead at Helmand,' *The British Journal of Sociology*, 6: 1 (2010), pp. 1–25 (pp. 2–3).

[65] King, 'The Afghan War,' p. 23.

[66] Henry Tudor, *Political Myth* (London: Pall Mall, 1972), p. 137.

[67] Ibid., p. 138.

asserted unity and belonging, both on the front and at home, despite the stark realities of class difference and political alienation.

The idea that the services of the postwar welfare state were a direct political recompense for wartime sacrifices can be found in a vast number of Powell's letters from the public. In this sense, the collective memory of the Second World War served as a touchstone, a point of departure, in conceiving of social justice and the responsibilities of state power in British society. This is quite different from the argument that collective memories of the war neatly and unequivocally produced an imagined transcendence of social divisions.[68] Instead, the memory of wartime sacrifice could be held up against postwar deprivation and an uncertain future. But the meaning of the victory of the Second World War transformed over time, subject to multiple and competing political contexts and ongoing reconstructions throughout the postwar period. Austerity rationing, the Cold War in Europe, the ending of National Service, the passing presence of the First World War generation and, even, greater access to home-centred consumption would all involve some reworking of what it was that the Second World War had been fought for.

While it may be clear that the myth of the Second World War was linked to shifting notions of the relationship between citizen and state in Britain's postwar era, it is less clear how the predominant myths of the war relate in complex ways to postwar beliefs about British international power, its history and its political legacies. Importantly, in the postwar years, the notion of wartime 'sacrifice' worked on both the domestic and international levels. Niall Ferguson has attempted to correct the dominant historical focus on the violence, racism and material exploitation of Britain's imperial activities.[69] He insists that, more than anything, it must be remembered that the British Empire brought modernity to the world via infrastructure, trade and education. This view relies on a particular construction of empire's end. It is that, in the end, Britain *nobly* sacrificed the empire – or more explicitly, British rule in India – to save the world for democracy against German barbarism. Like most myths, there is some truth to this: the eventual abandonment of the empire was a condition Winston Churchill traded for US military support in the Second World

---

[68] Chris Waters argues that working-class wartime sacrifices made it easier, during and after the war, 'to position the Black migrant against a national imaginary that now embodied the experiences of white Britons from all classes.' Thanks to the war, it became easier, according to Waters, to 'cement social cohesion through the exclusion of the racial other.' Chris Waters, '"Dark Strangers" in Our Midst: Discourses of Race and Nation in Britain, 1947–1963,' *Journal of British Studies*, 36: 2 (April 1997), pp. 207–238 (p. 212).

[69] Niall Ferguson, *Empire: How Britain Made the Modern World* (London: Allen Lane, 2003).

War (this is specifically mentioned in the Atlantic Charter). On the other hand, it obscures other truths, such as the power of anti-colonial revolt and prewar failures of political reform.[70] Importantly, this myth of noble sacrifice has a political life of its own. It contributes to the vision of British decline as a heroic sacrifice to the world, which (as the thousands of letters Powell received over the years make clear) can turn, in the context of the New Commonwealth immigration especially, into a myth of victimhood. The *English* people, after saving the world for democracy, are drawn as victims to excessive and ongoing postcolonial reprisals. Here, we begin to see more clearly the contours of a postcolonial Britain.

Bernard Porter, the most well-known and convincing sceptic of any widespread presence of popular imperialism in modern Britain, concedes that we cannot deny the empire's impact on the beliefs of Britain's political establishment in the postwar years. He presents the paternalism of postwar domestic politics, and Britain's welfare state, as an extension of the 'social imperialism' of the early 1900s and the ideas of economic development and protectionism emergent in the late British Empire.[71] Or, as Powell put it in 1970, 'One of the lessons to be drawn from the study of early-twentieth-century imperialism is the extraordinary durability of policies and programmes which lack all possibility of being realised.'[72] That imperialism would go 'hand-in-hand with prosperity for the working man' was the real genius of the 'myth of empire.'[73] Tellingly, Powell would draw a 'traceable line of descent' through Joseph Chamberlain's 'Imperial Union,' British Socialism and the likes of Oswald Mosley.[74] With this, Margaret Thatcher's doctrine of individualism and faith in the free market becomes a postcolonial revolt against a (still aristocratic) paternalism that survived into the twentieth century due to the needs of Britain's widening imperial bureaucracy. But recent historical scholarship has made further inroads into challenging the assumption that the history of the postwar settlement can be detached from the making of postcolonial Britain.[75] Alice

---

[70] Arthur Herman, *Gandhi and Churchill: The Epic Rivalry That Destroyed an Empire and Forged Our Age* (New York, Random House, 2008).

[71] Bernard Porter, 'The Empire Strikes Back,' *History Today*, 46: 9 (September 1996).

[72] Powell, 'The Myth of Empire,' in *Reflections of a Statesman*, pp. 589–595 (p. 589).

[73] Ibid., p. 594.   [74] Ibid.

[75] Wendy Webster, *Englishness and Empire, 1939–1965* (Oxford University Press, 2005); Schwarz, *The White Man's World*; Alice Ritscherle, 'Disturbing the People's Peace: Patriotism and "Respectable" Racism in British Responses to Rhodesian Independence' and Martin Francis, 'Men of the Royal Air Force, the Cultural Memory of the Second World War and the Twilight of the British Empire,' in Philippa Levine and Susan R. Grayzel (eds.), *Gender, Labour, War and Empire: Essays on Modern Britain* (Basingstoke: Palgrave Macmillan, 2009), pp. 179–196 and 197–218.

Ritscherle's research has revealed the contradictory role that memories of the 'People's War' played in the politics of Commonwealth immigration and race in British society – from the 'colour-blind' liberalism of the 1950s to the Powellite's 'free speech for the Britisher.'[76] Debates about race relations and immigration, and such reworking of the meaning of war, served – she argues – to introduce neo-liberalism into the political lexicon of the white working classes.[77] Jordanna Bailkin's *The Afterlife of Empire* meanwhile challenges the emphasis on high politics and diplomacy in our historical understanding of the end of empire in 1950s and 1960s Britain;[78] she reveals a social history of migrants and non-migrants – adopted children, families and the mentally ill – whose experiences were shaped in these years by global economic forces, by new legal regimes in Africa and Asia and by imperial decline. Convincingly, she argues that postwar welfare was never just a British story but was continually informed and transformed by these afterlives of empire. With these works, we see that greater understanding of the interconnected histories of the postwar settlement and postcolonial Britain – via, particularly, social memory and the understandings of legitimate state power – promises to give us far deeper insight into the impact of the end of empire in Britain.

Though British decolonization prior to 1968 was by no means peaceful (histories of the British suppression of Mau Mau in Kenya have been an important corrective to that misapprehension[79]), there was relatively little violence, unrest or political controversy in the metropole due to British decolonization in the 1950s and 1960s. Understanding this political 'silence' and Powell's part in its rupture is essential for any true comprehension of the end of imperial power in British public life. Explanations for the British public's silence on decolonization have largely taken two forms. One rests on the argument that a great majority of the British people, especially those of the working classes, were politically uncommitted or oblivious to the empire.[80] The other in essence argues that the British public experienced such a shock to their national identity in the

---

[76] Ritscherle, 'Opting out of Utopia: Race and Working-Class Political Culture in Britain during the Age of Decolonization, 1948–68.' PhD dissertation, University of Michigan, Ann Arbor, 2005, p. 4.

[77] Ibid., p. 9.

[78] Jordanna Bailkin, *The Afterlife of Empire* (Berkeley: University of California Press, 2012).

[79] See, especially, Caroline Elkins, *Britain's Gulag: The Brutal End of Empire in Kenya* (Pimlico: London, 2005) and David Anderson, *Histories of the Hanged: Britain's Dirty War in Kenya and the End of Empire* (London: Weidenfeld & Nicolson, 2005).

[80] See, for instance, Bernard Porter, *The Absent-minded Imperialists: Empire, Society, and Culture in Britain* (Oxford University Press, 2004).

loss of empire that it makes sense to read the deafening silence on the issue of decolonization as a sign of deep political trauma.[81] Britain, like the traumatized person, carried 'an impossible history' within itself, which caused a failure to understand the meaning of immediate events.[82] These two explanations rely on absolute or polarized views of the presence of the empire in British society. It was either so unimportant that nobody really cared, or so fundamental that no one could speak of it. To move beyond this historiographical stalemate, Stuart Ward insists that we must look to the ambivalences and anxieties brought about by imperial decline and consider the ways in which 'the rhetorical space within which any opposition or resistance [to decolonization] might have been articulated had been delegitimized.'[83] The words of Powell and his supporters seem to support this approach: they point to the possibility that the abiding beliefs about the Second World War – and the ideological parameters of the 'people's peace' of the postwar years – worked to placate concerns about decolonization. Particularly, their words point to the significance of Britain's 'finest hour' as a closure on the questions the history of the British Empire and anti-colonialism necessarily pose. The crisis of British authority – and the rise in (American?) middle-class values against the prewar order – was drawn out not as a consequence of anti-colonial forces but tied instead to the notion that Britain had found its liberal self through war. Again, the meaning of the war could serve multiple political purposes. The 'class peace' found within the war effort, particularly between the state and union power, underpinned an era of the imagined 'post-ideological' state, an 'endless era of pragmatic, class-less and antagonism-free politics' in which politics could be viewed as a 'management expertise.'[84] The structure of political power and the cross-party acceptance of reformed capitalism, Andrew Gamble argues, worked to muffle ideological debate at the popular level on the issue of decolonization.[85] By the 1950s, too, stories of the heroism of the nation at war – which often emphasized male bravery but also the benefits of modern, technological innovation – increasingly replaced that of the now less straightforward masculine, imperial adventure.[86]

[81] Anna Marie Smith, 'Powellism: The Black Immigrant as the Post-colonial Symptom and the Phantasmatic Re-closure of the British Nation,' in *New Right Discourse on Race and Sexuality: Britain, 1968–1990* (Cambridge University Press, 1994).

[82] Cathy Caruth, 'Introduction,' *Psychoanalysis, Culture and Trauma, American Imago*, 28: 1 (Spring 1991), pp. 1–12, as cited in Anna Marie Smith, *New Right Discourse*, p. 133.

[83] Stuart Ward, 'Introduction,' in *British Culture and the End of Empire* (Manchester University Press, 2001), p. 11.

[84] Anna Marie Smith, *New Right Discourse*, p. 137.

[85] Andrew Gamble, *The Conservative Nation* (London: Routledge, 1974), p. 62.

[86] For a discussion of the cultural memory of the Second World War in the 1950s and the emphasis, particularly, on masculine heroism, see Penny Summerfield,

Importantly, in 1968, Powell spoke at a moment when the moral coherence of the postwar era appeared to be in jeopardy. Alongside the divisive 'permissive society' ran political challenges to the 'class peace' of 1945. As Britain's mixed economy faltered, left-wing trade union opposition to prices and incomes policy and government efforts in both the Wilson and Heath administrations to restrict unions' right to strike indicated a breakdown in the relationship between state and union power. The women's Ford sewing machinists' strike for equal pay and the coming together of immigrant labour groups into the Black People's Alliance further challenged the limits of postwar trade unionism. Further, by 1968, the notion of a culturally coherent and politically unified people celebrated in the 'People's War' was increasingly problematized by questions over European membership, challenges to traditional sexual relations, the growth of Scottish and Welsh nationalisms, panics over immigration and race, not to mention the burgeoning civil rights movement in Northern Ireland. As in the past, unsettling the consensus by new political claims required a new vision of British history that would reposition the myth of the Second World War in popular understanding.[87]

When memories of war were applied to the question of immigration they underlined a contingent social contract between state and citizen, but not – at least for the Powellites – a sense of cross-class unity or classless experience. With Powell's help, the myth of the heroic sacrifice of 'the people' – a sacrifice that worked to resolve the contradictions of a classed society and legitimize the social peace of 1945 – could mature into a myth of sacrifice that revealed the victimization of the people by the political Establishment. Immigration was offered by Powell as a sign of the state prioritizing past international (post-imperial) obligations over the protection of the working classes – over the 'defence' of the nation. This struck a loud chord in Britain. Again, as Amy Whipple's analysis of Powell's letters from the public in 1968 reveals, the politics of race and nation did not subsume class identities or reinforce social cohesion in postwar Britain.[88] Black immigration

'Film and the Popular Memory of the Second World War in Britain 1950–1959,' in Levine and Grayzel (eds.), *Gender, Labour, War and Empire*, pp. 157–175.

[87] Geoff Eley, 'When Europe Was New: Liberation and the Making of the Post-War Era,' in Riera and Schaffer (eds.), *The Lasting War*, p. 20.

[88] Amy Whipple, 'Revisiting the "Rivers of Blood" Controversy: Letters to Enoch Powell,' *Journal of British Studies*, 46: 3 (July 2009), pp. 717–735. For other investigations that reveal the ways in which race and class are mutually constitutive in postwar Britain, see Ritscherle, 'Opting out of Utopia'; Anne Spry Rush, *Bonds of Empire: West Indians and Britishness from Victoria to Decolonization* (Oxford University Press, 2011) and Paul Gilroy, *'There Ain't No Black in the Union Jack': The Cultural Politics of Race and Nation* (London: Routledge, 2002).

was regularly viewed as a consequence of the actions of an irresponsible elite, or a distant and corrupt political Establishment. Powell's populist patriotism questioned the trustworthiness of state bureaucracy. The Home Office itself, charged by Powell with lying about the numbers of New Commonwealth immigrants, became the 'enemy within.' The white working class are redrawn, here, as *victims* of a traitorous state. Powell explicitly associated the Establishment at this moment with the appeasers of the 1930s.[89] This was, he insisted, an invasion not unlike that which was threatened in 1940. This is a populism that powerfully disrupts the fusion within social democracy of state and people. The migrant is drawn, in these terms, as a scrounger, an embodiment of all that is wrong with the (undemocratic and authoritarian) state. Even more, according to Powell and his supporters, race became (with the successes of anti-colonial nationalism) an unavoidable sign of the realignments of political allegiance after empire. As Stuart Hall powerfully articulated in 1978, the populist patriotism of Powellism enabled economic decline and the crises of the postwar settlement to be 'thematised through race.'[90] Via Powell, an economic crisis became a crisis of identity. Race became 'the prism through which the British people are called upon to live through, then to understand, and then to deal with the growing crisis.'[91]

As one woman put it to Powell: 'It would seem that we spent years fighting for our freedom only to find the Govt making us into the serfs of the "late comed" uns and, for the ordinary folk, plagued by these people, It just won't do.'[92] To this, via the repatriation of immigrants, Powell called for a reversal of history, a return to a certain world. Remarkably, we see a similar vision of a breakdown in social harmony due to the presence of black immigration in the words of the historian Andrew Roberts in 1994:

Part of the problem lay in the huge difference between those who were taking – or in this case refusing to take – the decisions over immigration and those upon whom the consequences of those decisions would fall. Of the seven Home Office ministers between October 1951 and January 1957 all

---

[89] For instance, speaking on his warnings of violence due to immigration, Powell noted, 'There are some so foolish as to imagine, or so malevolent as to pretend, that those who think they foresee danger or disaster, therefore desire it. One might as well accuse a man who warned against a rearming enemy of desiring the war he hoped to avert.' Enoch Powell, 11 June 1970, Wolverhampton, Election Meeting. POLL 3.2.1.20.

[90] Stuart Hall, 'Racism and Reaction,' in *Five Views of Multi-Racial Britain* (London: Commission for Racial Equality, 1978), p. 30, as cited in James Procter, *Stuart Hall* (London: Routledge, 2004), p. 83.

[91] Ibid.

[92] L. Windson to Powell, 23 April 1968. POLL 8.1.8.

were public school products and all but one Oxbridge-educated. A majority
sat for rural constituencies and had homes far removed from the areas which
were beginning to bear the brunt of immigration. It fell for the most part
upon ordinary working people at the bottom of the jobs and housing market
to pay the price for the Commonwealth idealism of their social superiors ...
The enormous social difference between governors and governed had not
been a malign force in the past. As officers in the two wars they had never
taken care of themselves before their men, and indeed managed to establish
a genuine sympathy with them. Yet over the question of immigration a profound gap opened up and widened between the opinions of the governors and
the governed.[93]

Roberts has made a stunning assertion here: until New Commonwealth
immigration, profound social inequality had not been a 'malign force.'
And, through war, class hierarchy could be steeped in 'genuine sympathy.' For Roberts, black immigration was the consequence of an ineffective patrician class. Crucially, this was what Powell feared most – this
was class disorder.

As R. J. Bosworth has noted, when compared to the rest of Europe,
Britain is a place for which the history of the Second World War 'matters
both too little and too much.'[94] The collective self-analysis of that history
in Britain 'is still riven by many gaps.'[95] Britain's unique history in the
Second World War as the nation that stood alone against fascism and,
therefore, is largely free of the complicated history of collaboration still
has the potential to explain something of the 'peace' of British decolonization as well as the relative peace of Britain in 1968. The People's War was
retold by Powell in 1968, not as a resolution of the class war of the interwar
years, but as an assertion of self-reliance – 'the people' against the liberal
state. As recent work on the interconnected histories of white populism
in South Africa, Rhodesia and Britain indicates, Powell's particular re-
envisioning of the meaning of the Second World War was not born in a
vacuum – it drew its language and imagery from, among other things,
the white colonial independence movements of the 1960s.[96] At this time,

[93] Andrew Roberts, *Eminent Churchillians* (London: Weidenfeld & Nicolson,
   1994), p. 223.
[94] R. J. Bosworth, 'Nations Examine Their Past: A Comparative Analysis of the
   Historiography of the "Long" Second World War,' *The History Teacher*, 29: 4 (August
   1996), pp. 499–523 (p. 506).
[95] Ibid.
[96] Alice Ritscherle, 'Disturbing the People's Peace: Patriotism and "Respectable"
   Racism in British Reponses to Rhodesian Independence,' in Levine and Grayzel
   (eds.), *Gender, Labour, War and Empire*, pp. 197–218; Martin Francis, 'Men of the
   Royal Air Force, the Cultural Memory of the Second World War and the Twilight
   of the British Empire,' in Levine and Grayzel (eds.), *Gender, Labour, War and
   Empire*, pp. 179–196; and Bill Schwarz, '"The Only White Man in There": The Re-
   Racialisation of England, 1956–1968,' *Race and Class*, 38: 1 (July 1966), pp. 65–78.

at the moment of decolonization and civil rights, 'amid all the rhetoric of families of nations, partnership and equality before the law,' emerged a counter language of the heroic and besieged white colonial.[97] On a subject that has remarkable parallels to the political work of 'Brigadier Powell,' Martin Francis has revealed the significance of the Rhodesian leader Ian Smith's persistent reference to his wartime service as an RAF pilot. As Francis notes, 'No white Rhodesian kitchen in the 1960s and 1970s was complete without an illustrated dishcloth featuring "Good Old Smithy" and his trusty Spitfire.'[98] Smith's associations with the loyal, heroic wartime flyboys helped Smith's white resistance to majority rule attain considerable support in Britain. Here, too, the British state (or, more specifically, Britain's 'liberal' elite) is viewed as failing to uphold the principles of self-determination, democratic spirit and heroic survival proven in the face of war. Here, Rhodesia is represented as the true inheritor of Britain's wartime spirit of self-reliance.[99] At the same time, the enlargement of the social responsibilities of that state, which had once been so intimately tied to the memory of the Second World War, could be viewed by Powell and the emerging New Right[100] as a *threat* to British values.[101]

Enoch Powell and the Making of Postcolonial Britain necessarily builds on a vast scholarship that investigates the changing political valences and collective and individual memories of the war in postwar Britain. But it also takes seriously the critique offered by Barnor Hesse and S. Sayyid, that continuing to invoke the term 'postwar' to describe the context and events in this period 'reiterates a descriptor' that is essentially incomplete, if not 'exhausted.'[102] The end of empire must be woven into the fabric of the story. For Powell, remembering war – and forgetting the black soldier – remained a crucial means by which to define Britain's political community after empire.[103] With Powell we see that non-white, New Commonwealth

[97] Schwarz, '"The Only White Man in There,"' p. 65. See Schwarz, *The White Man's World*.
[98] Martin Francis, *The Flyer: British Culture and the Royal Air Force, 1939–1945* (Oxford University Press, 2009), p. 192.
[99] See, too, Schwarz, 'Ian Smith: The last white man?' in *The White Man's World*, pp. 394–438.
[100] Emerging out of the economic crisis of the 1970s, the 'New Right' challenged the Conservative Party's postwar commitment to Keynesian economic planning and acceptance of trade union power.
[101] Bill Schwarz has recently made important inroads into establishing the links between white populism in Africa and the language of the New Right. See Schwarz, *The White Man's World*.
[102] Barnor Hesse and S. Sayyid, 'Narrating the Postcolonial Political and the Immigrant Imaginary,' in N. Ali , V. S. Kalra and S. Sayyid (eds.), *A Postcolonial Britain: South Asians in Britain* (London: Hurst & Company, 2006).
[103] See Gilroy, *Postcolonial Melancholia*, on race and memory. And for histories of national identity and the black soldier, see Marika Sherwood, *Many Struggles: West*

immigrants were not only, as Gilroy noted, the 'unwitting bearers of the imperial and colonial past,'[104] they were also the unwitting bearers of a wartime past – in that, for Powell's supporters, they represented a failure in the 'equality of sacrifice' of the postwar years. Immigrant communities represented, then, the consequences of an unsettled postwar settlement. In this sense, the making of postcolonial Britain occurred in conjunction with the *un-making* of the postwar settlement.

Enoch Powell and the making of postcolonial Britain

This book begins at the beginning. Not at the beginning of Powell's life, but at the beginning of a revolt that would culminate in 'the myth, bogyman' Enoch Powell.[105] We begin with imperial Powell – with Powell's experiences in the empire just prior to and during the Second World War as an academic and army officer. Chapter 1, 'Conservative war,' offers the story of the development of Powell's commitments to 'the unique structure of power' of British rule. This chapter reveals that Powell's conservative commitments were born in the context of a deep cynicism regarding the 'new world' of Australia and growing recognition of the profound challenges of American political hegemony. Here, we see Powell's experience of war as distinct in kind from the problematic and transformative domestic war found on Britain's home front, which has been so well documented in recent histories.[106] Powell's experience of war was *not* the 'People's War.' This opening chapter is far more personal than the chapters that follow, both due to the evidence available and because it is here, I argue, that we see much of the making of Powell's (post)colonial outlook.

In an effort to uncover something of the internal decolonization of Britain, Chapter 2, 'Liberal war, 1947–1959,' investigates Powell's initial turn away from Britain's imperial ambitions and the immediate consequences of decolonization for the Conservative Party in the context of the Cold War. As Powell saw it, Britain entered this time 'a sleep and a forgetting.'[107] There is a wealth of historical literature placing US race politics in its Cold War context that has no equivalent in postwar

Indian Workers and Service Personnel in Britain, 1939–1945 (London: Karia, 1985); Sonya O. Rose, *Which People's War? National Identity and Citizenship in Britain, 1939– 1945* (Oxford University Press, 2003); and Rush, *Bonds of Empire.*

[104] Gilroy, *Postcolonial Melancholia*, p. 101.

[105] Shrapnel and Phillips, 'Enoch Powell: An Enigma of Awkward Passions.'

[106] Summerfield, *Reconstructing Women's Wartime Lives*; Sonya Rose, *Which People's War?*; Francis, *The Flyer: British Culture and the Royal Air Force.*

[107] Enoch Powell, 'Oct 23 1959 International Commentary,' Radio Broadcast. POLL 4.1.27.

British history. But the management of race relations in Britain and efforts at the governmental level to maintain and control the *image* of a tolerant Britain were no doubt informed by international tensions. Here, we are reminded that decolonization is only one of many 'inchoate histories of postcolonial Britain.'[108] Memories of (imperial) wars, the politics of anti-racism, the ideological battleground of the Cold War and, even, the US civil rights movement cannot be written out of this complex history. In this sense, understanding Powell and 'Powellism' cannot offer a complete picture of the making of postcolonial Britain. Rather, they promise to tell us only one part of a much larger story.

Both Wendy Webster and Bill Schwarz have emphasized the ways in which the white colonial frontier and the 'disorder' of racial difference was imagined to come home to Britain in the postwar years.[109] The impact of the racial logics of white settler societies on postwar British politics and culture is highly controversial within the historical literature.[110] Still, as Chapter 3 will discuss, it is essential that historians work to place the maintenance and decline of the 'liberal race relations settlement'[111] – which sought to manage 'race' and, crucially, take it out of national political debate – in the context of international Cold War pressures and the fight for racial equality in the colonial world. Chapter 3, 'Without war? Commonwealth and consensus,' analyses Powell's revolt against the reconstruction of Britain's international role and the ways in which the politics of the Commonwealth – on South African membership, on Rhodesian independence, on Kenya's Africanization programmes – came home to Britain. Though the New Commonwealth, in many regards, lacked popular political currency in Britain and appears now as a largely vestigial, linguistic entity, it is still essential in understanding the relationship between the imperial legacy and Britain's postwar reconstructed state. Powell's revolt against the New Commonwealth was a revolt against a particular approach to international, Cold War politics and – linked to this – a liberal, progressive notion of British history as a moral crusade. In the idea of the

---

[108] Bill Schwarz cited by Stephen Howe, 'Internal Decolonization? British Politics since Thatcher as Post-colonial Trauma,' *Twentieth Century British History*, 14: 3 (2003), pp. 286–304 (p. 304).

[109] Schwarz, *The White Man's World*, and Wendy Webster, '"There'll Always be an England": Representations of Colonial Wars and Immigration, 1948–68,' *Journal of British Studies*, 40 (October 2001), pp. 557–584.

[110] See, for instance, John Mackenzie's review of Levine and Grayzel (eds.), *Gender, Labour, War and Empire* (John Mackenzie, 'Gender, Labour, War and Empire: Essays on Modern Britain,' *The Journal of Imperial and Commonwealth History*, 38: 4 (2010), pp. 657–658).

[111] Shamit Saggar, 'The Politics of "Race Policy" in Britain,' *Critical Social Policy*, 13: 37 (July 1993), pp. 32–51.

New Commonwealth, Britain's evangelical mission in the empire was reconstituted as a progressive ideal, imagined as a brotherhood free of racism, military oppression and economic exploitation. Britain's short romance with the ideal of the New Commonwealth served as an essential rhetorical bridge to Britain's post-imperial status and new 'moral' role in the Cold War and on the domestic front.[112] Powell's nationalism, his rejection of British (post)imperial international commitments and the transnational commitments of British citizens, is best understood as a revolt against this – against the new postwar forms of political thinking and action that were, in many ways, fruits of the Cold War. What is unique in Powell – as we shall see especially in the latter half of this book – is the way in which the prism of war left him at times highly sensitive and at times totally blind to the new political realities of the postwar period.

Chapters 4 and 5 set 'Powellism' – or the dramatic popular expressions of support for Powell in the post-1968 years – in the crucial context of political and social discontent. The former treats Powell's 'Rivers of Blood' speech much as Stuart Hall did decades ago, as a symptom of a crisis in the postwar social order. As the work of the Centre for Contemporary Cultural Studies at Birmingham University argued, the 'organic crisis' brought about by Britain's global decline – this 'deep-seated structural crisis of British social formation' – came to be blamed through Powell's rhetoric on the 'new' presence of a black population in British political life.[113] The chapter title, 'The war within,' highlights the profound preoccupation with wartime sacrifice in 1968 and, even more, signals the real key to Powell's anti-liberalism: namely, his opposition to the state's involvement in the moral 'war within' the individual (in this case, on the question of the sin of racism). The book returns in this chapter, then, to an essential aspect of Powell's conservatism, his opposition to the application of Christian (missionary) principles in the political world. Even more, it contends that the populist movement that emerged around Enoch Powell still has much to tell us about class identities and understandings of legitimate governance in postwar Britain. Here and in Chapter 3, we look to the letters to Enoch Powell in 1968. These letters are often highly personal, turning on a story of personal injustice. They read like offerings to Powell – sources to be quoted in

---

[112] Race relations experts would often, in one breath, refer both to Nazism and to Britain's special obligation to set an example of tolerance for the ex-colonies. See Andy Brown, *Political Languages of Race and the Politics of Exclusion* (Aldershot: Ashgate Publishing, 1999).

[113] Centre for Contemporary Cultural Studies, *The Empire Strikes Back: Race and Racism in 70s Britain* (London: Hutchinson, 1982), pp. 9, 32.

his next speech. In these letters, in the thousands of acts of writing to Powell and in Powell's uses of them, we see the translation of private histories into political meaning.

Chapter 5, 'Naming the crisis,' uncovers the logic behind Powell's turn to the politics of Ulster Unionism against European unity. Powellism is treated in this chapter as a revolt against new transnational thinking and action. Enoch Powell viewed extra-parliamentary political groups and supranational bodies as a consequence of forgetting the true nature of politics. New Left internationalism was born, in Powell's mind, out of a generation who had not seen the realities of war. Beyond Powell, we see, here, his contribution to a particular view of the social and political uncertainties of the 1970s. The enduring view, which really took hold in these years, that Britons must face a constant crisis of national identity is one key feature, I would argue, to understanding postcolonial British history. Lastly, the Postscript, 'Enoch Powell and Thatcherism,' questions the links between Thatcherism's evangelical mission and the politics of nation proposed and promoted by Enoch Powell.

This book is the story of a revolt. It treats Powell's life – his old eyes on new events – as a window into the dramatic shifts in meaning that were experienced in Britain in the postwar period. In civil society and in politics, the system of social difference that was once wedded to the imperial order was beginning to come unhinged. With such a perspective, it is possible to see that the black Briton was in no way a new political subject but came to embody for Powell – through the rise of the New Left especially – new political forms, new commitments and new transnational alliances that levelled a profound attack on the legitimacy of a once imperial order.

1   Conservative war, 1938–1947

> To be one of the diminishing number of those who actually witnessed the phenomenon of British India is like belonging to a dying race which cannot pass its secrets on.
>
> J. Enoch Powell, 1959[1]

In 1987, the Imperial War Museum began a series of interviews with Enoch Powell on his war memories.[2] He remarked then that the war, his experience of the war, 'my war' had ended 'with a blank.'[3] Though not clear, 'a blank' here probably represents a key absence, the absence of a memory, an unmarked, uncorrupted space – but it also potentially indicates the noun: a blank cartridge. Though a successful officer in the British Army, Powell shot no bullet while at war. When the interviewer asked Powell what he meant, Powell revealed perhaps the most defining feature of his war experience: by going to India, Powell had unwittingly left 'the theatre of war.' In telling the story of his war experience to the interviewer, he was suddenly struck by this discovery: 'It's something which I find almost impossible to believe now as I reproduce the narrative, that during the entire period from the landing of D-Day to VJ Day, I was in a sense encapsulated in India.'[4] He went on:

… I find it very strange that out of a war which for me lasted six and a half years, no less than two and half were spent away, out of the war, concentrating upon scenes – upon a theatre – which was part of a general history of centuries and not directly involved in continuing warfare. And that my mind should have been able to concentrate so intensely upon India, its present and its future while Europe was being pulverised. Japan of course was pulverised but then the length of time involved in that, between May and August 1945, was not really so significant.

When recalling all this, he could 'hardly believe the chronology.'[5] So separate was the Eastern theatre from the European, 'so back to back

[1] Enoch Powell, 'Passage to England,' *Birmingham Post*, 20 August 1959. POLL 6.1.1C.
[2] For the copies of the audio, see POLL 5.1. For transcripts, see POLL 1.6.26.
[3] 'JEP War Memories.' POLL 5.1.
[4] Ibid.   [5] Ibid.

were those views of the world and so inadequate in India,' that, 'my mind was totally unaffected by the gigantic struggle in which Germany was destroyed by the Allies in Europe.'[6] It seemed to both him and his wife 'simply incredible' that one could be 'so estranged [from] what I now see in retrospect was so large a fraction of the total war,' so completely estranged from the European war.[7] The import of Powell's response to the radio interviewer's question in 1986, 'How would you like to be remembered?' – which was 'I should like to have been killed in the war' – cannot be exaggerated.[8] Still, he emphasized, the war as he experienced it in India was to make a lasting imprint.

As noted in 1970 by the *People's Voice* (Wolverhampton's short-lived local anti-racist newspaper), after Powell came to be identified by protesters with the leader of the Third Reich, 'an account of his heroic exploits in the Indian Army served as a preface to almost every address.'[9] Much of the literature on Powell takes Powell's love and loss of the British Raj as a starting point in understanding his later nationalism.[10] While Powell's absolute obedience to the disciplines of military life in Britain, North Africa and India has been offered as a telling indicator of Powell's character,[11] the extent to which Powell understood the empire – and the British Raj particularly – through the prism of war has been largely neglected. Crucially, this is not unique to Powell: military service was the key avenue by which British men experienced imperialism on the ground. As this chapter will explore, Powell believed that the unity of the British Empire, across the borders of difference, was a product of war.

Powell's political formation is mapped onto a life lived day by day – a life which had a material geography and an uncertain future. This chapter is, in large part, concerned with the singular life of Enoch Powell, in adult years, prior to his emergence as a political figure. As John Dryden wrote while preparing an edition of Plutarch over three centuries ago, 'There [in the works of political history] you are conducted only into the Rooms of State; but here [in biography] you are led into the private lodgings of the hero: you see him undress ... The pageantry of life is taken away; you see the poor reasonable animal, as naked as ever Nature made him.'[12] The humanized Powell, 'the poor

[6] Ibid.   [7] Ibid.
[8] Cited in Heffer, *Like the Roman*, p. 901.
[9] *People's Voice* (1970). Collected by J. Enoch Powell in SRO D4490/49.
[10] Rutherford, *Forever England*; Peter Brooke, 'India, Post-Imperialism and the Origins of Enoch Powell's "Rivers of Blood" Speech,' *Historical Journal*, 50: 3 (2007), pp. 668–687.
[11] Cosgrave, *The Lives of Enoch Powell*; Heffer, *Like the Roman*.
[12] Cited in Richard Holmes, 'The Proper Study?' in Peter France and William St Clair (eds.), *Mapping Lives: The Uses of Biography* (Oxford University Press, 2002), p. 10.

reasonable animal' must be found, somehow, in conjunction with the Powell found in published texts. Powell himself was acutely conscious during these war years of his own self-construction over time, writing to his mother and father perpetually about his future career. Powell's own schema of his life – his first, second and (as yet undefined) 'third life' in politics – would later define the chapters of his biographies.[13] As he wrote in 1944:

I also spend much mental leisure in hard and deliberate reflection upon the strategy of my own personal life campaign – a problem harder than any purely military one, if only from the inherent difficulty of defining the object, or, more accurately, of legislating for a single human being whose object is a variable, grows and changes with his own growth and change. It is this baffling instability of the individual, as opposed to the national, purpose, which mocks the philosopher's attempts to reason his way through.

Powell's difficulty with self-construction reminds us to beware a telescoped view of Powell's life – reading his pre-1968 self as singularly a reflection of and explanation for his post-1968 self. Henry James is helpful here, noting that the trouble with death is that it 'smoothes the folds' of a person. 'The figure retained by memory is compressed and intensified; accidents have dropped away from it and shades have ceased to count; it stands sharply, for a few estimated and cherished things, rather than nebulously, for a swarm of possibilities.'[14] The accidents, the alternatives, 'the swarm of possibilities' in Powell's life still, though, do not offer an alternative ending.

Vast, sprawling suburbs

As an impressionable young man of twenty-five, Powell arrived to a new colonial life in Australia in 1938. He had secured a Chair in Greek at the University of Sydney. He officially became, in 1938, the youngest professor in the British Empire.[15] Before Sydney, he had taken a distinguished first class degree in classics from Trinity College, Cambridge and, at the very young age of twenty-two, was named a fellow of the college. He was, according to one professor there, considered 'something of a prodigy,'[16] teaching and publishing prolifically. Importantly, he was a prodigy from humble beginnings – a diligent outsider, the son

[13] Cosgrave, *The Lives of Enoch Powell*; Heffer, 'The third life,' in *Like the Roman*.
[14] Henry James, 'James Russell Lowell,' *Atlantic Monthly*, February 1892; cited in Hermione Lee, *Body Parts: Essays in Life-Writing* (London: Chatto & Windus, 2005), p. 2.
[15] Heffer, *Like the Roman*, p. 35.   [16] Ibid., p. 25.

of a Birmingham elementary schoolmaster and a teacher. His interest in the philosophy of history – by historians of war – was already clear at this young age, working as he did on 'The Moral and Political Ideas of Thucydides' as an undergraduate and then, as a fellow, on *The Lexicon of Herodotus*, which remained in print until 1977.[17] Powell's understanding of international relations was at least in part touched by his work on Thucydides, now read by students of international relations as one of the first proponents of a 'realist' approach. When Powell later sought out a professorship, British universities were unwilling to hire someone so young. And so, he took the best job he could find: a Chair in Greek in Sydney, Australia. Emigration to Australia functioned for Powell as it had done for many other Britons: as a means of social mobility.

When Australian journalist Luke Slattery first uncovered the letters between Powell and his parents held at the University of Sydney – letters closed from view until Powell's death – he emphasized the possible significance of prewar Australia in Powell's 'preparation for the political life.'[18] The letters, he tentatively proposes, could help to resolve the paradox of outspoken xenophobia touching such a highly educated man.[19] Slattery sees in these letters 'a lost era com[ing] to life; these were the last days of a charmed pre-war empire viewed with a sharp eye from its furthest colonial fringe.'[20] The letters, at very least, tell us of prewar Powell. As Slattery puts it, they introduce us to a man with a 'prematurely crusty disposition' and a 'strange, intense, personality, and … overweening self belief.'[21]

This chapter tells the story of one young man in the empire, of his disorientation, crisis and ensuing political commitment. It begins with 'Jack' Powell alone and over 13,000 miles from home in 1938 in Sydney, Australia. Like many millions of Britons, Powell wrote home from the empire. The living out of empire, through the lives and letters of men and women across the globe, still has much to tell us of imperial Britain. Powell, in these letters home right before and during the war, is at times xenophobic, at times curious, at times deeply disorientated. However, what marks Powell's letters out – especially at the cusp of imperial dissolution – is most of all his clearly blossoming commitment to 'our Far Eastern Empire.'[22] While the British wartime public in large part turned inwards,[23] Powell was turned out: as he said, to 'India to touch

[17] J. Enoch Powell, 'The Moral and Political Ideas of Thucydides,' POLL 1.6.21 and J. Enoch Powell, *Lexicon of Herodotus* (Cambridge University Press, 1938).
[18] Luke Slattery, 'Letters Home,' *The Australian*, 4 March 1998.
[19] Ibid.   [20] Ibid.   [21] Ibid.
[22] Powell to Ellen and Albert Powell, 25 July 1943. POLL 1.1.5.
[23] See, for instance, J. B. Priestley, *Postscripts* (London: William Heinemann, 1940).

the hem of the British Raj, which can be described to no one who has not experienced it.'[24] Powell's experience of war was distinct in kind, then, from the transformative domestic war found on Britain's home front.[25] This was, for Powell, a conservative war – a war to preserve, not transform, the imperial nation. This commitment to the survival of the imperial nation took hold of him at the same time as did a deep anti-Americanism. Even the origins of Powell's political views cannot be understood outside of the context of rising American power. While in North Africa in 1943, Powell became obsessed with the encroaching dominance of the United States. At that time, he explicitly told his parents that he sought a military appointment in the Far East because 'the survival of the British Empire' depended on British recovery of the Far East before it became 'occupied by the United States.'[26] How Powell conceived of the validity of British rule against American power would continue to have an impact on his thinking for the rest of his life.

Powell's understanding of British rule was consequently structured by three colonial worlds which were introduced to him over these years: the world of the Australian suburbs, the world of the American mess hall in Algiers and the world of the Indian Army. In his responses to these cultures of empire we can see the development of a very specific, conservative understanding of the limits and possibilities of British imperial rule. Most of all, we can see Powell developing a belief in 'natural' rule versus 'impersonation' – and an obsession with the linkage between historical consciousness and political legitimacy.

While in India, Powell felt himself become a 'natural' part of the scene, convinced of his place as an Englishman in India's history (he later called this an illusion);[27] the *tabula rasa* of the 'new world,' however, disturbed Powell. As he later put it of Australia and the United States, the new world gave him a 'dull pang,' 'the heartache of the exile, the oppressive sense of being remote, so remote, from everything that ultimately mattered, from all that gave one birth.'[28] Due to its colonial nature, the allegiance of Australia to British imperial rule was fragile at best. In Powell's mind, Britishness as a liberal project that could transform the world into Britain's likeness – into a political community of culture and ideas – had already proven itself to be a failure. Neither

[24] J. Enoch Powell, 'Pommy Professor,' *The Times Educational Supplement*, 28 February 1964.
[25] Summerfield, *Reconstructing Women's Wartime Lives*; Sonya Rose, *Which People's War?*
[26] As cited in Cosgrave, *The Lives of Enoch Powell*, p. 81.
[27] J. Enoch Powell, 'A Passage to India,' *Folio*, Summer 1983, pp. 15–22 (p. 21).
[28] J. Enoch Powell, 'The Great American Dilemma,' *Sunday Telegraph*, 17 March 1968.

whiteness nor 'colourblind' Britishness was enough to produce political unity across the geography of divergent defence interests.

Still, Powell's understanding of his place in the British Raj was absolutely a product of his vision of the historical role of the 'white man.' What Powell believed Australia lacked (an organic, hierarchical community connected to and sanctified by history) Powell found in the British Raj – specifically in the Indian Army. The paradox of empire – as both a place of subjugation and ordered difference as well as a place of change, assimilation and hybridity[29] – is present in this story of imperial Powell. In many respects, military allegiance as that which defines political community avoids the goal of assimilation and the inevitable question, following on from the promise of assimilation, of equality. No doubt, war – as ever-present threat and source of history – is a particularly useful logic of belonging in a historically imperial, multinational, multicultural and classed political body. As Powell's later arguments concerning the fall of the British Raj make clear, Powell's focus on the historical institution of war service as that which defines political community resulted in a highly gendered understanding of citizenship. Even more, Powell's conception of the relationship between hierarchy, political identity and war service – born, again, in the context of the Indian Army – underpinned his later concerns over Britain's increasing reliance on nuclear defence after 1957.

In later chapters, I hope to show that these two understandings of belonging – the centrality of war in defining who could be called British versus Britishness as a liberal project (which was to be remade after the war to fit the ideological parameters of the Cold War) – are both artefacts of empire. Powell's story highlights the ways in which these two historical visions of political belonging came into conflict as a result of decolonization. This adds a dimension to the significant work that Bill Schwarz has done on the ideological valences between the populism of Powell's supporters in the 1960s and 1970s and the ethnic populisms of Australia, South Africa and Rhodesia.[30] Here, in Powell at least, we see a preoccupation with the limits of British culture in Australia and an embrace, in India, of a near-defunct racial order (embedded, he believed, in institutions, history and social memory). Over the years, these experiences continued to structure Powell's views on political identity. Powell's conception of national belonging as fragile, contingent and constructed is no doubt linked to his experience of the 'new world' and Britain's fall from power. As Bernard Porter has noted,

[29] Homi Bhabha, *The Location of Culture* (New York: Routledge, 1994).
[30] Schwarz, *The White Man's World*.

Powell's view in the early 1960s that 'all history is myth'[31] was ahead of his time.[32] This view of history as political myth has gained popularity due to the profound influence that postcolonial criticism had on the discipline of history. Powell's thinking about the relationship between culture and political power was, as the story of imperial Powell makes clear, similarly born out of the imperial experience.

Powell called the journey over to Australia by flying-boat an 'immense revelation.' 'It was a living geography and imperial lesson … the extraordinary sense of the inevitability – an apparently strange word to use – of British power was very strongly borne in upon me,' he remembered. 'It seemed to me that the combination of sea power and air power which Britain still exhibited, gave to the structure of a British Empire an inherent strength which I was later to learn it didn't possess.'[33] This is Powell's first vision of the natural, the inevitable nature of British power – a vision that would be attenuated by experiences on the ground. Writing to his parents on arrival in Australia, Powell's first account of India on a stopover during this journey was, however, by no means indicative of his later 'love affair':

I was glad to be through India, where I felt a certain oppressiveness in the atmosphere difficult to describe. The people have not the spontaneity which makes the populations further east attractive, but a kind of dumb, almost animal, servility which to me came as a painful affront; largely, but not entirely, I think this is a projection of a fundamentally insubordinate nature. I do not find that others are affected in the same way.[34]

Race appears very seldom in the eight years of letters – posted usually once a week – which Powell wrote to his parents. But it appeared again only a month later; this time when speaking of Australians. In both, it seems that young Jack Powell found, or tested, a racial explanation for the inevitability of British power. In this letter, Powell described the '4 best classical men I have met' in Sydney. Three have 'nervous mannerisms and are ugly to the degree of deformity,' the fourth is an exception. 'Why? He is the son of a professor at the University who came from Scotland 25 years ago … courtly, clever, handsome, fit, mentally and physically supple, I realize there are good reasons for our Empire and that in England we take for granted a standard of human material which is elsewhere hard to seek.'[35]

[31] J. Enoch Powell, speech at Trinity College, Dublin, 13 November 1964, in Powell, *Freedom and Reality*, ed. John Wood (London: B. T. Batsford, 1969), p. 324.
[32] Porter, *The Absent-minded Imperialists*, p. 4.
[33] 'JEP War Memories.' POLL 5.1.
[34] Powell to Ellen and Albert Powell, 25 February 1938. POLL 1.1.4.
[35] Powell to Ellen and Albert Powell, 19 March 1938. POLL 1.1.4.

Patrick Cosgrave, Powell's one-time biographer, remarks that Powell was, 'greatly attracted to the virginity of the soil, both intellectual and physical ... [and] rightly praised the Australians for their eagerness and energy in all fields, and derided by comparison the slothful and self-indulgent fellow countrymen he had left behind.'[36] But Cosgrave, in his analysis, did not have access to Powell's private letters. There is evidence of an acute ambiguity to this 'virginity of the soil' in Powell. The problem in Australia was not merely racial, but also a problem of class: 'The dreadful thing about this country is its dead level, without ostentatious wealth or (the necessary complement) abject poverty ... It is not that there is a big proportion of "tikes" in the country; there is literally nobody here who is not a "tike."'[37] The 'dead level' that Powell noted here was a problem of cultural, historical 'cultivation' – which was in no small way linked in Powell's mind to Australia's weakening connections to and dependency on British imperial power.

There in Australia, Powell travelled the country, as well as throughout New Zealand and Tasmania, lobbying for the need for strengthened Greek education in secondary schools and universities. He spoke on Australian radio, gave lectures and wrote papers on the case for Greek in national education. He believed, he said, that the study of Greek civilization challenged the uncritical acceptance of social and moral convention; in the vast hinterland of the antipodes, the Australian needed more than ever to be brought 'face to face' with the Greek.[38] Powell found an audience of like-minded men and women who were similarly concerned with the state of Australia, such as those who supported Australia's English Association. Powell even chaired the Syllabus Committee for Greek, which would report to Australia's Department of Education in 1939.

Through this work especially, Powell considered the future prospects of the British colonial empire as 'new world.' Australia was a fragile partner, in a critical state of transition in terms of its defence interests and cultural identity. Australia was a world, for Powell, of 'vast, sprawling suburbs' which, without continuous dialogue with Europe, was in danger of complacency and 'a kind of cultural solipsism.'[39] It was a world, Powell feared, that had more in common with the United States than with Britain. The insoluble problem for Powell was this:

[It is] the dilemma of a population the English-speaking part of which is to an increasingly degree Australian by birth and environment, but which nevertheless

[36] Cosgrave, *The Lives of Enoch Powell*, p. 57.
[37] Ibid.   [38] Ibid.
[39] J. Enoch Powell, 'Pommy Professor,' *The Times Educational Supplement*, 28 February 1964.

can have no culture that does not derive, or rather import, from Europe and
in particular England. Not in centuries of placid development could Australia
acquire so much native culture that this would cease to be true.

Powell then referred obliquely to the fact that the likely solution to this
dilemma was independence – a 'rough' solution:

But long before then events which neither know nor care anything for culture
or education will probably have solved the dilemma, and solved it roughly.
Meanwhile the only reasonable policy for education in Australia is to foster
every possible way its connection with the English education of which it is a
remote and unhappily situated fragment.[40]

Australia, though it had strong Greek and Latin programmes, was
unlike Britain where classics was an educational pursuit of the upper
classes and where 'a good degree in classics offers on the whole the
best prospects not only in the employ of the government, such as the
civil, diplomatic, colonial and consular services, but also in such non-
governmental enterprise as the railways.'[41] The land of 'tikes' – the land
of the uncouth and boorish – gave no such weight, Powell found, to the
moral refinement of its political leaders and industrialists. But, Powell
emphasized in another lecture, 'You may conclude that I am cynical or
sordid: but I believe that friends of classical scholarship would profit
their cause more if they allowed as little as possible to be heard about
cultural values ... and addressed themselves instead to the hard lousi-
ness of making the education of which they preach the gospel a practical and, above all, a paying business.'[42] In other words, 'culture' and
power needed to be made stronger allies. He argued that the future
of classics – 'and so of humanistic education generally' – in Australia
depended on the state and federal governments recruiting their staff on
the same basis as done in Britain.

Despite this emphasis on practicalities, Powell's views on education
were at this time also clearly informed by the work of Friedrich Nietzsche
and that 'mighty river of German nineteenth-century philosophy.'[43]

---

[40] J. Enoch Powell, 'Greek in Australia,' 1939. POLL 1.1.2.
[41] J. Enoch Powell, 'Greek in New Zealand,' 1939. POLL 1.1.2.
[42] J. Enoch Powell, 'Greek in Australia,' 1939. POLL 1.1.2.
[43] J. Enoch Powell, 'Sentimental Journey,' from *A Second* Listener *Anthology*, BBC
Publications, London, 1970 in *Reflections of a Statesman*, pp. 104–111 (p. 108). 'The
young Friedrich Nietzsche was destined to be my companion through every published scrap of his writing from the opening bars of *The Birth of Tragedy* right on into
the ultimate explosion into insanity of *Ecce Homo*. The journey ran parallel in the
years from 1933 to 1939 with the collapse of the Germany of Beethoven and Goethe,
the enthronement of Satan upon its ruins, and the launching of war in Europe.
Meanwhile I dived in and out of the mighty river of German nineteenth-century
philosophy – itself, despite the often less than sensuous language clothing it, as much

This prefigured in Powell's thinking a (very Nietzschean) understanding of the social value of national myths, which would in later years colour Powell's views on political identity in Britain. On education, Powell argued via Nietzsche that training in the classics might serve as an antidote to the modern conditions of Australia.

Ours is an age when the engines for the diffusion of bad taste possess great force. With rare exceptions, the cinema, the newspaper and the wireless tend powerfully to promote vulgarity. By day and night in our cities the eye and the ear are continually assaulted by objects of bad taste. And the need of counteracting these influences is not at its least among a nation like the Australian, which has no tradition to fall back upon, and none of the sobering and steadying influences of a 'past at its doors.'[44]

As he later explained: 'Training in the recognition of *style* sharpens, according to Nietzsche, our perception and disgust for the medley of all styles in the modern world, which in *Zarathustra* he satirizes under the name "the city called 'bunte kuh,' the cow of many colours."'[45] Against the anarchy of competing cultural forms and 'vulgarity' of the modern world, a Greek education offers a sense of a hierarchy of (aesthetic) value and, via the history of translation, a history of culture. This was the best hope, Powell asserted, for the work of making Australians into Nietzsche's vision of 'good Europeans': 'a sound and broad understanding of the history, and consequently of the nature, of our culture itself, is the best antidote to that barbarism of a present without a past.'[46]

Powell was, then in 1939, no technocratic modernizer, embracing the brutal 'eagerness and energy' of the Australian suburbs. Powell felt both at home and at odds with his surroundings in Australia. It was a place for him of uncanny resemblances and impersonations. He wrote home to his parents, 'It's weird. We are standing at the moment at a covered station platform, indistinguishable from an English one, with WARWICK written on the seats,'[47] and wrote again, 'What struck me most about the ceremony was a kind of religious awe at the "impersonation"; that is to say, the Governor is not himself but an impersonation

poetry as pure reason. In particular, for one torn between myth and reality, poetry and prose, Schopenhauer was unavoidable. His *World as Will and Imagination* was consumed in half-hour stretches day by day on Sydney tramcars that clanged their way through the hot Australian sunlight.'

[44] J. Enoch Powell, 'Greek in the University,' Inaugural Lecture, Sydney University, 7 May 1938, in *Reflections of a Statesman*, pp. 87–96 (pp. 88–89).

[45] J. Enoch Powell, 'Nietzsche on Education,' 1939. POLL 1.1.12.

[46] J. Enoch Powell, 'Greek in the University,' 1938, in *Reflections of a Statesman*, p. 95.

[47] Powell to Ellen and Albert Powell, 22 May 1939. POLL 1.1.4.

of the King, receiving largely the same forms, which creates a very peculiar psychological atmosphere.'[48] Australia posed a fundamental problem to Powell: the artificiality of the new world. The political and cultural disjuncture of the 'new world' was mirrored, too, in Powell's feeling of being taken out of the stream of his own history. It was 'the oppressive sense of being remote, from everything that ultimately mattered, from all that gave one birth.'[49] He found himself 'disposed to view my own life and ambitions, as well as those of others, with a more theoretical detachment. But perhaps this is after all a natural result of the almost complete break with my past,' which leaving Britain had brought about.[50] The next month he wrote of his trans-continental journeying as making him 'feel as though the force of gravity has ceased to operate and I were in danger of dropping off the bottom of the world into space.'[51]

Powell's preoccupation with being taken outside the stream of history was only heightened by the lead-up to war. There was in Australia, he noted, the 'unreal sensation in those two years of 1938 and 1939' that everything that was happening in Europe 'was happening in a different world altogether.'[52] Powell wrote that he felt he alone could hear German divisions marching across Europe: 'I could hear this drumming coming through the earth and coming up again in Australia where no one else could hear it.'[53] One specific historic moment which likewise touched Powell occurred on 27 April 1939, when the British Parliament enacted the Conscription Law, bringing compulsory military service to Britain. Two days later, Powell found that, 'After advocating it for years at almost personal risk, [he] was grieved when it happened.' He was, he wrote: 'Grieved because the step is irrevocable, and cannot be traced as long as there is an England at all, so that the Old England, "England before conscription" … is gone forever; grieved also because I thereby feel myself suddenly become a generation older, for a gulf will hereafter separate those who were over 21 in 1939 from those who were under. What I left, I shall not return to.'[54] History was happening without him.

At this time, Powell yearned for the onset of war, and condemned the 'madness' of appeasement. He had what he later called 'a repugnance'

[48] Powell to Ellen and Albert Powell, 12 June 1938. POLL 1.1.4.
[49] J. Enoch Powell, 'The Great American Dilemma.'
[50] Powell to Ellen and Albert Powell, 26 August 1938. POLL 1.1.4.
[51] Powell to Ellen and Albert Powell, 18 September 1938. POLL 1.1.4.
[52] 'JEP War Memories.' POLL 5.1.
[53] J. Enoch Powell, 'My Early Life,' The Listener, vol. 80, no. 2074, 26 December 1968.
[54] Powell to Ellen and Albert Powell, 29 April 1939. POLL 1.1.4.

for 'the 1930s legacy of [Stanley] Baldwin ... of the dangerous insularity, if you like, of Baldwin.'[55] Powell's opposition to peace at any cost was long and thoroughgoing. Powell readied himself for war with the 'picture of the trenches, it was the picture of war as it was in 1918, the picture of war as it was when an infantry officer's expectation of life was three weeks.'[56] He had seen the war coming for five years and regarded it as 'a resumption where war left off in November, 1918.'[57] Powell felt 'ashamed of my own country [during] the Chamberlainite appeasement era of 1937–1939, and I recall to this day my sensation of embarrassment on producing a British passport at the German frontier in December 1938,' on his way to Britain during the Australian summer holidays.[58] He had travelled there to Germany to secure a British visa for his friend, the German Jewish classicist Paul Maas, staying three weeks there in the winter of 1938 mostly in the homes of German Jews. By this visit, he later recalled, he had begun to equate Nazi Germany with 'satanic power.'[59]

Three days after Prime Minister Neville Chamberlain met with Hitler and agreed to Hitler's demand to annex the Czech area of Sudetenland, he wrote angrily to his parents,

I do here in the most solemn and bitter manner curse the Prime Minister of England for having cumulated all his other betrayals of the national interest and honour, by his last terrible exhibition of dishonour, weakness and gullibility. The depths of infamy to which our accurst 'love of peace' can lower us are unfathomable. And I also state here that I desire war, and war now, and that I have no higher ambition than that all three of us should in our several ways meet our deaths in the service of the King, 'where unto we are bound' (Coriolanus).[60]

This outburst – which Powell probably wrote while sitting alone in a vast, sprawling suburb of Australia – is one of many of Powell's assertions of absolute deference, body and soul, to British rule. From the artificiality of Britishness abroad, Powell found himself in an oath to the King. From disorientation and isolation in Australia, Powell sought the certainty of war. Six months later he wrote: 'Oh to be at war to have

---

[55] J. Enoch Powell, Bill Schwarz interview, 26 April 1988. Powell had been 'so sickened' by Baldwin's policy of insularity and commitment to peace that he had even asked, in 1935, if his fellowship at Cambridge University could be put on hold so that he could go fight the Italians in Abyssinia.

[56] 'JEP War Memories.' POLL 5.1.

[57] Ibid.

[58] Cited in Cosgrave, *The Lives of Enoch Powell*, p. 57.

[59] 'JEP War Memories.' POLL 5.1.

[60] Powell to Ellen and Albert Powell, 18 September 1938. POLL 1.1.4.

a chance to kill and be killed! I wish I were German and not an English cur. The fulsomeness of us is indescribable.'[61] This language of bellicosity and this sense of shame in the prewar years were not unique to Powell. The British press, though, in large part kept in line with the government policy of appeasement in the lead-up to the war[62] and, as one female Mass-Observation respondent noted in the 1990s (rationalizing her support for the first Gulf War), 'How relieved we felt – how misguided we were,' on Neville Chamberlain's return from Munich.[63] Powell, lost in the new world, looked on at his compatriots with anger and disbelief.

The colonial distance with which Powell viewed the coming war so heightened this emotional response that he was compelled, he later explained, to write poetry. 'All this painful emotion struggling into verse,' he later wrote, had 'crossed the world … to Australia, not undiminished, but rather heightened by the sensation of living amongst those to whom the sound of impending doom appeared to be inaudible.'[64] When an Englishman was killed by Japanese forces in the course of the Sino-Japanese war in June 1939, Powell offered one of his most bitter condemnations of the policy of appeasement:

> Murdered, deny who can,
> Here lies an Englishman;
> The steel that through him ran
> Was tempered in Japan.
>
> Who then the murderer?
> England, that would not stir,
> Not though he died for her;
> England, the slumberer.
>
> His cry she would not hear
> Because insensate fear
> Had stopped the mother's ear;
> But now revenge is near,
>
> For while his land forgets
> And bends the knee to threats,
> His vengeful spirit whets
> The German bayonets.[65]

[61] Powell to Ellen and Albert Powell, 19 March 1939. POLL 1.1.4.
[62] Anthony Adamthwaite, 'The British Government and the Media, 1937–1938,' *Journal of Contemporary History*, 18: 2 (April 1983), pp. 281–297.
[63] Noakes, *War and the British*, p. 153.
[64] J. Enoch Powell, cited in Shepherd, *Enoch Powell*, p. 36.
[65] Powell, *Collected Poems*, p. 115.

Powell's isolation in the new world, the distance he felt from the structures of feeling in Britain in the lead-up to the war, profoundly affected
his understanding and experiences of the war itself. As he remembered
it, 'The familiar 1914–18 shape of the impending doom I now perceived
increasingly in terms of the Pacific.'[66] Crucially, from the perspective
of Sydney, appeasement not only meant appeasement to Hitler but also
represented the threat of Britain's increasing imperial apathy.

The People's War

On 5 September 1939, two days after Britain and France declared
war on Germany, Powell was on an aeroplane back from Australia
to Britain, determined to join the war effort. Here we find Powell,
for the next two years in training, conspicuously out of step with the
new home front. He arrived to 'an England at war, it was an England
under the black-out, it was an England which hadn't yet discovered
that it could live with war and to which war was still an unknown
and therefore a terrifying quantity.'[67] When he attempted to enlist
as a private, however, he was turned away – the War Office did not
want professors with no Territorial Army background. Still, he had
heard elsewhere that men who travelled from the colonies to enlist
were being accepted. So he pursued this and, on the basis of his few
years in Sydney, the Australia House gave him a piece of paper cer-
tifying that he was in fact Australian. That document got him into
the army.[68] And so, he recounted, 'one of the happiest days' of his life
came on 'the 20th of October 1939. It was then for the first time I put
on the King's coat.'[69]

Powell therefore spent very little time in Britain as a civilian during
the war. Before being discovered by chance as 'officer material' (by making a joke in Greek to a visiting brigadier), Powell trained in Warwick
as a private soldier in the Royal Warwickshire Regiment. Here, in the
Warwickshire Regiment, Powell felt he finally had the chance to witness
history. This was England's professional army:

[T]here was a sense in those barracks which I strongly had, that I had rejoined
the army of the Peninsular War. It was the professional army, it was the army
of a series of professional soldier's wars. There's a passage in Carlyle when
he says, 'What would we not give to meet alive one of the hypaspists [foot

[66] J. Enoch Powell, cited in Shepherd, *Enoch Powell*, p. 37.
[67] 'JEP War Memories.' POLL 5.1.
[68] Heffer, *Like the Roman*, p. 56.
[69] *Sunday Telegraph*, 6 February 1966.

guardsmen] of Alexander?' Well, at least I felt I had just known before it disappeared forever, the army of Wellington.

Despite the enactment of conscription, Powell still felt he had witnessed
Old England, 'England before conscription.'

Powell recalled that he took to being a private soldier 'like a duck
to water. It's the nicest thing to be. It seemed to me such a congenial
environment, but the whole institution of the army, the framework of
discipline, the exactitude of rank, the precision of duty was something
almost restful and attractive to me.'[70] Powell's belief in institutional
order and his stark tendency to appear to live according to it – to find
mental freedom in the framework of institutional discipline – sheds
light on Powell's understanding and experience of community. Powell is
variously described in these years as awkward, stiff and competitive – a
'strange bird' was 'Cub' Alport's description.[71] Though there are certainly references, too, to Powell's sense of humour and charm, the persistence of his apparent social 'exactitude' challenges us to consider
the relationship between Powell's *experience* of class and cultural convention and his political ideas. As the aristocratic 'Cub' Alport put it
when interviewing Powell for a role in the research department of the
Conservative Party not long after the Second World War: 'He wasn't
the sort of brigadier I had been accustomed to in my own army career.
For all the shine of his buttons, I noticed his shoes were dirty.'[72] In this
perfectly constructed description, Powell is revealed as too shiny, too
exact, with too much effort, and essentially unkempt, without servants
(or wife). It is a perfect, pejorative description of class aspiration. Still,
Alport concedes: 'but he told me he had been a fellow of Trinity, which
always impresses someone like myself. I was very anxious to recruit
intellectuals, who before the war had been alienated by the Conservative
party.'[73] And so Powell was hired. In understanding Powell, it is insuf-
ficient to read him as merely a class outsider who ruthlessly pursued status and power. Rather, as the chapters that follow will indicate, Powell
remained acutely conscious, as he put it in 1988, of that 'web of understood relationships which sustains society.'[74] That social norms were
perhaps experienced by Powell as a performance rather than a natural
certainty may, too, have informed his views on the fragility of culture
and civility.

---

[70] Heffer, *Like the Roman*, p. 57.
[71] *Sunday Telegraph Magazine*, 28 August 1977, as cited in Heffer, *Like the Roman*, p. 101.
[72] Ibid.   [73] Ibid.
[74] Bill Schwarz interview with Enoch Powell, 26 April 1988 (private recording).

Powell remembered his fellow soldiers in the Warwickshire Regiment in an interview in 1980. Here, we see Powell attempting to describe his own political formation. Unlike himself, he noted in 1980, 'They were not keen to be soldiers and they were very conscious of the civil life that they'd left behind.'[75] He was friendly, for instance, with a fireman on a railway engine. He was 'very much a railwayman,' who expected to 'spend his lifetime, so far as it wasn't interrupted by the war' on the railway.[76] Despite their utter identification with their civilian selves, Powell was quick to note, they did not resent being called up as soldiers and 'were not irked by a discipline of the industrial life which most of them had been living.'[77] These soldiers were busy, not in the pursuit of a soldier's life, but in getting by: in 'Hanging out the washing on the Siegfried line.'[78] What struck Powell hardest at this time, his 'lesson ... about my fellow men,' was that, unlike Powell, these men did not seek out advancement. 'I wanted promotion, I wanted to get on, I wanted rank, I wanted authority. The lesson I learnt was that they didn't.'[79] Powell's experience of the privates in his regiment, though only at the beginning of the war, emphasizes and reasserts his focus on the conservative effects of war. The war, Powell believed, did not disrupt the soldiers' sense of place and the order of civilian society.[80]

In the winter of 1939, on his first weekend leave as a private, Powell visited Cambridge and found a copy of Carl von Clausewitz's *On War* in a second-hand bookshop. He stayed up night after night absorbed by it. This philosophy of war was to have a profound influence on his analysis of the next few years: 'it gripped my mind,' he said.[81] After three months of basic training at Budbrooke Barracks outside Warwick, he was sent in January 1940 to Aldershot to begin training as an officer.[82] In his memoirs of the war, one fellow officer in training remembered the impression Powell made at Aldershot: 'He was reserved,

---

[75] Heffer, *Like the Roman*, p. 17.
[76] Ibid.   [77] Ibid.   [78] Ibid.   [79] Ibid.
[80] Powell's emphasis on the conservative effects of war touches on a still contested historical issue. See Paul Addison, *The Road to 1945: British Politics and the Second World War* (London: Pimlico, 1975) for the argument that the experience of the war produced a political shift in public opinion towards the acceptance of social reform. In opposition, see Steven Fielding, Peter Thompson and Nick Tiratsoo, *'England Arise!': The Labour Party and Popular Politics in 1940s Britain* (Manchester University Press, 1995) that puts forward that, 'Above all else, the war had been extremely disruptive and so there was a common desire that it should be followed by a period of normalcy ... Wider [political] questions seemed less pressing,' p. 39.
[81] 'JEP War Memories.' POLL 5.1.   [82] Ibid.

taciturn and generally believed in the platoon to be modelling himself on the Prussian Great General Staff ... the rest of the platoon used to think ... he had quite a congenital sympathy with the ideas of Prussian militarism.'[83]

For all the 'Prussian militarism' of Powell's demeanour, Powell's views on German culture and politics were far from conciliatory. During his cadetship at Aldershot, he spent a short time as the editor of *Battledress*, 'The Cadet Magazine,' and in the spring of 1940 wrote an editorial on the 'metaphysical miscalculation' that led 'the people of Empire' – such as his acquaintances at Sydney – from apprehending 'the nightmare vastness of the struggle that is beginning.' This war, he argued, was like no other. In most wars, there is some 'ground of compromise, some basis of possible understanding,' but this war of 'unlimited objectives' was a war of 'opposing metaphysics, or, if you like it better, ideologies.'[84] This was not just a war with Nazism, he wrote, but was a war with the strongest traits of the German people: 'anti-Semitism, the faith in the hero-leader, the application of Darwinian "survival of the fittest" to foreign politics, the love and admiration of force and power for their own sake, and, above all, the readiness to sacrifice the present and the material for the future and the abstract.'[85] Here in the last line conservatism is drawn in opposition to fascism. Like the liberal imperialists of Britain or the United States, fascism attempts to remake the world. Powell was cynical about whether the British public were up to the task of fighting this 'opposing metaphysic,' writing of the need for a transformation in the national attitude: 'when I find German music enjoying an undiminished popularity in England, and when I notice the coolness of the nation and the public towards [the British] army ... which alone will have to achieve the almost impossible, then I cannot help but wonder.'[86] The British people's lack of commitment to India and the empire likewise frustrated Powell. The people of the home front – George Orwell's 'nation of flower-lovers ... stamp-collectors ... crossword-puzzle fans' – were perhaps, Powell offered, not up to the task of global war.[87]

In his 1958 memoir, Field Marshal Bernard Montgomery criticized the British public for treating the returning men of Dunkirk as heroes.[88]

---

[83] As cited in Heffer, *Like the Roman*, p. 59.
[84] J. Enoch Powell, *Battledress*, May/June 1940, as cited in Heffer, *Like the Roman*, p. 60.
[85] Ibid.   [86] Ibid.
[87] George Orwell, *The Lion and the Unicorn: Socialism and English Genius* (London: Secker and Warburg, 1941), p. 15.
[88] Bernard Law Montgomery, *The memoirs of Field-Marshal the Viscount Montgomery of Alamein* (London: Collins, 1958).

Montgomery himself had led the II Army Corps in France and had been forced to retreat to Dunkirk (he was later made a hero for his leadership in El Alamein). Powell was asked, in 1987, if he saw anything in Montgomery's criticisms, to which he replied, 'maybe Montgomery was wrong …' and maybe 'the British public were right.' Here was Powell talking from the perspective of 1987: a post-imperial Powell who above all recognized the importance of national myth. To his interviewer, he explained that behind that reception was the realization that without France, 'the ultimate defence and prospect, if there was one, of victory was for an insular Britain.'[89] The Battle of Dunkirk had meant, according to Powell, the 'recovery of our insularity' in the summer of 1940.[90] He warned his interviewer that this recollection had been 'fed' by later experiences, 'distilled' or 'grown' in the mind by the thoughts of almost fifty years. Still, he stressed, that is 'how I now see the kind of cheerful acceptance which was so much the prevalent mood in the summer of 1940.'[91]

The miracle of Dunkirk as well as the 'little ships of Dunkirk' – which refers to the civilian and merchant marine ships that went out to evacuate the retreating soldiers on the French coast – became at this time the archetypal representation of British civilian/military courage in the face of German advance. Four-fifths of the British Expeditionary Force (BEF), though surrounded by German forces, had been saved by civilian and (predominantly) military vessels at Dunkirk.[92] Anthony Eden, then Secretary of State for War, broadcast to the nation of the BEF's 'epic' battle against all odds and refusal to surrender: 'Four days ago not one of us would have dared to hope that the isolated Allied Armies could have fought their way through the bottle-neck to the coast. It is the spirit of the B.E.F. that has won through.'[93] After this spirited effort against the odds, Eden called on the civilians to 'make good our losses … Brave hearts alone cannot stand up against steel. We need more places, more tanks, more guns. The people of this country must work as never before. We must show the same qualities, the same discipline, and the same self-sacrifice at home as the B.E.F. have shown in the field.'[94] Churchill in the Commons the next day spoke of the BEF survival at Dunkirk as a, 'miracle of deliverance achieved by valour, by perseverance, by perfect discipline, by dauntless service, by resource, by skill, by unconquerable fidelity, [that] is manifest to us all.'[95]

[89] 'JEP War Memories.' POLI. 5.1.
[90] Ibid.   [91] Ibid.
[92] 'Triumph of an Army,' *The Times*, 3 June 1940.
[93] Ibid.   [94] Ibid.
[95] 'House of Commons,' *The Times*, 5 June 1940.

In the *Postscripts* broadcast, Priestley told of the 'little holiday steamers' and their associations before the war with 'high spirits and bottled beer' and 'pork pies,' which had 'made an excursion to hell and came back glorious' by rescuing the British soldiers.[96] Here was the indomitable spirit of the underdog, the reluctant soldier and the volunteering civilian.

In recent years historians of the Second World War have focused on the home front, on civilian death and scarcity. Civilian lives – in Poland, in Germany, in Japan, in France, in Britain – were in many ways on the very frontline of the war. As such, the violence against civilian lives has carried much of the historical meaning of the Second World War. The Blitz of 1940 stands at the centre of British narratives of the war.[97] This is not just a historical view. During the war we see the same emphasis: rhetorically, the home front and the battlefront were blurred. For instance, we see Churchill emphasizing in 1940, 'The front lines run through the factories. The workmen are soldiers with different weapons, but the same courage.'[98] Likewise, *Picture Post* had a piece on getting physically fit, because 'the civilian [man] is no longer behind the front. He is the front. So everywhere he is getting fit.'[99]

Crucially, unlike the millions of men and women whose war did not end in a 'blank,' who saw the brutality of total war, Powell's war would remain an abstract and romantic pursuit. Throughout the war, he wished for his heroic moment. 'I wanted to end the war so to speak ... riding into Berlin on a white horse.'[100] Though Powell was at times frustrated by the incompetence of his military superiors, he did not develop a sceptical view of institutional authority. The anti-authoritarian potential of the war experience – found, for instance, in the links many soldiers made between social inequality and wrongful death – did not touch Powell.[101] Though there is still much historical debate over whether the Labour victory of 1945 was a sign of new (though perhaps short-lived) political radicalism,[102]

---

[96] Priestley, *Postscripts*, pp. 1–4, cited in Webster, 'There'll Always be an England,' pp. 557–584 (p. 574).
[97] See Angus Calder, *The People's War: Britain 1939–1945* (London: Panther, 1971).
[98] Ibid., p. 20.
[99] Sonya Rose, *Which People's War?*, p. 166.
[100] Ibid.
[101] Paul Fussell, *Wartime: Understanding and Behavior in the Second World War* (New York: Oxford University Press, 1989).
[102] For the argument in favour of popular apoliticism, see the influential book by Fielding, Thompson and Tiratsoo, *'England Arise!'*; for a recent critique of this argument, see Eley, 'When Europe Was New,' in Riera and Schaffer (eds.), *The Lasting War*.

there is little doubt that the Second World War – and especially the blurring of home front and battlefront – changed the political landscape.[103]

Importantly, this experience of the war profoundly affected official and unofficial conceptions of citizenship and belonging in Britain. During and after the Battle of Britain, the press, radio and film, as well as official wartime propaganda, depicted the Second World War as a 'People's War.'[104] Wartime policy and rhetoric emphasized 'equality of sacrifice' across class.[105] This, in turn, gave wider scope for expressions of resentment against those of the privileged classes who were seen to be shirking wartime sacrifice/obligation.[106] As Sonya Rose argues, 'With nearly every major demand for additional contribution to the war effort, the rhetoric of equality of sacrifice led to the expression of class antagonism.'[107] Whatever the truth of the story of the 'People's War,' as an idea it contained both progressive power and normative constraints. Ross McKibbin suggests that, during the war, the rhetoric of national unity both enabled working Britain to make political claims at the same time as tempering working-class radicalism.[108] The social consensus of the postwar period was built on this tension.

While Powell regarded the cheerful acceptance of retreat at Dunkirk as a sort of discovery in 1987, his mood in the summer of 1940 was far from cheerful. In August 1940, when invasion was thought to be a threat, he made the decision with a fellow officer in training, that if the King made peace with Germany, they would shoot themselves with their service revolvers: because, they decided, 'if the King had been party to surrender … an officer had no justification for going on living.'[109] His entire being was consumed by the war effort; this was no reluctant citizen-soldier. This was not the mythic 'relentlessly cheerful,' 'inherently tolerant,' Briton willing to live with 'everyday sacrifice,' as in the myth of the Blitz.[110] In November 1940, he wrote to Commander Peploe at Western Command headquarters that he had been arguing

---

[103] Due to full employment in the traditional industries, working-class communities strengthened in the North and South, as did worker solidarity. This 'universalized' a working-class political culture, such that the Labour Party could recruit those who had previously identified themselves with conservatism. Ross McKibbin, *Class and Cultures: England, 1918–1951* (Oxford University Press, 1998), p. 531.

[104] Sonya Rose, *Which People's War?*, p. 29.

[105] Ibid., p. 31.   [106] Ibid., p. 34.   [107] Ibid., p. 36.

[108] McKibbin, *Class and Cultures*, p. 533.

[109] 'JEP War Memories.' POLL 5.1.

[110] Sonya Rose, *Which People's War?*, pp. 2–4.

'ad nauseam' throughout the summer that the danger of German invasion was not real. He even went so far as to question whether Churchill emphasized the threat so as to discredit Germany by making it appear that it had failed in the enterprise.[111] Still, the reports from German papers reprinted in Britain revealed a country on the brink of invasion. Crowds reportedly gathered on the streets of Berlin in June, singing the German war song, 'We are sailing for England.'[112] But even if Britain were as 'inviolate,' as Powell emphasized, it would not necessarily escape defeat. Powell wrote to the Commander: 'It is not England that is at war with Germany but the British Empire; it is not England territorially for which we are fighting, but the British Empire, unified by its allegiance to the Emperor which is also, and first and foremost, King of England.'[113] It was this that was now under threat.

Conservative war

In October 1941, Powell left the United Kingdom for Cairo, travelling undercover as a civilian through Ireland. There, Powell worked in the Joint Intelligence Committee gathering and analysing intelligence on Rommel's Afrika Korps. He wrote to his parents when he first arrived that, 'sometimes, especially at night, the illusion of being in Sydney is startling: the sky, the temperature, even something about the suburbs and way of life of the European community. But in Sydney we are not.'[114] Despite the uncanny resemblances, the British Empire was uneven and inconsistent. While in Cairo, Powell would have little interaction with Egyptians. Unlike in India, Powell noted later, Britain was perpetually there as a 'temporarily occupying power.'[115] Unlike in India, with its military collaboration, he knew that the severely qualified independence of Egypt, 'was bound to be irksome to nationalists.'[116] Powell felt that he and Britain in no sense belonged in Egypt.

We see in this period in the North Africa, however, Powell drawing out a conservative sense of himself. This was in dialogue largely with his father, Albert Powell. In a letter to both his parents, he wrote:

The tendency to repeat history is not, I think, isolated. I see reasons for believing that as I get older I shall wish more and more to read, say, do, think only

[111] Powell, Letter to Commander Peploe, H.Q. Western Command, 11 November 1940. POLL 3.1.1.4.
[112] 'At England's Doors: The Germany Threat of Invasion,' *The Times*, 25 June 1940.
[113] Ibid.
[114] Powell to Ellen and Albert Powell, 25 October 1941. POLL 1.1.5.
[115] 'JEP War Memories.' POLL 5.1.   [116] Ibid.

those things & in that way that my father before me read, said, did & thought. Conservatism could hardly be carried further; but war, I think, makes people conservative – English wars, at least – because in the last analysis the people undertakes to support them not for the present nor the future, but for the memory of a dream, the associations of infancy and childhood.[117]

In Albert Powell's letters to his son in Egypt, he frequently wrote romantically of the English countryside, reminding Powell of their long walks: 'the country [is] generally thickly wooded, with gentle undulations ... The villages with the distinctive style of cottages and thatching ... Needless to say we often think of you on these jaunts and wonder what the future holds.'[118] Enoch Powell replied to them that week of his experience sleeping out in the open in the desert and regaining his 'vitality.'[119] Albert Powell a few days later wrote back that Powell was showing signs that he had been 'tarred with the family brush': 'It will be interesting to notice whether this atavistic tendency develops or fades away as the years go on.'[120] The next month, Powell wrote of his postwar intentions, emphasizing, 'I have an overwhelming desire (not due, I am certain, to mere absence) to acquire that intimate knowledge of the British Isles and their inhabitants which to acquire requires more than the nasty glance which the person in employ can give.'[121] Not due to mere absence, perhaps, it was still in the Egyptian desert and at war that Powell first spoke of his need to gain that 'intimate knowledge' of Britain. It was via the colonial experience that Powell imagined England.

This nostalgia for Old England and home was heightened by Powell's rising anti-Americanism. In the winter of 1942, Powell worked on a report entitled '1943' for circulation among senior colleagues. It contained, he told his parents, 'my strategic and political convictions as they have built themselves up during the last three years.'[122] With defeat no longer likely after the victory at El Alamein, decisions about the future of the empire had to be taken. He argued that 'the decision of 1943 will determine our history and our greatness for centuries.'[123] The very meaning of the victory was in question.

It is a question which the soldier, or even the statesman, will decide. Those who think, plan, calculate are only bubbles on the stream of the nation, which wills.

[117] Powell to Ellen and Albert Powell, 23 May 1942. POLL 1.1.5.
[118] Albert Powell to Powell, 2 August 1942. POLL 1.1.5.
[119] Powell to Ellen and Albert Powell, 9 August 1942. POLL 1.1.5.
[120] Albert Powell to Powell, 12 August 1942. POLL 1.1.5.
[121] Powell to Ellen and Albert Powell, 18 September 1942. POLL 1.1.5.
[122] Powell to Ellen and Albert Powell, 5 January 1943. POLL 1.1.5.
[123] J. Enoch Powell, '1943,' 25 December 1942. POLL 1.6.2.

Against or without the national will they can do nothing; yet that will itself they are incapable of rousing, allaying or altering. Never, indeed, since ROME has there been a national will so strong, steady and persistent as BRITAIN'S. The moral counterpart of BRITAIN's unique strategic situation, it has given and preserved to us the Empire.[124]

Powell's main point on 'the decision of 1943' was clear in this report: America was Britain's next great rival, 'our terrible enemy,' in the survival of the British Empire.[125] Remarkably, in Powell's assertion at this moment, Britain's corollary was *not* Greece, facing its inevitable decline to the United States, but Rome. He later wrote to his parents, 'My thoughts range ... beyond the present war to the peace after it and to the war after that.'[126] The next war would be with the United States, in the Far East, 'fought by men in lounge suits or morning dress.'[127]

While in Algiers, after long days working for the Joint Intelligence Committee, Powell would go to an American Army mess hall for dinner. There and in professional intercourse, Powell spoke with American officers about the war. American attitudes towards war disturbed Powell. He described the Americans there as 'gauche and amateurish.'[128] When Germans forces near Gafsa captured fifty American tanks early in 1943, he recalled later in 1967 that, 'the British staff were almost as aghast as if the war had been lost; after fighting the Germans in the desert for two years, we knew what Rommel could do with a few captured tanks. The Americans couldn't understand. "Hell," they said, "there's plenty more where those came from."'[129] He was, too, critical of what he saw as the American approach to war, believing the growing demand among Americans for unconditional surrender to be 'the most barbaric and inhuman concept ... you do not have to destroy your opponent; you merely have to prove to him that he cannot win.'[130] It was not, then, just America's imperialist designs in the Far East and America's determination to undermine British power that disturbed Powell; it was what Powell regarded as America's entire approach to foreign policy. As he later put it, the Americans, in contrast to the British, were universalists. Their tendency to divide 'nations into "goodies" and "baddies" ... derives from the universalist outlook: there simply are only two catego-

[124] Ibid.
[125] Powell to Ellen and Albert Powell, 16 February 1943. POLL 1.1.5.
[126] Powell to Ellen and Albert Powell, 29 September 1943. POLL 1.1.5.
[127] Powell to Ellen and Albert Powell, 22 December 1945. POLL 1.1.10.
[128] Ibid.
[129] *Sunday Express*, 17 March 1967, as cited in Heffer, *Like the Roman*, p. 74.
[130] Cited in Heffer, *Like the Roman*, p. 71.

ries available – pro-American, or "free" or "democratic" ("please don't quibble, it all means the same thing") or else anti-American.'[131]

This first brush with America in Algiers occurred concurrently with a strengthened articulation of his conservative commitments. Just twelve days after naming the United States Britain's 'terrible enemy,' Powell told his parents, 'I don't think you could be more constantly in my mind, waking or sleeping. Last night, sleeping in an aircraft with 6 Americans, I dreamt of you and thought that Mother was in some trouble, whereupon I woke up and found I was crying freely.'[132] The mention of Powell's sleeping partners is probably not incidental here. America represented a new threat to home and family. Days later, he noted that he believed that,

almost unlimited sacrifices of individual life and happiness are worth while to preserve the unique structure of power of which the keystone (the only conceivable and indispensable keystone) is the English Crown. I for my part find it the nearest thing in the world to an absolute (as opposed to a relative) value: it is like the outer circle that bound my universe, so that I cannot conceive of anything beyond it.[133]

Powell's anti-Americanism is an absolutely essential aspect of his political outlook. His letter home to his parents about 'almost unlimited sacrifice' to the English Crown was written at the exact moment when, through conversations at the military base in Algiers, he found American officers openly committed to the end of the British Empire.[134] He wrote to his parents at this time that he saw a 'greater peril than Germany or Japan ever were,' the threat of America.[135] This realization, he explained, meant that 'our duty to our country may not terminate in peace ... it will remain for those of us who have the necessary knowledge and insight to do what we can where we can to help Britain be victorious in her next crisis.'[136] The next crisis Britain faced was against American power.

As previously discussed, Powell's nostalgia for home – his 'wish more and more to read, say, do, think only those things & in that way that my father before me read, said, did & thought' – emerged via the distance of war. In other words, it was through his experiences while in North Africa during the Second World War that Powell imagined the English

[131] J. Enoch Powell, 'The Great American Dilemma,' *Sunday Telegraph*, 17 March 1968.
[132] Powell to Ellen and Albert Powell, 16 February 1943. POLL 1.1.5.
[133] Powell to Ellen and Albert Powell, 9 March 1943. POLL 1.1.5.
[134] Heffer, *Like the Roman*, p. 74
[135] Powell to Ellen and Albert Powell, 16 February 1943. POLL 1.1.5.
[136] Ibid.

nation. It seems clear that this was not complicated, for Powell, by an experience of violence that might expose the human failures of hierarchy and deference. For Powell, it appears that an abstract, romantic war could be fought for an abstract, romantic nation.

The romantic nature of Powell's war is perhaps best exemplified in his obsession with finding one missing soldier with whom he had had a close relationship prior to the war. The probable death of this young man, Powell would often explain, became truly 'symbolic in my mind' of Powell's responsibilities to the empire-nation and the imagined home front.[137] At Cambridge University in 1936, 'Jack' Enoch Powell had supervised an undergraduate by the name of A. W. J. 'Tommy' Thomas. He was three years younger than Powell and became, according to Powell, Powell's earliest poetic muse.[138] Powell called Thomas a 'miracle.'[139] They would go on long walks together. Simon Heffer, Powell's official biographer, has been adamant that Powell's regard for Thomas in his poetry was less a sign of homosexuality than of Powell being 'socially and emotionally limited' both in the male-only world of Cambridge and then in the British Army. Powell was merely steeped in classical literature and Greek homoerotic poetry.[140] Powell had, Heffer claims, 'an almost childish regard for the hero whose heroism was rooted in physical courage, a regard which caused him to manifest affection in the form of a schoolboy crush.'[141] This was not sexual love, this was the love, Heffer explains, for A. E. Housman's 'lads who will die in their glory/And never grow old.'[142]

The truth of this claim is, of course, acutely dependent on how we define homosexuality – a social identity that, in these prewar years, was manifestly more porous than Heffer chooses to define it.[143] As Sonya Rose has aptly put it, 'masculinity is a field of gender meanings, the composition of which changes historically as does the particular constellation of meanings that predominate at a given historical conjuncture.'[144] Powell adored Thomas. There is little to indicate one way or

[137] Powell to Ellen and Albert Powell, 25 July 1943. POLL 1.1.7.
[138] Powell to A. W. J. Thomas, 10 November 1937, cited in Heffer, *Like the Roman*, p. 34.
[139] Powell to Ellen and Albert Powell, 25 July 1943. POLL 1.1.7.
[140] Shepherd, *Enoch Powell*, p. 25.
[141] Heffer, *Like the Roman*, p. 34.
[142] Ibid.
[143] For an argument regarding the establishment of homosexuality as an identity that can be recognized, performed, policed, see George Chauncey, *Gay New York: Gender, Urban Culture, and the Making of the Gay Male World, 1890–1940* (New York: Basic Books, 1994).
[144] Sonya Rose, *Which People's War?*, p. 153.

another if this love found physical expression. In all likelihood, this was a chaste affair – but not platonic. Powell himself described his mentor A. E. Housman's poems as offering 'irrefutable evidence' of Housman's 'emotional homosexuality.'[145] Powell's poems, at very least, offer sexual ambiguity:

> While yesteryear I tarried
>   In a garden in the south,
> I met a youth who carried
>   A rose-bud in his mouth
>
> I gave him chase and caught him,
>   And would not set him free,
> But held him and besought him
>   To give the flower to me.
>
> He smiled, and broke a petal
>   And laid it in my hand –
> It seared like molten metal,
>   And here is yet the brand.[146]

It is certain that Powell throughout the war did not think he would ever marry. As he explained to his parents, he held a 'conviction, deepened by further experience and observation, that a certain peculiarity of which you are aware is strong, real and deep-seated as to render the eventuality of marriage very improbable.'[147] Meanwhile, he referred to his married friends as 'dead.'[148]

Here we can begin to see that Powell's ordered world, that 'web of understood relationships which sustains society,'[149] was at this time very much a male-only world. At the University of Sydney, Powell had been known for his misogyny and atheism. In Powell's view, social order was not sanctioned by God, but by historical institutions; importantly, the history and historical institutions that sanctified the structures of society were the domain of men. 'I found that I enjoyed the Army,' he told an interviewer in 1986, 'I enjoyed its discipline; I enjoyed its institutionality; the framework in which men understand one another because they live subject to the same conventions, the same rules. It's the kind

---

[145] As cited by Shepherd, *Enoch Powell*, p. 24.
[146] Ibid., pp. 24–25.
[147] Powell to Ellen and Albert Powell, 21 May 1944, POLL 1.1.7.
[148] Thomas was, meanwhile, less affected or serious about his marriage prospects, writing while in Singapore: 'I am forgoing further consideration of marriage, until I see a real woman again. Here they are largely Russian and dangerous, besides loving the bottle.' A. W. J. Thomas to J. Enoch Powell, 20 October 1940, POLL 1.6.12.
[149] J. Enoch Powell, Bill Schwarz interview, 26 April 1988.

of environment in which I've always flourished – Commons, college, or regiment.'[150] As is clear in Powell's later views on the break-up of the British Raj, women brought disorder – not via their sexuality exactly, but as the carriers of cultural difference.

In 1937, Thomas was posted to Malaya as a civilian in the colonial service. The next time Powell saw Thomas was to be the last. He visited him briefly in Singapore on his way to Australia in February 1939, before the outbreak of the war. Powell remembered his leaving him then as 'the most horrible parting of my life.'[151] He explained in a letter to his parents that, 'I think I have never spent any time with him without feeling at the end that this pain [of leaving] outweighed the pleasure. But I always forget this again. It's the story of the moth and the candle.'[152] He burst into tears twice on his way back to Sydney.[153] Back in Australia, the 'familiar 1914–1918 shape of impending doom I now perceived increasingly in terms of the Pacific' had been given emotional force, 'after my last parting at Changi airfield in Singapore in 1939 from a younger friend who was in fact, as we fore-knew that he would be, killed by the Japanese on the Johore Straits in 1942.'[154]

Close to the end of his life, when asked about the homoerotic con-tent of his poetry, Powell explained, 'Does one not love young men, from being young?' adding, 'One's love is for a whole generation that is doomed.'[155] Powell had adopted the language of the Great War. During the war, he came to the conclusion that the appeasers had 'the blood of Thomas and a hundred thousand Thomas's' on their hands.[156] No doubt Thomas represented something irretrievably lost in war. Visiting Thomas's parents while in officer training in 1940, Powell described it as making him feel – more than anything – 'shriv-elled and dried up.'

The plain fact is that I have had my cake and eaten it. With the wrong sex and in unfavourable circumstances I have had and finished what is likely to be the one real love affair of my life, together with its accompanying minor ones, like the satellites of a planet.[157]

[150] J. Enoch Powell interviewed on BBC Radio by Anne Brown, 13 April 1986. Cited in Shepherd, *Enoch Powell*, p. 39.
[151] As cited in Heffer, *Like the Roman*, p. 48.
[152] Powell to Ellen and Albert Powell, 8 March 1939. POLL 1.1.4.
[153] Powell to Ellen and Albert Powell, 10 March 1939. POLL 1.1.4.
[154] Powell, *Collected Poems*, p. viii.
[155] Transcript of an interview with J. Enoch Powell by Michael Cockerell for 1995 BBC documentary on Powell. Cited in Heffer, *Like the Roman*, p. 34.
[156] Powell to Ellen and Albert Powell, 22 December 1945. POLL 1.1.10.
[157] Powell to Ellen and Albert Powell, 26 June 1940. POLL 1.1.10.

Powell therefore wished to die in the conflict, a sentiment he continued to express throughout his life:

Henceforward the only emotions [of] which I am capable seem to be hatred, ambition and selfishness, and I feel possessed and burnt up with them. If I survive the present hostilities, which I increasingly pray God I may not, there will be little humanity left in me at all, and certainly no poetry.[158]

Thomas's death occurred at the fall of Singapore to the Japanese, an event which John Darwin pinpoints in a study of four centuries as then indicating to the world that 'Britain's century of dominance in South and South East Asia had come to an end.'[159] Thomas had joined the frontline of British opposition to Japan while working as a civilian in Singapore. At the time, Powell was stationed in Cairo as Secretary to the Joint Intelligence Committee.

Powell yearned to see the frontline of battle. He wrote to his parents that his beloved friend Thomas had become 'the personification of my conscience; as though my military omissions and commissions were seen and silently rebuked by him.'[160] Writing three days later to explain his 'determination to go East': if substantially British forces did not reconquer Burma and Malaya, then Australia and New Zealand were likely to renounce their allegiance to the Crown after the war. And so,

From this consequence alone ... the disappearance of the Empire itself would probably follow not later than the lifetime of my children, should I have any. These convictions of mine take on a certain lively reality and pathetic force from my relationship with Thomas, the circumstances of whose probable death render him symbolic in my mind. Believing all this, then, I am obliged, though in isolation and possibly even ridicule, to place myself in a position to act ...[161]

After victory at El Alamein, Powell turned down a promotion to colonel that would have kept him in North Africa indefinitely – the war was no longer in North Africa.[162] In November 1942, Powell wrote to his parents, 'I must ask for your understanding and sympathy with a resolution which I have already begun to try to put into effect,' which had come to him, 'more suddenly, decidedly and utterly imperatively than any since I became a soldier. I have this day asked my chief to assist me in getting to the Far East.' He felt himself, 'bidden, beckoned by the ghost of

---

[158] Ibid.
[159] John Darwin, *After Tamerlane: The Global History of Empire since 1405* (London: Penguin, 2007), p. 431.
[160] Powell to Ellen and Albert Powell, 22 July 1943. POLL 1.1.5.
[161] Powell to Ellen and Albert Powell, 25 July 1943. POLL 1.1.7.
[162] Heffer, *Like the Roman*, p. 81.

Thomas, living or dead.'[163] In a definitively romantic act, Powell went east to rescue Thomas as a prisoner of war in Malaya or at least to uncover the details of his death. Powell took the first job that would take him closest to this end, which was work on intelligence against the Japanese in Dehra Dun, India, outside of Delhi.

Becoming Indian

Powell's opportunity to go east arrived when General Auchinleck, who had been stationed in Cairo, was transferred back to his old post in 1943 as Commander-in-Chief of India. The British government was concerned at the time that Indian nationalism could greatly influence the rapidly expanded Indian Army. Powell arrived to an India that summer when the Bengal Famine raged, during which as many as three million people were to die of starvation. And when Subhash Chandra Bose's Indian National Army, recruited in the main from disaffected Indian Army soldiers, captured the news as they fought on the Japanese side. Powell saw these events as transitional and temporary troubles.[164]

India was, Powell hoped, a 'stepping stone' to the war with Japan.[165] He went there to assist General Cawthorn, the Director of Military Intelligence in India. Powell at this time, as he often noted later in life, fell 'hopelessly and helplessly in love with India,' and refused to transfer to Ceylon (now Sri Lanka) when Mountbatten's South-East Asia Command headquarters moved there from Delhi in 1944.[166] Powell served as an officer in India for two and a half years, between August 1943 and February 1946.[167] He had by now spent two years' service in the Middle East and North Africa Commands. 'War is a strange thing,' Powell wrote a few months after arrival in India, 'and strange are the ways it takes people ... Thomas, in his one brief contact with it, perishes like Oates in the blizzard; and I, who for over four years now have assiduously followed and embraced it, have never seen a dead body and, apart from air raids, only hear shots fired in anger.'[168]

In November 1944, Powell began work on the Willcox Report to advise on the future of the armed forces in India. He had been selected by Auchinleck personally, he was told. Auchinleck had insisted that the committee, including a lieutenant general and senior representatives from all the services, include an officer from army intelligence who

[163] Powell to Ellen and Albert Powell, 11 November 1942. POLL 1.1.5.
[164] Roth, *Enoch Powell: Tory Tribune*, p. 43.
[165] Ibid., p. 15.   [166] Ibid.
[167] Powell, 'A Passage to India,' p. 15.
[168] Powell to Ellen and Albert Powell, 15 October 1943. POLL 1.1.7.

was not a professional soldier.[169] Powell told his parents that he had been surprised by his appointment and was therefore unable to prevent it from going through at an earlier stage. He described the posting as 'honorific enough' supposing that 'one can forget the objects for which I joined the army ... It might be described as a "painless" introduction to peace.'[170] And so, '[t]herefore Thomas (if he is still alive) will sit in his prison-camp, Wickenden [another close friend] will fight in the Burma jungle, and I, who forced my way here for very other purposes ... shall travel across India in the utmost pomp with a lot of brass hats, expressing opinions upon subjects of which I know nothing. This is one of God's little jokes.'[171]

The crisis of British imperial power, in the double loss of Singapore and his most loved student Thomas, would find resolution for Powell in India. He wanted to be on the frontline of the war in Burma but would spend the last few years of the war in India, first as Assistant Director of Military Intelligence in India and then, after actually declining a job in the Far East in 1944, as a British serviceman in the Indian Army.[172] He had discovered in India a sensation 'not unlike falling in love,' which was an 'inheritance' experienced 'by successive generations of Englishmen.'[173] This was the experience of being 'part of the fabric of the country.'[174] Powell became 'fascinated by the effortlessness' of the British Raj.[175] He studied Urdu and the architecture and history of his surroundings – he modelled himself, he said, on the early nineteenth-century imperialist. On a journey through Bihar, he wrote, 'It struck me almost as a blinding revelation that I was the only Englishman within thirty, forty, maybe fifty or sixty miles, and *that this was the natural order of things.*'[176]

Unlike the French in Indochina, with their *mission civilisatrice*, the English came to India 'to become a part of India.'[177] He shared, he said, the 'orthodox British view' that where you governed, 'there you put yourself as far as possible within the skin, within the culture of those whom you governed ... to represent, as it were, the people of that

[169] Foot, *The Rise of Enoch Powell*, p. 11.
[170] Powell to Ellen and Albert Powell, 4 November 1944. POLL 1.1.7.
[171] Ibid.
[172] 'JEP War Memories.' POLL 5.1.
[173] J. Enoch Powell, 'Encountering the Great Indian Mystery,' *Sources: Revue d'études anglophones* 4 (Printemps 1998), pp. 91–97 (pp. 93, 94).
[174] 'JEP War Memories.' POLL 5.1.
[175] Peter Beswick, 'The Lone Wolves,' 1964 in Powell's scrapbook. POLL 12.1.7.
[176] Patrick Cosgrave interview with J. Enoch Powell in Cosgrave, *The Lives of Enoch Powell*, p. 87 (my emphasis).
[177] Powell, 'Encountering the Great Indian Mystery,' p. 94.

country.'[178] As Simon Heffer described this experience for Powell, 'By the end of his two and a half years there, he would feel as much Indian as British.'[179] By the beginning of 1944, Powell felt he had become 'Indianized.' It was, in his opinion, a 'disgrace' if a British officer did not have a fair knowledge of Urdu. He looked at things 'through the same spectacles as people who have served here 30 years.'[180] Powell belonged there, he believed, thanks to a history of the men who came before him. Powell had risen in the ranks, over the course of the war, from private to brigadier. Powell's character – particularly his movement across class – is recounted as self-conscious and unnatural in critical readings of Enoch Powell. As Paul Foot wrote in 1969 concerning Powell's time in Dehra Dun:

Powell's fellow-officers found him prickly, over-sensitive about his Midland middle-class background, which contrasted with their own simulated orthodoxy. He was at once hypnotized and irritated by the ease and arrogance of the officer class, and, while carefully studying every aspect of officer manners, he seldom missed a chance to demonstrate that he was 'different' – a cut below by birth, perhaps, but a cut above in every other way.

Again, Powell's subjective experience of class identity – his difference – accentuated the ritual performance of hierarchy and belonging. Powell recounted in 1974, the story of drinking water from an earthen tumbler as a guest of a Brahmin in India. When finished, Powell 'smashed [it] on the ground to show that I knew it could not anyhow be used again. "He is a Hindu," they said to one another with a smile. There is a sense in which it had been true: the British were married to India, as Venice was married to the sea.'[181] As is clear by Powell's later pronouncements on British immigration, however, this was no reciprocal process: 'The West Indian or Indian does not, by being born in England, become an Englishman. In law he becomes a United Kingdom citizen by birth; in fact he is a West Indian or an Asian still.'[182]

Powell believed that the Indian Army was as its name declared, 'not an extension or a detachment of the British Army, but an army Indian in composition, in language and in loyalty.'[183] He was no longer disoriented by empire but as an Englishman found himself a 'natural' part of the scene: 'The British seemed – seemed, I say, for all is hallucination – a

---

[178] 'JEP War Memories.' POLL 5.1.
[179] Heffer, *Like the Roman*, p. 82
[180] Powell to Ellen and Albert Powell, 13 January 1944. POLL 1.1.7.
[181] Cited in Heffer, *Like the Roman*, p. 98.
[182] Cited in Kathleen Paul, *Whitewashing Britain: Race and Citizenship in the Postwar Era* (Ithaca, NY: Cornell University Press, 1997), p. 178.
[183] Ibid.

natural part of the scene. The moon rose, the cow walked through the village, the British magistrate or officer went about his duties, as if from time immemorial.'[184] In the homo-social and hierarchical world of the Indian Army, Powell believed, the Indian and the Briton became one. In his first political speeches after the war, he would argue for the possibility of one imperial *nation* of India and Britain based on this model. This was a construction of the nation as an ordered and hierarchical, male-only fraternity.[185]

In 1959, Powell reviewed Nirad C. Chaudhuri's *A Passage to England*, a travelogue of a 57-year-old Bengali's experiences travelling for five weeks in England in the spring of 1955. The title was a play, clearly, on E. M. Forster's *A Passage to India*, which Chaudhuri associated with the growth of 'the mood which enabled the British people to leave India with an almost Pilate-like gesture of washing their hands of a disagreeable affair' and which, it perhaps should be noted, in 1959 Powell had not yet read.[186] Powell wrote that Chaudhuri's work could inform the English reader on England, but more so on (British) India. By this time, Powell agreed with Chaudhuri that the 'much-talked-about Indo-British friendship since 1947' was a myth.[187] In British India, Powell explained, the British had loved India and had hated it; likewise the Indian had hated the British and admired them, because 'each was locked to the other in an embrace which was both voluntary and constrained, for Britain ruled India not by force but yet by necessity.'[188] The 'inevitability' and 'natural order' of Britain in India had evolved in Powell's thinking into a 'locked embrace' of 'necessity.' But, importantly, Powell found in reading Chaudhuri that it could only be a man who had experienced the British Raj, a man like himself, who could appreciate the authenticity of Chaudhuri's experience of England. The visitor to England from India or Pakistan, Powell seemed to say, already had a mutual understanding with the Briton who had inhabited the British Raj. And this was a mutual understanding that could not be explained. He and Chaudhuri were men of 'the diminishing number of

---

[184] Powell, 'A Passage to India,' p. 21.

[185] For analysis of the nation as fraternity, see George L. Mosse, *Nationalism and Sexuality* (New York: Howard Fertig, 1997), p. 91; Anne McClintock, *Imperial Leather: Race, Gender and Sexuality in the Colonial Contest* (New York: Routledge, 1995), p. 352; and Sonya Rose, *Which People's War*, p. 6.

[186] J. Enoch Powell, 'The Imperfect Dream: A Return Passage to India,' *The Times*, 7 May 1983.

[187] J. Enoch Powell, 'Passage to England,' *Birmingham Post*, 20 August 1959, in File 3 of 'Publications 1, 1946–66' POLL 6.1.1C.

[188] Ibid.

those who actually witnessed the phenomenon of British India [which] is like belonging to a dying race which cannot pass its secrets on.'[189]

Decades later, in 1983, in an article entitled 'The imperfect dream: a return passage to India,' Powell reminisced on his time in India. He had read Forster's work for the first time only the year before.[190] It read like 'a deliberate caricature.'[191] Forster's book did not ring true for Powell. Forster, who had spent fourteen months in total in India, looked to Powell as bad as 'the proverbial fun-figure Paget MP, who spent "twenty-one days in India" before writing his authoritative accounts.'[192] But the crucial difference between Powell and Forster, according to Powell, was women. Set against the backdrop of the Raj in the 1920s, *A Passage to India* highlights the racial tensions and prejudices of the Raj via a story of the trial of an Indian doctor falsely accused by a young British schoolmistress of sexual assault. In reading *A Passage to India*, Powell understood the reason for Forster's pessimism on British India. Forster's India is India without the army. Any attempt to understand British India with this omission was 'foredoomed.' For, Powell explained,

The dream that the British and the Indians dreamed together for so long, a dream unique in human history in its strangeness and its improbability ... was always imperfect: it was a dream that only the men would ever dream.[193]

This was necessarily true because of the different social conventions governing the life of Indian women, Muslim and Hindu, and European women. This was a barrier, Powell explained, 'to which no obstacle between European and Indian men was in any way comparable.' In the camp, on tour, in wartime, in medicine or missionary work, the European woman could never be 'other than a stranger at a distance in a strange land.'[194] This was the core of truth beneath 'the crudity and bias with which, for all its literary skill, the plot of *A Passage to India* is woven.'[195] As Powell stressed here, it was the hierarchical, masculine world of the Indian Army that Powell committed himself to in 1944.

Despite stark political differences, it is possible to see that both Forster's and Powell's words rest on overlapping visions of the corruption of empire, on what Margaret Strobel calls the 'myth of the destructive female.'[196] In 1984, one year after Powell's discussion of *A Passage to*

[189] Ibid.
[190] Powell, 'A Passage to India,' p. 15 and also printed as 'The Imperfect Dream: A Return Passage to India,' *The Times*, 7 May 1983.
[191] Ibid.   [192] Ibid.   [193] Ibid.   [194] Ibid.   [195] Ibid.
[196] Margaret Strobel, *European Women and the Second British Empire* (Bloomington, IN: Indiana University Press, 1991), pp. 1–16.

India, its film adaptation written and directed by David Lean came out. As Lean put it at the time: 'It's a well-known saying that the women lost us the Empire. It's true.'[197] This myth – which was, importantly, largely accepted in the field of imperial history prior to the feminist scholarship of the 1980s and 1990s – assumes that the settlement of British women in the Raj produced a destructive, destabilizing distance between white administrators and those governed. In this neat little argument, the arrival of substantial numbers of white women occasioned the decline of Indian mistresses and, simultaneously, bred anxieties about protecting supposedly vulnerable (white) women from the alleged sexual appetites of indigenous men.[198] With this, their arrival contributed to the formation of a socially distant, exclusive and itself hierarchical British community. Interestingly, in this view, too, British women led the rituals that maintained class and racial boundaries within colonial society. They are, again, the carriers of culture; 'culture' is essentially domestic. The fact that Powell did not, after the Second World War, see the child of a (white) British woman and (black) British man or immigrant as British of course belies the simple construction, in Powell's thinking, of women as the carriers of cultural difference and national belonging. Powell would, in fact, take an unpopular stand against the British Nationality Act of 1981, arguing against the extension of British citizenship through the maternal line. He insisted then that nationality in the last resort was 'tested by fighting'; 'primary allegiance' was expressed, therefore, through the male.[199]

Among its many limitations, the 'destructive female' explanation of racist division in the administration of the Raj underplays and naturalizes power relations between white administrators and indigenous mistresses. Again, Strobel explains: 'The fact that such a structurally unequal relationship has been taken as evidence of closeness between the two communities indicates how little understanding there was and

---

[197] Ibid., p. 1.
[198] Ibid. For work that has contributed to a feminist analysis of the colonial world, see Helen Callaway, *Gender, Culture and Empire: European Women in Colonial Nigeria* (London: Macmillan, 1987); Claudia Knapman, *White Women in Fiji, 1835–1930: The Ruin of Empire?* (London: Allen & Unwin, 1986); McClintock, *Imperial Leather*; Antoinette Burton, *At the Heart of Empire: Indians and the Colonial Encounter in Late-Victorian Britain* (Berkeley, CA: University of California Press, 1998); Diana Jeater, *Marriage, Perversion and Power: The Construction of Moral Discourse in Southern Rhodesia, 1894–1930* (Oxford: Clarendon Press, 1993); Mrinalini Sinha, *Colonial Masculinity: The 'Manly' Englishman and the 'Effeminate' Bengali in the Late Nineteenth Century* (Manchester University Press, 1995).
[199] 'Mr Powell's views "will encourage thugs"', *The Times* (20 February 1981).

is of gender and power in the dynamics of colonialism. Only if one ignores the element of subordination in the concubinage relationship can it be read as closeness.'[200] As Claudia Knapman put it in 1986, 'to fall back on a gender explanation for the failure of British colonialism obscures the realities of the power relationship between ruler and ruled.' It obscures, among other things, institutionalized inequalities and the massive appropriation of land and resources. Even more, '[It] leaves the imperial idea itself intact, the men who affected it inviolable ... [and] excuses men of the ultimate responsibility for what is now both unpopular and assessed as a failure.'[201] Knapman is, here, pointing to the contemporary purchase of this explanation in the 1980s. As we shall see, Powell was not alone in his nostalgic views of the comradeship of a male-only empire. But, remarkably, in Powell's recollections of empire, women – both British and Indian – are completely invisible. By this point, by the 1980s, the debate on South Asian immigration into Britain had turned, more and more, to questions surrounding the rights of entry of family dependants, women and children. And so, as Powell wrote of male comradeship in the Indian Army in 1983, his arguments concerning non-white communities in Britain had turned, more and more, to women, to birth-rates and to the repatriation of now second- and third- generation Britons.

But let us return to the world that for Powell was, by the postwar years, lost: the Indian Army. It was in 1944, under Lieutenant General Willcox, that Powell began work with three other officers on the reform and reorganization of the postwar Indian Army. This work on the Indian Army reflected recognition of the future strategic importance of India as an arsenal East of Suez after the war.[202] Control over defence had been a major issue of debate between Indian nationalists and the British government throughout the war. In fact, the famous failure of Sir Stafford Cripps' mission to India in 1942 to secure cooperation from Indian leaders in the war effort came down to the question of who would control India's military resources.[203] Jawaharlal Nehru and Maulana Abul Kalam Azad (then president of the Indian National Congress) insisted during the negotiations on an Indian defence minister.[204] The organization and leadership of Indian manpower stood at the centre of the debate surrounding the nature of India's eventual independence.

[200] Strobel, *European Women and the Second British Empire*, p. 6.
[201] Knapman, *White Women in Fiji*, p. 179.
[202] A. Martin Wainwright, *Inheritance of Empire: Britain, India, and the Balance of Power* (Westport, CT: Praeger Publishers, 1994), p. 61.
[203] Ibid., p. 32.   [204] Ibid., p. 33.

The necessities of the Second World War had significantly transformed the make-up of the army and challenged the Indian Army's loyalty to the Raj. General Auchinleck, Commander-in-Chief of the Indian Army in 1941 and from 1943 onwards, had abandoned the traditional 'martial races' policy of recruitment in order to expand the number of potential recruits.[205] With this increased recruitment and with emergency commissioned officers, greater numbers of soldiers with nationalist beliefs joined the military effort. Auchinleck had been given the task of investigating the army's morale.[206] The defection of prisoners of war to the Japanese-supported Indian National Army had in part induced this investigation.

Significantly, the formation of the Willcox Committee occurred at the tail end of controversy between Leo Amery, British Secretary of State for India, and William Phillips, personal ambassador to Franklin D. Roosevelt, serving in India. In September 1944, a confidential report from Ambassador William Phillips to the president was leaked to the press.[207] The report criticized the 'purely mercenary' character and the 'inertia' of the Indian Army, noted that the British would only likely give token assistance in the war against Japan, and treated India in general as merely a base for American operations.[208] Phillips's criticism of the Indian Army was a prime example of the problem of empire – and the problem of the now tenuous European promise of the *mission civilisatrice* – in the ideological structures of the Second World War. Leo Amery would go on to repudiate Phillips's libel against the Indian Army and the subsequent 'muck-raking' journalism of Drew Pearson. The success of the Indian Army, which had a long, prestigious tradition, was rather proof of Britain's good governance in India: 'There were 2,000,000 volunteers, and from that it would appear that these people did not believe the Government oppressive or unjust or the cause unworthy.'[209] If this is mercenary, then so too was the British Army, 'which fought so heroically in the last war.'[210]

These criticisms of the Indian Army and the British Empire in general, Amery stressed, were more than anything an electioneering manoeuvre for the US elections. Amery had, elsewhere, described the Indian

[205] Ibid., p. 35.
[206] Cosgrave, *The Lives of Enoch Powell*, p. 84.
[207] 'Indian Army's Good Name: American's Slights Resented,' *The Times*, 6 September 1944.
[208] Ibid.
[209] 'Libels on Indian Army: Mr. Amery's Emphatic Repudiation,' *The Times*, 27 September 1944.
[210] Ibid.

Army much as Powell did: it was 'based on loyalty and affection between the British and Indian elements' and was recently forming 'a new comradeship ... of equal status.' 'In her Army, India personified a true unity,' he stressed, 'transcending religion, class, or language, and also a true identity between Indians and British.'[211] A copy of a short piece in *The Spectator* that month on the topic of American criticisms was typed out for Churchill.[212] Defending the Indian Army from 'irresponsible' American journalism and the notion that 'volunteers [are] apparently of a lower status than 'draft' men,' *The Spectator* would quote for the readers Housman's poem, 'Epitaph on an Army of Mercenaries':

> These, in the days when heaven was falling,
>   The hour when earth's foundations fled,
> Followed their mercenary calling,
>   And took their wages and are dead.
>
> Their shoulders held the sky suspended;
>   They stood, and earth's foundations stay;
> What God abandoned these defended,
>   And saved the sum of things for pay.

Housman's poem was published in *The Times* in 1917 on the anniversary of the Battle of Ypres. The article concluded, 'There is the stuff of immortality in this.'[213]

As A. Martin Wainwright has argued, the British government's attachment and traditional connections to the Indian Army resulted in an 'unrealistic assessment of Britain's popularity among Indians.'[214] Indian officers in the Indian Army who opposed Congress and the shifts in power that independence would bring were often in the best position to advise British officials in the Raj.[215] For instance, Auchinleck's private secretary, Major General Shahid Hamid, described the officers of the Indian National Army as 'cowards' who were simply 'not prepared to face the hardships of the prisoner of war camps.'[216] Many of these Indian officers had strong loyalties to the Raj based on social position and family tradition – crucially, for these men at least, this was not a loyalty based, as Amery put it, on new ideas of 'comradeship ... of equal status.'

The Willcox Report held that India required the expansion of a peacetime army – what was described by Powell as a 'very un-English

[211] 'Unity Through Service,' *The Times*, 19 November 1943.
[212] *The Spectator*, 29 September 1944. CHUR 2/42B.
[213] Ibid.
[214] Wainwright, *Inheritance of Empire*, p. 35.
[215] Ibid.   [216] Cited ibid.

approach.'[217] Powell told his friend Michael Wickenden just after its completion that he had been the 'anonymous father' of this two-volume, 570-page report, 'from my pen and 95% from my brain.'[218] The report maintained that it would take India twenty-five years to pre-pare militarily for independence. In the meantime, Powell argued that the Indian Army would require up to half of its officers to be British, basing his argument on tours of all the major military establishments from Peshawar to Calcutta and on elaborate calculations estimating how many Indians would reach the educational standards required to be officers. 'We believed,' with education, said Powell, 'that a gradual loosening of the class composition of the army was both possible and desirable, though it would have taken place much more slowly than I think it was envisaged by the successor Government.'[219]

Against the changes brought about by Auchinleck in order to increase recruitment, however, the report argued for a return to a modified form of the racial doctrine of recruiting from the traditional 'martial races.'[220] Whatever the settlement that was to be reached with the Indian National Congress, the report assumed that India would remain a military arse-nal of British imperial power. It argued that industrial development in India be fundamentally restructured for further strategic military value, not in the direction of self-sufficiency but as a means of imperial defence: 'A plan to ensure supply of equipment and munitions at the rate and scale necessary in war is not synonymous with a plan to make India self-sufficient. We do not believe that it would be desirable, even if it were possible, for India to aim at producing all the equipment and material required by her own forces. Self-sufficiency in this sense is an unsound conception.'[221] The notion of fundamentally restructuring India's industrial economy for the purposes of imperial war sits uneas-ily with Powell's view of his role there as traditional, conservative and 'natural.' As one historian has noted, this was one of many reports in this period that attempted to 'apply nineteenth-century British impe-rial solutions to the Cold War.'[222]

Powell's failure to see that Indian antipathy towards British imperial control was a factor in explaining the low levels of recruitment into the Indian Army in 1944 is striking.[223] For all his hopes for the widespread influence of the Willcox Report, Powell's absolute failure to account for

[217] 'JEP War Memories.' POLL 5.1.
[218] Powell to James Wickenden, 10 November 1945. POLL 1.1.10.
[219] 'JEP War Memories.' POLL 5.1.
[220] Wainwright, *Inheritance of Empire*, p. 35.
[221] Ibid., p. 61.   [222] Ibid., p. 62.
[223] Rutherford, *Forever England*, p. 108.

the political realities of pre-independence India largely discredited the report. It was dismissed by Auchinleck as off the mark.[224] Despite this, Powell was convinced of its lasting influence. Copies of the Willcox Report were apparently divided up at partition and, Powell believed, 'dominated for a long time, the military planning both of India and of Pakistan.' 'I would think that for twenty years or so it probably was fairly frequently referred to, both in Delhi and in Karachi.'[225]

An undated report that Powell is likely to have written while working for the Willcox Committee is a good indicator of Powell's view of Indian national consciousness throughout this period. It reveals something of Powell's cynicism in regard to Indian self-determination and self-knowledge. The report argues for the development of 'Indian Studies' in universities throughout Britain based on the principle of classical studies as a single and systematic subject. Powell noted that while there were hundreds of students who finished classics degrees every year, who possessed ten years' worth of knowledge of the language, customs and history of ancient Greece, it was 'an ironical thought that the equivalent knowledge of India would be the envy of men who had spent a lifetime's distinguished service' in India.[226] The study of the equivalent knowledge of India would be the proper preparation for the Indian Civil Service. This pursuit of knowledge in India was practically necessary, Powell claimed, because the Indian himself does not pursue it:

All experience tends to show that the natives of India unaided and unencouraged have neither the impulse nor the capacity to do work of the kind that needs doing. On the other hand there exists a real, though rather a barren, pride in what is and has been in India, which tends to render association and intercourse between Europeans and Indians in this sphere exceptionally easy and harmonious.[227]

Indians, Powell implies here, are not alone capable of cultural self-knowledge. Their self-knowledge depended on the British. As this report makes clear, Powell's seemingly liberal arguments regarding Indian development were fixed in a deeply conservative mindset. Powell loved India, but it was only as an Englishman that he could know it. In many ways, Powell's belief that the study of Urdu could replace the study of the classics indicates the limits of Powell's seeming 'liberalism.' The moral value of the 'language, customs, and history of ancient Greece' was not sufficient to rule India – to replicate or impersonate European

[224] Ibid.
[225] 'JEP War Memories.' POLL 5.1.
[226] J. Enoch Powell, 'Indian Studies.' POLL 3.1.1, File 3.
[227] Ibid.

civilization in the Indian subcontinent was never Powell's impulse. At the same time, the report makes clear that in Powell's mind 'the Indian' was not yet 'a political entity' because he failed to vote according to his class interest but *also* because he had 'neither the impulse nor the capacity' to know himself. While Heffer asserts that the main legacy of Powell's time in India was 'his optimistic view of what could be achieved by Europeans and Asians working together,'[228] Powell's views remained remarkably pessimistic about Indian national consciousness.

Reconquering the Raj

While in India in the army in Dehra Dun as an officer under General Cawthorn from 1943 to 1946 and while working for the Conservative Party Secretariat as a researcher from 1947 to 1950, Powell wrote literally dozens of lengthy reports and speeches on India. These reports were his first foray into domestic political analysis. In them, Powell consistently argued for a strengthened commitment to India, more manpower and greater British control – against the policy of 'Indianization' of the civil service and the army. The British Raj was failing, Powell believed, due to British apathy. For some reason, the British had become 'introverted and apathetic about her prospects in the East.'[229] When still in India, he read in the papers the things said in England and would 'writhe.' 'Is there no way,' he asked, 'of stopping the airing of the "delirious vapourings" of people that know nothing of India?' Going on, he wrote:

Lord Curzon said justly that 'the British dominion in India is one of the wonders of the world.' The history of it is one which I should have thought no Englishman could read without emotion and pride. Why should this be slandered and abused and dragged in the mud not by our enemies, not even by our pseudo-allies, but by our own kindred? Lies and falsehoods and fallacies, and never a courageous and defiant justification. My old fears that filled my letters from Sydney in 1938–1939 are coming upon me again.[230]

These 'kindred' knew nothing of India, Powell emphasized. In January 1946, just a month before he left India, he witnessed the changing scene:

[T]he capital is today the proud sojourning place of a body of gentlemen who wish themselves to be considered as 'human beings'! Most of them have now for the first time so much as set eyes upon the country about which they have for so many years favoured us with their advice or rather criticism, based

[228] Heffer, *Like the Roman*, p. 106.
[229] Powell to Ellen and Albert Powell, 16 October 1944. POLL 1.1.7.
[230] Powell to Ellen and Albert Powell, 27 January 1944. POLL 1.1.7.

invariably on the assumption that their fellow countrymen here are activated only by malevolence, ignorance and incapacity.[231]

This was the consequence of a shift in opinion in Britain that was foreign to him – a political shift that had amounted to Labour's victory in 1945. Indeed, Powell returned to Britain to enter politics, following Edmund Burke's line 160 years prior, because 'the keys of India'[232] were in the House of Commons. He returned to England to save the British Raj from the arrogance of these gentlemen who wished to end the empire, not for Britain or for India, but so that they might be 'considered as "human beings."'

Powell returned in 1946, thirty-three years old and a brigadier.[233] The day he arrived back in England, he called the Conservative Party central office looking for work. He soon took up a post in the Conservative Party Secretariat as a researcher. He continued to study Urdu until 1947 – until the moment of Indian independence – at the School of Oriental and African Studies in London, in an effort, he made explicit, to one day attain the title of Viceroy of India. Patrick Cosgrave's work *The Lives of Enoch Powell* recounts a story of Enoch Powell bursting into Churchill's office offering to reconquer India if given ten army divisions. The story of him saying this is still heavily disputed. Cosgrave attributes the story to R. A. Butler's high-table gossip at Trinity College, Cambridge.[234] Though this may be an apocryphal tale, a similar argument can also be found in a report that Powell delivered to Churchill in 1946. Powell, at the time, saw Labour's failure to plan for civil unrest in India as a chance for Conservatives to show their political sense. In May, while working in the Conservative Parliamentary Secretariat with special responsibility in imperial matters, Powell delivered a preliminary report in which he maintained that, 'after the legal moment of transfer of power an outbreak of violence in India such as will dwarf 1857 is not only likely but certain ... Terrible though the immediate and direct consequences of such a disaster would be, it is difficult to see how without it either Britain or India can make their escape back to reality from the political make-believe of the last 30 years.'[235] Sounding much like he would in 1970 regarding the 'anarcho-student movement,' Powell warned that 'the forces of disorder are endemic.'[236] The Royal

[231] Powell to Ellen and Albert Powell, 6 January 1946. POLL 1.1.10.
[232] Berkeley, *The Odyssey of Enoch*, p. 51.
[233] Rutherford, *Forever England*, p. 108.
[234] Cosgrave, *The Lives of Enoch Powell*, p. 115.
[235] J. Enoch Powell, *Memorandum on Indian Policy* (Conservative Parliamentary Secretariat), 16 May 1946, p. 15. POLL 3.1.1.4.
[236] Cited in Heffer, *Like the Roman*, p. 107.

Indian Navy mutiny three months previously was 'the infallible precursor of the coming storm.'[237] The result of this upheaval in India would be that Indians would 'look to British order as a welcome salvation from chaos and strife.'[238] The tragedy would be Britain's responsibility. In essence, this would be Britain's moment to reclaim its special role – its role as the rulers of India. Thanks to India's need for order, 'for some two generations ahead ultimate responsibility for the government of India will continue to be with Britain.'[239]

In his preliminary report, Powell argued that the Conservative Party needed to work in private on a policy that the party could adopt at the moment when India fell into civil war.[240] This was the party's chance to ensure that the impending catastrophe would be blamed on the Labour government. And so, Powell went to work, producing a report six months later. In these reports, Powell made clear something of his thoughts on the centrality of social and economic motivation in politics. Communalism was the central factor in India that, according to Powell, indicated that India was unready for self-government. As Peter Brooke has rightly noted, at times Powell's arguments read as though he were a committed liberal imperialist.[241] Indeed Powell even spoke of the need to make 'the individual Indian a political entity.'[242] In his preliminary report, he wrote:

When the ordinary India citizen has a position and a value in the economic structure of the nation, is sufficiently informed and educated to form opinions on the manner in which one policy or another would affect it, and has attained some conception of the state and of his relation to it, then truly political parties will of their own accord come into existence.[243]

Via martial law, Britain could support the formation of nationwide trade unions that would cut across communal divisions. Democracy, Powell noted, depended on voters who change their political allegiance according to the circumstances of the day. Without a 'fluid electorate,' majority decision becomes 'a tyranny of the majority over the minority.'[244] Already Powell was arguing that the cleavage of the electorate on

---

[237] Ibid.
[238] J. Enoch Powell, *Memorandum on Indian Policy* (Conservative Parliamentary Secretariat), 16 May 1946, p. 15. POLL 3.1.1.4.
[239] Cited in Heffer, *Like the Roman*, p. 107.
[240] J. Enoch Powell, *Memorandum on Indian Policy*, p. 17.
[241] Brooke, 'India, Post-Imperialism and the Origins of Enoch Powell's "Rivers of Blood" Speech,' pp. 669–687.
[242] J. Enoch Powell, *Memorandum on Indian Policy*, p. 17.
[243] Ibid., p. 10.   [244] Ibid., p. 6.

racial or religious grounds automatically precluded the essential fluidity of democracy; only when they were politically irrelevant could parliamentary government truly exist in India. That was Powell's position in May 1946. And so, Powell argued that Britain needed to 'institute a social and economic revolution in India before she can bring about a satisfactory constitutional settlement.'[245]

In December 1946, Powell submitted his final report to Butler, who then passed it on to Churchill. Butler wrote to Churchill: 'It is impossible, at present, to foresee the turn events will take; but I trust you will find it valuable to have available some positive suggestions in the event of our being obliged to resume a large measure of control in India.'[246] The background of the study assumed a total breakdown of law and order in India and that Britain had restored order by armed force. Britain would, on the request of the Indian people, bring in martial law. Powell argued for a return to first principles. He maintained that such an event would 'offer a unique but fleeting opportunity to do those things which have been left undone in India during the past generations, and to undo much that has proved ... to have been wrongly done.'[247] This was Britain's chance at a 'fresh start' that would break through the 'atmosphere of hallucination which surrounds Indian politics.'[248] The policy of the 'Indianization' of the leadership of India's government, army and police would be called to a halt. Civil war would break from that narrative of political progress in India which, according to Powell, 'consisted largely of rearing up one superstructure of words and forms upon another, until little correspondence remains between realities and the political organization which appears to have been attained ... By breaking the spell, or assuming it broken, we escape back to real objects, real factors and real methods.'[249] There was, Powell insisted, 'clearly a limit' to the 'reduction of the British element in the Government of India itself, in the officering of the Police and in the Civil Service which is consistent with the British Government being sure of its intentions and decisions being carried out.'[250] Without responsibility to Westminster, no cabinet responsibility could yet exist. Independence was a leap in the dark.

Here, Powell speaks of breaking the spell – breaking the spell of what Powell regards as an immature will to independence. Political

---

[245] As cited in Letter from Powell to R. A. Butler, 3 December 1946. CHUR 2/42A.
[246] Letter from R. A. Butler to Winston Churchill, 18 December 1946. CHUR 2/42A.
[247] J. Enoch Powell, *India Report*, 3 December 1946, p. 1. CHUR 2/42A.
[248] Ibid.   [249] Ibid.
[250] Cited in Heffer, *Like the Roman*, p. 106.

myth-making – in this instance the belief in the Indian nation – would be cured by violent revolution and a return to sustained British control. Already, Powell regards political action as the interplay between reality and (historical) myth. As the previous section discussed, even before 1947, Powell was never convinced by the idea of Britishness as an ideological project. While in Australia before the war, Powell was deeply cynical about the survival of a British Australia. Its imperial ceremonies required 'impersonation.'[251] He did, however, embrace the historical role of British power in India, the ideal of the Indian Army's allegiance to the English Crown, and the 'natural' role of the Englishman he believed he found there.[252]

Churchill read Powell's December report and is said to have called Powell mad.[253] Powell sent the report to friends also. One missionary worker in India replied, 'I have read your brochure on a new move in India ... You haven't said half enough about securing the cooperation of the people ... You expect the people to acquiesce in the breaking down of all their pet customs, which militate against progress ... The incentive and the work of securing cooperation must be colossal.'[254]

Powell's arguments for the institution of temporary martial law in India were not wholly concerned with the eventual attainment of Indian democracy and independence. This was, even more, about the unique and necessary role of the Englishman in India. What is most striking in Powell's report to Churchill is Powell's fundamental failure to see the power of Indian anti-colonialism and assertions of equality against imperial dominance at this time. Like his report on the reorganization of the Indian Army, Powell was blind to Indian antipathy towards British control. In fact, Powell regarded the independence movement as having little relation to the actual commitments of the Indian people. 'The political campaign against Britain,' he wrote, 'has no relation to the actual feeling or behaviour of the peoples of India towards the individual Englishman or the British in India collectively. It is possible for an Englishman, in or out of uniform, to move freely up and down India, its industrial cities and its rural areas, from one year's end to another without encountering a single case of hostility, while, on the other hand, he will still be met with innumerable marks of his acceptance as an integral part of the structure of the country.'

[251] Powell to Ellen and Albert Powell, 12 June 1938. POLL 1.1.4.
[252] Powell, 'A Passage to India,' p. 21.
[253] Cosgrave, *The Lives of Enoch Powell*, p. 115.
[254] Frank Brayne to J. Enoch Powell, 27 December 1946. POLL 3.1.7.

This was because, Powell insisted, 'modern India is so much a creation of Britain.'[255] Even 'the so-called nationalists' did not actually contemplate the 'literal removal' of British control.[256]

This is where Powell's thinking failed him. Both in Britain and in India, the 'hallucination' of the British Raj was over. This Powell did not see. He wrote that, as in 1857, 'it is surely not unreasonable to imagine that after witnessing in India the catastrophic outcome of recent policy, opinion in Britain would be prepared to back the measures necessary to restore order and administration throughout the sub-continent.'[257] However, both in India and in Britain, no call to power or acceptance of British responsibility materialized.

Conclusion

Recognizing Powell's commitment to a (once imperial) order goes far in explaining why historian Peter Brooke could unearth in Powell's papers evidence of arguments against black migration into Britain prior to decolonization. Black migration to the metropole, both before and after the successes of the anti-colonial independence movements, threatened to disrupt the hierarchical whole on which British power depended. Brooke has deduced from Powell's opposition to black migration in 1946 that Powell's views on immigration into Britain in 1968 were less a reflection of the cultural and political consequences of the end of empire than Powell's 'repackaging [of] a colonial apology for racial inequity rooted in the language of liberalism.'[258] Powell's insistence that Britain close its borders to 'New Commonwealth' citizens was, according to Brooke, a consequence of his fear that rigid communal (racial) divisions could threaten Britain's democratic system.[259] This fear of communalism was, this argument emphasizes, 'rooted in assumptions typical of liberal colonial governors' and 'established long before the end of empire.'[260] In Brooke's view, Powell's later anti-immigration speeches were based, then, on the very same liberal imperial precepts as his argument in 1946 against the idea that an ethnically divided India could be ready to form an independent, democratic state.

---

[255] J. Enoch Powell, 'Memorandum on India Policy,' 16 May 1946, cited in Heffer, *Like the Roman*, p. 106.
[256] Ibid.   [257] Ibid.
[258] Brooke, 'India, Post-Imperialism and the Origins of Enoch Powell's "Rivers of Blood" Speech,' p. 670.
[259] Ibid.   [260] Ibid., p. 671.

This effort to reveal that Powell was a liberal – or that his ideas on race and immigration were based in 'a distinctive liberal philosophy'[261] – is a curious historical intervention. Powell's reports on India in 1946 do reveal his belief that increased social and economic motivation in India could be the key to making 'innocuous the differences of race and religion.'[262] But Powell's primary interest in India was hardly democracy per se, nor was it the cultivation of liberal development along the lines of the British or European example. Rather Powell, as he would be throughout his political career, was preoccupied by the health and limits of governing institutions – again, the 'unique structure of power' of British rule. Tellingly, Powell's 1946 report on India was based on an imagined scenario of India falling into absolute anarchy and the Indian people looking to British military power to restore order. In this report on India – in which Brooke uncovers Powell's liberal creed – Powell was, it should be noted, arguing for the introduction of a police state.

As his later preoccupation in the 1960s and 1970s with social anarchy emphasizes, in Powell's mind, the fabrication of society could not be the goal – society was a delicate and vulnerable phenomenon:

Anarchy is a very striking encounter for a conservative. It is a striking encounter for a conservative more than for anybody else because he is more conscious than anyone else of the delicacy and vulnerability of that which sustains society.

When asked to further expound on this idea of the vulnerability of society, he explained:

that the web of understood relationships which sustains society is an object, to a degree, of veneration as something which cannot be without danger tampered with, which arguably once injured may not be capable of being restored. So the phenomenon of anarchy is philosophically very impressive to a Tory.[263]

Again, the *raison d'être* of imperial rule was not its transformative potential nor its role in preserving a liberal space for individual development and freedom, but its (natural) role in preserving the web of intricate, organic and historically understood relationships.

As this chapter has emphasized, it is possible to see Powell's cynicism regarding Britishness as a liberal project if one looks not only to

---

[261] Brooke, 'Indian, Post-Imperialism and the Origins of Enoch Powell's "Rivers of Blood" Speech,' p. 687.

[262] J. Enoch Powell, *Memorandum on Indian Policy* (Conservative Parliamentary Secretariat), 16 May 1946, p. 10. POLL 3.1.1.4. In this report on India in 1946 – in which Brooke uncovers Powell's liberal creed – Powell was, it should be noted, arguing for the introduction of a police state.

[263] J. Enoch Powell, Bill Schwarz interview, 26 April 1988.

India but also to his views on Australia and the United States. The American, in Powell's mind, had no idea of the (natural) nation, of hierarchical unity and international variety. The American vision of the world was, as Powell decided while in North Africa during the Second World War, Britain's most 'terrible enemy.'[264] It is worth quoting Powell's view of America in 1968 at length, for in his formulation of American identity we can begin to see the outline of Powell's conservative, postwar revolt:

One flies for hour after hour at near sonic speeds, across a territory of endless continental variety, and at the other end – this again, a typical Australian sensation – one still finds just more America, more Americans ... The distance has made no difference. There are no foreigners, only reservations, like zoological gardens or geological museums, for the aborigines or the Indians. How could such a nation avoid the assumption, source of all their mistakes and disillusionments, that the earth is inhabited either by Americans or by those whose manifest destiny, however long or laborious its achievement, is to become a passable imitation of Americans? This, too, is the voice of the colonist, the frontiersman in the empty or inhospitable land: in all that variety and wonder which lies to be explored in the 'out beyond,' one thing there will not be – other nations, with other values, assumptions and standards, as true, as valid...

Here Powell reveals what he believes divides British rule from American power:

The Americans, in contrast [to the British] are universalists, bred and brought up to believe that the same rules apply everywhere. The propensity to divide the world into 'East' and 'West,' and the nations into 'goodies' and 'baddies' ... derives from the universalist outlook: there simply are only two categories available – pro-American, or 'free' or 'democratic' ('please don't quibble, it all means the same thing') or else anti-American ... A recent freak result is the American's reinterpretation of the British Empire. In the course of defending the American way of life in South-East Asia, they noticed that there were some other Europeans near by. As it happened, these were the last outposts of the British Empire in India, which were in course of being closed down following liquidation – a consummation which American policy from time immemorial had favoured and even promoted ... The Americans jumped to the conclusion that the British must be engaged on the same missionary enterprise as themselves, embraced them cordially, and transferred the British soldier and administrator from the ranks of Satan to the legions of the Lord ... This sort of thing makes one crimson with embarrassment. One wants to reply: 'You were nearer right before, as a matter of fact' ....[265]

---

[264] Powell to Ellen and Albert Powell, 16 February 1943, POLL 1.1.5.
[265] J. Enoch Powell, 'The Great American Dilemma,' *Sunday Telegraph* (17 March 1968).

In this sense, Powell's anti-Americanism is not just another symptom of Powell's eccentric personality.[266] It is a window into Powell's confrontation with the postwar world. Crucially, out of the Second World War, there grew a liberal consensus on the need to reconstruct the international order on a new basis, one that rested on commitments beyond the maintenance of state sovereignty.[267] In the wake of millions of displaced persons, Europe faced a 'human rights revolution.'[268] According to Powell, this 'new order' of human rights and international law asserted a moral righteousness that disguised (material) domination. He opposed both the 'moral' politics of postwar internationalism and the further expansion of the state into the economic and moral life of the individual. Powell's protests over the postwar period might best be viewed as a consequence of these transformations in the political order.

Again, as Powell's 1987 interview makes clear, Powell's memory of war was not the potentially transformative 'People's War' of Britain, removed as he was from both the European theatre of war and the home front. At the same time, Powell's experiences of empire – his sense of dislocation in Australia and his subsequent embrace of the politics of war in wartime India – left him with an ongoing faith in war as the foundation of politics and community. In the following years, this commitment to the nation-at-war as the foundation of politics and his rejection of Britain's international ('civilizing') role had profound consequences. Powell's notion of the naturalness of the unity of the Englishman and Indian in the Indian Army combined with a blindness to the violence present in the imperial arrangement. As he put it while in North Africa in 1943:

I do abhor this use of the word 'imperial' with its connotations. I doubt whether the charge of believing in the British mission to rule over palm and pine can ever be authenticated. I've used the term 'inevitability', and I've used it as a qualification for righteousness in terms of the Raj but ... Dominion founded on force, on compulsion, has never been something which I recognized or still less have been attracted by.[269]

---

[266] For a discussion on Powell's and Margaret Thatcher's differing views on the United States, see Richard Vinen, 'Thatcherism before Thatcher? Enoch Powell,' in *Thatcher's Britain: The Politics and Social Upheaval of the 1980s* (London: Simon & Schuster, 2009), pp. 45–59.

[267] Jay Winter, 'From War Talk to Rights Talk: Exile Politics, Human Rights, and the Two World Wars,' in Menno Spiering and Michael Wintle (eds.), *European Identity and the Second World War* (London: Palgrave Macmillan, 2011), pp. 65–66.

[268] G. Daniel Cohen, 'The "Human Rights Revolution" at Work: Displaced Persons in Postwar Europe,' in Stefan-Ludwig Hoffman (ed.), *Human Rights in the Twentieth Century* (Cambridge University Press, 2011), pp. 45–61.

[269] J. Enoch Powell, cited in Cosgrave, *The Lives of Enoch Powell*, p. 82.

For Powell, militarism and martial institutions were the necessary result of their exact opposite: an absence of coercion and a love of peace. In the British defence of the status quo – for all that already existed – in India, Powell envisioned a prioritization of life over abstraction. This was the prioritization of meaningful everyday order over the false promise of an abstract and perpetual peace. Ironically, Powell's fantasy of the weightlessness of Britain's military institutions – his belief that Britain's presence in India was a 'conservative' force – was in direct contradiction to the dramatic restructuring of India's political economy that the Willcox Report demanded (for the empire in a Cold War world).

Meanwhile, the liberal vision of empire was, for Powell, intimately linked to his vision of a totalitarian infiltration and regulation of everyday life. His use of the word 'imperial' – his disdain for it – is precisely in its relationship to the liberal (American) project as Powell envisioned it. In other words, with 'righteousness,' with a splitting of the world into 'goodies' and 'baddies,' Powell feared that war would be declared upon everyday life. This would, in the years ahead, underpin both Powell's belief in the market (as the expression of everyday social life) and Powell's refusal to condemn popular racism. The following chapters will track Powell's revolt against the postwar world. There, we will see the ongoing significance of Powell's particular experience of war and empire.

Powell's experience of WW2 was not the 'People's War' experienced by those who wrote to him in 1968.

2 Liberal war, 1947–1960

> One can never resolve in the span of a human lifetime that kind of a revolution [the end of empire] without the marks being left of a struggle. I confess to you that for all that I write, for all that I think, for all that I try to demonstrate to myself and others I shall go to the grave with a conviction at the back of my mind that Her Majesty's ships still sweep the oceans of the world ... That hallucination will be there when the mind stops.
>
> J. Enoch Powell, 1965[1]

As we have seen in the previous chapter, Enoch Powell was thoroughly committed to the maintenance of British imperial power during and after the Second World. He took up military employment in Asia during the war because he believed, as he wrote to a friend in 1944, that, 'the Far East was in the beginning, is now, and ever shall be the only source of world power.'[2] This chapter charts Powell's dramatic turn away from Britain's imperial ambitions and turn toward the (territorial) nation as the touchstone for all political action and thinking. This is, then, the story of the emergence of Powell the 'post-imperialist.'

Historians and cultural theorists have long argued that Powell's later views against black immigration must be tied to his prescient rejection of Britain's commitment to the empire in the early 1950s and subsequent embrace of English nationalism.[3] Simon Heffer argues that the divorce of British nationality from allegiance to the Crown – brought about by the British Nationality Act of 1948 – is the root of

---

[1] J. Enoch Powell, 'The Consequences of the General Election,' *Swinton College Journal* (Summer 1965).

[2] Heffer, *Like the Roman*, p. 92.

[3] See Brooke, 'India, Post-Imperialism and the Origins of Enoch Powell's "Rivers of Blood" Speech,' p. 670, fn. 5; J. Barnes, 'Ideology and Factions,' in Anthony Seldon and Stuart Ball (eds.), *Conservative Century: The Conservative Party since 1900* (Oxford University Press, 1994), p. 338; Berkeley, *The Odyssey of Enoch*, p. 46; Cosgrave, *The Lives of Powell*, p. 130; Gilroy, *There Ain't No Black in the Union Jack*, p. 48; Heffer, *Like the Roman*, pp. 120–121.

Powell's revolt against black immigration.[4] With this Act, the people of ex-colonial nations who had gained independence still retained rights to enter Britain as 'Commonwealth citizens.' In essence, Heffer insists that Powell's revolt against black immigration was, more than anything, a pragmatic assertion that British citizenship law needed to reflect the transformations in allegiance that were unfolding due to the accelerating disintegration of the British Empire. Meanwhile, those critical of Powell, many writing from the cultural studies tradition, have argued that it was the traumatic loss of the British Raj in 1947 that caused Powell to embrace ethnic nationalism.[5] This work has revealed the way in which, through Powellism, the black immigrant came to then embody imperial decline, or Britain's loss of identity in the loss of the imperial project.[6] The black immigrant was, in this sense, a reminder of Britain's loss of dominance and a representative of a world turned upside down.[7] In both of these arguments, the historical rupture of end of empire is the key to understanding Powell's thoughts on black immigration.

Others argue that Powell made the arguments he made about immigration because he was, above all else, concerned with the prospects of democracy in Britain. At a small conference to mark the opening of Powell's papers to the public in 2004, Powell's long-time assistant Richard Ritchie was heckled for repeatedly asserting that for Powell, 'this was about democracy.'[8] Powell was, Ritchie insisted, not concerned with race per se; he simply believed that parliamentary democracy required a degree of homogeneity and cultural unity in order to truly function. As discussed in the proceeding chapter, this argument is most developed and most nuanced in the writing of Peter Brooke. Brooke argues that Powell's speeches in favour of keeping Britain white do not reflect any post-imperialist resurgence of English ethnic nationalism. In Powell's thinking, there was no intellectual *rupture*. Rather, in 1960s Britain as in the British Raj, Powell believed that liberal democracy could not flourish in the face of communalism.[9] Democracy depends,

---

[4] Heffer, *Like the Roman*, p. 121.

[5] Rutherford, *Forever England*.

[6] For a discussion of the way in which Powellism linked the imperial 'race problem' to immigration, see Webster, *Englishness and Empire*, pp. 149–150.

[7] Anna Marie Smith, 'Powellism: The Black Immigrant as the Post-colonial Symptom and the Phantasmatic Re-closure of the British Nation,' in *New Right Discourse*.

[8] 'Enoch Powell and the Politics of Immigration,' conference sponsored by the Centre for Research in the Arts, Social Sciences and Humanities, at Churchill College, Cambridge (21 February 2004).

[9] Brooke, 'India, Post-Imperialism and the Origins of Enoch Powell's "Rivers of Blood" Speech,' pp. 669–687.

argued Powell, on the individual voter free of group identification –
according to Brooke, then, Powell based his arguments on immigration on a 'distinctive liberal philosophy.'[10] During and just after the
Second World War, Powell argued like many others in the Conservative
Party that Indians, due to ethnic and religious divisions, were not yet
ready for political independence. His worst fears, he found, were proven
legitimate by the ensuing communal violence. Brooke emphasizes an
absolute coherence of thought for Powell from the Punjab to the West
Midlands.

The emphasis on (imperial) continuity versus (post-imperial) rupture in the above analyses offers a false dichotomy in understanding the
life of Enoch Powell. Powell retained many of his wartime views about
human nature and the limits of stable political organization. There is
certainly continuity in his belief in the need for historically sanctioned
institutions and in his preoccupation with the fragility of political community. In many ways, the logic of war – his imperial war – remained
the prism through which he understood a changing, postwar world.
But it is also clear that Powell's experience of the social, cultural and
political changes that rocked Britain and the empire in the postwar
years set the trajectory of his thinking and spurred many of his public arguments. In this way, Powell is far from unique. The fact that
Powell carried an ideological filter constituted by past experiences gets
at the straightforward historical value of biography. That individual
lives are an accumulation of innumerable subject positions – that lives
are experienced across many decades and through seismic historical
events – forces historians to take account of the fact that the events
of history are connected most of all by the men and women who witness change and carry an understanding of the past with them. What is
unique in Powell – as we shall see especially in Chapter 4 and Chapter 5
of this book – is the way in which the prism of war left him at times
acutely sensitive and at times blind to the new political realities of the
postwar period.

In August 1947, India was partitioned. As Powell put it, with this,
'One's whole world had been altered.'[11] As is often remembered, he
walked the streets of London all night on the night of Independence in
a state of shock.[12] While working as the head of the Conservative Party's
research committee on India, Powell received regular reports on the
violence in the Punjab from two acquaintances who remained there.

---

[10] Ibid., p. 687.
[11] Rutherford, *Forever England*, p. 109.
[12] Ibid.

Gordon Thompson, commander of Calcutta sub-area, wrote personal letters to Powell on the situation and Frank Brayne, a former Indian civil servant, sent Powell confidential leaked reports on the violence as they were released.[13] They tell of horrific suffering. Like many others who remained critical of British withdrawal, Powell believed the responsibility for the bloodshed lay with, as he put it in 1946, that 'body of gentlemen who wish themselves to be considered as "human beings."'[14] While there remains an ongoing historical debate on whether it is appropriate to read the 1945–1951 Labour government's approach to decolonization and colonial rule as essentially altruistic or even liberal, we can begin to see one key strand in Powell's political thinking in this single line of condemnation. Namely, Powell opposed the application of progressive principles – or that effort to be considered as moral 'human beings' – over the protection of social and political order. As we shall see, Powell was at this time swimming against the tide.

The years of austerity after the war contributed to Labour's loss in the general election of 1951. As Andrew Gamble has explained in his classic work *The Conservative Nation*, the postwar Conservative Party, rather than representing a clear ideological alternative to Labour, succeeded in presenting itself in the 1950s as the best party to *manage* reformed capitalism and, linked to this, the best party to maintain Britain's capital wealth in the empire.[15] Despite Britain's dramatic strategic loss of the Suez Canal and military base and despite war in Malaya and Kenya, the Conservative Party – the party of empire – managed to stay in power throughout the 1950s. Though Kenya's anti-colonial movement Mau Mau became a household name and wars in Kenya and Malaya made headlines, the 'internal decolonization' of Britain, the effects of Britain's transformation from imperial to national status, did not result in the loss of Conservative hegemony at this time.[16] Rather, by 1959, Harold Macmillan's election campaign told Britain that the people had 'never had it so good,' and the Conservatives would win in October 1959 with a landslide victory. When the news spoke of chaos and violence in the Belgian Congo and France raged with war in Algeria and state killing in the metropole, it served as further proof of Britain's stability in the face of decolonization. In these years, Powell offered a sustained critique of his party's imperial policy. He described the Suez Crisis and the resultant backbench rebellions of 1954 and 1957 as an 'agony of soul through which the Conservative party passed,' in

---

[13] 'Personal letters on India.' POLL 3.1.7.
[14] Powell to Ellen and Albert Powell, 6 January 1946. POLL 1.1.10.
[15] Gamble, *The Conservative Nation*, pp. 38–86.
[16] Webster, 'There'll Always be an England,' pp. 557–584.

which 'the country at large barely participated.'[17] This agony of soul
and the party's subsequent eschewal of imperial and national pride led
Conservatives, according to Powell, to turn to a 'cult of newness,' to
modernization and technocratic planning – all best represented, Powell
believed, in the character of Harold Macmillan.

Along with the story of Powell's turn from imperial ambitions, this
chapter will also seek, then, to present this world of 1950s Britain
through Powell's eyes. Words such as 'mesmerized,' profound public 'forgetting' and 'collective wilful amnesia' enter into his lexicon
in these years to describe the British public's failure to appreciate the
significance of the surrender of imperial power.[18] Powell was at times
shocked by the public's silence on decolonization: in 1959, surprised by
the lack of public scrutiny regarding the Suez Crisis during the 1959
general election campaign, he surmised that 'the public mind had sustained a deep trauma, irrespective of party and irrespective of opinion'
due to the crisis.[19] Ironically, Powell's words echo much of the analysis
of British racism – which read it as a failure of historical consciousness – that would emerge in the wake of his 'Rivers of Blood' speech.[20]
Britain was what Powell called in 'a sleep and a forgetting.'[21] At times,
Powell associated this quiet consent around decolonization as the mark
of the historic character of Britain, as a mark of a deferential nation,
and a benefit to the British government's freedom of action in foreign
policy. But by the mid-1960s, as we shall see in the following chapter,
Powell offered an alternative to the public: a 'new patriotism' that challenged the approach of his party and the widespread assumptions about
Britain's constructive role in the world.

Liberal order

Powell was highly sceptical of the new ideology of imperialism which,
coming out of the manpower necessities and symbolic politics of the
Second World War, emphasized welfare, development and multiracial
partnership.[22] A reconstructed imperial state was born in these years

[17] J. Enoch Powell, 'A Party in Search of a Pattern: From the Years of Protest to the Year
of Disaster,' *The Times*, 1 April 1964.
[18] J. Enoch Powell, 'International Commentary,' 23 October 1959, Radio Broadcast.
POLL 4.1.27.
[19] Ibid.
[20] See, for instance, Centre for Contemporary Cultural Studies, *The Empire
Strikes Back*.
[21] J. Enoch Powell, 'International Commentary,' 23 October 1959, Radio Broadcast.
POLL 4.1.27.
[22] Webster, *Englishness and Empire*.

to garner colonial support, which employed newly accepted theories of planned economic development. In 1949, the Conservative Party published a pamphlet entitled *Imperial Policy*. This was one of a string of Conservative pamphlets that are now remembered in the history of postwar Britain as a sign of the party's effort to reform and broaden its appeal after its electoral defeat of 1945. Among other things, the pamphlet accepted the consequences of Indian independence and stressed the value of modernization, economic cooperation and education in both the colonies and the Commonwealth. The pamphlet became one of the 'intellectual cornerstones' of modern, postwar conservatism and laid the foundation for Prime Minister Harold Macmillan's 'Wind of Change' speech in support of African nationalism in 1960.[23] The pamphlet begins with a history of imperial expansion and, interestingly, tells a story of an empire built on the working man's entrepreneurial spirit and the prospect of social mobility. Here, 'the greatest seafaring explorer' Captain Cook is remembered as the 'son of a Yorkshire farm-bailiff,' the explorer and missionary David Livingstone is described as a 'cotton worker' and 'the great Englishman' Cecil Rhodes 'the son of a clergyman.'[24] The history of the British Empire is, the pamphlet argues, 'not so much the history of Governments' but a history of individuals spreading 'ideals of humanity, tolerance and justice.'[25] We see condensed in this pamphlet the effort to repackage the British Empire as a modern, forward-thinking and essentially middle-class national project. Echoing the Labour foreign secretary Ernest Bevin's views on the value of imperial trade and explicitly quoting Joseph Chamberlain's social imperialism of fifty years earlier, the pamphlet presents the promises of postwar reconstruction, the welfare state and full employment, as dependent on Britain's ability to develop resources in the empire.[26]

But as well as this emphasis on the British Empire as a distinctly *modern* project of development, the pamphlet highlights another critical feature of imperial rhetoric at this moment – the character of which is really essential to any appreciation of Britain's decolonizing state. The pamphlet speaks of Britain's 'most precious possession' which is, the pamphlet argues, 'the word of the Englishman' and, conflating Englishness and the British nation, the 'good name of Britain.'[27] In the face of material decline and the loss of the British Raj, it was the British Empire's 'great moral standing' as a missionary project of

---

[23] Rutherford, *Forever England*, p. 109.
[24] *Imperial Policy: A Statement of Conservative Policy for the British Empire and Commonwealth* (Conservative and Unionist Central Office, June 1949), p. 2.
[25] Ibid.   [26] Ibid., p. 3.   [27] Ibid., p. 17.

economic and political development that is presented here as the basis of Britain's continued influence in the world. Britain emerged from the Second World War gripped by war loans, lost export markets and the costs of both reconstruction and the maintenance of a huge air force and conscript army. Still, British policy-makers after the war continued to assert, alongside the United States, a certain moral authority as the nation who 'saved the world for democracy.' Even within the Second World War itself – and especially after the United States officially entered the war in December 1941 – there was a marked shift in imperial rhetoric in the BBC's Empire Service, for instance, from a focus on colonial loyalty and dependence towards partnership and development. This was essentially a rebranding exercise: a new paternalism. Importantly, within the *Imperial Policy* pamphlet, Britain's 'moral leadership' in this reformed egalitarian empire and its public image of tolerance and good governance are presented as vital in facing a new liberal war, a war against a 'new barbarism':

[W]e live in a dangerous world and it would be sheer folly to ignore the threat to democratic freedom which Soviet aggression presents. The British Commonwealth has greater resources of political experience than any other nation. Moral leadership in the 'cold war' against the new barbarism must, therefore, devolve upon its shoulders. To those who believe that the days of world leadership for the British Empire and Commonwealth are over, we reply 'British leadership is more vital to the future of civilization now than at any time in history.'[28]

As this pamphlet explains, in this liberal war, the British government's weapons on the international stage are not only economic and military might but the hearts and minds of colonial university students, the improvement of standards of living in the colonies, agricultural development and nutrition, a British Commonwealth defence system coordinated with the United States and, finally, the explicit acceptance of the eventual self-government of colonial peoples.[29] All this represented 'a vigorous policy aimed at restoring the British Empire and Commonwealth to its role as a leader of free peoples against the encroachments of world Communism.'[30] These assertions reveal a significant line of thinking in the shifting terrain of postwar narratives of empire, which – as Wendy Webster describes it – 'spilled into narratives of British-American relations … [and] were variously modernized, disavowed, lampooned, or reclaimed as heritage in a volatile, shifting, and contradictory narrative of the nation.'[31]

[28] Ibid., p. 8.   [29] Ibid., p. 19.   [30] Ibid., p. 8.
[31] Webster, *Englishness and Empire*, p. 4.

Critical to this transformation, too, was an emphasis on the political promises of the Commonwealth. The Commonwealth was a voluntary association of independent states – all of which were once British territories – that promoted the avowedly British traditions of democracy, the rule of law and good governance, as well as economic and social development. As Louis St Laurent, the Canadian Prime Minister, put it in 1951, the Commonwealth was 'a community of interest on matters that really count ... a common attachment to certain political ideals, such as the maintenance of a large measure of freedom for the individual within the community, and the upholding of genuine control by the citizens over their governments.'[32] Here was the optimism of the liberal postwar moment. In Powell's mind, the political effort to resurrect Britain's national role as moral leader of the empire or Commonwealth failed to recognize the material realities of power. Critically, for all the talk of 'a common attachment to certain political ideals,' the postwar Commonwealth failed to produce (military or economic) unity. John Darwin has, similarly, referred to public discourse on decolonization – and the widespread commitment to Britain's 'world role' as leader in the Commonwealth – as an effective 'anaesthetizing rhetoric' against the realities of decline.[33]

As the analysis below of Powell's responses to the Suez Crisis and African decolonization reveals, Powell's turn away from imperial ambitions would involve a very specific articulation of the meaning of sovereignty and political responsibility – or the character of political power – against America's rising international dominance. At very least, Powell's 'post-imperial' understandings of state power, citizenship and national belonging must be firmly set in the historical context of the Cold War. Similarly, the making of a postcolonial Britain – and, relatedly, the shifting understandings of race after empire – were structured and contained by a Cold War world.[34]

Importantly, it was not simply imperial rupture and transformation that challenged Powell's thinking in the immediate postwar years. Powell refused the intellectual innovations and political and legal initiatives wrought by the Second World War that challenged the sanctity

[32] As cited in J. A. Cross, 'Appraising the Commonwealth,' *Political Studies*, 32 (1984), pp. 107–112 (p. 107).

[33] John Darwin, 'Decolonization and the End of Empire,' in Robin W. Winks (ed.), *The Oxford History of the British Empire, Vol. V: Historiography* (Oxford University Press, 1999), p. 547.

[34] For a convincing discussion of the limits of postwar labour radicalism in this regard, see Eley, 'When Europe Was New,' in Riera and Schaffer (eds.), *The Lasting War*, pp. 17–43.

of state sovereignty. In response to the state-sanctioned atrocities and genocide of the war and the abundance of displaced, stateless peoples in Europe at the war's end, the United Nations and the Council of Europe established 'human rights' monitoring committees which defied the notion that rights were dependent on political membership. The distinguished lawyer Hersch Lauterpacht, who drafted the influential 'International Bill of the Rights of Man' in 1945, hailed the postwar moment as the dawn of a new era. Like many others, his was a vision of an 'international society' based on the human rights of the individual.[35] Powell remained consistently critical of the new international human rights regimes that emerged after the war. Rights, he insisted, 'flow from the constitution and nature of a particular society'; human rights – 'in abstraction from a given society' – are 'an absurdity.'[36] Here was a Tory critique of postwar internationalism and liberal humanism. Powell's 'realist' critique went further. He saw the United Nations not as a new political innovation that might truly protect the refugee (and the world) from repeating past violence but as a means of American domination. He distinguished himself from the 'victors of 1945' who were 'mesmerized by the memories of 1918, which they seemed to be reliving with a determination "not to make the same mistakes again."'[37] Here, again, his profound anti-Americanism continued to structure his postwar thinking. He would not accept the validity of the UN as 'a kind of super-state, with its own armed forces' nor would he accept the postwar 'project of sinking national sovereignty in organizations for uniting the world.'[38] In many ways, Powell's preoccupation with the nature of national sovereignty and political consent seems to be directly born out of his opposition to this internationalist thinking.

Powell was, in fact, not alone in his concerns about the consequences of humanitarian international law and the UN Human Rights Commission for the maintenance of British power. In a secret circular to the British colonies in 1949, Labour's Secretary of State for the Colonies, Arthur Creech-Jones, referred to the Universal Declaration of Human Rights as a potential 'source of embarrassment' that could cause undesirable consequences in Britain's colonies.[39] Meanwhile,

[35] Hersch Lauterpacht, *International Law and Human Rights*, p. 4, as cited in Cohen, 'The "Human Rights Revolution" at Work,' p. 53.
[36] Powell, *Wrestling with the Angel*, p. 27.
[37] Enoch Powell and Angus Maude, *Biography of a Nation: A Short History of Britain* (London: John Baker, 1970), p. 224.
[38] Ibid., pp. 224, 225.
[39] Secret Circular 25102/2/49, 28 March 1949, as cited in Fabian Klose, '"Source of Embarrassment": Human Rights, State of Emergency, and the Wars of Decolonization,'

the Governor of Nairobi, Sir Philip Mitchell, argued that the right for individuals or non-governmental organizations to actually petition the UN Human Rights Commission would be a threat to world peace.[40] While both Britain and France took part in the creation of the post-war human rights regime, both colonial powers attempted to prevent its extension to their colonial possessions.[41] Both France and Britain were, by the 1950s, fighting bloody guerrilla wars – and, in Britain's case, undertaking massive internment and resettlement of populations. A 'state of emergency' was declared by British colonial authorities during disturbances in Malaya, British Guiana, the Gold Coast, Nigeria, Uganda, Nyasaland and Kenya. In fact, Britain's efforts to retain control of the Crown Colony of Kenya between 1952 and 1959 were not so far from what Powell imagined Britain might do in his report to Churchill in 1946 to regain order in the British Raj. Importantly, as Fabian Klose argues, the use of the declaration of a 'state of emergency' in British colonies as a means to control colonial 'chaos' created a legal framework to enable Britain to break humanitarian restrictions.[42]

Like 'human rights,' it is possible to see the legacy of Europe's total wars – and, particularly, the intrusion of the state into civilian life – in the character of Britain's suppression of anti-colonial subversion: via the significant extension of the secret service, forced labour and torture, and mass internment and resettlement, Britain attempted to break subversive activity by gaining 'total control' of indigenous populations.[43] The effort to control and transform colonial societies – and the subsequent destruction of files that document the radicalization of colonial violence that this effort entailed – must sit awkwardly at the very centre of our understanding of Britain's image of moral leadership and 'liberal war.' In the context of both Communist and subaltern 'barbarism,' this was, as Jordanna Bailkin argues, the era of the 'activist colonial state at its most intrusively ambitious, eager to obtain knowledge about all dimensions of life, from labor to public health.'[44] Ironically, the process of decolonization – whether guerrilla warfare or 'peaceful transition' – could intensify rather than weaken the British state's involvement in the economic and social life of newly independent states.[45]

Both the Labour and Conservative parties of the 1950s spoke similarly of the need to protect Britain's liberal reputation and project a

in Stefan-Ludwig Hoffman (ed.), *Human Rights in the Twentieth Century* (Cambridge University Press, 2011), p. 242.
[40] Ibid., p. 244.   [41] Ibid., pp. 237–238.   [42] Ibid., pp. 249, 248.
[43] Ibid.
[44] Jordanna Bailkin, *The Afterlife of Empire*, p. 4.
[45] Ibid.

vision of tolerance, democratic freedom and fair play in both domestic and foreign policy. Hence, Britain's military intervention to regain control of the Suez Canal from Egypt in 1956 and subsequent retreat was as much a moral embarrassment as a sign of lost strength. Similarly, after the assertion of Afro-Asian solidarity and non-alignment at the Bandung Conference of 1955, non-democratic, white-minority rule in colonial Africa was increasingly recognized as a threat to the basis of Commonwealth unity (and that anxiously projected image of democracy and freedom in 'the West'). And, like the United States, and especially after Britain's Notting Hill race riots of 1958, domestic racism in the United Kingdom continued to be treated as an *international* issue as much as a social problem – again, a political liability in an uncertain world. As the National Council for Civil Liberties put it in its 1956 leaflet, *It isn't a Colour bar but ...*, these years were a 'testing time':

All over the world the eyes of coloured people – and of colour conscious whites too – are on Britain. Are we to become the laughing stock of all the negro baiters everywhere, because we who were once bold and high principled in our condemnation of them now crudely submit to their dogmas and imitate their practices?[46]

International Soviet propaganda did indeed emphasize racist oppression in the West; domestic racism would come to be seen as a problematic source of political radicalization among colonial students attending university in Britain who were nervously viewed, by British government officials, as the future leaders of their homelands.[47] Remarkably, progressive opinion in 1950s Britain still spoke of the 'bold and high principled' Englishman and, in this way, sustained an idea of Britain's 'civilizing mission' of tolerance in the world.[48] Libertarians, Labour and Conservatives alike, tended to overlook the long tradition of British racism within imperial governance and, by the end of the decade, insistently juxtaposed Britain's 'liberal traditions' to race politics in the Central African Federation and South Africa. As we shall see in the last sections of this chapter, Powell's words on colonial violence and British power must be understood in this light, as working to affirm the identity of the Englishman in the face of this crisis of confidence in the white colonial.

Critically, the rhetorical emphasis on Britain's 'liberal traditions' against colonial racism and its moral mission against a 'new barbarism'

---

[46] As cited in Paul Rich, 'Black People in Britain: Response and Reaction, 1945–62,' *History Today*, 36: 1 (January 1986).
[47] Jordanna Bailkin, *The Afterlife of Empire*, pp. 112, 131.
[48] Ibid.

do not tell the full history of the end of the British Empire. Thanks to the continued legal efforts of the victims and witnesses of British authority in 1950s Kenya – who successfully sued the British government in 2012 for the release of the most sensitive colonial documents of this period – we now know that some ministers in London were well aware of the torture and murder of anti-colonial insurgents during Kenya's years of 'emergency.'[49] An official review in 2012 of the Foreign Office's secret archive of colonial papers at Hanslope Park has revealed the extent to which Britain used force to retain its colonial possessions after the Second World War. But, perhaps even more tellingly, this official review has exposed the systemic destruction of the most sensitive of colonial documents. Iain Macleod, Secretary of State for the Colonies under Harold Macmillan's Conservative government, is remembered in the history of British decolonization for presiding over the massive and remarkably quick decolonization of British Africa between 1959 and 1961, despite protestations from the right of his party. But it was also Iain Macleod who, in 1961, ordered that all sensitive colonial documents be destroyed before files were passed on to newly independent nations if documents 'might embarrass Her Majesty's government' or 'embarrass members of the police, military forces, public servants or others eg police informers,' compromise intelligence sources or could 'be used unethically by ministers in the successor government.'[50] Though it is certainly understandable that local informants be protected in this way, the destruction of files was focused primarily on protecting Britain's reputation – and therefore its capital and defence interests in former colonies. The documents destroyed are thought to include reports about an alleged massacre of twenty-four unarmed villagers in Malaya by soldiers of the Scots Guards in 1948; records of abuse, torture and murder of insurgents detained by British authorities in Kenya; the papers of the Army's Intelligence Corps in Aden, where a secret torture centre operated for several years in the 1960s; and all sensitive documents kept by the colonial authorities in British Guiana.[51]

British Guiana perhaps most clearly underlines that this 'information war' was a product of a Cold War world. There, British colonial authorities tapped phones, intercepted letters and maintained constant surveillance of Guianese political activities and, in 1953, eventually suspended British Guiana's new constitution and overthrew the elected, left-leaning leader, Cheddi Jagan, because – an MI5 archive now reveals – it

---

[49] Ian Cobain, Owen Bowcott and Richard Norton-Taylor, 'Britain Destroyed Records of Colonial Crimes,' *The Guardian*, 18 April 2012.
[50] Ibid.   [51] Ibid.

was feared that his party, the People's Progressive Party, would lead the country to Communism.[52] After this, successive British governments gave in to pressure from the United States to allow the CIA to use subterranean methods to ensure that Jagan would not be the first leader of his country in 1966. Macleod's order to destroy colonial files must be recognized as another arm of this information war. In Uganda, the process of destroying files was codenamed Operation Legacy. In Kenya, the purge was led by Special Branch officers who followed the strict instruction that no Africans be involved in the operation but only individuals who were 'a servant of the Kenya government who is a British subject of European descent.'[53] Proof of violence in these colonies could, it was feared, provide fodder for Communist propaganda against the new 'informal imperialism' of the West. Perhaps due to the success of these legacy operations, British decolonization in the 1950s and early 1960s is still understood to have been a relatively painless enterprise.[54] But recent revelations challenge us to fundamentally reconsider the image that Macleod worked to construct of Britain's 'civilized' transformation. We need, with this, to understand the broader consequences of the maintenance of a liberal vision of British power, into the postcolonial period, as the redemptive continuation of 'civilization.'

David Anderson argues that the radicalization of colonial violence that occurred in Kenya was not due to chaotic instability but because the 'state of emergency' there was so effectively bureaucratic: political imprisonment, mass detention and hangings were contained within a state system of rules, courts and regulations such that violent suppression could be presented as good governance.[55] With all this, it is clear that colonial violence and the cover-up of files is not a side story in the history of Britain's 'successful' decolonization, a quiet embarrassment, which merely reveals the inevitable and even innate troubles associated with colonial withdrawal. These efforts speak to the fragility of British power and the belief by policy-makers in the 1950s that the 'good name

[52] 'M15 Files Reveal Details of 1953 Coup that Overthrew British Guiana's Leaders,' *The Guardian*, 26 August 2011.
[53] Ibid.
[54] W. David McIntyre, *British Decolonization, 1946–1997: When, Why, and How did the British Empire Fall?* (Basingstoke: Macmillan, 1998); Edward Grierson, *Death of the Imperial Dream: The British Commonwealth and Empire, 1775–1969* (Garden City: Doubleday & Company, 1972); D. A. Low, *Eclipse of Empire* (Cambridge University Press, 1993); John Darwin, *End of the British Empire: the Historical Debate* (London: Wiley-Blackwell, 1991).
[55] For an excellent description of the state of the literature on Mau Mau as well as a discussion of Anderson's work, see Joanna Lewis, 'Nasty, Brutish and in Shorts? British Colonial Rule, Violence and the Historians of Mau Mau,' *The Round Table*, vol. 96, no. 389 (2007), pp. 201–223, particularly p. 204.

of Britain' was essential to the maintenance of the political status quo
in both Britain and the Commonwealth, and – with waning material
power – critical to Britain's influence in a Cold War world. Powell's
revolt against the direction of both imperial and domestic policy in
these years, his loss of faith in Britain's (liberal) empire and his Tory
perspective on the limits of state power at home and abroad shed light
on this process and on the politics of Britain's decolonizing state.

Bonds of empire

The years of Labour's postwar government were for Powell, as he later
remembered, 'a period of more drastic change and revision of ideas
than I ever experienced before or since.'[56] Most of all, this period saw
Powell embrace the limits of the nation:

So by the early '50s, despite the long story of colonial disentanglement which
still lay ahead, it was for me as if the nation and the monarchy had come back
home again ... I had now understood that the sovereign was not the Crown in
abstract but the Crown in Parliament – and not in Parliament in general, nor
in a parliament here, a parliament there and a parliament somewhere else, but
in the Parliament in the United Kingdom, or, to name it less exactly but more
truthfully, the English Parliament. Herein lay the necessity of the limitation of
the nation and the allegiance to those who physically, politically and spiritually
could be represented in Parliament. It was the key which interpreted our past
imperial history and accurately forecast how its terminal stages would run.[57]

Allegiance remained centrally important for Powell, but now it was not
allegiance in the 'abstract.' Rather, political authority relied on the limits of consent, on historical legitimacy and social practice. Even prior
to his election as Member of Parliament for Wolverhampton in 1950,
Powell regularly attended parliamentary debates. As he noted himself, much like his embrace of military life, here Powell was drawn to
the institutional structure, homo-social world and historically sanctioned rules of Parliament. As he put it in the late 1970s, the House of
Commons became, 'almost literally, my home.'[58] Unlike 'the Congress
of the United States any more than of the representative assemblies
which other Western nations have erected at various stages in their
history,' he could imagine Parliament as the historical *embodiment* of
British history and national values, 'a kind of ecological exception,'
whose 'common root' was the feudal court.[59] This would develop into

[56] Powell, *Wrestling with the Angel*, p. 2.
[57] Ibid., pp. 3–4.   [58] Ibid., p. 4.
[59] J. Enoch Powell, 19 December 1974, cited in Cosgrave, *The Lives of Enoch Powell*, p. 94.

a recognition that Britain was a 'prescriptive monarchy,' meaning that sovereign power exercised through Parliament was not derived from a document but 'from the fact that it has been so from time immemorial – that it is immanent in the nation itself.'[60] Crucially, Britain, unlike France, could not with colonial independence transfer 'prescriptive authority' – the historically sanctioned hierarchy of British rule – which was 'the essence of our own state' to new nations.[61] As he found a new 'home' in Parliament, we see Powell turn from a commitment to formal imperialism to a belief that its disintegration was, and always had been, inevitable.

During the infamously harsh winter of 1947, Powell ran for a seat in Parliament for the first time. He lost. It was a by-election for Normanton in south Yorkshire. And it was an easy seat to lose: since 1885, a miner's representative had held the seat and Powell's opponent, George Sylvester – a miner himself – defended a Labour majority of 19,979.[62] Still, we see in this campaign an emerging picture of Powell's public persona. He ran as a soldier; he appealed as 'Brigadier Powell' to the 1,500 ex-servicemen in the constituency.[63] Citing the 'danger and humiliation' brought to British soldiers, he criticized Labour's policies in Egypt, Palestine and Burma.[64] In this year, too, Powell led the Conservative Party Secretariat's defence studies group and, in this capacity, attended the Conservative backbench Army Committee. He was there also known as 'Brigadier Powell' and, via this work on defence, developed working relationships with other former soldiers – fellow brigadiers – within the party, such as Anthony Head, Otho Prior-Palmer and Toby Law.[65] Powell's experience as a brigadier remained significant throughout his political career, but in these early years it served as the basis of his public persona and, perhaps even more, as a means of social mobility within the party. Like many others, Powell's (meteoric) military career bled into his political life and postwar preoccupations.

In 1948, the Labour government introduced the British Nationality Bill that established the distinction between Commonwealth citizens and British subjects who were citizens of the United Kingdom and colonies. The bill ensured that, despite Indian and Pakistani independence and break from allegiance to the English Crown, citizens of the Commonwealth would continue to have the legal right to settle in Britain. Powell and Angus Maude would later describe the British Nationality Act as, 'the contrivance by which the British endeavoured

---

[60] J. Enoch Powell, 'Commonwealth Morning After the Imperial Night Before,' *Daily Telegraph*, 22 November 1983.
[61] Ibid.
[62] Heffer, *Like the Roman*, p. 112.
[63] Ibid., p. 113.   [64] Ibid., p. 112.   [65] Ibid., p. 117.

to conceal from themselves the reality of [the empire's] dissolution' –
an assertion of unity and belonging without military obligation or
true membership.[66] This was, in Powell's mind, the make-believe of
the Commonwealth in practice. While the Nationality Bill was a sign
of the new political environment of the 1940s, some Conservatives,
such as David Maxwell Fyfe, supported the bill as a continuation of
Britain's imperial tradition, calling for no distinction between citizen
of Commonwealth or colony so as to 'maintain our great metropolitan
tradition of hospitality to everyone from every part of our Empire.'[67]
Notably, something of Maxwell Fyfe's commitment to British (imperial)
responsibility found expression in the next few years in his work drafting the European Convention on Human Rights.[68] Despite the prevalent rhetoric of the possibilities of a multiracial 'New' Commonwealth,
there were certainly limits to its influence even in relation to the British
Nationality Act. As Randall Hansen has convincingly argued, it was a
commitment to the loyalties of the Old Commonwealth, to the inherent connectedness of Australia, Canada, New Zealand and South
Africa, rather than any belief in racial equality, that caused so many
British politicians to reject restrictions on Commonwealth immigration after 1948.[69] As early as 1952, one colonial correspondent argued
that the British were in fact experiencing a 'protective psychological
retreat' from the promises of racial egalitarianism written into the New
Commonwealth, turning away from any expansive, multiracial view of
'Britishness.'[70] Powell, meanwhile, described the British Nationality
Act as 'that most evil Statute' which had 'effected a complete revolution
in the basis of British subjecthood.'[71] With the British Nationality Act
'common status was reduced to a nullity' as 'common status and common authority had ceased.' The 'whole contraption' of citizenship law
was 'a humbug, a pretence and a self-deception'; and Powell, he later
explained, 'came to hate it.'[72]

    In 1950, Powell successfully ran for a Conservative seat in
Wolverhampton.[73] As he entered into his political career, Powell began
to expound a political philosophy of imperialism born out of this
moment of imperial uncertainty. Insisting that late imperial governance

---

[66] Powell and Maude, *Biography of a Nation*, p. 235.
[67] HC, vol. 453, col. 411, 7 July 1948.
[68] A. W. Brian Simpson, *Human Rights and the End of Empire: Britain and the Genesis of the European Convention* (Oxford University Press, 2001).
[69] Randall Hansen, *Citizenship and Immigration in Post-war Britain* (Oxford University Press, 2000).
[70] A colonial correspondent, 'African Attitudes' *Twentieth Century*, 151 (1952), pp. 19–25, as cited in Waters, '"Dark Strangers" in Our Midst,' pp. 207–238.
[71] Heffer, *Like the Roman*, p. 173.   [72] Ibid.
[73] Powell, *Wrestling with the Angel*, p. 2.

promised only to destroy the fabric of the British Empire, he reasoned in 1950 that if the Conservatives' stated policy of working for greater imperial unity was real, it required a 'new conception of sovereignty, or rather an old one reinterpreted; the beginning of a new evolutionary phase in British history.'[74] This would require the recognition that the political consent of the governed could be secured in better ways than through republicanism, or what he called 'paper constitutions of Western invention,' that offered only 'sham independence and real chaos.'[75] He drew a connection, here, between the promise of republicanism and the threat of social anarchy and violent disorder. This argument that the call for democratic representation – and, implicitly, non-white self-governance – threatened chaos is not unique to Powell; it is an ever-present refrain within white colonial nationalisms in Africa at this time. Order meant for Powell a reaffirmation of allegiance to the King: overt dependence, rather than the 'sham independence' of international membership to the Commonwealth or United Nations, coupled with economic and military dependency.

On 16 March 1950, Powell gave his maiden speech in the House. In it, his background in the Indian Army and martial view of imperial power were clear. The debate was on defence spending. Emanuel Shinwell, Labour's Defence Minister, maintained that the economy was already too badly stretched to increase spending on the Armed Forces, while Churchill insisted that whatever resources were necessary must be found: the need for increased defence against the threat of Soviet aggression in West Germany and the Middle East was irrefutable. In the context of debates about the inefficiencies of National Service and the need to build a European army to represent the 'Western Union,' Powell offered another solution: train a new colonial army. The (lost) Indian Army had been, in Powell's mind, the heart of imperial power:

...we have lost the greatest non-European army which the world has ever seen, an army which made possible, as did no other institution in the world, the active and affectionate co-operation of European and non-European.[76]

The increase in British manpower in the colonies, in the Middle and Far East, and the decline in colonial forces was 'moving in the wrong direction.'[77] National Service, a conscript army, was, he argued, a drain on the human resources of Britain's economy. And the British manpower

---

[74] J. Enoch Powell, speech to Penn Fields, 16 February 1950. 'Constituency Special Subjects,' SRO, D3123/223.
[75] Ibid.
[76] J. Enoch Powell, HC, vol. 472, col. 1317, 16 March 1950.
[77] J. Enoch Powell, HC, vol. 472, col. 1318, 16 March 1950.

required to police the empire was politically unpopular in a society still exhausted by the Second World War. The building of a new colonial army led by the 'virtues' of British officers was essential:

If we are an Empire defending the Empire, we must draw far more than we do on the vast reserves of Colonial manpower which exist within the Empire. The virtues which enabled British officers and British administrators to create the Indian Army are not dead ... Not only is it not impossible, it is imperative that we should create from the other parts of His Majesty's Dominions a replace-ment for that which we have lost ... I am well aware that such a demand raises far reaching political implications. I am not afraid of those implications, indeed I desire them, for I am certain that unless we summon to the defence of this worldwide Empire all its resources, be they European or non-European, we shall fall under the load which we are attempting to bear.[78]

The Conservative member and Anglo-Irish Brigadier Otho Prior-Palmer agreed. It was, according to him, 'a terrible waste of first-class [British] fighting troops to station them in places like Gibraltar, Malta and Aden.'[79] Likewise, he agreed with Powell on the potential of colonial troops in the East African forces. This was Britain's 'immense reserve.'[80]

The next year, Powell made his views on the future of the British Empire even more explicit, when writing to the *Birmingham Gazette* on the Tory vision of 'Britain's Position in the World.' This he juxtaposed against a world divided into 'Western' and 'Eastern' power. Here, again, we see Powell believing that without greater unity all was lost:

It is the essence of Toryism to view the British nation as something natural and organic – the creation of time, nature and (I do not shrink from the word) Providence – but to look with scepticism upon dogmas, whether political or economic, which are supposed to be valid for all races and climes and a sure guide for reforming all constitutions. From such a Britain the Tory cannot look out upon a world merely divided into two, 'democratic' or 'Communist,' 'free' or not free, 'Western' or 'Eastern'. He sees instead a wide scene peopled with various individual nations, obeying the respective laws of their being. Nations, to him, and national sovereignty, so far from being artificial barriers, are the inevitable framework within which mankind lives and associates ... Our mis-sion towards the colonies is to educate them not to independence but to inter-dependence, to a more and more conscious and positive unity with the rest. Our mission towards the dominions is to find means whereby ... our separate identities can still be sunk in common action. In its widest sense the Empire is the nation. The Empire should always be becoming one nation.[81]

[78] J. Enoch Powell, HC, vol. 472, cols. 1318–1319, 16 March 1950.
[79] Otho Prior-Palmer, HC, vol. 472, col. 1337, 16 March 1950.
[80] Ibid.
[81] J. Enoch Powell, 'Britain's Position in the World,' sent to the editor of the *Birmingham Gazette*, 15 October 1951. 'Constituency Special Subjects,' SRO, D3123/223.

As he put it in his election address of 1951: 'I BELIEVE IN THE BRITISH EMPIRE. Without the Empire, Britain would be like a head without a body.'[82] Both in Powell's 1946 report to Churchill and in his early political speeches, Powell spoke of an imperial nationalism that promised to save itself from the chaos of national self-determination. Arguing against federation or indirect rule, Powell was here attempting to save the empire by solving the problem of difference in imperial governance. Importantly, he is not making an argument for the expansion of British ideals, for the application of 'dogmas, whether political or economic, which are supposed to be valid for all races and climes and a sure guide for reforming all constitutions.' Rather, he maintains a Tory vision of political unity as essentially historical and bound by common action (found, most of all, in the unity of the armed forces) – again, not by any pro-capitalist or pro-democratic 'dogma.' For the true Tory, political community would be defined by men's 'respective laws of their being.' Importantly, this 'essence of Toryism' – which recognized a historically sanctioned social (or racial and class) order – would continue to underpin his profound Cold War scepticism.

But Powell's focus was, of course, not only imperial affairs. Powell's protests were protests against the expanding parameters of state power in these decolonizing years. As in the empire, in Britain, state-led social and economic development threatened the 'laws of their being.' According to Powell, the war had brought with it public control over the economy such that, he believed, control itself had become too familiar and too acceptable in British society. He later imagined the average person's response to further state controls as, 'Isn't there something familiar about this?' To which he replied, 'Why yes, of course, that was in war ... That is the ideal towards which every good socialist strains – a siege economy.'[83] Despite Powell's activity in the One Nation group and close connections to the influential centrist Conservative Rab Butler, Powell remained adamantly opposed to the limited economic planning and nationalization of industries which lay at the heart of the postwar settlement. In this, Powell opposed Harold Macmillan's long campaign in favour of pro-capitalist government spending which had gained ground within government circles during the war effort. Prior to the war, Macmillan had produced several pamphlets, speeches, a book and numerous articles which 'attested to his crusading devotion

---

[82] J. Enoch Powell, 'A Letter from your Conservative Candidate, Enoch Powell,' general election 1951, as cited in Heffer, *Like the Roman*, p. 169.
[83] J. Enoch Powell, speech to a public meeting at Queen's Hall Barnstaple, Devon, 28 April 1967.

to the new concept' of a planned economy.[84] A planned economy found fertile ground within the economic mobilization of the war effort. This 'middle way' of reformed capitalism was imagined after the war as a representation, on the governmental level, of 'class peace' between capital and labour. Powell's opposition to public control, controls which had been brought about by the necessities of war and made familiar by the war experience, was a consistent theme in his political commentary. In 1947, echoing Churchill's unpopular comparison of Labour and the Gestapo, Powell drew a parallel between Britain in 1947 and his experience of Nazi Germany in 1938. In postwar Britain, according to Powell, private life itself was under threat. As reported in the *Yorkshire Post*, Powell stated:

People are already in many parts of this country reluctant to disclose their political views for fear of jeopardising their employment or livelihood under the State or a public authority. Parliament is treated more and more like a rubber stamp Reichstag, while the real legislative powers are translated to Ministers of the Crown. The Gestapo, as yet in a mild form and under the reassuring title of inspectors or enforcement officers, pry into our private affairs to see if we are breaking any of the multitudinous orders and regulations by which our lives and actions are restricted, and actually try to tempt us into committing offences so that they can prosecute us.[85]

Against the 'inspectors and enforcement officers,' Powell advocated the reintroduction of market forces over state control in housing, social services, trade unions, nationalized industries and exchange rates.[86] Due to Powell's commitment to the principles of liberal economics and his refusal to support the intervention of government to support big businesses, Powell came to be viewed as a spokesman for small capital and found his support in the West Midlands amongst local businessmen and shopkeepers.[87]

Still, as a One Nation conservative, Powell sought to present a Tory vision of welfare services against the socialist state.[88] He supported some social provisions, such as the National Health Service, but insisted that

[84] Daniel Ritschel, *The Politics of Planning: The Debate on Economic Planning in Britain in the 1930s* (Oxford University Press, 1997), p. 191.
[85] As cited in Heffer, *Like the Roman*, p. 113.
[86] Gamble, *The Conservative Nation*, p. 116.
[87] Ibid., p. 117.
[88] As a member of the One Nation Group of 1950, Powell worked to modernize and broaden the appeal of the party in domestic affairs. This backbench discussion group, which brought together Iain Macleod, Edward Heath, Angus Maude and Robert Carr among others, got its name from its first publication *One Nation: A Tory Approach to Social Problems*. The group came to represent a new political generation entering Parliament in 1950 that worked to reform the party towards managed capitalism and the expansion of social services. They focused on domestic policy and, by

social services 'ought to flow from the nature and organization of the community itself' and that 'community' is 'not necessarily the state.'[89] Against public control, Powell juxtaposed the bonds of community. 'Socialism has always seen social services as an engine for dominating the social life of the nation to the State,' he argued, 'as completely as they would subject its economic life: nationalisation of our society, as the companion piece to nationalisation of our economy.'[90] This insistence on the need to protect 'community' and the moral order from the encroachments of the state – from the 'nationalisation of our society' – would structure his views on welfare provisions throughout his career. Again, the blind acceptance of the 'nationalisation of our society' was, in Powell's mind, linked to Britain's experience of total war. The social memory and acceptance of an economy at war remained a threat to the survival of Britain's national community.

But Powell's critique of the postwar state went beyond the war. While writing on the history of the House of Lords, Powell would go so far as to consider the significance of the Reformation in understanding the postwar welfare state. The conflict of church and state, symbolized by the separate houses of clerical and lay baronage, had ended with the Reformation. 'Henry VIII had cut the Gordian knot of the Middle Ages.'[91] Yet, Powell asserted, the conflict remained. While it was no longer given shape by Britain's political institutions, still 'beneath the surface' the community still had to face 'the dilemma of the moral and the material, between the authority within and the authority without.'[92] The divide is everywhere:

What we today call the Welfare State can be traced back along an unbroken line of development to the endeavours of the Reformation to replace the functions of the Church in education and in the care for want and suffering. The secular state has grown a whole new organ to meet demands and to obey requirements which in the last analysis are moral rather than material.[93]

The politics of the previous four centuries was, according to Powell, best viewed as an attempt to cope with the consequences of the Reformation.

emphasizing economic opportunity alongside the need for welfare provisions, aspired to break down the perceived class divide of Britain's 'two nations.' With the publication of a number of pamphlets in its name, the group became an important voice for reform within the party, providing ministers with a language and rationale with which to base Conservative acceptance of the postwar settlement.

[89] J. Enoch Powell, 'Conservatives and Social Services,' *The Political Quarterly* (April–June 1953) in POLL 6.1.1E.
[90] J. Enoch Powell, 'Compassion, or Domination?' *West Midlands Review*, no. 1, Sept/Oct. 1963. POLL 6.1.1E.
[91] J. Enoch Powell, 'Bishops and Kings,' *The Listener*, 16 October 1958.
[92] Ibid.   [93] Ibid.

Aspects of community life which were once religious in character were, with the Reformation, suddenly secularized and individual conscience was 'enthroned' as arbiter over the community.[94] 'What is common to the 16th and 17th and the 19th and 20th centuries is the disruption of the natural and organic unity of the nation's life.'[95] Class war and communism, Powell argued, were merely symptoms of the fact that the individual had lost his place in the community; the community – as a religious and political entity – no longer satisfied both his spiritual and physical wants.[96] These arguments had some corollaries in the work of both Richard Law, the son of the former Conservative Prime Minister Andrew Bonar Law, and Maurice Cowling, an influential British political theorist at this time. Cowling viewed secular liberalism as a destructive force and insisted that Christianity was the essential glue of English culture. Likewise, in *Return from Utopia* in 1950, Law argued that the survival of the nation relied on a moral order that was substantiated by religious belief in the Church.[97]

Remarkably, Powell argued, in 1951, that recognition of the essential role of Church and nation in British society was more possible after the war than it had been in a long time for two important and related reasons – namely, the failure of liberalism and rationalism manifest in the war itself:

In the last thirty years two idols have come loose from their clay feet and toppled down, amongst whose debris we now live. One is liberalism, which proclaimed that the secret of human happiness lay in liberating the individual and freeing him to the greatest extent possible from the ties and limitations imposed by his human environment. The other, which begot 'democratic Socialism', declared that by common sense men could lay down the objects of his society and … apply methods to achieve them, if only sufficiently complete control could be placed in the hands of those who happened to be possessed of the right sort of common sense.[98]

The war's 'bitter discovery that both gospels were fallacies' would lead people back, Powell believed, to the 'two-fold conception of nation and Church,' which he called 'the heart of Toryism.'[99] This was, of course, not universally regarded as the lesson of the war. But it was, for Powell, perhaps the lesson of his imperial war and empire's end. Powell claimed that contemporary anxieties about the power of the state against the

---

[94] J. Enoch Powell, 'The Church,' part of unpublished One Nation Book, 1951. POLL 3.2.1.1.
[95] Ibid.   [96] Ibid.
[97] Geoffrey Foote, *The Republican Transformation of Modern British Politics* (Basingstoke: Palgrave Macmillan, 2006), p. 121.
[98] Ibid.   [99] Ibid.

individual arose from the recognition 'that somehow there should be more than one source of authority in society: that the state has not a monopoly of the imperative, but somewhere there is an antithesis, an opposite magnetic pole, a co-ordinate authority.'[100] Personally, Powell was, at this time, a newly committed Anglican. His arguments against aspects of the postwar settlement were, importantly, not for the individual against state power. It was not for the individual liberated from the imperatives of institutional structure. Powell's argument was, in fact, the very opposite: 'an authority which is merely abstract – be it individual conscience, or the instinct of liberty, or the moral sense of a nominally Christian country – is not effective substitute or counterpart for an authority endued with the personality of an institution.'[101] Powell argued, then, both for unity of the community under Church and state and for the consequential end of the state's 'authority within.' This (Anglican) commitment to structure, ritual and hierarchy – rather than individual belief – in the making of community was reflected, too, in Powell's reverence for the army as the basis of common action in defining the nation.

As will be discussed in depth in Chapter 4, Powell would use the above insistence on the divide between the material and the moral – the political and the religious, the 'authority without' and the 'authority within' – to oppose the validity of anti-discrimination law. Powell's position on racism – and moral 'decline' generally – was tied up with his views on the false promise of the moral state. In 1955, well before Powell became the spokesman for those opposed to 'New Commonwealth' immigration, he wrote to the Bishop of Lichfield on similar grounds. The local transport authorities of West Bromwich had hired one Indian immigrant as a conductor. The West Bromwich transport workers went out on strike, against the advice and policy of the Transport and General Workers Union. Dr J. L. Wilson, Bishop of Birmingham (and Bishop of Singapore at the close of the Japanese invasion), and Dr A. S. Reeve, Bishop of Lichfield, wrote a public appeal to the West Bromwich bus strikers.[102] Five hundred white workers and one Indian worker were involved in the dispute in West Bromwich. While the proportion of non-whites in Britain was still less than 1 per cent,[103] large West Indian, Pakistani and Indian immigrant communities had already

[100] J. Enoch Powell, 'Bishops and Kings,' *The Listener*, 16 October 1958.
[101] Ibid.
[102] 'Bishops Appeal to West Bromwich Bus Strikers,' *Express and Star*, February, 1955. POLL 3.1.12.
[103] E. J. B. Rose, *Colour and Citizenship: A Report on British Race Relations* (London: Oxford University Press, 1969), p. 97.

developed in London and the industrial areas of the West Midlands, like West Bromwich. These transport workers were for the next decade on the front line of race disputes in Britain.

The colour bar, Wilson and Reeve wrote, was not reconcilable with Christianity or human freedom: 'We rely on the kindliness of the British working man to uphold the call of human freedom and realise that a colour bar is humanly indefensible.' Powell had a problem with this. Would it have been racist if the conductor had been Italian? Was any national border reconcilable with Christianity or human freedom? Was the Commonwealth sanctioned by God? Crucially, the British state in Powell's eyes held no Christian obligation to the Indian immigrant. Powell refused to condemn public intolerance because, he argued, to condemn sin was the job of the moralist not the politician. This belief in a necessary divide between moral and political arguments would also structure his response to the controversies surrounding decolonization and the violence of colonial Africa.

On 3 March 1953, in a debate on the Royal Titles Bill, Powell acted as the lone voice in support of the 'indivisible' sovereign Crown of the British Empire – against what he imagined amounted to only political disunity. Powell's argument that day was an argument for formal imperialism. Labour MP Patrick Gordon Walker, speaking in support of the Royal Titles Bill, argued that the government had to face the fact that the Crown meant different things in different parts of the world, that the doctrine of the indivisibility of the Crown would impose upon Commonwealth peoples feelings which would only be appropriate to those of 'British stock,' and that therefore to unify the Commonwealth the Crown must be 'set free to find its own national and emotional levels.'[104] The bill worked to solve the constitutional problem of bringing a republic into the Commonwealth. It introduced the term 'Head of Commonwealth' (which Powell called a 'sham') and took British out of the name 'British Commonwealth.' The whole thing was evil, Powell argued, as it was something which Britain had invented to blind itself to reality.[105] Britain was no longer politically united with India and was wrongly substituting unity for a 'fortuitous aggregation of a number of separate entities.'[106] In many ways echoing Powell, the Scottish Labour MP William Ross noted that Conservatives had 'clung tenaciously to the word "Empire". This Bill kills the idea of the British Empire.'[107]

---

[104] HC, vol. 512, col. 198, 3 March 1953.
[105] HC, vol. 512, col. 242, 3 March 1953.
[106] Ibid.
[107] HC, vol. 512, col. 239, 3 March 1953.

The government was doing this, Powell believed, not for 'friends' but for those to whom the name British was 'repugnant.'[108]

At this point, the Labour opposition jeered Powell. And Conservative MP Godfrey Nicholson interrupted the speech, 'They died in thousands during the war.' And Nicholson continued, 'I beg him to measure his words and to remember the vast sacrifices and the oceans of blood that India has poured out in the past, and to recognise the deep affection and feeling that exist throughout India towards this country.'[109] Powell replied:

I, who have had the advantage and privilege of serving with the Indian Army in the War, am not likely to be unmindful of it; but it was an army which owed allegiance to the Crown, an enthusiastic allegiance, which was its very principle of existence and its binding force. That allegiance, for good or for evil, has been cast off, with all that follows.[110]

The oceans of blood meant nothing, Powell believed, if they bound no allegiance now.

At the close of his emotional speech, Powell made it clear that he was under no delusion that his words would have any 'practical effect.' He was speaking for the historical record:

Sometimes, elements which are essential to the life, growth and existence of Britain seem for a time to be cast into shadow, obscured, and even destroyed. Yet in the past they have remained alive; they have survived; they have come to the surface again, and they have been the means of a new flowering, which no one had suspected. It is because I believe that, in a sense, for a brief moment, I represent and speak for an indispensable element in the British Constitution and in British life that I have spoken. I pray, not entirely in vain.[111]

We see here the emergence of Powell's view that the political establishment was caught in a state of collective blindness, wherein certain elements of the British Constitution were 'cast into shadow, obscured.' Already, Powell has taken on the prophetic tone that would mark his 'Rivers of Blood' speech. Like Powell's 1939 poem, Britain appeared to Powell a 'slumberer.' For the rest of his life, Powell regarded this speech on the Royal Titles Bill as the best he had ever delivered.[112] Iain Macleod wrote to him afterwards that, 'You may have been foolish to say what you did, but it was nobly said. And that is enough.'[113] Like the influential historian Lionel Curtis and politician Leo Amery in the decades before him, Powell rejected the reality of a compromise

---

[108] HC, vol. 512, col. 247, 3 March 1953.
[109] HC, vol. 512, cols. 247–248, 3 March 1953,
[110] HC, vol. 512, col. 248, 3 March 1953.   [111] Ibid.
[112] Simon Heffer, *Like the Roman*, p. 182.   [113] Ibid.

between the idea of one, unified, Britannic Realm and the alternative, the Dominions going the way of that 'American Commonwealth.'[114]

Powell's historical – and constitutional – consciousness is significant here. Forty years later, in a speech to the Edmund Burke Society, Powell would liken the making of the Commonwealth to the opening of that 'new can of worms labelled America' in the eighteenth century.[115] Parliamentary sovereignty had solved the 'old monster' of internal rebellion only to replace it with a 'new monster, the monster of secession.' With the United States, Powell noted, a new axiom had been born: populations that could not or would not be represented in the English Parliament could not be part of the same state or nation.[116] The people of Great Britain were governed by the middle of the eighteenth century, 'however tortuous and artificial the modalities,' by the authority of a Parliament that was seen to represent the people. The axiom to which the United States confronted Great Britain was that a government so designed could not govern any population not represented in that Parliament. The disintegration of the empire was, with that rebellion, written into the very nature of Britain's domestic politics.[117] The Whig Edmund Burke craftily replaced the bond that parliamentary sovereignty broke with the ideal of 'affection.' In 1953, Powell explained to his audience, when faced with the inevitable spread of democratic self-government in the colonies, 'Britain adopted Burke's method: they refused to accept the logical consequences of their constitution and took refuge in bluff. They invented the Commonwealth and declared, for good measure, that the Queen of the United Kingdom was something called "the Head" of it.' In 1994, Britain was, 'still striving to escape from the clutches of the same logic.' At that point, the 'clutches' were foreign development aid and New Commonwealth immigration. In other words, 'affection' had to be bought at a price.

In 1954, lecturing at the Conservative Political Centre summer school, Powell explained the ending of empire to young Conservatives in a talk on 'the Empire in England.'[118] There he argued that the very concept of sovereignty (as 'a group to all of whose members, but to no

---

[114] W. David McIntyre, 'Clio and Britannia's Lost Dream: Historians and the British Commonwealth of Nations in the First Half of the 20th Century,' *The Round Table*, vol. 93, no. 376 (September 2004), p. 529.

[115] J. Enoch Powell, 'Address to the Edmund Burke Society,' 2 February 1994. POLL 4.1.26.

[116] Ibid.

[117] Enoch Powell, 'The UK and Commonwealth,' Lecture at Sydney University, 7 September 1988, in *Reflections of a Statesman*, pp. 608–615.

[118] J. Enoch Powell, Lecture to the National Union of Conservative and Constitutional Associations (England) at Oxford, 11 July 1954. Reprinted in *Tradition and Change*

others, a single authority is able to give commands') had been defied by the creation of the British Empire.[119] Authority could not extend over those who did not elect that authority. Both a domestic and imperial parliament, a type of federation, would have been needed to sustain the life of the empire.[120] The 'can of worms' of secession had been there from the beginning. The end of the British Empire had been written into it from the start; nothing could have prevented it.[121] The empire was, by its very nature, unsustainable: 'a connection originally formed by force or necessity could not in the long run be maintained by an executive responsible to a Parliament.'[122] Explaining his own imperial past, he noted in 1953 that the inherent instability of Britain's connection with 'large populations unconnected in origin with the United Kingdom and potentially antipathetic to it by tradition or colour' was 'for a long period veiled by the circumstances of time – by the overwhelming preponderance of British power.'[123] The British Empire – and the white Englishman's superiority – appeared, in a word, *natural*.

Although it apparently 'troubled many members' – and just embarrassed others – Powell's position on the Royal Titles Bill got no support in Parliament.[124] Instead, he appeared all over the papers, in Birmingham a 'strained but soldierly figure,' in the *Evening News*, 'sincere and courageous,' in *The Times*, 'impassioned.'[125] One letter Powell received in response noted that Powell could not be Christian, 'with Pagan feudal views and outlook.'[126] Powell's local paper, Wolverhampton's *Express and Star*, meanwhile proclaimed that Powell spoke the 'Feelings of Millions.' Along with an exotic reference to a Fijian who had written to Powell in support, they published one of Powell's 'typical' letters. It came from an ex-army officer: 'You may have felt alone in the House of Commons, but what you spoke were the hidden feelings of millions of Britishers in this country and in the empire.' This ex-army officer had, also, been in the Indian Army. He had been there through the

---

(*Nine Oxford lectures*) [*by*] the Rt. Hon. R.A. Butler [*and others*], etc. (London, 1954). CPA PUB 165/18.

[119] Ibid., p. 41.
[120] Ibid., p. 49.   [121] Ibid., p. 52.   [122] Ibid., p. 50.   [123] Ibid.
[124] 'The Queen's New Title "a Sham" Says M.P.: Attack by Lone Tory,' *Express and Star*, 4 March 1953. The only sustained protest came from Scotland: Scottish MPs protested that the Queen could not be crowned Elizabeth II in Scotland, as they had had no Elizabeth I. Enough post boxes across Scotland marked 'EIIR' were blown up that the British Government changed the royal insignia on Scottish post boxes.
[125] Ibid. See also: 'Courageous,' *Evening News*, 4 March 1953; 'Objections to the Royal Title,' *The Times*, 4 March 1953; and 'A Conservative Critic,' *The Times*, 4 March 1953.
[126] Letter to Powell, 4 March 1953. POLL 3.1.9.

bloodshed of partition and Britain's 'disgraceful scramble.' It was, he agreed, only 'the haters of the British, men like Nehru,' who called the tune to which Britain now danced. 'Your speech may have seemed to you a small voice crying in the wilderness, but, believe me, it rang a true note in the hearts of millions of still loyal servants of the Crown.'[127] The *Express and Star* cut out the final lines of the letter, which read:

...believe me, it rang a true note in the hearts of millions of still loyal serv-ants of the Crown and the hearts of many (like the Sepoys, Naihs, Harridars, Jemadars, SM's, headmen, etc etc) who would, if they had a voice in India, still be proud to belong to the British Raj. But in this democracy of ours, and in the phoney democracy we have raised in India and Burma, it is the vociferous minority that wins the battles.[128]

Powell replied to the letter, 'Amongst the very many expressions of sup-port and sympathy which I received, [your letter] was one of the few which I appreciated the most.'[129] A businessman in the Empire Industries and British Empire League, also wrote in support, as did a member of the old Indian Civil Service.[130] The letters came from all over, but many tell of a personal connection with India and indicate an enduring sense that the 'Englishman' had broken the trust of those loyal to the Raj.

A week later, again in the local paper, a letter to the editor appeared on the same issue. Powell had some local opposition. The writer, J. W. Goodwin, first shared some 'heart-warming experiences' to show that the term 'Head of the Commonwealth' was not a sham. He had been on a decrepit, rattling bus in Panama, when:

[A] swarthy Jamaican had put his ham-sized hand on my knee and his grin, as wide as a slice of water-melon, made the brass rings twinkle in his ears. 'You are British.' He seemed to swell with manly pride, and then all at once he was as a child, bubbling over with irrepressible joy. 'I've seen the duchess. Yes, I've seen the duchess.'[131]

The stark racism of Goodwin's description, the representation of the Jamaican as a child, seems to imply that there is nothing to fear in the loss of Britain's formal status – Britain will remain like a parent to Jamaica. Next, Goodwin described being in India, at the King's death:

… it was a moving experience to find that the bearded Sikh doorkeepers, the little Bangali [sic] clerks, the midnight black Tamils of the lowly caste who

---

[127] 'The Queen's New Title "a Sham" Says M.P.: Attack by Lone Tory,' *Express and Star*, 4 March 1953.
[128] Letter to Powell, 4 March 1953. POLL 3.1.9.
[129] Powell, Letter to S. J. H. Green. POLL 3.1.9.   [130] Ibid.
[131] J. W. Goodwin, 'The Crown and the Commonwealth: A reply to Mr. Enoch Powell, M.P.,' *Express and Star*, 12 March 1953.

swept the railway carriages all spoke in their varying forms of English as if George VI had been a respected family friend.[132]

Much like the ex-army officer's list of loyal servants, a panoply of racial types are displayed here as an imperial family. Goodwin could not accept Powell's argument. 'Constitutional lawyers alone can neither make nor mar personal loyalty or the bonds of common interest.'[133] There was enough love and loyalty there. The bonds of the past, in J. W. Goodwin's eyes, were strong enough.

In May 1953, Elizabeth II became Queen of the United Kingdom and Head of the Commonwealth. That month, at the Imperial Institute in London, an exhibition opened entitled 'Queen and Commonwealth.' Life-sized effigies of the people of the colonies in their 'native environments' were exhibited in the section 'Focus on Colonial Progress.' Other sections included 'Parliament, Past and Present,' which was a recycled exhibit from the Festival of Britain that had opened two years earlier.[134] That week, too, the Arts Council exhibition of 'Pictures of British Life' opened, with paintings by mostly unknown artists that were 'designed to throw some sort of light on the life of the British from the time of Queen Elizabeth I onwards.'[135] The exhibit offered an optimistic collapse of time and space, with the Commonwealth – at least at the Imperial Institute – as a shared historical endpoint. Meanwhile, as Powell warned, the truth of New Commonwealth unity was not so clear. The Prime Ministers of the Commonwealth, after attending the coronation, met early the next month for the Commonwealth Prime Ministers' Conference. Even before the meeting, the press speculated on their political disagreements: Prime Minister Malan of South Africa and Prime Minister Nehru of India would disagree on South African apartheid, Prime Minister Huggins of Southern Rhodesia and Nehru on the Central African Federation, and, again, Prime Minister Bogra of Pakistan and Nehru on Kashmir.[136] Malan, leader of the Afrikaner National Party, gathered criticism as soon as he arrived in London for warning Britain not to support the creation of another English-speaking Ulster in South Africa by opposing Afrikaner republicanism.[137] But these controversial political subjects were not to be discussed formally.

[132] Ibid.
[133] Ibid.
[134] 'Commonwealth and the Queen: Livingstone Relics in New Exhibition,' *The Times*, 27 May 1953.
[135] 'Pictures of British Life: From Queen Elizabeth I to the Present Day,' *The Times*, 28 May 1953.
[136] 'Commonwealth Conference,' *The Times*, 1 May 1953.
[137] 'Dr. Malan's Pea to Britain,' *The Times*, 30 May 1953.

Instead, the focus was the preparation of a united Commonwealth position for Churchill's meeting in Bermuda with the United States and France. Still, only days before the meeting, ten Indian women and their children who had travelled by ship from India to South Africa to join their husbands were prevented from landing in Durban by South African immigration officials. They appealed by telegram to the Queen, 'as a wife and mother,' to intervene and use her 'good offices as Queen of the Commonwealth' to prevent their suffering. Earlier in the year, the South African government had announced its intention to withdraw the concession to allow Indian women to enter South Africa. The Natal Indian Congress telegraphed Nehru to urge Malan in London to lift this restriction. It was unsuccessful. While Nehru and Malan sat at the Queen's coronation luncheon, ten families tested the reality of any unity across a mounting political divide. The following month, Malan called for 'freedom in the Commonwealth,' which he defined as freedom from interference in domestic South African affairs.[138] By 1953, 'affection' and 'ideals' across the Commonwealth were strained by the politics of racism.

The Suez Crisis

It was in 1954 that Powell recognized that the British Empire as he knew it was lost, and that the tenuous and problematic bonds of 'affection' were to replace Britain's material power. In 1953, Powell made the headlines as an influential member of a new radical right-wing group of forty or so backbench MPs, led by Julian Amery, who attempted to pressure the government to maintain military control over the Suez Canal in Egypt. Critically, these backbenchers called the 'Suez Group' could rob the Conservative government of its weak majority of 18.[139] As Powell told a Wolverhampton audience, it was not only Britain's Asian colonies but 'the entire British position in Eastern and Central Africa [that was] at stake' in the control of the canal.[140] In 1953, Britain had a vast military complex, with a garrison of 80,000, at Suez. As Daniel Yergin explains, 'In 1948, the canal abruptly lost its traditional rationale ... [British] control over the canal could no longer be preserved on grounds that it was critical to the defence either of India or of an empire that was being liquidated. And yet, at exactly the same moment, the canal was gaining a new role – as the

[138] 'Freedom in the Commonwealth,' *The Times*, 8 July 1953.
[139] '25 Tory "Rebels" Defy Churchill,' *Sunday Express*, 15 November 1953.
[140] J. Enoch Powell, speech to South West Wolverhampton Conservative and Unionist Association, 4 December 1953. SRO, D3123/223.

highway not of empire, but of oil.'[141] By mid century, the economic and geo-strategic importance of the canal was beyond refute: two-thirds of Western Europe's oil imports passed through the canal.

But maintaining control was becoming increasingly problematic. In 1951, the Egyptian government rescinded its commitment to the Anglo-Egyptian Treaty of 1936, which had granted Britain's lease of the base at Suez until 1956. And in 1952, anti-Western riots in Cairo and escalating opposition to Britain's presence at Suez contributed to a military coup led by the Free Officers Movement which overthrew King Farouk and established an Egyptian republic. Meanwhile, the Free Officers coup and Colonel Gamal Abdul Nasser's subsequent government, the Revolutionary Command Council, was welcomed by Washington as a forward-thinking and, they hoped, pro-Western government in the Middle East. Despite ongoing hostility towards British troops in Egypt and American pressure, the backbench Suez Group insisted that any military withdrawal would be catastrophic: Suez Group reports emphasized that withdrawal would destroy British prestige and open the doors to Soviet predominance in the Middle East.[142] The House of Lords backed the Suez Group and for a while they managed to halt British concessions to Egypt.[143]

Despite the group's preoccupation with Soviet influence in the Middle East, Powell's eyes were of course on another enemy. At the height of his association with the group, in 1953, Powell gave a 'shocking' speech to Parliament against an 'advancing American imperialism' that was trying to eliminate British influence around the world and especially in the Suez Canal region.[144] As Powell told the Commons, 'Whatever might be the attitude of the American government and people to the United Kingdom as such, American policy over the past decade has been directed towards the weakening and destruction of the links which bound the British Empire together.'[145] The United States was initiating construction of a naval base in Crete and pouring troops into Malta, Powell reminded the Commons. While planting bases on the territory of the sovereign countries of Greece and Spain, the United States was not only 'standing by with folded arms but was assisting the process of eliminating us from the base we had maintained for American and British interests with the

---

[141] Daniel Yergin, *The Prize: The Epic Quest for Oil, Money, and Power* (New York: Simon & Schuster, 1991), p. 480.
[142] See 'Suez Canal Zone,' 3 March 1953. POLL 3.1.11.
[143] 'Peers Back Tory Rebels,' *Daily Express*, 16 November 1953.
[144] '"Shock" Attack by Tory MP,' 'Suez Correspondence.' POLL 3.1.12.
[145] J. Enoch Powell, 'Conservative Critic of America,' *The Times*, 6 November 1953.

blood of imperial troops in two wars.'[146] This was Powell's first public articulation of opposition to British concessions to American power. Powell received a round of letters from the public in support of his arguments against 'American imperialism'. As one man wrote from London: 'Russian tyranny is bloody for all the world to see' while 'American tyranny is wrapped up in cellophane but is no less real.'[147] Another man, who had served in the navy off the coast of China in 1907 and 1909, offered this:

Our politicians, pulled and pushed by parish and priest, take refuge in treating anti-British movements among backward peoples all over the world as indications of nationalism and a desire for progress, whereas they are the manifestations of the need of human beings for physical control, and of the knowledge that Britain ceased to exercise it.[148]

Political realism – the recognition that human beings need 'physical control' – is here a close cousin of social Darwinism.

The next year, British forces would, with the Suez Agreement, pull out of the canal zone. Against the opinion of the parliamentary party, Powell was one of twenty-six Conservative MPs to vote against the government when the decision came up for a vote in the Commons in July.[149] He described the withdrawal, the belief that '4,000 technicians will fare better than 80,000 troops,' as 'an optimism which has no place in foreign relations.'[150] Powell's experience of Egypt during the Second World War gave him little reason to trust this optimism.[151] British trade had been put in the hands of the goodwill of Egypt. Speaking at a local annual Conservative Association meeting on 14 November 1954, Powell explained that the Suez Agreement had been a turning point. Territories that had value as part of a world system now in isolation may have no value at all. Henceforward the members of the audience were to ask themselves not, as in the past, 'Why should we give up this or that territory or position?' but 'Exactly why and how does it pay the United Kingdom to keep it?'[152] The agreement was, he told Israeli radio listeners years later, 'a tremendous break in British history.'[153] When a

---

[146] 'Conservative Critic of America: Weakening the Empire,' *The Times*, 6 November 1953.
[147] Letter to Powell, 7 November 1953, 'Suez Correspondence.' POLL 3.1.12.
[148] Letter to Powell, 8 November 1953, 'Suez Correspondence.' POLL 3.1.12.
[149] Heffer, *Like the Roman*, p. 193.
[150] J. Enoch Powell in *New Commonwealth* (4 January 1954) as cited in Cosgrave, *The Lives of Enoch Powell*, p. 130.
[151] 'JEP War Memories.' POLL 5.1.
[152] J. Enoch Powell, speech to the Annual General Penn Ward Branch Conservative Association, 12 November 1954. SRO, D3123/223.
[153] J. Enoch Powell, 'International Commentary,' February, 1960. POLL 4.1.27.5.

colleague in the Suez Group reportedly asked him at the time, 'Well, Enoch, what's the next move?' he answered, 'I don't understand.' 'Well, how do we go on fighting for the Empire?' Powell replied, 'I don't know what you mean. It's over.'[154] For Powell, British imperial power finally shattered in 1954.

The following year, Nasser refused to join Turkey, Pakistan, Iraq and Iran in the US-sponsored Baghdad pact against Soviet influence in the Middle East. Nasser's refusal contributed to the United States and Britain withdrawing their financial support for the construction of the Aswan high dam, a project considered essential to Egypt's economic development. Here were the limits of Britain's moral commitment to an empire of development. In July 1956, in order to finance the Aswan project, Nasser announced the nationalization of the canal and froze all assets of the Suez Canal Company. He also closed the canal to Israeli shipping. With this, Nasser would be condemned by much of the British press as a dictator. And in the autumn of 1956, with the help of Israel and France, a Conservative government led by Anthony Eden attempted to recapture control of the canal. Remarkably, the invasion was organized without consultation with the United States. At the time of the invasion, Eden made a direct comparison between the events of that year and the Munich Agreement of 1938. The invasion itself involved a bombing campaign, paratroopers, an Israeli invasion of Gaza and the storming of Egypt's beaches at Port Said; approximately one thousand Egyptian civilians were killed.[155] Immediately, the United States and the UN condemned the military operation in the name of Egypt's national sovereignty and, as Britain was too financially weak to act outside of US foreign policy considerations, Britain withdrew. Nasser called it a people's war. The Suez Crisis shattered British 'prestige' and dramatically demonstrated that Britain could no longer act independently of US foreign policy. Powell was, from the beginning, against the military operation. Once Britain's military bases were given up, Powell maintained, Britain and Egypt's Treaty of 1936 no longer held and, therefore, no longer made lawful Britain's presence at Suez.

In the lead-up to the invasion, the managing director of the polling group Research Services Ltd told the influential Labour MP Richard Crossman that 'there has never been a subject on which there is more genuine bewilderment and divided don't knowism.'[156] As the British forces went in, the country was divided both on and across party

[154] J. Enoch Powell, *Sunday Telegraph*, 19 January 1986.
[155] Derek Varble, *The Suez Crisis 1956* (London: Osprey, 2003).
[156] Richard Crossman, *The Backbench Diaries of Richard Crossman* (London: Hamish Hamilton, 1981), p. 517.

lines.[157] As Crossman noted in his published diary: 'There are many more Labour people ... who feel they would like to have a go at Nasser and who, when faced with the prospect of Britain's ceasing to be a great Power, are emotionally repelled.' Equally, 'there are also any number of Tories who are deeply shocked by the idea of an Anglo-French attempt to impose internationalization by military sanctions.' The socialists were not, Crossman emphasized, 'Little Englanders' ready to accept Britain's reduced status. Radicalism – 'the kind ... which made Byron fight for the Greeks' – was, likewise, rare in the Labour Party.[158] Though London saw protests against the war, notably a large rally organized by the Suez Emergency Committee at Trafalgar Square at the beginning of November, public meetings of the Suez Emergency Committee – as Crossman describes them – leading up to the invasion were not popular or highly politicized, '[p]eople weren't there to demonstrate but to try to understand what on earth was going on and to sort out their own minds.'[159] Though we must take Crossman's assertions with a grain of salt, it is clear that *after* the invasion the public response to it was far more unanimous.

In November 1956, when Britain withdrew, Powell received a flood of constituency letters from both Conservative and Labour voters condemning Eden and the government for the attempted recapture of the canal. One wrote: 'This is one of the few occasions in my life when I have been ashamed of being British.'[160] As one self-described 'Angry Young Tory' wrote in 1958 in *Crossbow* (the magazine of young conservatism): until the Suez Crisis, 'Politics were for Indians.'[161] Until that moment, this line seems to imply, the nature of decision-making in British foreign policy was unproblematic, unpolitical and inevitable. Public uncertainty about British power and subordination to the United States felt, in this Angry Young Tory's mind, like Britons were becoming a subject people. Meanwhile, while publicly condemned by much of the Commonwealth, the catastrophic Suez invasion did not in fact stem the flow of rhetoric on the benefits of (New) Commonwealth unity. Instead, it shook the foundations of British dominance within the Commonwealth and demonstrated that its members were, in fact, witnessing the birth of a new era in international relations. Nasser's triumph was read, by some, as further proof that the 'epoch of the white man was drawing to a close.'[162] At the time, Powell's condemnations of the campaign were kept private. Powell sent a stock reply to letters he received after the crisis supporting the intervention. Exactly eight out of the

[157] Ibid.   [158] Ibid.   [159] Ibid., p. 518.
[160] Letter to Powell, November 1956. SRO, D3123/223.
[161] 'The Angry Young Tory,' *Crossbow*, Spring, 1958.
[162] Schwarz, *The White Man's World*, vol. 1, p. 182.

many hundreds of letters Powell received from the public supported the military action.[163] The failure at Suez underlined a mounting sense that the British Empire (and all the military commitment that was required to maintain it), far from being a modern project, was behind the times. The great majority of the letters to *The Times*, meanwhile, captured the mood of the country by opposing military intervention.[164]

The *moral* embarrassment of the intervention was further heightened by another critical event which dramatically occurred in October and November of 1956 in parallel with the Suez invasion. This was the Hungarian Uprising, the spontaneous, nationwide revolt that momentarily toppled the People's Republic of Hungary and its Soviet-imposed policies. While Britain insisted on the need to regain control of the Suez Canal to control Soviet influence in the Middle East, Soviet tanks rolled into Budapest to suppress the uprising, resulting in thousands of casualties, mass arrests and 200,000 Hungarian refugees fleeing the country. Some Britons opposed to the Suez intervention would not separate the two events. As journalist Malcolm Muggeridge and actor Robert Speaight wrote in a public letter:

The bitter division in public opinion provoked by the British intervention in the Middle East has already had one disastrous consequence. It has deflected popular attention from the far more important struggle in Hungary. A week ago the feelings of the British people were fused in a single flame of admiration for the courage and apparent success of the Hungarian revolt. Now, that success seems threatened by Russian treachery and brute force, and Hungary has appealed to the West ... The Prime Minister has told us that 50 million tons of British shipping are at stake in his dispute with President Nasser. What is at stake in Central Europe are rather more than 50 million souls. It may be objected that it is not so easy to help the Hungarians; to this excuse they are entitled to reply that it was not so easy to help themselves.[165]

Similarly, the influential Liberal Party member, Lady Violet Bonham Carter, wrote to *The Times:*

I am one of the millions who watching the martyrdom of Hungary and listening yesterday to the transmission of her agonizing appeals of help (immediately followed by our 'successful bombings' of Egyptian 'targets') who have felt a humiliation, shame and anger which are beyond expression. At a moment when our moral authority and leadership are most direly needed to meet this brutal assault on freedom we find ourselves bereft of both by our own Government's

---

[163] POLL 3.1.12. As the research of Nicholas Swatman reveals, letters written from the public to both Anthony Eden and Enoch Powell during and after the Suez crisis indicate, perhaps more than anything, growing public frustration with National Service and, with this, military engagements in the empire.

[164] A. N. Wilson, *Our Times* (London: Hutchinson, 2008), p. 65.

[165] Cited ibid., pp. 65–66.

action. For the first time in our history our country has been reduced to moral impotence. We cannot order Soviet Russia to obey the edict of the United Nations which we ourselves have defied, nor to withdraw her tanks and guns from Hungary while we are bombing and invading Egypt. Today we are standing in the dock with Russia. Like us she claims to be conducting a 'police action.' We have coined a phrase which has already become part of the currency of aggression. Never in my lifetime has our name stood so low in the eyes of the world. Never have we stood so ingloriously alone.[166]

Like many others, Bonham Carter called for a change in government. Though there was no such change, Eden stepped down, citing ill health, and Harold Macmillan took the premiership. This was Britain's lowest moment. Bonham Carter is one example of a broad range of political opinion which held up the present against the imagined values of the past: 'For the first time in our history our country has been reduced to moral impotence.' Like many of Powell's constituency letters, Bonham Carter offers an emotive mix of postcolonial shame – of immorality and impotence. The effort to draw Colonel Nasser as a most evil enemy, likened to Adolf Hitler himself, had failed. The 'good name of Britain' was, in Bonham Carter's view, in crisis.

By 1956, we see Powell's path clearly diverging from the committed imperialism of the Suez Group. In the wake of the retreat from Suez, many of that group joined together as the '1957 Group,' and became, as Robert Holland put it, 'the keeper of the flame of a British Cyprus.'[167] In a debate on the independence of Cyprus and its membership in the Commonwealth, Powell told the Commons that Britain had to divest itself of the notion that British sovereignty in the colonies conferred any political advantages when it did not rest upon the real circumstances of the places concerned: 'Sovereignty itself is a mere form. The realities within it are the will of the people and the power of the sovereign.' The United States had airbases in England without any share in British sovereignty. Why could Britain not do the same in Cyprus? In the preceding twenty years, the reality inside Britain's sovereignty abroad had been gradually 'hollowed out.' All that was left was 'the shell of sovereignty':

Both the physical and the moral or sentimental reality of sovereignty have gradually fallen away – the physical reality by the loss of Britain's absolute and relative economic and military preponderance in the world, and the moral reality by the spread of what we ineffectually call 'nationalism', but is really the projection of all that Europe has given over the last two centuries to people of different races and circumstances throughout the world.[168]

---

[166] 'Landings in Egypt,' *The Times* (6 November 1956).
[167] Robert F. Holland, *Britain and the Revolt in Cyprus, 1954–1959* (Oxford University Press, 1998), p. 197.
[168] HC, vol. 602, col. 697, 19 March 1959.

Powell called Britain's colonial position a 'tragedy.' British power was no longer natural. British sovereignty existed now only within the limits of the nation.

To Powell's consternation, the Suez Crisis resulted in the Conservative government drawing itself closer to the United States. In 1957, the new Prime Minister, Harold Macmillan, and his closest advisers would meet President Eisenhower in Bermuda. There, Macmillan announced:

> Britain, my Government, will be staying in the game and pulling our weight. That is why I welcome free restoration of confidence and cooperation between our two countries. You need us: for ourselves, for our commonwealth, and as leaders of Europe. Powerful as you are, I don't believe you can do it alone. Chiefly because without a common front and true partnership between us I do not know whether the principles we believe in can win.[169]

In preparing his speech, Macmillan wrote in his notes, 'For about 2,500 years Whites have had their way. Now revolution: Asia/Africa.'[170] He reminisced about his own Victorian childhood and expressed fears that the West's colonial, Christian civilization, from which he came, was near its end.[171] The 'principles we believe in' and (white) civilization were one in the same. Macmillan emphasized that without a joint alliance, the Soviets could take hold of the Middle East. If that happened, Macmillan told Eden, 'Europe is finished.'[172] The Bermuda conference resulted in increased American involvement in the Middle East and, most importantly, the stationing of American-made intermediate-range ballistic missiles in Britain. That year, too, the government announced future restructuring of the British Army with the 1957 Defence White Paper which would result, in an effort to reduce the costs of defence, in the ending of conscription and the turn toward nuclear defence. From this point on, Powell would remain critical of Britain's reliance on the nuclear deterrent and consequential dependence on the United States for its 'mini-arsenal.'[173] In Powell's mind, a world truly 'poised between the hope of total peace and the fear of total war,' as the British defence White Paper of 1957 put it, would be a world without the nation.[174]

Soon after Macmillan assumed office in January 1957 after Eden's resignation, Rab Butler persuaded him of the need for a committee, a

---

[169] Cited in E. Bruce Geelhoed and Anthony O. Edmonds, *Eisenhower, Macmillan and Allied Unity, 1957–1961* (New York: Palgrave Macmillan, 2003), p. 15.

[170] Cited in Schwarz, *The White Man's World*, p. 182.

[171] Ibid.

[172] Cited in Geelhoed and Edmonds, *Eisenhower, Macmillan, and Allied Unity*, p. 15.

[173] J. Enoch Powell, 'Why I Don't Believe We Need to Keep the Bomb,' *Today on Sunday*, 30 November 1986.

[174] Cited in J. Enoch Powell, 'Nuclear Weapons and World Power,' *The Listener*, 17 February 1966.

policy study group, to consider the contents of the next Conservative manifesto. Britain's failure at Suez the previous year had seriously weakened Conservative support. The group's main goal was the reform of the party so as to appeal to the middle-class voter. In the language of One Nation conservatism, the group sought to attack Labour's rhetoric of equality with a focus on the 'Opportunity State.' In a letter to Iain Macleod early in 1957, Powell put forward what he regarded as the most pressing issues for reform in the Conservative Party, namely the turn to the Tory nation. The letter was to be circulated and discussed on 15 February at the first meeting of the policy study group to which Powell and Macleod both belonged. In that circulated letter, Powell set out the policy areas which he believed needed reform:

First I put without hesitation external relations, and here I see two main tasks. The Tory Party must find the means to interpret its membership of international organisations in a manner which shall not be repugnant to its deep sense of nationhood and shall also not be verbiage and humbug. In this I am myself only beginning to grope; but I wonder if concepts like 'The Concert of Europe' and securus judicat orbis terrarum might not prove on study to offer an alternative to the mad theory of universal democracy which UNO had tried to live on. This is one salve that must be applied to the deep Suez wound.

The future was not 'universal democracy' and not the Commonwealth but a return to the true identity of the nation:

The other task is curative too: the Tory Party must be cured of the British Empire, of the pitiful yearning to cling to relics of a bygone system (and fight for them if necessary at the barricades and in the wrong division lobby), while at the same time proclaiming the wonders of a new system whose foster parents were Attlee and Nehru. Economically and politically, we need what the Younger Pitt of 1784 stands for: what (and why) the Empire was and what (if anything) the Commonwealth is, must be made clear to ourselves till it hurts no longer. The courage to act rationally will flow from the courage to see things as they are. The Tory Party has to find its patriotism again, and to find it, as of old, in 'this England'. This too will be a salve to the wound of Suez.[175]

In a public speech the same day as his first meeting with the group, Powell told his local Wolverhampton audience that Britain must recreate the best of the nineteenth century: 'Britain must recreate what was good, dynamic and creative in the first half of the 19th century.'[176] The policy study group produced studies of the political potential of

---

[175] Circulated letter from J. Enoch Powell to Iain Macleod to members of the Policy Study Group for consideration at the meeting on 15 February 1957. POLL 3.2.1.2. File 4.

[176] J. Enoch Powell, 'Britain must recreate best of 19th Century,' Express and Star, 16 February 1957.

middle-class organizations, such as the Middle Class Alliance, on how they voted, their associations with the Liberal Party and on whether they advised their members regarding Britain's actions over Suez.[177] These organizations were, one study noted, the home of the discontented conservative.[178] These were the home of fixed income groups – such as landlords – who were increasingly susceptible to inflation in Britain's economy, and therefore most opposed to the government's fiscal policies. At their third meeting, the guest expert Dr Charles Hill came to speak to the group. Hill argued that the 'mood of frustration' that stemmed from Suez needed to be dispelled by a clear policy, so, he asked, 'Could we clothe the bones of the Opportunity State with some attractive flesh to give pleasure to the middle class?'[179] For Powell, the 'attractive flesh' for the Conservative voter was no doubt the nation.

Never had it so good

In Powell's eyes, the Suez operation had been the most dramatic political event in Britain since the end of the Second World War – it had split both parties, with the Suez Group on the right and the Suez Emergency Committee on the left. The following years saw the direct consequences of the invasion, in negotiations with Egypt, in refugees, in altered international relationships. After the invasion, Powell argued, 'Nothing, one supposed, could ever be quite the same again.' Because of this, Powell did not understand, 'when the electorate was called upon to pass judgment, barely three years later, on a government substantially the same,' why did it seem to have no effect at all?[180] Powell himself had prepared for criticisms against the party in the 1959 general election campaign. As a junior member of the government during the Suez operation, he thought it right to make a full and prominent reference to it in his election letter that he sent to each elector in his constituency. He armed himself with a full argument in favour of the Conservative government's actions when he went out to public meetings before the election. And then, he told a radio audience, the most astonishing thing happened.[181] At one meeting after another, not only in his constituency, but wherever he spoke, up and down the country, no one asked him a question

---

[177] 'Policy Study Group Minutes of First Meeting,' 15 February 1957. POLL 3.2.1.2.
[178] *The People's League for the Defence of Freedom/The Middle Class Alliance Report of the Committee of Investigation,* November, 1956, p. 2. POLL 3.2.1.2.
[179] 'Minutes of the Third Meeting of the Policy Study Group,' 1 April 1957. POLL 3.2.1.2.
[180] Ibid.
[181] J. Enoch Powell, 'International Commentary,' 23 October 1959, Radio Broadcast. POLL 4.1.27.

on the subject of the Suez operation.[182] What did this mean, Powell asked, for Britain's policy in the Middle East and its foreign policy in general? It surprised Powell, but this 'wilful amnesia' was not necessarily an obstacle to Britain's foreign policy. Rather, it could be the very opposite. There was, he realized, value in forgetting the empire: the Anglo-American intervention in the Lebanon and Jordan in 1958 was conducted with 'notable coolness,' which was made possible by public amnesia, by the public's lack of concern for 'sentiments born of conditions that no longer exist.'[183]

Voters clearly concentrated on domestic issues and the domestic security of Macmillan's 'sound and prosperous' society took the attention of the British voter, but Powell 'did not believe that the full answer to the question lies here.'[184] Rather, he argued, Britain had entered 'a sleep and a forgetting.' And this 'act of collective wilful amnesia' was made possible by the succession of Harold Macmillan to the premiership. Despite Macmillan's involvement in the Suez operation, 'the public mind has rewritten history to its own purpose and has decided that Eden is to be the symbol of Suez and Macmillan the symbol of forgetting.'[185] To this, he warned, a 'part of a man's mind can be at work while the rest is asleep.'[186] The consequences of the end of empire in Britain were still to come.

This description of Harold Macmillan as a 'symbol of forgetting' came only one year after Powell's resignation as Financial Secretary under the Chancellor of the Exchequer, Peter Thorneycroft. In 1958, Powell resigned alongside Thorneycroft and Nigel Birch in opposition to increased government expenditure. Crucially, Powell believed that Macmillan refused to take Thorneycroft's advice on restricting the budget simply because it would have been electorally damaging. Powell, Thorneycroft and Birch were swimming against the tide of the Conservative Party's 'middle way' of reformed capitalism; but their revolt can be aligned, too, with emerging criticisms of redistributive taxation and public spending found in such lobbyist groups as the Middle Class Alliance and at the grassroots of the Conservative Party, in the Conservative Political Centre (CPC) and the Young Conservatives.[187] As one chairman of a London CPC branch recalled in 1970, 'Back in the 1950s, when I was a young Y.C., I wanted to see Enoch Powell as Chancellor of the Exchequer, a viewpoint which, needless to say, was not well received in the days of Conservative planning.' In Powell's

---

[182] Ibid.   [183]Ibid.   [184] Ibid.   [185] Ibid.   [186] Ibid.
[187] See E. H. H. Green, *Ideologies of Conservatism: Conservative Political Ideas in the Twentieth Century* (Oxford University Press, 2002).

mind, Macmillan had sacrificed the health of the national economy for the maintenance of Conservative power. From that moment on, Macmillan came to embody all that Powell distrusted in the party. For Powell, 1958 was 'the great turning point that marked the beginning of the Macmillan Era,' the era of inflation.[188] As Powell described it, Macmillan's political cynicism, his willingness to bend to the 'cult of newness' for the sake of political expediency, had resulted in the 'expansionist' economic policies and reforms of the Macmillan era. This had, Powell argued, put the country to sleep. When Powell was sympathetic to Macmillan, he emphasized the ideological constraints of Macmillan's (patrician) past and, particularly, Macmillan's experiences of dealing with large numbers of unemployed in his constituency in the interwar years. As Macmillan himself explained:

I look back with gratitude to the twenty-odd years of my association with Stockton and the North-East coast. I learned there lessons which I have never forgotten. If, in some respects, they may have left too deep an impression on my mind, the gain was greater than the loss.[189]

Still tax on capital gains, a National Economic Development Council, a National Incomes Commission, House of Lords reform, a consumers council and development planning for the north-east and central Scotland are all marked out, by Powell, as essentially un-Tory. Crucially, Macmillan's commitment to economic 'modernization' masked, Powell believed, a lack of faith in social traditions and an implicit rejection of national and imperial pride. In the following years, Powell would become the leading critic of the government's interventionist state.

Later, Powell went so far as to describe Macmillan's politics at this time as a politics of 'chicanery,'[190] a technocratic politics of consensus-building by any means necessary. He described him as having 'all the skill of an old actor-manager.'[191] But perhaps the best description that Powell offers of Macmillan came in 1987 in *The Spectator*:

Macmillan was a Whig, not a Tory ... he had no use for Conservative loyalties and affections; they interfered too much with the Whig's true vocation of detecting trends in events and riding them skilfully so as to preserve the privileges, property and interests of his class.[192]

[188] Cosgrave, *The Lives of Enoch Powell*, p. 160.
[189] Harold Macmillan as quoted in J. Enoch Powell, 'Winds of Change,' *Glasgow Herald* (1963) in *Reflections of a Statesman*, pp. 321–324 (p. 322).
[190] J. Enoch Powell, Bill Schwarz interview, 26 April 1988.
[191] As cited in Cosgrave, *The Lives of Enoch Powell*, p. 150.
[192] J Enoch Powell, *The Spectator* (10 January 1987), as cited in Heffer, *Like the Roman*, p. 210.

Between Macmillan and himself, Powell juxtaposed class interest and Tory belief. The influential historian Andrew Gamble similarly described the significance of Macmillan's class identity as follows:

The shock of Britain's decline was ... softened through the adroit leadership of Macmillan, whose aristocratic pose and unflappable manner managed to suggest that nothing was changing at the very moment the most radical developments were taking place.[193]

Powell's own assessment of this (fortuitous) misreading of Macmillan fits with that of Gamble. No doubt, Gamble himself read the words of an anonymous article published in *The Times* in April 1964 (and written by Powell), which caused major ripples within the party:

In assessing him commentators and public alike fall into the crudest of fallacies when they conclude that *because* he was elderly, looked old-fashioned and enjoyed aristocratic poses, *therefore* he must be right wing or reactionary. It was the reverse of the truth; he was profoundly un-conservative and innovating by temperament. Novelty attracted him for its own sake. The contradictory term 'new tradition', which he personally when Minister of Housing insisted on applying to non-traditional forms of construction, was a gem-like reflection of his cynicism.[194]

Both Gamble's and Powell's descriptions point to the complex way in which public perceptions of the class identity of Britain's political elite were significant – and, for a short while, stabilizing – at a moment of dramatic social and political change.

Alongside public perceptions of Macmillan, we see in this postwar state of reformed capitalism and planning, less a clean break from class paternalism than the complex persistence of hierarchical thinking, patrician idioms and corporate identities, embedded in the social and political system.[195] The expansion of state power in the postwar years was

---

[193] Gamble, *The Conservative Nation*, p. 62.

[194] 'A Conservative' [Enoch Powell], 'From the Years of Protest to the Year of Disasters,' *The Times*, 1 April 1964.

[195] Lawrence, 'Paternalism, Class, and the British Path to Modernity,' in Gunn and Vernon (eds.), *The Peculiarities of Liberal Modernity in Imperial Britain*; and Conekin, Mort and Waters (eds.), *Moments of Modernity*. For a critique of historians' treatment of British modernization, see David Edgerton, 'Anti-histories and technocrats: revisiting the technocratic moment, 1959–64,' in *Warfare Britain: Britain, 1920–1970* (Cambridge University Press, 2006), pp. 191–229. In part, the 'disciplinary dimension' of the postwar consensus – in which political forces were to find representation within a 'neutral' and 'post-ideological' state – was buttressed by both the Labour and Conservative Parties' commitments to the 'special relationship' with the United States and the Cold War world order. The politics of anti-communism established, in a divided Europe, the need for the collective defence of reformed capitalism in 'the West' against Soviet power. Marshall Aid from the United States economically underpinned a particular reformist agenda in Britain, which promoted high

underpinned, in other words, by a conservative nationalism or a belief in the 'inexhaustible wisdom of Institutions and their custodians.'[196] Linked to this, despite the extension of the state's role in economic and social planning, 'one of the most important distinguishing features of English polity in the 1950s' was, according to the political scientist Jim Bulpitt, a 'divorce between centre and periphery' – between the management of the postwar state and grassroots issues.[197] The emerging criticisms against government spending from the Conservative Political Centre and the Young Conservatives would have, at this stage, little effect. Bulpitt goes on to explain that the government's laissez-faire approach to immigrant welfare and 'race relations' was in part a product of this representative structure. A pragmatic, non-populist state system held sway. Powell's own concerns about centralized power were, as we have seen, focused on the management of the economy. But, in 1958, even Powell embraced a top-down approach to the question of immigration law, explaining his refusal to support Cyril Osborne and emerging activist groups in public opposition to the British Nationality Law, because he thought that 'such a fundamental change in the law of the country was a monkey which was easier caught softly.'[198]

Yet by the late 1950s cracks in this 'aristocratic pose' were already beginning to show. The Suez Crisis, the suppression of the Hungarian Revolution, rapid decolonization and the domestic political constraints of the Cold War led some, in elite circles, to critique bureaucratic centralization as well as the sway of party discipline.[199] At this moment, critics on both the left and right of the political spectrum began to look to the importance of custom and community – though very differently defined – as that which might sustain participatory democracy and decentralize political power. Powell was not alone in understanding the significance of 'traditional' community via work in a (rapidly transforming) colonial world. Echoing Powell's belief that the nation was

wages, redistributive taxes and mass consumption. Anna Marie Smith, *New Right Discourse*, p. 137.

[196] Unlike modern nationalisms, Tom Nairn explains, '[t]he dominant *Gestalt* of political England is patrician, not popular: it perceives a grateful People, allowed to advance ... Not the self-action of *Volk*, but inexhaustible wisdom of Institutions and their custodians; not a belief that the People can do anything, in the last resort, but the conviction that popular aspirations will always, in the end, be attended to *up there*.' Tom Nairn, *The Break-Up of Britain: Crisis and Neo-Nationalism* (Altona, Vic.: Common Ground Publishing, 2003), p. 284.

[197] Jim Bulpitt, 'Continuity, Autonomy and Peripheralisation: the Anatomy of the Centre's Race Statecraft in England,' in Zig Layton-Henry and Paul B. Rich (eds.), *Race, Government and Politics in Britain* (Basingstoke: Macmillan, 1986), pp. 17–44 (p. 26).

[198] As cited in Cosgrave, *The Lives of Enoch Powell*, p. 169.

[199] Foote, *The Republican Transformation of Modern British Politics*, p. 189.

'asleep,' left-wing critics voiced concerns about widespread political apathy – produced by full employment, economic planning and, with this, the effective social engineering of the working classes by Britain's ruling elite.[200] Planning and reconstruction were, they feared, destroying traditional communities and the radical base of local politics. As we have seen, Powell similarly spoke of the need to protect the (religious) community from the encroachments of economic planning and the welfare state. We see at this time Stuart Hall, one of the founders of the New Left, arguing that the new consumer capitalism of the period had caused working-class people to renounce their traditional opposition to the capitalist elite; consumer society had replaced traditional communities with 'a permanently exploited, permanently alienated mass of consumers,' who were now caged morally and mentally (rather than materially) via advertising and status anxiety.[201] Further, economic affluence and the Cold War's yawning gap between the military expert and the ignorant majority had generated, according to E. P. Thompson, a 'Great Apathy.'[202] Britain had become, as he later called it, a 'Natopolitan' culture: 'at the heart of a disintegrating imperial system, with weapons of annihilation posed over the earth, the Natopolitan walks carefully down well-known streets, putting his securities in the bank.'[203]

Critical to these debates, too, were concerns about the moral make-up of Britain and anxiety about a transformation in Britain's national character. The 'nation' was, some believed, losing itself. This was tied, by some, to concerns about the weakening influence of the Church. For others, again, this was a consequence of mass affluence. A Conservative Cabinet meeting in December 1958 pointed out that the 'increase of young offenders was striking evidence of a decline in spiritual values.'[204] Anxieties about juvenile delinquency and moral decline found expression, too, in One Nation's 1959 pamphlet *Responsible Society*. Much like criticism on the left, here a shift in social mores was chiefly discussed as a consequence of postwar affluence.[205] Sir David Eccles, Minister of Education, told Macmillan in 1961 that full employment and welfare had damaged the incentive to work.[206] But he also argued that 'materialism' had induced women to abandon the responsibilities of child care for paid employment, while delinquents grew up in an education system which did not instil traditional values.[207] Eccles went so far as to warn

[200] Ibid., p. 34.   [201] As ibid., p. 37.
[202] Ibid., p. 27.   [203] Ibid., p. 28.
[204] Mark Jarvis, *Conservative Governments, Morality and Social Change in Affluent Britain, 1957–64* (Manchester University Press, 2005), p. 25.
[205] Ibid., p. 24.   [206] Ibid., p. 25.   [207] Ibid.

Macmillan that many teachers believed that the 'Tory pre-occupation with financial incentives could easily be pursued to an extent that would cause further deterioration in morals.'[208] The party's macro-economic vision of full employment and high consumer spending was failing Britain, according to Eccles, at the grassroots.

These anxieties about social transformation were occurring at a moment, too, of massive diversification in mass entertainment, resulting in as yet poorly understood shifts in cultural authority, 'the axis turning sharply – in an age of Americanized mass culture – to the popular.'[209] New popular forms, the romance of Hollywood as well as African-American and rock 'n' roll music, were working to destabilize and displace state-directed displays and rituals of the (imperial) nation. As Schwarz argues: 'the tempo of these new cultures could make the old seem very old.'[210] And so, as Macmillan maintained his 'unflappable manner', state-directed narratives of empire, which even in the 1940s registered powerfully in public life, looked increasingly out-of-date and, for some, even inconsequential.[211] In contrast to the optimistic rhetoric of the *Imperial Policy* pamphlet, then, 'by the end of the 1950s, the empire was coming so completely to signify the past that it was almost impossible to remember that once it had symbolized the future.'[212]

Linked to concerns about juvenile delinquency and cultural change were the various readings of the race riots that rocked Notting Hill in 1958. The presence of racism in Britain was ambiguously read, across the political spectrum, as a symptom of national decay. Critics on the left viewed the Notting Hill riots – in which blacks were attacked by white working-class youths – as a sign of the corruption of working-class culture. For instance, the *Universities and Left Review* editors wrote that 'it reflects the decline of a number of human responses and values – from fair-minded liberalism to working-class international solidarity – which this country is going to need, more and more, if Britain is to pass peacefully out of colonialism into a new relationship with the nations of Africa and Asia.'[213] On the other side of the coin, those opposed to black immigration often did so via a concern for the moral integrity of the nation. As Esme Wynne-Tyson put it in *The Contemporary Review*, the 'Teddy Boys' of the 1958 riots were a sign, again, of working-class *moral* decline. The so-called 'enforced intermingling' of races in Britain threatened the nation's moral future:

---

[208] As cited ibid., p. 25.
[209] Schwarz, *The White Man's World*, p. 335.
[210] Ibid., pp. 336–337.   [211] Ibid.   [212] Ibid., p. 338.
[213] As cited in Foote, *The Republican Transformation of Modern British Politics*, p. 36.

The 'hot' music, primitive dances, and other sensual practices of the coloured races, have permeated with their devolutionary influences every corner of a once proud civilization, debasing and obstructing the process of an originally highly ethical people.[214]

Ironically, in Wynne-Tyson's argument, the influence of black culture on white communities is read as the *cause* of white violence against the black community. Again, these concerns revolved around the fragile moral character of the working classes and, often, white working-class women particularly. Much of the public discussions on mixed-race couples and bi-racial children couched overtly racist, eugenic anxieties in terms of concerns about female promiscuity. The 'myth of the destructive female' had taken on a new form. Structured by elite concerns about the decline of traditional culture within working-class communities, recycled images of 'civilization' and 'barbarism' came home to the metropole to comprehend a society that had 'never had it so good.'

Reckoning with Hola Camp

Powell gave speeches and joined pressures groups throughout the 1950s that were concerned with questions of imperial policy and decolonization. He spoke, until the Suez Agreement, of the need to protect Britain's formal empire. But Powell's hope of a unified Britannic realm under the Crown, manifest in a new colonial army, was by 1957 entirely lost. Powell argued, then, that the Tory party needed to be 'cured' of the British Empire. It needed to face the harsh realities of Britain's place in the world and turn away from the false promise that Britain's 'civilizing mission' and global influence would continue, via Western opposition to the 'new barbarism' of Soviet power. But Powell's persistent Tory critique of the direction of imperial policy did not always speak at cross-purposes to the shifting rhetorical terrain of empire and nation at this time. Powell's insistence that Britain needed to find itself, to return to 'the nation,' came at a moment when we see clear anxiety in intellectual circles about the 'moral make-up' of the British people. At the same time, the Suez Crisis and the calls for fair African political representation in parts of British Africa called into question the moral limits of Britain's new imperialism. In July 1959, Powell's words on empire were to have a significant effect. At that point, in response to the torture and death of eleven men in a British detention camp in Kenya, Powell did not rely on humanitarian or universal moral principles.

---

[214] As cited in Rich, 'Black People in Britain,' p. 19.

Rather, he emphasized good governance and, importantly, the identity of the Englishman.

On 3 March 1959, eleven men lay near death in a remote detention camp in Kenya. They lay in a pile on the ground, beaten with batons by colonial guards. Due to exhaustion or political defiance, they could not complete a menial task, and so the guards followed the orders of the 'Cowan Plan' against the prisoners. These eleven men had been some of the remaining 'hard core' of Kenya's Mau Mau movement. Colonial security forces explained their actions by stating that they found that the hard core responded only to the blunt 'compelling force' of forced labour.[215] As the *Daily Telegraph* described it on 27 July of that year, this was a 'highly successful technique of rehabilitation to a hard core of spell-bound Mau Mau members who had lately become idle, insolent and undisciplined.' And so, 'The problem before the officers and their 105 African warders on March 3 was to get 85 fanatical resisters to work so that the spell of the Mau Mau oath not to work with the Government could be broken ... Difficulty was to be expected, but not disaster.'[216] Survivor John Maina Kahihu remembered that morning he was one of eight-five men who were marched outside and ordered to work, but 'We refused to do this work. We were fighting for our freedom. We were not slaves.' Violence followed:

One hundred and seventy [guards] stood around us with machine guns. Thirty guards were inside the trench with us. The white man in charge blew his whistle and the guards started beating us. They beat us from 8am to 11:30. They were beating us like dogs. I was covered by other bodies – just my arms and legs were exposed. I was very lucky to survive. But the others were still being beaten. There was no escape for them.[217]

In addition to the eleven who died, sixty men were seriously injured at Hola that morning.[218]

The prison initially covered up the cause of death of the men at Hola Camp: disobeying orders, they had died drinking 'infected water.'[219] When the truth came out, it became clear that their deaths had been a direct and anticipated consequence of the prison's official policy. J. B. T. Cowan, District Officer in the Colonial Army at the time, had developed a system of abuse to break the prisoners' resistance to work. A minute that soon became public sent by the Commissioner of Prisons

[215] *Documents Relating to the Death of Eleven Mau Mau Detainees at Hola Camp in Kenya*, Parliamentary Papers, Cmnd. 778 of 1959. PP.

[216] 'More Facts About Hola,' *Daily Telegraph and Morning Post*, 27 July 1959.

[217] *Documents Relating to the Death of Eleven Mau Mau Detainees at Hola Camp in Kenya*, Parliamentary Papers, Cmnd. 778 of 1959. PP.

[218] Ibid.   [219] Ibid.

to the Minister of Defence, on 17 February of that year, seeking further authorization from the administration's Security Council, read: 'The plans Mr. Cowan worked out ... could be undertaken by us, but it would mean the use of a certain degree of force, to which operation someone might get hurt or even killed.'[220] Nonetheless, the Minister of Defence and the Minister of African Affairs authorized Cowan's plan directly.

On the very same day as these eleven men were beaten in Hola, Sir Robert Armitage declared a state of emergency in Nyasaland. In February 1959, riots had broken out there. Southern and Northern Rhodesia and Nyasaland had, for six years, been politically federated within the settler-dominated Central African Federation. African nationalism in these countries focused on opposition to the Federation, demands for the franchise and representation in the territorial legislatures.[221] When the political protests broke out – as the Devlin Commission Report would reveal alongside publicity over Hola later in the year – the Federation responded with brutal force. Federal troops burnt the houses of suspected nationalist sympathizers. They beat protesters.[222] Troop actions heightened nationalist opposition in the country. Dr Hastings Banda, leader of Nyasaland's Congress Party, had returned to his country the previous year after forty-three years in exile in South Africa, the United States, Britain and Ghana. Dr Banda was imprisoned indefinitely. The government suppressed all nationalist political expression. In March 1959, public opinion polls revealed that, even among Conservative voters, many now had more sympathy for the African majority than for the white settler minorities in British Africa.[223]

At 1.15 a.m. in the early morning of 28 July 1959, after hours of debate on Africa, Powell got up in the House of Commons in London to give a speech. In *The Penguin Book of Twentieth Century Speeches*, this speech appears alongside 'I have a dream' and 'Ask not what your country can do for you' (as well as Powell's own 'Rivers of Blood' speech), set down as one of the English-speaking world's most important political performances.[224] That night, Parliament debated who was to be held accountable for the deaths of the eleven Kenyan men in Hola Camp. Controversy in Britain over the prisoners' deaths had led to the

---

[220] As quoted by J. Enoch Powell, HC, vol. 610, col. 232, 27 July 1959.
[221] McIntyre, *British Decolonization, 1946–1997*, p. 51.
[222] 'The Massacre Plot that Never Was,' *Daily Mail*, 24 July 1959.
[223] David French, *The Army, Empire and Cold War: The British Army and Military Policy, 1945–1971* (Oxford University Press, 2012), p. 281.
[224] Brian MacArthur (ed.), *The Penguin Book of Twentieth-Century Speeches* (London: Viking, 1999).

Conroy Inquiry into disciplinary charges against two low-level prison officers. The results of this inquiry had been published in a government White Paper the week before, and it was the ramifications of the contents of that White Paper that Parliament debated.[225] Alongside the government's Devlin Commission Report on the political unrest and state of emergency in Nyasaland, which dubbed that area a temporary 'police state,' the deaths at Hola Camp seemed to indicate a complete unravelling of colonial authority in Africa. In May, press reports covered the 144 Mau Mau detainees at the camp who went on a hunger strike.[226] 'Police state' captured the headlines; the reports of an administrative cover-up regarding the deaths of the prisoners in Kenya took the headlines too.

The Hola Camp atrocity occurred after over seven years of conflict between colonial security forces and Mau Mau insurgency and after seven years of a declared state of emergency in Kenya. The insurgency was largely the struggle of the Kikuyu, Kenya's major ethnic group. By the early 1950s, 30,000 British settlers lived in Kenya along with 5 million indigenous Kenyans. Owing to this colonial settlement, the Kikuyu had lost millions of acres of agricultural land to white farmers and had been forced to continue farming as tenants or move into crowded native reserves. Reclaiming this land was the greatest single issue in the rebellion. Between October 1952 and January 1960 – the month the emergency officially ended – Mau Mau supporters killed approximately 2,000 African 'loyalist' civilians and caused 200 casualties among the army and police force. Thirty-two white settlers died in total. Meanwhile, British forces hanged more than 1,000 Kenyans, killed somewhere between 12,000 and 20,000 in combat and detained at least 150,000.[227] Caroline Elkins maintains that, in those seven years, as many as 100,000 Kenyans may have died in British detention camps. As Elkins describes it, this war in the forests of the central highlands against Kenya's Kikuyu people and, even more, the detention of and violence against thousands – perhaps hundreds of thousands – of Kenyan nationalists[228] was no doubt Britain's 'imperial

---

[225] *Documents Relating to the Deaths of Eleven Mau Mau Detainees at Hola Camp in Kenya*, Cmnd 778, 1959, PP; Henry Rice, 'The Week in Westminster,' 1 August 1959. POLL 3.1.18. The investigation itself was castigated as a cover-up. The doctor who inspected the bodies made no mention of the bruises caused by the beating on the death certificates, indicating only pneumonia.

[226] 'Mau Mau Detainees' Hunger Strike,' *The Times*, 27 May 1959.

[227] Bernard Porter, 'How Did They Get Away With It?,' *London Review of Books*, 27: 5 (3 March 2005), pp. 3–6.

[228] For the historiographic debate on Mau Mau as a *nationalist* movement, see Susan Carruthers, '"Worse Than Communists": Propaganda and the Mau Mau Insurgency

reckoning.'[229] Or, more accurately, if a failed war to recapture the Suez Canal from Egypt was the reckoning and loss of Britain's imperial position to American dominance, the war in Kenya was the reckoning and failure of British colonial Africa and Britain's requisite support of white domination in Africa.

As we shall see, Powell's speech worked to affirm the political tradition of Britain – and the character of the Englishman – at the exact point when an important political rift had begun to develop between the British government and settler communities. At this historic moment, colonial violence was essentially redrawn, by Powell and others, as distinctly un-British. Powell's speech on Hola Camp is best understood in this light, in light of a postwar crisis in the (moral) superiority of the white man. This holds, too, a wider significance. The effort to assert British moral superiority (and rhetorically distance the British state from the realities of colonial violence) is a key building block in the making of postcolonial Britain.

As the deaths at Hola Camp became worldwide news, Iain Macleod, Powell's friend and colleague, who was then Minister of Labour, was in Geneva at an International Labour Organization conference. There, he found himself having to defend Britain's use of forced labour on Mau Mau detainees.[230] 'Operation Anvil' – which a Conservative Cabinet had approved in 1954 – had caused the further detention of tens of thousands of Kenyans and for these detainees to be 'usefully employed in work which the officer in charge is satisfied will assist in bringing the Emergency to an end.'[231] This was technically a carefully worded breach of the International Labour Organization Forced Labour Convention of 1930. Throughout the years of violence in Kenya, British newsreels and news reports had portrayed the situation in terms fundamentally sympathetic to the white settlers, tending to characterize it as a battle between black savagery and white civilization. Violence against white settler families, though in no way representative of the vast majority of deaths in Kenya, came to symbolize the true nature of Mau Mau in Britain. Mau Mau infamously engaged in tribal oaths and wore traditional, 'uncivilized' dress. As Wendy Webster has emphasized, this image of Mau Mau was highly gendered: here was the African male revealed as a

in Kenya, 1952–1960,' in *Winning Hearts and Minds: British Governments, the Media and Colonial Counter-Insurgency 1944–1960* (London: Leicester University Press, 1995), pp. 128–193.

[229] Elkins, *Britain's Gulag*. Elkins convincingly argues that the number of Kenyans detained during the state of emergency was far higher than the official 70,000.

[230] Madeleine Bunting, 'Is this Our Hola camp?' *The Guardian*, 15 March 2004.

[231] *Kenya: Rehabilitation Policy and the Use of Forced Labour*, 10 June 1959. CAB 129/97. C. (59) 97.

fundamental threat to the white domestic sphere.[232] Critically, by many, Mau Mau was not envisioned as a valid political or national movement but a sign of the essential fragility of civilization in Africa. The war to control Mau Mau could then be told as a war for (white) civilization. Hola Camp broke this narrative, however. Joanna Lewis has shown that it was Kenya's Hola Camp massacre that convinced Macleod that the empire was becoming a serious political liability.[233] Macleod would soon after warn Macmillan that the situation in Africa threatened to alienate the 'middle voter' from the Conservative Party.[234] In October 1959, with the appointment of Macleod as the new Colonial Secretary, the government officially scrapped the Colonial Office's 'gradualist timetable' of decolonization.[235] Macmillan would early in the next year, after finishing off a tour of Ghana, Nigeria, Central Africa and South Africa, give his 'Wind of Change' speech to the South African Parliament in Cape Town, recognizing the legitimacy of growing nationalisms across Africa and indicating a policy turn away from perpetual support of Africa's white settler communities. In that speech, Macmillan would contend that some South African policies were 'impossible' for the British government to support 'without being false to our own deep convictions about the political destinies of free men.'[236] This was an attack on apartheid – again, an assertion of Britain's liberal tradition against the racial politics of colonial Africa.[237]

And so, Powell stood up at the end of a very long night in the Commons. At this point in his career, Powell had already established himself in opposition to the moderates of the Conservative Party, against the fiscal policies and economic planning of the postwar consensus. At the beginning of the previous year, he and Nigel Birch, as Financial Secretaries of the Treasury, had resigned with Peter Thorneycroft, then Chancellor of the Exchequer, because Macmillan had not accepted Thorneycroft's refusal to permit an increase in the current expenditure of government. Supplementing his lost income with regular journalism and business consultancy, Powell returned to the life of an active backbencher.[238] It was 1959, with an election coming and a weak Conservative government on the defensive. The Labour opposition, led by Barbara Castle

---

[232] See Webster, 'There'll Always be an England,' pp. 557–584.
[233] Joanna Lewis, 'Nasty, Brutish and in Shorts?,' pp. 201–223.
[234] Ibid.
[235] W. David McIntyre, *British Decolonization, 1946–1997*, p. 47.
[236] Ibid.
[237] Anderson, *Histories of the Hanged*, p. 3.
[238] After leaving his job in the Treasury, Powell increasingly took to journalism to supplement his income. Tony Benn remembers Powell in those years resenting the fact that he was offered no good job in the City, in finance, because, Powell believed, he was not born of the right class. Tony Benn, Interview with the Author, November 2005.

and Dingle Foot, had spent the last few hours pushing for further investigation into the deaths at Hola. They argued that Parliament could not accept the White Paper, which called only for the early retirement, without loss of retirement funds, of the Kenyan Commissioner of Prisons and the Hola Camp Superintendent.[239] They called for the resignation of the Colonial Secretary, Alan Lennox-Boyd. Barbara Castle had for years campaigned to reveal the abuses of the detention camps in Kenya and had even visited Kenya to report on the situation. The debate that night in Parliament was the climax of her campaign: 'If this White Paper is accepted by the House, there will have been one of the gravest miscarriages of justice in British Colonial history.' It was, she went on, an 'insult to Africans unparalleled in British Colonial history' for an official found guilty of three counts of grave dereliction of duty causing the deaths of eleven men to be retired without a penny lost to himself. Instead of retribution, the month before the Queen had awarded John Cowan, author of the 'Cowan Plan,' the MBE – against protests from a young Labour backbench MP, Tony Benn. As the debate developed, wrote one reporter, few Kenyan officials escaped criticism and 'tempers rose as the Government was accused of "white-washing" and the opposition of "mud-slinging."'[240] Until Powell's speech, wrote the (conservative) *Daily Telegraph*, the heated debate seemed to be entirely overshadowed by party politics.[241]

Unlike all Conservative speakers before him that night, Powell argued that the responsibility for the deaths at Hola lay with Kenyan Ministers. Colonial Secretary Lennox-Boyd knew nothing of the Cowan Plan, Powell maintained, but Kenya's Minister of Defence and Minister of Africa Affairs had to be held accountable. Unlike those speaking up on the other side of the aisle, however, Powell made no appeal to any universal principle of decency or justice. Rather, his was above all else a political argument. Though appointed civil servants, Kenya's Minister of Defence and Minister of African Affairs were not free from political responsibility.[242] Africa was no longer a political vacuum for the neutral civil servant:

... it is argued that this is Africa, that things are different there. Of course they are. The question is whether the difference between things there and here is such that the taking of responsibility there and here should be upon different

---

[239] '3am: Lennox-Boyd Fights,' *Daily Mail*, 28 July 1959.

[240] Henry Rise, 'The Week in Westminster,' 1 August 1959. POLL 3.1.18.

[241] *Daily Telegraph and Morning Post*, 29 July 1959.

[242] Ibid. Among the pile of newspaper clippings in Powell's 'Hola Camp' file is a lone academic article, written by G. Kitson Clark and published earlier that same year: '"Statesmen in Disguise": Reflexions on the History of the Neutrality of the Civil Service.' The article discusses the history of both domestic and imperial civil service: particularly, the 'neutralization' of civil service from 'political jobbery' in the mid-

principles. We claim that it is our object – and this is something which united both sides of the House – to leave representative institutions behind us wherever we give up our rule. I cannot imagine that it is a way to plant representative institutions to be seen to shirk the acceptance and the assignment of responsibility, which is the very essence of responsible Government.

Britain could not lose itself in that remote detention camp in Kenya. Powell's speech called for a return to their own national standards:

> Nor can we ourselves pick and choose where and in what parts of the world we shall use this or that kind of standard. We cannot say, 'We will have African standards in Africa, Asian standards in Asia and perhaps British standards here at home.' We have not that choice to make. We must be consistent with ourselves everywhere. All Government, all influence of man upon man, rests upon opinion. What we can do in Africa, where we still govern and where we no longer govern, depends upon the opinion which is entertained of the way in which this country acts and the way in which Englishmen act. We cannot, we dare not, in Africa of all places, fall below our own highest standards in the acceptance of responsibility.[243]

Again, Powell's speech worked to affirm the political tradition of Britain – and the character of the Englishman – at a key moment when a rift had begun to develop between the British government and the white settler communities. Powell's words in favour of good governance and colonial responsibility in Kenya worked to distance the 'good word of the Englishman' from the realities of colonial violence. The call to 'be consistent with ourselves' and to uphold the good character of the 'Englishman' resonated with Parliament at a moment when Britain's political elite – and, more broadly, the assumed superiority of 'white civilization' – faced an increasing crisis of authority. As a parliamentary reporter described it, six hundred Members of Parliament on both sides of the aisle sat 'spell bound' by the logic of Powell's argument.[244] This was 'one of the finest parliamentary speeches of the last ten years.'[245]

Importantly, the sense that Britain was 'losing herself' in Africa was directly linked by one MP to Britain's Cold War defence policy. As George Wigg, an influential Labour MP with close contacts in the Security Service, put it that night:

> We have a nuclear deterrent. I do not think that it is very much. I do not think that by any standards it is a deterrent. It is not a deterrent because it is not

---

nineteenth century. The problem in the empire of governance outside of political representation looks to have been a concern of Powell's at this time.

[243] HC, vol. 610, col. 237, 27 July 1959.
[244] Henry Rice, 'The Week in Westminster,' 1 August 1959, p. 3.
[245] Ibid.

credible. We cannot commit national suicide and call it a defence policy; it is not national defence policy.[246]

It was not a national defence policy – it threatened 'national suicide' – because, without armed forces, Britain could not uphold a British standard of 'the rule of law':

> If the worst comes and it is total war and cataclysmic oblivion, it is the end for all of us, but if it does not come the well-being of the society in which we live, the standard of life which we have attained and our civilised way of life can be maintained only by the application of the rule of law, not only in this country, but in those parts of the world for which we are responsible.[247]

Wigg offered an important link here between post-Suez defence policy and Britain's post-imperial identity. In an effort to make substantial cuts to the defence budget, Minister of Defence Duncan Sandys' White Paper of 1957 heralded the ending of conscription and increased reliance on nuclear deterrence. Conscription was to be phased out by 1960. In 1958, Britain signed the US–UK Mutual Defence Agreement which further established Britain's close cooperation with the United States on nuclear policy. This was a moment, then, not only of an increasingly assertive anti-colonialism; it also marks a key shift in the nature of the armed forces, which would, in Wigg's mind, have a profound effect on the ability to rely on the 'good word of the Englishman.' Without British armed forces, Britain had to rely on colonial forces:

> It therefore seems to me that the top priority should not be the bomb or talks about tactical atomic weapons which we have not got and will never get, but the provision of those conventional forces which will maintain the viability of the sterling area, the rule of law and the honour and good name of Britain. I do not think it is an accident that we are concerned at the moment about what happened at Hola and in Nyasaland. There we had the breakdown of the rule of law. What has happened there can be directly attributed to the defence policy of the right hon. Gentleman. If we had had a battalion there – not a battalion of Askaris, with whom I have had the honour to serve – British troops would never have behaved in a way to occasion some of the things stated in the Devlin Report.

The Hola Camp massacre and the police state in Nyasaland are, in this retelling, essentially un-British. They represented, rather, the actions of colonial forces without British leadership. Echoing Powell's arguments for 'British standards,' Wigg used the deaths to criticize defence policy – and a world increasingly not led by Britain's 'civilized way of life.' His words point to an anxiety about the maintenance of that 'civilized way of life' in a Cold War world.

---

[246] HC, vol. 610, col. 86, 27 July 1959.   [247] Ibid.

Powell's Hola Camp speech is today used as the ideal counterpoint to the proposition that Powell was a racist and that therefore Powell's position on immigration was racist. That night on 27 July Barbara Castle asked the Conservative government whether, 'sincerely, and genuinely, without even being aware of it, honourable members opposite do not believe that an African life is as important as a white man's life.'[248] John Hall, the Conservative MP for Leicester South and former Colonial Service member, would argue that the deaths of the eleven men were inevitable and unavoidable because these men were 'sub-human.'[249] Castle had her answer. It was on this point, however, that Powell would help to clear his future name: 'It has been said – and it is fact that these eleven men were the lowest of the low: sub-human was the word which one of my hon. Friends used. So be it. But that cannot be relevant to the acceptance of responsibility for their death.'[250] Further, he insisted, if the government accepted the very premise of the British camps – i.e. rehabilitation – then they must accept Mau Mau insurgents' ability to be human.

Many, on both left and right, argue that Powell's position in the Hola Camp debate proves that he did not believe in the inherent inferiority of the eleven Kenyans. Michael Foot, former leader of the Labour Party, when interviewed by *The Observer* at Powell's death, agreed: 'In 1956 [sic], he spoke brilliantly in the Commons, denouncing the ill-treatment of Mau Mau prisoners in the Hola Camp in Kenya. For this reason I do not think he was ever a racist.'[251] The Conservative Lord William Deedes would write of the speech in *The Telegraph* in 2005 that, 'For good measure, no racist could have made it.'[252] Simon Heffer's official biography on Powell made similar use of the Hola Camp speech. The speech is remembered as a moral, politically defiant act against the party line. However, for all the drama surrounding the debate and Powell's speech and for all the importance of clearing Powell's name, little is actually made of the contents of his argument. For Powell, it was less about the victims than about the character of power. In other words, it was less about liberal belief than about political responsibility.

In Bill Schwarz's three-volume work on race and the memory of the empire, Schwarz takes as his starting point Powell's 'Rivers of Blood' speech in 1968. He argues that the positive response to Powell's speech

---

[248] HC, vol. 610, col. 220, 27 July 1959.
[249] 'Lennox-Boyd Reply,' *Daily Mail*, 28 July 1959.
[250] Ibid.
[251] John Sweeney, 'Powell's Heart of Darkness,' *The Observer*, 15 February 1998.
[252] W. F. Deedes, 'Parliamentary Democracy Needs More Enochs,' *The Telegraph*, 21 October 2005.

was so large and so passionate, because (as Stephen Howe surmised) 'within British civil life there operated self-consciously white identities which echoed or adapted the experience, and imagery, of whites on the frontiers of imperial settler societies – the "white man's countries."'[253] The Powellism of the late 1960s was in large part, Schwarz argues, the 'retrieval and re-articulation' of this identity in Britain.[254] Again, Powell's Hola Camp speech can be understood in this light, as working to affirm the identity of the (colonial) Englishman in the face of a crisis of confidence in the white colonial. Yet this reading must not be detached from Powell's position on national sovereignty – in the specific context of the Cold War and increasing American power abroad.

A year after the Hola Camp deaths, on 21 March 1960, unarmed African protesters were gunned down by South African police in Sharpeville. Sixty-seven were killed and 186 injured.[255] The Pan-Africanist Congress of South Africa had set that day as a day of protest against the pass laws imposed on non-whites in South Africa. A crowd of men, women and children, three thousand in all, had surrounded the Sharpeville police station. Some in the crowd began to throw stones. 'Hands went up in the Africanist salute. Then the shooting started. We heard the chatter of a machine gun, then another, then another ... Before the shooting, I heard no warning to the crowd to disperse.'[256] Powell gave a radio broadcast that week to Israeli listeners. This international broadcast reveals an important corollary to Powell's arguments concerning responsible government in British Kenya. Here, Powell focuses on the international condemnation of the Sharpeville Massacre, especially the condemnation from the United States. According to Powell, by condemning the measures taken against the demonstrators, the United States had committed itself unequivocally to the cause of the bloodshed: 'That is, the blame lay with the authorities.' This was not all. By expressing support for South Africans obtaining redress for their 'legitimate grievances,' America effectively widened the blame beyond the Sharpeville police to include the policy of the

---

[253] Stephen Howe, 'When (If Ever) Did Empire End?: "Internal Decolonisation" in British Culture Since the 1950s,' in Martin Lynn (ed.), *The British Empire in the 1950s: Retreat or Revival?* (Basingstoke: Palgrave Macmillan, 2006), p. 219.

[254] Ibid. In 1968, Powell quotes a 'man on the street' who tells Powell that the black man will have the 'whip hand' over the white man in Britain in a few years – so he is moving his family to Australia. Here is an uncanny re-enactment of colonial settlement. See also Tom Nairn, 'Enoch Powell: The New Right.'

[255] Thomas Patrick Melady, *The Revolution of Color* (New York: Hawthorn Books, 1966), p. 15.

[256] Eyewitness report by Humphrey Tyler, editor of *Drum*, quoted in *Africa Today*, May 1960.

South African government itself. And 'the hope that the aggrieved "will be able" to obtain redress "by peaceful means" became not an exhortation to the aggrieved to be peaceable but a warning to the government not to apply force. The United States has taken up a position, not only against apartheid in South Africa, but against resistance by force to the African peoples of efforts to redress any grievances which the United States judges to be "legitimate."'[257] This was, for Powell, a serious and deeply threatening political transformation. This was the pressure of American power detached from political responsibility.

In Britain, Powell noted approvingly, things had been different. Sharpeville would not be debated in Parliament. Parliament would not debate the domestic actions of a foreign government. That, it is important to note, had already been set down as a parliamentary rule in order to silence the political claims of the Northern Irish in the metropole – they had a Stormont Parliament. Britain was, however, falling under the sway of new thinking. If the events had occurred in Russia, Powell noted, 'the British government would not in the same way have been felt to have some kind of moral responsibility. The contrast with the United States, jerked into public condemnation of a foreign government, is all the sharper. It is a pointer to the kind of dilemma in which Britain is increasingly involved by the modern law and theory of the Commonwealth.'[258] In both the Hola Camp speech and in the Sharpeville broadcast, Powell emphasized the essential link between political responsibility and power. The character of Powell's nationalism – and his thoughts on national sovereignty – were born out of a critique of postwar internationalism. The moral character of this critique, especially in regard to racism, is entirely ambiguous.

About a week prior to Powell's 1959 speech, just across town at the Royal Court Theatre, another group of men and women reacted to the government's report on the Hola Camp deaths. As a Sunday night experimental performance, this group of actors and writers played out the gruesome details of the White Paper itself: men and women improvised as one man stood at a lectern and dispassionately read aloud the report from Hansard to the audience.[259] They acted out the men dying from contaminated water, which had been the official cover-up, and the beating itself. One white officer seized a baton and demonstrated how to beat a man without leaving a mark. Black guards began beating the prisoners 'almost ritualistically' as white camp commandants gave the

---

[257] 'International Commentary,' Broadcast 25 March 1960. POLL 4.1.27.5.
[258] Ibid.
[259] Wole Soyinka, *Ibadan: The Penkelemes Years, A Memoir, 1946–1965* (London: Methuen, 1994), p. 26.

orders: 'one to the left side, then the back, the arms – right, left, front, back. Rhythmically, the cudgels swing in unison … In terms of images, a fluid, near balletic scene.'[260]

William Gaskill, an organizer of the performance, later described it as 'a dramatized protest.' He explained, 'We had never done anything as positively political as this before and the Council was shit-scared.'[261] Reviewed in *The Times* the next day, it was dismissed as 'a loosely documentary charade.'[262] The reviewer went on, 'When he turned to the Cowan [sic] report and the inquest on the dead men the dramatic pressure rose as if by the turn of a switch and now the coloured actors, whose improvisation lost bite from doggedly Brechtian attempts to distance them, could be men in a given situation.'[263] This one-off performance is now better remembered, less for its originality as a dramatized protest, but rather for its reappearance in a speech given in 1986 by one of the play's participants that night: Wole Soyinka.

On 8 December 1986, Wole Soyinka gave a lecture entitled 'This Past Must Address Its Present.'[264] Dedicated to Nelson Mandela, the lecture was given in acceptance of the Nobel Prize that year for Soyinka's work as a playwright. Soyinka is Nigerian, a writer and political activist, but in the late 1950s, he explained, he lived for a short time in England. There, he was active with the Royal Court Theatre in London. On the night of that play, Soyinka sang folk songs at the beginning but refused to participate in the improvisation of the beating. He was pulled onto the stage by the black South African actor Bloke Modisone. They struggled in front of the audience. Soyinka refused to join the performance.

Soyinka's refusal is revealing because it stands in stark contrast to Powell's Hola Camp speech. Soyinka remembered the night as follows:

[The] profound unease, which paralysed my creative will, therefore reached beyond the audience and, finally, I traced its roots to my own feelings of assaulted humanity, and its clamour for a different form of response. It provoked a feeling of indecency about that presentation, rather like the deformed arm of a leper which is thrust at the healthy to provoke a charitable sentiment. This, I believe, was the cause of that intangible, but totally visceral rejection which thwarted the demands of my calling, rendered it inadequate and mocked

---

[260] Wole Soyinka, 'This Past Must Address Its Present,' Nobel Lecture, 8 December 1986.

[261] William Gaskill, *A Sense of Direction* (New York: Limelight Editions, 1990), pp. 37–38.

[262] 'Eleven Men Dead at Hola Camp,' *The Times*, 20 July 1959.

[263] Ibid.

[264] http://nobelprize.org/nobel_prizes/literature/laureates/1986/soyinka-lecture.html.

the empathy of my colleagues. It was as if the inhuman totality, of which that scene was a mere fragment, was saying to us: Kindly keep your comfortable sentiments to yourselves.[265]

Soyinka there felt the fundamental inexpressibility of the Hola Camp massacre. All their 'Brechtian' distance was not enough. While Powell looked for a simple cause and effect, blaming the most recent policy shift toward the Cowan Plan and a failing on the part of the ministers in charge, Soyinka resisted the Hola Camp enactment as an 'exorcism,' for the audience, 'a certificate of release or indeed … a soporific.'[266] The deaths would remain outside a comprehensible, linear narrative of cause and effect.[267] The 'inhuman totality' of the colonial project revealed the truth of Britain's liberal tradition.

With the work of Mahmood Mamdani on the legacies of British imperialism in the Ugandan state, we are reminded of the essential link between the maintenance of state power and the constant construction of political identity:

Whether in its uni- or multicultural version, liberalism presumes the self in self-determination as a cultural self, the 'nation.' Yet, so long as the link between power and identity is obscured, we remain ignorant about how power reproduces certain identities and erodes others. The result is a notion of politics that focuses one sidedly on aggregating given preferences, but not on politics as the changing of preferences. It is the creative dimension of politics – politics as the changing of preferences – that highlights the relationship between power and responses to it, between power and consent, and teaches us that these are not simple opposites, but that power can and does generate its own form of consent.[268]

Whether Powell was conscious of it or not, his Hola Camp speech was, in this sense, a political performance – part of that 'creative dimension in politics' – that exorcised accusations against the party and the government of systemic racism and offered a rewritten narrative of decolonization to the British public, around which Conservative Party power could coalesce. Rather than a picture of decolonization as the British guard ordering the beating to death of a starving Kikuyu man, Powell's speech offered a picture instead of moral outrage and moral rectitude back in London which asserted a divide between Britain's 'civilized way of life' and the actions of white and black Africans. In this sense, Powell – like Macmillan – became 'a symbol of forgetting.'

---

[265] Ibid.   [266] Ibid.
[267] For a discussion of the politics of linear versus traumatic time, see Jenny Edkins, *Trauma and the Memory of Politics* (New York: Cambridge University Press, 2003).
[268] Mahmood Mamdani, 'Historicizing Power and Responses to Power: Indirect Rule and Its Reform,' *Social Research*, 66: 3 (1999), pp. 859–886.

Powell's Hola camp speech: Britain can't apply different standards O/seas to those at home

Clearly, Powell believed that the Kenyan Ministers had to be held responsible for the deaths at Hola. However, Powell's response to the Sharpeville Massacre reveals that Powell's Hola Camp protest cannot be read as a sign of his general opposition to state-led violence against colonial disorder. Nor was Powell's cause anti-racism. Ironically, Powell's speech was a major factor in Macmillan's decision to deliver his 'Wind of Change' speech to the South African Parliament the following year. There, Macmillan dramatically supported the political validity and viability of African nationalisms. As Ritchie Ovendale describes it:

Macmillan himself, though sceptical of universal suffrage, appears in the end to have been most influenced by the moral aspect and its effect on young people of all parties, outlined by Enoch Powell in his speech to the house of commons in which he attacked his own government and said that Britain could not apply different standards in Africa to those at home. That consideration prompted Macmillan to visit Africa.[269]

Cabinet records make clear that foreign policy considerations – 'the need to sustain the revived Anglo-American relationship' and 'the need of the West to maintain a common front in Africa to prevent Soviet penetration'[270] – substantially contributed to Britain's decision to support African majority rule. Yet the violence of white minority rule in British Africa and the deaths at Hola Camp were also increasingly regarded as a political liability at home. Despite the distinct philosophical divide between Macmillan and Powell, the domestic political purchase of Powell's Hola Camp speech set the tone for the Conservative government's subsequent policy of African decolonization.

The day after Powell gave his Hola Camp speech, in the debate on the Devlin Commission Report, Aneurin Bevan told the Commons:

This is the worst Parliament I have been in. Some Parliaments have been called Long Parliaments, some Rump Parliaments. This will be known to history as the Squalid Parliament. It reached its natural end in 1956. It has been kept going all along to try to revive the political fortunes of the Conservative Party. They have made mistake after mistake for which people have had to suffer. There are Africans now lying in their graves who are there as a consequence of the conduct...[271]

The rest of the sentence was lost in the noise, but he pointed dramatically to the Conservative front bench. He then went on to argue that the Conservatives had done more damage to the reputation of Britain in

[269] Ritchie Overdale, 'Macmillan and the Wind of Change in Africa, 1957–1960,' *Historical Journal*, 38: 2 (June 1995), pp. 455–477 (p. 457).
[270] Ibid., pp. 456–457.
[271] 'This Squalid Parliament, Says Bevan,' *Daily Mail*, 29 July 1959.

1956 than any government had done in three centuries. Bevan went so far as to read the words of Lord Malvern, former Prime Minister of the Central African Federation, in the Federal Assembly in 1956: 'We have complete control over our own defence forces,' he said, 'I only hope we shall not have to use them as the North American colonies had to use theirs, because we are dealing with a stupid Government in the United Kingdom.'[272] After the laughter had died down, he pointed to the front bench again, 'Stupid Government – that's them. The new George III.'

All this talk would come to fruition again in only a few years when Rhodesia declared independence. But then in 1959, it served as a condemnation of the Conservative government's credibility and its double standard on Africa. While Dr Banda was seized and imprisoned for being a political leader, white African leaders could freely taunt Britain. This was a government of the past, of an unsuccessful and embarrassing imperialism, the 'new George III.' After Bevan, Labour MP James Callaghan told the Commons that Macmillan, by refusing to ask for the resignation of Colonial Secretary Lennox-Boyd after his mismanagement of the unrest in Nyasaland, indicated that the Prime Minister was 'prepared to sacrifice the future of the people of Nyasaland for the sake of winning a General Election.'[273] This does not appear to be far from the truth. Cabinet papers over these weeks, discussing Hola Camp and the Devlin Report, are clearly far more concerned with the political consequences at home in the run-up to the general election than with violence in Nyasaland or Kenya – revealing the hope that the British voters would remain apathetic to the goings-on of colonial Africa in an economy in which they had 'never had it so good.' The Cabinet discussed the possibility of a 'disciplinary inquiry' into the Hola Camp murders to 'satisfy public opinion in this country,' but this course was rejected, because it was unclear what ground it should cover, '[they] would appear to the public to have given way to Opposition pressure,' and '[i]t would be very difficult to avoid a complete examination by any inquiry of the whole policy of forced labour in rehabilitation … caus[ing] grave embarrassment if through lack of understanding of the circumstances in 1954 it criticized what had been done.'[274] As for Nyasaland, the Monckton Commission, which at the time was criticized for its colonial leanings – would publish a report on constitutional change in Nyasaland and Rhodesia by 1961.

---

[272] Ibid.   [273] Ibid.
[274] 'Hola Detention Camp: Memorandum by the Secretary of State for the Colonies,' CAB 129/97, p. 2.

While Bevan spoke of George III, Macmillan in a speech before the election instead praised the 'humble' empire builders.[275] He had noticed, he said, left-wing speeches and propaganda that praised the Commonwealth and attacked the British Empire, but this was illogical as there would have been no Commonwealth without empire. The empire had brought independence about: 'Where would have been the possibility of making these recent strides forward to liberty and self-government if men and women had not gone out, sometimes to populate the empty lands of the New World and Antipodes, sometimes to bring order and development to backward and primitive peoples in many regions?' He told his audience to disregard the critics and to remember, instead, the humble folk that peopled the empire: 'They have come from the cottage, the vicarage, the manse – aye, from every home throughout this country, for a century of more.' Macmillan still carried the language of that imperial policy pamphlet of 1949. But, for Macmillan, the answer to the lack of public scrutiny about Suez, Hola Camp or Nyasaland was simple. At the next Conservative Party conference in 1960, he offered an answer. In the lead-up to the 1959 general election, Macmillan had also been concerned with the opinion of 'middle voters' regarding Suez and the controversies in colonial Africa. But after twelve months of surveys and articles and political talk about the images of the political parties, it had become clear that the answer to the question 'What is it that the people of Britain, especially young people, want in the 1960s?' was that 'They want to see their country economically sound and prosperous ... They want to earn more ... They want their houses to belong increasingly not to a local council but to them. That is Conservative policy.'[276]

Without further debate in the Commons on the events in British Africa, the Conservatives won the general election. An editorial in *The Times* argued that Labour's failing was that it remained by tradition and popular assumption a party of economic doctrine.[277] It went on:

If the Opposition fixed their point of attack by noting where many Conservatives feel uneasy, they would choose Hola. That is the point at which the Government are most vulnerable ... Hola makes it more plausible for Labour to depict the Conservatives as a party of force and callousness ... But will the country see the Labour Party as the natural and effective guardians of individual liberties, blacks' and whites'? And has the party a Gladstone whom Hola could stir into a campaign of 'righteous passion' ... [The] people would not instinctively look

[275] 'Mr. Macmillan Praises the "Humble Empire Builders,"' *The Times*, 24 September 1959.
[276] 'Macmillan's Hope of Continuing African Federation,' *The Times*, 17 October 1960.
[277] 'In the Country,' *The Times*, 31 July 1959.

to Labour, with its collectivist tradition and the narrow outlook of its rank and file, in the same way as they would look to Liberalism, as the ordained champion of liberty and human rights.[278]

That was, at least according to one observer, the problem: the Labour Party apparently did not stand for 'liberty.' Instead, the Tories were able to successfully play against Labour's disunity on foreign affairs and, most surprisingly to the Labour MP Richard Crossman, their lack of patriotism on Suez.[279] Liberal progressivism, according to this *Times* editorial, had no political home.

Conclusion

Powell was not alone in his concerns about what social planning and mass affluence were doing to 'traditional societies' in Britain. As we have seen, in British civil society at this moment, the systems of social difference that were once wedded to the imperial order were beginning to come unhinged. Britain was, Powell insisted, in a state of 'collective wilful amnesia' about imperial decline, thanks in part to the postwar state's 'expansionist' social and economic policies.[280] In this context, in 1959, at a moment of anxiety about 'national character' and social change in Britain, Powell spoke to the political elite of his generation by insisting that 'the way in which Englishmen act' must be protected through the processes of decolonization. Via Powell, the violence of Hola Camp was, essentially, rewritten as un-British. Powell asserted a divide between their 'civilized way of life' and the actions of white and black Africans. In this sense, Powell became, like Harold Macmillan, another 'symbol of forgetting.' Even more, this ideological response to the violence of decolonization was quite clearly taken up by Harold Macmillan in the 'Wind of Change' speech.

This chapter has tracked Powell's turn from the British Empire, both as a formal body of allegiance and – in its 'modern' form – as a liberal project of development within the Cold War. While Powell's revolt against the ongoing commitment to Britain's liberal mission after empire drew him to the far right politically (causing him to speak out, for instance, against human rights law and, later, in opposition to British sanctions against South Africa), his insistence that the end of empire revealed the failure of this liberal impulse has corollaries on the left. The most famous example is Jean-Paul Sartre.

---

[278] Ibid.
[279] Crossman, *The Backbench Diaries of Richard Crossman*, p. 787.
[280] J. Enoch Powell, 'International Commentary,' 23 October 1959, Radio Broadcast. POLL 4.1.27.

For we in Europe too are being decolonized ... that is to say that the settler which is in every one of us is being savagely rooted out. Let us look at ourselves, if we can bear to, and see what is becoming of us. First, we must face that unexpected revelation, the striptease of our humanism. There you can see it, quite naked, and it's not a pretty sight. It was nothing but an ideology of lies, a perfect justification for pillage; its honeyed words, its affectation of sensibility were only alibis for our aggressions.[281]

Like Sartre, for Powell, the rupture of empire's end revealed the truth of Britain's missionary purpose. The limits of the empire and the nation had been and always would be delineated by material power. As the next chapter will investigate, Powell's refusal to accept the premise that affection or political ideals could constitute a political community eventually found a home – in the race politics of 1960s Britain.

---

[281] Jean-Paul Sartre, 'Preface,' in *The Wretched of the Earth* (New York: Grove Press, 1963), p. 24.

3 Without war? Commonwealth and consensus

Ryan: If one day you form a Ministry – I know you've great feeling for the past of the party – do you see the Tory Party having quite a new image in the rest of the century?

Powell: It will always have to have new clothes. Its worst mistakes have been when it was wearing the external fashions that were half a generation out …

Ryan: Such as when?

Powell: Well, I wonder if we're in danger of it at the moment.

Ryan: Where does that take us back to?

Powell: It takes us back to the wartime and I think much of the post war politics can't be understood without intense study of the last two or three years and the age of the White Papers in the coalition government.

Bowen: You yourself, although you admire the hierarchical principle, would not, would you, describe yourself as being of the Tory Party's hierarchy?

Powell: Let's take the word hierarchical which I used. I mean that the subordination by rank of one man to another – one set of men to another – need not, and in a good society should not, be an affront to the dignity of either. And I believe those societies are happiest and most successful where rank is organic.

Bowen: It is not elective hierarchy that you prefer. You said organic, this suggests hierarchy of birth.

Powell: No. I think anything which is to command authority – or which is to command it most successfully – must exercise that authority because it is accepted. It's acceptance of a form of functioning which is the essence of the happy and successful society – Disraeli again – and the function of the statesman is to make men love their

140

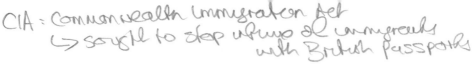

institutions. If that is to be so, the statesman is striving to maintain a harmony between the institutions and the men.

'Frankly Speaking,' Radio Broadcast, 1964[1]

On 12 January 1969, somewhere between four thousand and eight thousand people participated in a march in London against the regime of white minority rule in Rhodesia. The Commonwealth Prime Ministers' conference was going on close by that week at Marlborough House. That day, Prime Minister Harold Wilson's policy of denying Rhodesian independence without a promise of African majority rule was announced by newspapers to be 'dead.'[2] There, too, Home Secretary James Callaghan met with the East African leaders of Uganda, Kenya and Tanzania in an attempt to discuss their policies towards Asian communities, and to negotiate a controlled and staggered emigration of Asians (with British passports) into Britain. During the late 1960s, the Kenyan government, as a nationalist campaign, began to deny Kenyan Asians access to work permits and business licences. Asians in East Africa, especially in rural areas, faced ever-harsher economic constraints. On the day of the march in London, Jagmohan Joshi, a leader of the Indian Workers' Association and organizer of the march, delivered a memorandum to Wilson at 10 Downing Street, calling for the government to stop capitulating to racism, and demanding a repeal of Britain's new racially restrictive immigration law, the Commonwealth Immigrants Act.[3] The Act had been designed to stop the flow of Kenyan Asians with British passports entering Britain. The march, called the 'March for Dignity,' was one of the first major activities that the Indian Workers' Association participated in as a member organization of the newly formed Black People's Alliance.[4] The mile-long procession began at Speakers' Corner at Hyde Park, where it was joined by the Zimbabwe Solidarity Committee. Five thousand protesters marched to 10 Downing Street. Others picketed the South African and Rhodesian embassies. Violence broke out at Rhodesia House when police drove back several waves of demonstrators, then at South Africa House when 400 protesters rushed the building breaking windows and trying to break down doors to enter the

---

[1] 'Frankly Speaking,' 28 February 1964. POLL 4.1.27.

[2] Roy Lewis, 'Africans Seek New Pledge,' *The Times*, 13 January 1969.

[3] 'Battle of the Strand in South Africa and Rhodesia Protest,' *The Times*, 13 January 1969.

[4] J. Joshi, 'Report of the General Secretary: Presented at the National Conference of the Indian Workers' Association, Nottingham on November 7–8 1970,' p. 21. IWA, MS 2141 10/3.

building. Two white protesters, Ian Middlehurst and Jon Coles, tore down the Rhodesian flag and hoisted the Union Jack over Rhodesia House – there they remained with the Union Jack on the roof until midnight. Perhaps only unwittingly reasserting British responsibility, they later explained to reporters that they had not known which flag to fly to represent freedom.[5]

Meanwhile, Joshi and other members of the Black Peoples' Alliance delivered their memorandum to Wilson at Downing Street. As well as arguing for a repeal of the Commonwealth Immigrants Act (passed under a Labour government in 1968), they called for 'the equal treatment of all peoples' and for the strengthening of anti-discrimination laws in employment and housing.[6] By this time, after the 'Rivers of Blood' speech, Enoch Powell had already become a rallying point for black Britons; he had become the veritable symbol of the racist Establishment. And so, the Indian Workers' Association carried an effigy of Enoch Powell in a coffin. The demonstrators chanted against Powell in this funeral procession. Outside No. 10, the effigy of Enoch Powell was taken from his coffin and set alight in the middle of the road.[7]

The meaning of Powell's burning effigy at No. 10 is not exactly the story of this chapter. Rather, we must focus now on the coffin. To indicate what the Black People's Alliance thought of the remaining value of the Commonwealth, the coffin was painted black on one side – labelled *Common* – and white on the other – labelled *wealth*.[8] The 'Common/ wealth' was condemned as morally bankrupt. Immigration restrictions and the failure to stop white minority rule in Africa had underlined the truth of the political order. Powell and the Commonwealth were ritually denounced, remarkably, as one. In 1969, Powell and the Commonwealth, or the hope of an imperial past made good and profitable, were, in one act, put to death.

This chapter focuses, then, on what the Rhodesian newspaper *The Chronicle* dismissively called: 'the most malleable body in history, twisting, turning and contorting itself to accommodate new ideas and ideologies.'[9] The Commonwealth, as a collection of independent states that shared a history of empire, served as an essential rhetorical bridge to Britain's post-imperial status and new 'moral' role in the Cold War. Its twists and turns and contortions outline a politics in transition. As the

---

[5] *Wolverhampton Express and Star*, 13 January 1969.
[6] 'Battle of the Strand in South Africa and Rhodesia Protest,' *The Times*, 13 January 1969.
[7] Ibid.   [8] Ibid.
[9] 'Kissing in the Club,' *The Chronicle*, 17 January 1966. SRO, D3123/240.

previous chapter emphasized, Powell's political frustrations within the Conservative Party in the postwar years reveal something of the ideological parameters of Conservative thinking on decolonization. From a lone figure opposing 'American imperialism' in 1953, Powell emerged in 1965 as the man who, to a standing ovation, told the Conservative Party conference that Britain was a 'European power' that needed to refrain from involvement in the fight against communism 'East of Suez' (in other words, in America's war in Vietnam).[10] As the *New York Times* put it, Powell enunciated 'the potential declaration of independence from American foreign policy.'[11] There, Powell argued against Britain's continued involvement in the newly independent countries of Asia and Africa. He insisted on the need for non-nuclear military defence. There, we see an implicit connection between the presence of war and the command of authority – or national defence and that 'harmony between the institutions and the men.' This chapter charts the connections Powell drew between foreign and domestic policy and his efforts to construct a new post-imperial nationalism. For Powell, the nation-state was the 'ultimate political reality.' There was 'no political reality beyond it.'[12] In an effort to salvage that reality, Powell in 1963 argued for a 'new patriotism' – oriented towards entrepreneurship and a post-imperial national pride.[13] Critically, Powell argued that this post-imperial pride required a 'clean break' from Britain's imperial past.[14] This was a past that doomed Britain to a state of decline—or a present continually overshadowed by lost glory.

This chapter concludes in Africa, with Rhodesia's Unilateral Declaration of Independence and the Kenyan Asian refugee crisis, where Britain's relationship to the imperial past was put to the test. Beyond Powell, it begins to tell the story of the break-up of the 'anaesthetizing rhetoric' of British political discourse on decolonization – or the widespread (though, by the 1960s, faltering) commitment to Britain's 'world role' as moral leader in the Commonwealth.[15] It is possible to see, in the twists and turns of the Commonwealth and in the language

---

[10] J. Enoch Powell, 'To the Brighton Conference,' October 1965, in *Reflections of a Statesman*, pp. 624–627 (p. 624).

[11] Cited in Heffer, *Like the Roman*, pp. 391–392.

[12] Ibid., p. 153.

[13] See, for instance: J. Enoch Powell, speech at the S.W. Norfolk Conservative Fete, 15 June 1963. POLL 4.1.1.

[14] 'A Conservative' [J. Enoch Powell], 'Patriotism Based on Reality Not Dreams,' *The Times*, 2 April 1964.

[15] John Darwin, 'Decolonization and the End of Empire,' in Robin W. Winks (ed.), *The Oxford History of the British Empire, Vol. V: Historiography* (Oxford University Press, 1999), p. 547.

of the Unilateral Declaration of Independence, the uncertain legacy of the Second World War. In a variety of ways, Powell contributed to a loss of faith in the British state's moral role – both inside and outside of Britain. Broadly, this was a rejection of a reconstructed 'peaceful' empire of welfare and development. This was a rejection of utopian visions of the reconstructed state. And it is in this political work that Powell's role in the making of postcolonial Britain truly begins.

Commonwealth in transition

In the early 1960s, in the wake of anti-colonial political successes and increasing international criticism of racism in Africa, a notable number of academic publications began work to historicize the very notion of political authority and empire.[16] Margery Perham – one of the last famous civil servants of colonial Africa – offered one such example in a series of Reith Lectures in 1961 on BBC Radio entitled 'The Colonial Reckoning.' Perham told her radio listeners that despite the widespread moral condemnations that Britain faced, the British Empire – and Britain's imperial mission – could not be judged by contemporary moral standards. It was and had been too large and diverse, too alive and changing. She insisted, rather, that due to anti-colonialism – and, in part, as a consequence of the United States' and the Soviet Union's stake in anti-colonialism – the world had forsaken the colonial 'partnership' and had divided instead into a terrible conflict between white and black: Congo troubles, Mau Mau in Kenya, the Algerian War and the violence against West Indian immigrants in Notting Hill she mentioned in one breath.[17] The desire to morally reckon with the British Empire, Perham concluded, was an unfortunate consequence of the Cold War politicization of race. The anti-colonialist was encouraged to criticize the morality of the past and present 'British Empire' without boundaries:

What confuses the issue is that they constantly extend the idea from the British colonial empire to that of all European powers and slide into a denunciation of Western domination in general. *They shift from past to present and to even future fears* … It seems that not only are the Western empires to be regarded as an evil, but the very possession of economic and military power is itself to be considered discreditable.[18]

---

[16] For an influential example, see also Richard Koebner, *Empire* (New York: Cambridge University Press, 1962). See also Margery Perham (ed.), *Diaries of Lord Lugard*, vols. I, II, III, IV (London: Faber and Faber, 1959 and 1963).
[17] Margery Perham, *The Colonial Reckoning: The End of Imperial Rule in Africa in the Light of British Experience* (London: Alfred A. Knopf, 1962), p. 4.
[18] Ibid., p. 14 (my emphasis).

The anti-colonialist failed, Perham argued, to appreciate changes in the 'established order' over time. Condemning all authority, what Perham calls the recent 'escape from authority' found throughout the world, reverses sixty centuries of esteem.[19] Here, we see an echo of Powell's concerns over the 'moral' politics of new international thinking and the Americanization of the international order. 'Today' in 1961, she argued, was unlike the past and the difference between past and present could not be traversed by moral judgment: 'Today we are at least *trying* to escape, through international cooperation ... from the old law of the jungle. But this was the law which ruled international relations through all the years of our empire until the very latest, and which bound men in the dilemma between moral man and immoral society.'[20] Perham would in the years ahead be active in promoting the protection of the historical archives of the British Empire for prosperity – from leading protests against the British state's systematic destruction of documents concerning Mau Mau suppression in 1961 to creating, after seeing the 'sense of rejection' of those in the colonial service and the devaluation of their achievements, the Oxford University Colonial Records Project in 1963.[21]

While historians largely concur that in these years Britain faced 'a veritable crisis of national self-representation,'[22] they do not agree on the relative significance of the loss of the empire in that crisis.[23] As well as losing an empire, they remind us, the British state faced an end to its national purpose found in war, a decline in global economic status and the growing dominance of the United States and Cold War political tensions.[24] But is there historical evidence to suggest a *postcolonial* crisis? Within the historical literature, it remains strongly disputed whether such evidence can be found, especially at the level of popular culture, and – perhaps even more – what would constitute a sign of any

[19] Ibid., p. 15.   [20] Ibid., p. 22.

[21] Musila Musembi, *Archives Management: The Kenyan Experience* (Africa Book Services, 1985) and Margery Perham, 'Reappraisal of the Colonial Bogey,' *The Times*, 23 June 1971.

[22] Waters, '"Dark Strangers" in Our Midst,' p. 208.

[23] See Howe, 'Internal Decolonization?,' pp. 286–304. Perhaps the most widely read opposition to the argument that the empire mattered to British national identity can be found in Bernard Porter, in his *The Absent-minded Imperialists*. Porter argues that between 1815 and 1914 Britain's domestic political culture (if such a thing could exist across the cultures of class) was actually profoundly detached from British imperialism – even at its height. Against the current trend of 'cultural "theorists" who have teased imperial subtexts from the most unlikely cultural products,' he argues that the empire really *happened* on the periphery, not to the British but to the Americans, the Canadians, the Australians and the South Africans. The white frontier identity had very little parlance, Porter argues, inside Britain itself.

[24] Paul Addison, *Now the War is Over: A Social History of Britain, 1945–1951* (London: Jonathan Cape, 1985).

postcolonial crisis in postwar Britain. As will be discussed below, we do see concern among Powell and some of his contemporaries that traditional society in Britain, or the legitimacy of the class order, was married in some way to imperial power.[25] And we see increasing criticism, from the late 1950s onwards, over the state of national culture within British intellectual circles, which was concerned – at least in part – with imperial decline.[26] But Perham's words point to an understanding of Britain's postcolonial crisis as more than mere declinism. She points to a (moral) crisis of state authority.

This particular vision of Britain's postcolonial crisis, this colonial reckoning, is not entirely separate from the broad critique of the international order which emerged in response to the state-sanctioned atrocities and genocide of the Second World War. Out of war, there grew a liberal consensus on the need to reconstruct the international order on a new basis, one that rested on commitments beyond the maintenance of state sovereignty and protected the 'human rights' of the individual.[27] Despite the efforts of colonial authorities to limit the reach of 'human rights' in their colonial affairs, Perham's words emphasize that the moral challenge of the Second World War could not be contained. As one Canadian commentator argued, it was in remembering the Nazis that the meaning and value of the Commonwealth became clear.[28] Likewise, parliamentarians and, later, British race relations experts would frequently refer to the spectre of fascism to prove Britain's special obligation to set an example of racial tolerance at home and abroad.[29]

The shifting popular understandings of the international order that Perham describes have links, too, to the emerging ideological significance of 'development aid' in the Commonwealth. Alongside the inward-looking postwar cultural politics of the home and 'never had it so good' consumerism – and (as Wendy Webster argues) the turn to the inviolate, incorruptible 'Little England' – ran awkwardly for a short time a politically expansive idea in the Commonwealth of an imperial past made good.[30] A major government inquiry on the empire resulted in two reports

[25] See Porter, 'The Empire Strikes Back,' pp. 11–13, and David Cannadine, *Class in Britain* (Harmondsworth: Penguin, 1998).

[26] Ward, *British Culture and the End of Empire*, pp. 8–9.

[27] Jay Winter, 'From War Talk to Rights Talk: Exile Politics, Human Rights, and the Two World Wars,' in Spiering and Wintle (eds.), *European Identity and the Second World War*, pp. 65–66.

[28] See Pierre Berton in the CBC Radio Special, 'Canada must "show some moral guts" against apartheid' (23 February 1961), CBC Digital Archive.

[29] See Brown, *Political Languages of Race*.

[30] Webster, *Englishness and Empire*. As Webster explains, the ideal was born in the war years so as to ensure political allegiance and manpower and due, also, to newly accepted theories of planned economic development.

delivered to Cabinet in 1957 and 1958; these insisted that Britain's future was not the surrender of international power but, in fact, a transformation in the nature of power into informal control over former colonies through the Commonwealth. Influence *required* formal withdrawal: 'We shall not maintain our influence if we appear to be clinging obstinately to the shadow of our old Imperial power after its substance has gone.'[31] As we shall see, this concerted effort to maintain influence via informal imperialism sat uneasily alongside the language of racial partnership and political development in the Commonwealth. And so, at its political height, between 1957 and 1961, international aid from the British government more than doubled (from 81 to 180 million pounds).[32] Five-sixths of this aid would be administered through bilateral channels, not international agencies like the World Bank or the UN. This, controversially, avoided 'anonymity' and stressed 'our historic ties,' as well as Britain's continued economic power.[33]

Despite its significance in understanding Britain's decolonizing state, the problem with writing about the Commonwealth in the domestic history of 1960s Britain is that it appears, at first glance, so uncontentious that it does not require a close analysis. Despite its twists and turns and contortions, there was no significant national debate on the merits of the Commonwealth in the lead-up to the 1959, 1964 or 1966 general elections. It was, rather, a seemingly insignificant component of the political consensus – taken for granted and taken up by both Labour and Conservative.[34] In the larger political narrative now told, its role has been as obstacle to a viable future in the European Economic Community (EEC).[35] It did not carry the force of history, as many of its proponents imagined; it rather hung on, morbidly, to an unforgivable past. Yet the Commonwealth concept may still tell us a great deal about the political imagination of various communities in postwar Britain and diverse understandings of Britain's transition to postcolonial status. For instance, at the elite level, it was a commitment to the loyalties of the Old Commonwealth, to the inherent connectedness of Australia, Canada, New Zealand and South

[31] July 1958 report as cited in French, *The British Way in Counter-Insurgency, 1945–1967*, p. 236.
[32] *A Changing Partnership: A Report by the Young Conservatives on Problems of the Commonwealth* (London: Conservative Political Centre No. 248, 1962), p. 18.
[33] Ibid., p. 21.
[34] John W. Young, 'International Factors and the 1964 Election,' *Contemporary British History*, 21: 3 (2007), pp. 351–371 and Hugo Young, *This Blessed Plot: Britain and Europe from Churchill to Blair* (Basingstoke: Macmillan, 1998), pp. 139, 156.
[35] For a discussion of this historiography, see Gabriele Clemens, 'A History of Failure and Miscalculations? Britain's Relationship to the European Communities in the Postwar Era (1945–1973),' *Contemporary European History*, 13, 2 (2004), pp. 223–232.

Africa, rather than a belief in racial equality, that caused many British politicians to oppose immigration restrictions from the Commonwealth after the Second World War.[36] But, in this section, we will turn to a particular point of transition in the Commonwealth, to its rapid expansion in the early 1960s and to the debates within Britain about the meaning of that expansion. This will uncover aspects of Perham's 'colonial reckoning' and will provide the crucial backdrop to Powell's nationalist arguments prior to and after Labour's victory in 1964 – when, in opposition, Powell argued that the Conservative Party had to find itself (or find its Tory authority) again.

The expansion of the Commonwealth from 'Old' to 'New' – with the membership of India, Pakistan, Ghana, Malaysia and Nigeria by 1960 – required a transformation in its public meaning. What had once represented the natural rise of settler colonies to independence – or the natural political proclivities of the British race around the globe – could, by 1960, represent for some of its supporters the future possibilities of an 'intimate inter-relationship' with 'inherent moral ends' of a 'Euro-Afro-Asian Commonwealth.'[37] This new endpoint required a rewriting of Britain's imperial history that legitimized Britain's role at independence;[38] it also, just as importantly, required a move to define the ties of the Commonwealth, both literally and metaphorically, as something other than the ties of race and family. As renowned Commonwealth historian Keith Hancock put it in 1937, the Commonwealth was 'nothing else than the "nature" of the British Empire, defined, in Aristotelian fashion, by its end.'[39] Because his generation, unlike those before or after, had been uniquely born into a 'heritage of the Empire,' noted Powell, they wrongly believed the end of empire to be 'the culmination of a majestic pre-determined historical process.'[40] His generation faced a political challenge:

We have continuously to adjust ourselves to a world not that in which I was born … a world in which there is no longer a British Viceroy and Governor General on the throne of the Moguls in Delhi … [which was] bred into the bone of our thinking and talking. This creates a difficult and also dangerous ambivalence and psychological tension between our emotions and observable reality. It is the business of politics to mediate the resolution of such tensions.[41]

---

[36] Hansen, *Citizenship and Immigration in Post-war Britain*.
[37] Patrick Gordon Walker, *The Commonwealth* (London: Secker & Warburg, 1962), pp. 381, 382.
[38] Cannadine, *Ornamentalism*, p. 189.
[39] W. David McIntyre, 'Clio and Britannia's Lost Dream,' p. 525.
[40] Enoch Powell, 'German Service,' 17 June 1965, Radio Broadcast. POLL 4.1.26.
[41] J. Enoch Powell, Interview with Julian Critchley, *Crossbow* (April–June 1966), as cited in Berkeley, *The Odyssey of Enoch*, p. 59.

Rather than courageously recognizing Britain's place in the world and the threatening hegemony of the United States, the political elite of his generation – especially the Conservative elite – were, according to Powell, showing themselves to be cowards, working to ensure that a self-consoling narrative of Britain's noble civilizing mission continue, in theory at least, via the United Nations, colonial development and the Commonwealth.[42] Powell's answer to the question, 'What has happened to the British Empire on which the sun never sets?' was that 'It never existed.' It was not, he explained, the more conventional answer, 'It has changed into something better and nobler still, which we would like to call the British Commonwealth.'[43]

The years that brought the emergence of the 'New Commonwealth' saw 'history' and 'friendship' in print and in public speeches increasingly replace the traditional political focus on the Commonwealth 'family.' Instead of blood and iron, instead of war and allegiance, Britain was to be a 'first-rate *moral* leader, setting an example for the rest of the world.'[44] Both the Conservative and Labour governments spoke similarly in these years in terms of the promotion of trade, economic aid and development as the means of forging stronger political links.[45] It was described, by its supporters, as the ultimate political bridge: 'between the continents of the world,'[46] 'between the Western bloc and the Communist bloc,'[47] and the 'arch linking North America to Asia with the United Kingdom as always in the position of the keystone.'[48] For a while, the Commonwealth ideal had the advantage in Britain of what writer Paul Foot in 1965 called 'electoral irrelevance.'[49] It would, however, be firmly linked by 1965 – by Powell and others – under the shadow of news from South Africa, Rhodesia and the United States, to a 'colour problem' that was seen to exactly threaten the culture of (white) domesticity and the promises of postwar reconstruction.

At the beginning of 1960 – after Iain Macleod's decisive appointment as Minister of Colonial Affairs and Macmillan's 'Wind of Change' speech – the Conservative Party, for the first time, embraced the rapid

---

[42] J. Enoch Powell, 'German Service,' 17 June 1965, Radio Broadcast. POLL 4.1.26.
[43] Ibid.
[44] Dilip Hiro, *Black British, White British* (Middlesex: Penguin, 1971), p. 189.
[45] Trevor R. Reese, 'Keeping Calm About the Commonwealth,' *International Affairs*, 41: 3 (July 1965), pp. 451–462 (p. 455).
[46] Cmnd 2276: Plowden Report on Representational Services Overseas (London: HMSO. 1964), in Reese, 'Keeping Calm,' p. 452.
[47] M. S. Rajan, *The Post-War Transformation of the Commmonwealth* (London: Asia Publishing House, 1963), review in *International Affairs* (October 1964) in Reese, 'Keeping Calm,' p. 452.
[48] *The Round Table*, vol. 53, no. 211 (June 1963).
[49] Paul Foot, *Immigration and Race in British Politics* (Harmondsworth: Penguin Books, 1965), p. 174.

decolonization of British Africa.[50] As Powell's biographer, T. E. Utley, noted at the time, Toryism was, consequently, at a crossroads with the Commonwealth. He asked, '[I]s there still a case for this institution? If so, what is it? The Conservative answer is no doubt an automatic "yes"; but what are the implications of this affirmative?' Utley drew out the implications for the party. African independence struggles were presented by Utley as the beginning of inevitable racial violence and disorder. In South Africa, in the Central African Federation, in Kenya, Britain was to face in the Commonwealth the task of 'holding the ring' in 'the fiercest of human conflicts, the conflict of the races.'[51]

At the same time, the emphasis on a kind of moral development – and notion of British 'moral' leadership – would increasingly come to the fore when discussing 'race relations' in Britain in these years. As in the United States, racism in Britain carried an international meaning. It was, for both, a Cold War liability.[52] A political language of moral superiority and capital development continued to require Britain to be 'above' the 'colour problem' at home. Meanwhile, Perham's and Utley's warnings of a 'race war' reflect an emerging language of race in Britain, one that cannot be entirely divorced from the increasingly significant US civil rights movement and an American or 'Atlantocentric' black/white construction of race.[53]

Critics of the Commonwealth such as conservative journalist Peregrine Worsthorne rejected the possibility that its success would be possible by 'polite pressures,' without force and with only friendship in 'a world in revolution.'[54] The idea that 'Britain is not losing an Empire but gaining a Commonwealth' was comforting to conservative sensibilities but this 'attractive picture' amounted to 'nothing less than a world-wide diplomatic and political self-denying ordinance.'[55] Worsthorne concluded with a call for political 'realism':

Is it a true masterpiece of statesmanship or a brilliantly varnished forgery that cannot bear close examination? … I have a suspicion that the Commonwealth idea, civilised, urbane, subtle as it is, also overlooks the true nature of the contemporary world and the role which force must still play in it. It is a method, in short, of escaping from, rather than dealing with, international reality.[56]

---

[50] Peregrine Worsthorne, 'Bonds that Could Become Fetters,' *Daily Telegraph* (5 March 1960).

[51] T. E. Utley, 'Toryism at the Cross-roads,' *Daily Telegraph* (18 February 1960).

[52] For discussion of the 'colour problem' in the United States as a Cold War problem, see for instance, Mary Dudziak, 'Brown as a Cold War Case,' *The Journal of American History*, 91: 1 (2004), pp. 32–42.

[53] For a critique of this, see Tariq Mamood, *Not Easy Being British: Colour, Culture and Citizenship* (London, 1992).

[54] Worsthorne, 'Bonds that Could Become Fetters.'

[55] Ibid.   [56] Ibid.

Powell kept Worsthorne's article in his scrapbook, wherein he usually saved only articles by or about himself.[57] Worsthorne's rejection of the Commonwealth as a forgery would be echoed only a few years later in Powell's description of it as 'farce': what had once been real power – and therefore unity – was pathetically re-enacted without meaning.[58]

But there was a fine line between conservative scepticism regarding the Commonwealth and thinly veiled assumptions about racial superiority. Worsthorne's view of Ghanaian membership in the Commonwealth, expressed in a published letter from Ghana in 1959, is a case in point. Ghana was the Commonwealth's first African-led government. In Worsthorne's mind, Ghana was not ready, in the deepest sense, for parliamentary democracy:

Before granting independence the British … dressed up Ghana's infant body politics in a political uniform which was so vastly too large that any movement at all involved contortions bound to be both ridiculous and destructive. The truth is that whereas Ghanaians were quite capable of defending their primitive liberties under the kind of limited autocracy to which they were accustomed, they have proved quite incapable of defending the grandiose liberties provided by a parliamentary democracy.[59]

Worsthorne called Ghana's leader, Kwame Nkrumah, a bull in a china shop, with the 'rule of law, freedom of opposition, two-party Government, habeas corpus – lying shattered and trodden underfoot.'[60] The inevitable failure of parliamentary democracy is proven in the Ghanaian government's efforts to squash the political opposition at this time. Any other African leader would have done the same, he says. And 'Nobody with any sense of history should find this at all surprising.'[61] Except, that is, for the British:

It only surprises the British because they took their own imperial propaganda seriously. Unwilling to admit that they were withdrawing from the Gold Coast because they were not prepared to make the effort to stay, they pretended they were withdrawing because the Africans were ripe for parliamentary self-government.[62]

Again, we see a critique of the liberal belief in a reconstructed empire of development. John Hatch, the Labour Party's Commonwealth Officer, rightly criticizes Worsthorne's tendency here to view 'everything which

[57] See POLL 12.1.3.
[58] 'A Conservative' [J. Enoch Powell], 'Patriotism Based on Reality Not on Dreams,' *The Times*, 2 April 1964.
[59] Peregrine Worsthorne, 'Trouble in the Air: Letter from Ghana,' *Encounter* (May 1958), pp. 3–13 (p. 3).
[60] Ibid.
[61] Ibid., p. 6.   [62] Ibid.

he either does not understand or disagrees with' in Ghana as having 'some connection with racial origins.'[63] Worsthorne, meanwhile, (superficially) applauds the lessening of prejudice based on the colour of skin but, from there, argues that his own colour-blindness revealed the true depth of difference between himself and Ghanaians. In this, we find an acceptance of a postwar shift in the language of race alongside the maintenance of race as a facile marker of political development. African politics, which at one time could be dismissed as an 'elaborate charade,' was now, with African power, a fact that had to be taken seriously:

The truth is that far from closing the gap between Africa and Europe, the evaporation of colour prejudice may well tend to widen it. So long as white men and black men were separated by irrational colour prejudice which kept them at arm's-length, neither bothered to get to know the other ... The whites regarded the blacks as unassimilable, and the blacks regarded the whites as unapproachable. Neither took the other seriously. Today they take each other very seriously indeed. When I first arrived in Ghana it seemed rather comic; it all seemed an elaborate charade, as indeed it used to be in the colonial days. But now that the Ministers really are Ministers and exercise real power, one soon forgets how they are dressed and how they talk. These characteristics no longer seem worth noticing. One listens to what they have to say instead of being amused by how they say it ... one seeks to discover what is going on beneath the skin instead of being fascinated by its colour.

But, to Worsthorne, what lies beneath the skin is a disappointment: these men are not Europeans.

The point is surely that so long as the colour of the black man was the most interesting thing about him the whites never bothered with other differences. Now that the colour bar is ended and the black man has achieved his independence, we are being forced to probe a little deeper. My own impression is that this process, far from leading to an inter-racial 'synthesis,' has instead created a clearer awareness of basic antithesis. I found it impossible, for example, to discuss politics with a great majority of Ghanaians whom I met. One gets on all right for the first half hour, which in the old days would have been all that was called for. But once the conversation descends below the level of banality all contact is lost. So long as one does not try to analyse what is actually meant by 'freedom,' 'democracy,' etc., everything goes swimmingly. But once the conversation launches out into the meaning behind these words it soon dries up.[64]

Worsthorne underlines the limited reach of the new language of racial equality, even questioning Ghanaian leaders' ability to understand the true meaning of the words 'freedom' and 'democracy.' But even more

[63] John Hatch, 'Africa, in Black and White,' *Encounter* (June 1959), pp. 64–65 (p. 64).
[64] Worsthorne, 'Trouble in the Air,' pp. 12–13.

surprising is – linked to this – his view that Ghana could not live up to membership in the Commonwealth. He goes so far as to argue that Britain's efforts to support Ghana's Commonwealth membership, and forgive the limits of parliamentary democracy there, threatened Britain's own political integrity with a double standard of values. As the South African journalist Colin Legum writes in response in Worsthorne: 'if there is a doctrinal affinity that would justify Ghana's exclusion from the Commonwealth, what of Pakistan with its military dictatorship ... or of South Africa with its denial of the basic ethic of Western democracy?'[65] At this time, double standards in the Commonwealth were no new thing – what was new was that Africans now exercised real power within it.

It was due to South Africa, not Ghana, that Britain's double standard in values first reached a point of crisis. In the spring of 1960, the Sharpeville massacre led to international condemnation of the system of apartheid. That same year, South Africa's continued membership was in question, after the National Party government declared South Africa would become a republic the following year. While representatives of Britain denied the legal legitimacy of Commonwealth or UN pressure on the domestic political affairs of its member states according to their official charters, five Commonwealth members in Africa and Asia joined the South African United Front against South Africa's continued membership.[66] They, in essence, redrew the political parameters of the Commonwealth by insisting on their power to influence South Africa's domestic life. 'Friendship' meant a shared set of political principles. As an assertion of sovereignty and independence (to maintain white minority rule), the South African Prime Minister, H. F. Verwoerd, withdrew South Africa's application, as a republic, for membership in the Commonwealth at the Commonwealth Prime Ministers' Conference of 1961.

For Powell, Sharpeville revealed the kind of dilemma Britain increasingly faced due to 'the modern law and theory of the Commonwealth.'[67] The Commonwealth, he argued immediately after Sharpeville, held no common denominator at all – 'neither origin, law, constitution nor policy.' It was, rather, a political fiction, which in theory can be 'serviceable, or at least harmless' but which, in this case, had outlived its usefulness for Britain and could 'do actual harm.'[68] Britain held responsibilities in

[65] Colin Legum, 'Politics and Race,' *Encounter* (June 1959), p. 66.
[66] 'Preview of 1961 Commonwealth Prime Ministers' Conference,' CBC Television News, 22 January 1961.
[67] J. Enoch Powell, 'International Commentary 25 March 1960.' POLL 4.1.27.
[68] Ibid.

Central Africa, to the Federation and to the British settler. Holding within the same system, however 'shadowy and fictitious,' an increasing number of independent states in West and East Africa as well as Rhodesia and the Union of South Africa was, Powell argued, close to impossible. Britain's task, rather than an obligation to an ideal, was to bring about the transition to 'inevitable African self-government and independence' without both avoidable injustice and violence and avoidable economic loss.[69] As will be discussed below, this was a task that Powell would quickly give up when it came to Rhodesia's Unilateral Declaration of Independence.

Racism in Africa remained, throughout the decades to come, the touchstone of debate on the meaning of post-imperial community. On 23 February 1961, the Committee of Concern for South Africa gathered at Toronto's Massey Hall to pressure Canadian Prime Minister John Diefenbaker to refuse the readmittance of the new Republic of South Africa into the Commonwealth. The speech delivered by the author and commentator Pierre Berton was broadcast to Canadian radio-listeners that night. Here, too, we see a liberal effort to break with the 'myth' of the Commonwealth. Berton maintained that, if the Republic of South Africa were readmitted, the Commonwealth would have 'lost its meaning' and become 'an umbrella for hypocrisy.'[70] With South African membership, the Commonwealth was little more than a gentlemen's club:

We've raised the victims of half a dozen sovereign states which don't belong to the so-called 'free world', but because South Africa still remains a cozy member of the cozy little club, we haven't uttered a peep. Why? Because of this myth that however hideously its members may act, the Commonwealth is somehow sacred and must be held together at all costs even if the cost is that silence which has been our shame. Now over the past year, especially since the Sharpeville Massacre, a great many people have started to ask themselves exactly what it is the Commonwealth stands for.[71]

Those who believed in the polite pressures of the Commonwealth suffered, he argued, from 'the same kind of wishful thinking that produced the gibberish of Munich.'[72] Berton ridiculed the notion that Canada shared any 'common ground of British tradition' with 'the Malans, the Strijdoms and the Verwoerds.'[73] This was, rather, history repeating itself: 'These "let's not be beastly to the South Africans" discussions remind me of bull sessions I used to have back in college on what we should or shouldn't do about the Nazis around 1936 and '37.'[74] The analogy continued throughout the speech. By remembering Nazism, the value of the Commonwealth was clear.

[69] Ibid.
[70] Pierre Berton in the CBC Radio Special, 'Canada must "show some moral guts" against apartheid' (23 February 1961), CBC Digital Archive.
[71] Ibid.   [72] Ibid.   [73] Ibid.   [74] Ibid.

Berton insisted on the need for economic sanctions. Without sanctions against South Africa, Berton warned: 'We are dangerously close to having two Commonwealths, one marked white and the other marked black. And that's what's going to happen if the white nations all vote one way at the Commonwealth conference, and the coloured nations vote the other way. Nothing could be worse; it would be the end of it.'[75] According to Berton, this was a defining moment for Canada; this was a moment that required not Britain but Canada – as 'the oldest and most powerful member of the Commonwealth' – to lead the countries of Africa and Asia.[76]

In the immediate aftermath of the critical and divisive 1961 Commonwealth Prime Ministers' Conference, Macmillan instructed the Commonwealth Relations Office to push for a redefinition of the term 'British' in official usage.[77] What had once been used to refer to all 'British' governments around the globe was to refer solely to the narrower 'home' constituency of the United Kingdom.[78] Stuart Ward cites this moment as a critical turn away from expansive ideas of Britishness – as either racial category or historical/political concept. In 1962, Macmillan told the next Commonwealth Prime Ministers' Conference that, 'It used to be fashionable to refer to the Commonwealth as a family ... But now ... we can best think of the Commonwealth as a group of friends and relations.'[79] At the same time, as Britain's economic relationship with the Common Market increased in significance and as the international tariff negotiations via GATT further eroded the value of Commonwealth trade preferences, so too did government concern over Commonwealth reactions to Britain's immigration policy fade.[80]

Meanwhile public sentiment for the Commonwealth – found for instance in the 1961 Gallup Poll that found that 48 per cent of respondents named the Commonwealth 'the most important to Britain' compared to 19 per cent for America and 18 per cent for Europe[81] – was, Macmillan asserted, really limited to the old Commonwealth countries.[82] BBC television

---

[75] Ibid.   [76] Ibid.
[77] Stuart Ward, 'The End of Empire and the Fate of Britishness,' in Helen Brocklehurst and Robert Phillips (eds.), *History, Nationhood and the Question of Britain* (Basingstoke: Palgrave Macmillan, 2004), p. 251.
[78] Macmillan to Sandys, 20 June 1961, in Ward, 'The End of Empire,' p. 251.
[79] Cited in Harold Macmillan, *At the End of the Day, 1961–1963* (London: Macmillan, 1973), pp. 527–528.
[80] Webster, *Englishness and Empire*, p. 175.
[81] Stuart Ward, '"Commonwealth or Europe?" Macmillan's Dilemma, 1961–1963,' in Alex May (ed.), *Britain, the Commonwealth and Europe: The Commonwealth and Britain's Application to Join the European Communities* (Basingstoke: Palgrave, 2001), pp. 97–98.
[82] Cited in Webster, *Englishness and Empire*, p. 175.

programmes such as *Commonwealth Crisis: Britain and the Old Dominions* echoed Macmillan's assertion by representing Britain's entry into Europe as a crisis of loyalty to Britons around the globe.[83] Still in 1961, Britain's possible entry into the Common Market was largely seen in Britain as something that would economically strengthen the country and therefore the Commonwealth. The notion that the Commonwealth with its variety of interests was an obstacle to British membership of the EEC only became clear in the ensuing debates between 1961 and 1963.[84] In these debates, it was the Old Dominions – Canada, Australia and New Zealand – that were Britain's severest critics. Britain's application to the EEC revealed that economic self-interest trumped Commonwealth loyalties. Articles, books and speeches began to appear in the early 1960s on Britain's failure to join Continental Europe's 'economic miracle.'[85]

After the Tory annual conference in October 1961, which passed by a massive majority the motion demanding control of Commonwealth immigration, the then Prime Minister of the West Indian Federation, Grantley Adams, cabled Macmillan that 'West Indians are convinced that Britain has begun to take steps which are no different in kind to the basis on which the system of apartheid in South Africa is based.'[86] Those at the Colonial Office did not want to sabotage the chances of Jamaica's continued involvement in the West Indian Federation, and it was believed that any restrictions on Jamaicans' freedom of movement into Britain would result in the Jamaican electorate voting against joining the Federation at independence.[87] When the Jamaican people voted against Federation anyway, 'the final impediment' to the adoption of control was removed.[88] The need for legislation to restrict immigration was read by some as another sign that the politics of the Commonwealth had failed: the West Indies had refused to restrict emigration at their end, and Pakistan's and India's attempts to control emigration were, apparently, ineffective.

The 1961 Commonwealth Immigrants Bill marked a decisive shift in the Conservative Party away from the recent political challenges and assertions of equality and anti-racism in the New Commonwealth towards

---

[83] Ibid., p. 176.

[84] Clemens, 'A History of Failure,' p. 226.

[85] For Powell's take on the European economic 'miracles', see 'Introduction' in Jossleyn Hennessy (ed.), *Economic 'Miracles': Studies in the Resurgence of the French, German and Italian Economies since the Second World War* (London: The Institute of Economic Affairs, 1964), pp. ix–xvii. He argues there that economic planning impeded rather than assisted economic growth in Western Europe.

[86] Webster, *Englishness and Empire*, p. 47.

[87] Hansen, *Citizenship and Immigration in Post-war Britain*, pp. 106–107.

[88] Ibid.

negotiation with Europe.[89] The turn to Europe was, as Powell described it, imagined as 'the substitution of one system of trading preference for another.'[90] Those supporting the EEC, including Enoch Powell, viewed it as a 'commercial' rather than political event – this was in the context of an expansion of trading opportunities which had been taking place: the liberalization measures in OECD, the negotiation for a Free Trade Area with the Rome Treaty countries and the proposal of a European Free Trade Area.[91] But when President de Gaulle's veto of Britain's entry into the EEC in January 1963 revealed concern with 'Skybolt and Polaris, Americans and Ango-Saxons,' Macmillan's government was, as Powell described it, astonished: 'What on earth had that to do with being inside or outside a customs union or with what had seemed to us the only burning issue – Commonwealth preference?'[92] To this, Powell notes, 'Of course, we were wrong.'[93] As de Gaulle's veto made clear, the EEC was about more than trading preference. The 'humiliation of Britain' brought by de Gaulle's veto was even greater because it immediately followed 'her most recent pretensions to independent military power.'[94] Over the previous five years, via the acceptance of the theory of nuclear deterrence, Britain made large reductions in its conventional forces on the continent and ended conscription. This shift in policy relied on Britain's continued nuclear capability. However, at the end of 1962, the United States abandoned the joint US–UK project of producing the airborne rocket Skybolt and turned instead to the development of their own Polaris missiles from nuclear-powered submarines. As Powell put it, Britain was left to purchase Polaris missiles from the United States, and thus 'stood revealed as dependent on America for the very weapon on which it had exclusively rested its own defence.'[95]

The New Commonwealth ideal was taken up briefly by the Labour Party after the Commonwealth Immigrants Act. In 1962, Hugh Gaitskell delivered a still famous speech to the Labour Party conference, claiming that Labour were now the defenders of the Commonwealth. Opposed as he was to deregulation in the Common Market, Gaitskell argued that Britain's entry into Europe meant 'an end to 1,000 years of history.' It meant 'the end of the Commonwealth.' 'For how could we serve as the centre of the Commonwealth when we had become

---

[89] The legislation instituted a voucher system by which the right of entry of Commonwealth citizens was based upon employment skills, passport and the British labour market.
[90] Powell speaks to an audience in France, 1971, about 1963, as cited in *Enoch Powell on 1992*, ed. Richard Ritchie (London: Anaya Publishers, 1989), p. 7.
[91] Ibid.   [92] Ibid.   [93] Ibid.
[94] Powell and Maude, *Biography of a Nation*, p. 237.
[95] Ibid.

a province of Europe?'[96] The American magazine *Time* said he was 'more and more resembling a Tory empire-firster.'[97] Yet he got massive applause from his party, especially when he emphasized some old loyalties, refusing to forget 'Vimy Ridge and Gallipoli.'[98] Here, memories of the Old Dominions at war remained more potent than any 'new' multiracial Commonwealth. Still, in the coming years, as the new party of the Commonwealth, Labour leaders were keen to emphasize the potential of the Commonwealth in 'helping rich and poor and in bringing different races and colours closer together.'[99] In 1962, the Labour MP Patrick Gordon Walker, outspoken proponent of the Commonwealth and opponent of the Commonwealth Immigrants Act 1962 (and, significantly, loser of his Smethwick seat in 1964 to Peter Griffiths in an overtly racist campaign), put the meaning of the Commonwealth this way: '[T]he cohesion and reality of the Commonwealth is at root historical. Everything about the Commonwealth springs from the historical association of the members. It came into existence, evolved and will survive because it has a connected, coherent and intelligible history ...'[100] Gordon Walker had grown up in the Punjab and, while working for the Commonwealth Relations Office in 1947, had had the task of finding a way to accommodate membership for the future Indian republic.[101] His work contributed to the divisible Crown of the Royal Titles Bill. While Gordon Walker argued that history was what ensured the Commonwealth its substance through political difficulties, *history* could, of course, mean something entirely different. As it did in 1964 when the pro-European Lord Gladwyn Jebb compared Commonwealth sentiment to the lingering smile on the face of the Cheshire cat (and dismissed its modern form as just 'playing cricket with fuzzy-wuzzies').[102] The Commonwealth was, for Lord Gladwyn, a ghost. *The Economist* would go so far as to call it 'the world's biggest experiment yet in sustained and creative historical humour.'[103]

Importantly, the competing nationalisms of the British (ex)colonies – their turn to sovereign independence and representative assemblies – were, in Powell's mind, not a historical endpoint in any political evolutionary process to be supported by the Commonwealth but 'a phenomenon (or even a device) of transition' in the transfer of

---

[96] 'Even if You Win, You'll Lose,' *Time*, 12 October 1962.
[97] Ibid.   [98] Ibid.
[99] Elspeth Huxley, 'Is the Commonwealth a Farce? An Answer to "A Conservative",' *The Round Table*, vol. 54, no. 215 (June 1964).
[100] Gordon Walker, *The Commonwealth*, p. 9.
[101] McIntyre, 'Clio and Britannia's Lost Dream,' p. 527.
[102] Huxley, 'Is the Commonwealth a Farce?'.
[103] *The Economist*, 6 June 1964.

power.[104] The nations formed at the transfer of power were, in Powell's mind, necessarily transitional. Was 'Western nationhood export-able?' Powell asked at a Conservative Summer School in 1955, 'The answer is, no.' The actual stuff of nationhood (not shared political principles, but the 'sentiments, habits and acceptances' of a constitu-ency) emerged through a unique historical process that took time.[105] Rather than the stable completion of an evolutionary process, decolo-nization involved a 'sudden release' of forces, internal and external, which would work to determine a new equilibrium, a new sovereign entity. An honourable exit therefore did not require continued politi-cal ties and obligations after independence – this only suspended the attainment of political equilibrium. Powell would argue this again ten years later, against Britain's military involvement East of Suez, and specifically against Britain's commitments to the United States' intervention in Vietnam (what he derisively called 'the post-colonial problem ... in absolutely classic form'[106]).

When Labour took office in 1964, the centre of Commonwealth lead-ership shifted dramatically from the UK government's Commonwealth Relations Office to intergovernmental control at Marlborough House. This restructuring in 1965 came after a succession of crises in Commonwealth unity that centred around the politics of British Africa. The change was implemented as an explicit attempt to reinvigorate the group by decentralizing decision-making power and further reducing the British state's responsibility for the group's continued political survival. The Commonwealth's transformation from 'family' to the more contin-gent 'partnership' was complete. The words 'Vimy Ridge and Gallipoli' were no longer an invocation of Commonwealth loyalty.[107] One-party rule, military regimes and racial antagonism – against the backdrop of violence in the (ex-Belgian) Congo – were seen now to dominate the African political scene. The Commonwealth had become, for many in Britain, less representative of worldwide British parliamentary design and economic influence than a (left-wing dominated) Third World forum.[108]

---

[104] Enoch Powell, 'Nationalism' (London: C.P.C., 1955), p. 41 (PUB 165/22, Conservative Party Archive, Special Collections & Western Manuscripts, Bodleian Library).
[105] Ibid.
[106] Enoch Powell, 'Southern European Programme 1 March 1965' (POLL 4.1.27). Then, he would argue, 'It could be that in the absence of the American [forces] the com-munists would not necessarily prevail in Viet Nam. It could also be that if the com-munists did prevail in Viet Nam, the resultant regrouping of forces, ... would prove a stronger not a weaker obstacle to the further extension of communist power.'
[107] Ibid.
[108] Krishnan Srinivasan, 'Nobody's Commonwealth? The Commonwealth in Britain's Post Imperial Adjustment,' *Commonwealth and Comparative Politics*, 44: 2 (July 2006), pp. 257–269 (p. 263).

In this regard, Powell was an absolutely central figure, before taking up the mantle of anti-immigration, in giving voice to British resentment about a perceived lack of gratitude in the former colonies. As the reputation of the Commonwealth faltered in Britain, nativist racism also gathered momentum and liberal values on race in Britain – formerly politically attached to the Commonwealth ideal or the postwar 'people's empire' – were left on the defensive, cut adrift from public support for an imperial past made good.[109]

Post-imperial neurosis

In September 1953, Enoch Powell participated in a forum on tradition in culture and in politics alongside Hannah Arendt and Gabriel Marcel to argue that all government rests not merely on authority but on consent.[110] Powell wrote that this consent relied on political myth. These myths are neither true nor false, Powell explained, but when destroyed, 'men and societies go mad. It is revolution.'[111] The British nation was peculiar, Powell explained, because 'the evolution of its myths has been far longer and less interrupted than those of any other society in recorded history.'[112] Britain was 'mythologically speaking a kind of Midway Island or St. Helena,' because the British have 'a capacity for make-believe which almost exceeds credibility.'[113] Importantly, Powell emphasized that Britain was unique because it could contain both the *myth* of democracy – Britain was not, he noted, a democracy: the Crown, the Courts, and the Church were irreconcilable with that – and the myth of the Crown. Still, the 'democratic myth' persisted, right alongside the contradictory 'monarchic myth.' Powell called Britain's democratic theory, 'a kind of vaccination' against revolution – 'a cowpox' that saved the life of the monarchic myth.[114] The year was 1953, the year of Queen Elizabeth II's Coronation. The very act of crowning a sovereign in the year 1953, he insisted, called for an 'almost superhuman effort of reinterpretation and adaptation of the facts to the myths and the myth to the facts.' And, '[t]o believe that the British can accomplish so plain an impossibility, one requires to be British oneself.'[115]

---

[109] Paul Rich, *Race and Empire in British Politics* (Cambridge University Press, 1986), p. 200.

[110] Enoch Powell, 'Tradition in Culture and in Politics,' *Confluence: An International Forum*, 2: 3 (September 1953), p. 22. The other contributors to theories of tradition in the forum that month were Gabriel Marcel, Carl J. Friedrich, Bertrand de Jouvenel, Oscar Handlin and Hannah Arendt.

[111] Ibid., p. 18.   [112] Ibid.

[113] Ibid.

[114] Ibid., p. 18.   [115] Ibid., p. 22.

In 1953, Powell kept the faith. The British still knew themselves and loved their institutions. The Crown, that pinnacle of Britain's class order, remained compatible with 'the nation.' It was the year that Governor Baring declared a state of emergency in Kenya. It was the year that saw the formation of the undemocratic Central African Federation, against nationalist opposition from Africans in Rhodesia and Nyasaland and considerable public opinion in Britain.[116] It was the year that the Royal Titles Bill passed, redefining the very meaning of the Commonwealth. And it was the year that Powell joined the Suez Group, against Britain's initial withdrawal of troops from the Suez Canal. Despite all this, Britain's political tradition was still, mythologically speaking, 'St Helena.'

A decade later, Powell saw a different Britain. It had lost Suez. It had entered under America's nuclear umbrella. It had tried – and failed – to become a member of the EEC. After economic stagnation and a sex scandal under a Conservative government, Labour was about to win the general election. Britain's Central African Federation was breaking up with Zambian and Malawi independence and the Rhodesian crisis was soon to begin. And, despite the Commonwealth Immigrants Act of 1962, hundreds of thousands of dependants of newly settled immigrants could legally reunite with family members in Britain. The world had changed. The myths no longer held: Britain was going mad. Powell called it 'post-imperial neurosis.'[117]

In the conclusion to his long history of paternalism in British political life – entitled *The Habit of Authority* (1966) – historian A. P. Thornton's considers the consequences of decolonization on notions of class and political authority. In stark contrast to the new political environment of the postwar period, he describes imperial power as follows:

Public opinion, as in the case of Eyre in Jamaica in 1865, might later force [a Colonial Governor's] recall or repudiation: but that was an aftermath of the exercise of power, which did not diminish its efficacy. The essence of empire was control; the confidence to wield it; the capacity to enforce it if necessary. These were the three indivisibles of British authority overseas – and at home.[118]

In contrast to empire, the Commonwealth had 'too little that was concrete, and lacked authority accordingly.'[119] Commonwealth members came and went according to national interests. Thornton notes that with its loss in

---

[116] MacIntyre, *British Decolonization, 1946–1997*, p. 51.
[117] Enoch Powell, German Service, 17 June 1965. POLL 4.1.27.
[118] A. P. Thornton, *The Habit of Authority: Paternalism in British History* (London: George Allen & Unwin, 1966), p. 378.
[119] Ibid., p. 383.

authority abroad, the British upper classes lost their *raison d'être*. This was fundamental: 'however necessary it was to cut the imperial ties' for financial reasons, 'decolonization was not carried out without damage to the Tory concept of authority itself, with all its duty and habit.'[120] Thornton connects the decline in the 'three indivisibles of British authority overseas' to a turn to 'pragmatism' in both parties. He ties it to a turn, as historian Anne Marie Smith describes it, to the 'post-ideological' state, to the pragmatic, 'class-less' and antagonism-free politics of the Macmillan era.[121] In place of authority came the economic efficiency and management of the consensus. In other words, at least in Thornton's eyes in 1966, the consensus was at least as much a product of the damage to the concept of 'authority itself, with all its duty and habit,' as a product of the political gains of the working and middle classes.

The crisis of authority that Thornton describes had, of course, a racial dimension. The assertion of racial equality in the Commonwealth could be experienced as a revolutionary break in history, a devastating break in the order of things. According to Prime Minister Harold Macmillan in a private telegram to the Australian Prime Minister, Robert Menzies, in 1962, it was the world wars that fundamentally challenged the acceptance of white racial dominance and superiority.[122] European civilization and 'the automatic leadership of the whites' was, he offered, in crisis:

By folly and weakness on the one side, and incredible wickedness on the other, Europe has twice pulled itself to pieces in a single generation. I do not think the loss of life, terrible as it has been (especially since it always takes its toll on the best), has been the chief loss. Nor does the squandering of money and materials amount to much: these can be replaced. What has really gone is the prestige of the Europeans – British, French, Germans, call them what you will. Whether in the Old World, or migrated to the New World, or settled in Australasia, or in Africa, Europeans have broadly governed the world for over 2,000 years in a more or less coherent unit ... But, as I say, what the two wars did was to destroy the prestige of the white people. For not only did the yellows and blacks watch them tear each other apart, committing the more frightful crimes and acts of barbarism against each other, but they actually saw them enlisting each their own yellows and blacks to fight other Europeans, other whites. It was bad enough for the white men to fight each other, but it was worse when they brought in their dependants. And what we have really seen since the war is the revolt of the yellows and blacks from the automatic leadership of the whites.[123]

[120] Ibid., p. 377.
[121] Anna Marie Smith, *New Right Discourse*, p. 137.
[122] Harold Macmillan, 'The Commonwealth: Reflections on Commonwealth and other changes in the post-war world': personal telegram (reply), Mr Macmillan to Mr Menzies, 8 February 1962, PREM 11/3644, T 51/62.
[123] Ibid.

According to Powell, the confusion and (class and racial) bewilderment of this moment needed to be resolved politically. It was via political debate that 'the picture of [Britain's] own nature, its past and future, its place among other nations in the world, which it carries in its imagination' would be revealed. Specifically, Powell argued that the Conservative Party needed a 'new patriotism' which put Britain at the centre of its political world and banished the delusion of international dominance and control.[124] Britain could no longer, with the Commonwealth, carry responsibilities with lost power nor rely on moralism *as* power. In other words, in order to salvage any Tory concept of authority, Britain needed a post-imperial life-story. Powell perhaps gave the clearest sense of this life-story when he spoke to a Manchester audience in 1965:

> I am not quite saying that the new history will be 'Britain without Empire,' but it will be very nearly 'Britain with the imperial episode in parenthesis.' We might do worse than start reading again the histories of Britain written in the two generations before 1880 ... But the perspective we need for 1980 has much more in common with that of before 1890 than with any view that could be taken in the years since then.[125]

It was the job of politics – it was his job, Powell explained – to now rewrite Britain's national story. It was his function as a 'statesman' to make 'men love their institutions' again.[126] Because 'Nations, like women, cannot resist looking at themselves in the mirror.'[127] By 1965, Powell had an audience. As John M. Mackenzie has noted, after the massive decolonization of Africa between 1961 and 1965, both popular and political circles became conscious of the underlying realities of British power and the extent to which the British Empire was over in 'economic, political, military and conceptual terms.'[128] No longer could the British 'trade off (in both literal and metaphorical terms) a richly powerful imperial past.'[129] In Powell's words, Britain was, it seemed, waking up from 'a sleep and a forgetting.'[130]

[124] J. Enoch Powell, speech delivered at the S.W. Norfolk Conservative fete, 15 June 1963. POLL 4.1.1.
[125] J. Enoch Powell, 'Power and glory: the nation in the mirror,' speech to Manchester Convention Dinner, 6 November 1965. POLL 4.1.2.
[126] J. Enoch Powell, 'Frankly Speaking,' Radio Broadcast, 28 February 1964. POLL 4.1.27.
[127] J. Enoch Powell, speech to Manchester Convention Dinner, 6 November 1965. POLL 4.1.2.
[128] John M. Mackenzie, 'The Persistence of Empire in Metropolitan Culture,' in Ward (ed.), *British Culture and the End of Empire*, p. 32.
[129] Ibid.   [130] Ibid.

In these years, critiquing the British government's 'imperial delusions' and its 'pretence of Commonwealth,'[131] he spoke consistently of the need for 'a clean break with the imperial past' which would enable 'a future dependent on competitive development of ... abilities and resources.'[132] Britain's national self-consciousness obscured the true nature of national achievement – which was, in the modern world, essentially economic viability. Despite the shared desire to construct a national identity based in 'entrepreneurial spirit,' Powellism is no simple precursor to the Thatcherite revolution. As will be discussed in the Postscript ('Enoch Powell and Thatcherism'), Powell's insistence on the need to untether market relations in British society from the constraints of economic planning was less a precursor to (Thatcher's) moral revolution of the market than it was a sign of his overriding concerns about sovereignty and consent in the context of American global power. Michael Oakeshott's later notion of 'enterprise' versus 'civil' association – which appeared in his text *On Human Conduct* in 1975 – contributes, too, to our understanding of Powell's conservative revolt. Here, Oakeshott critiques a notion of the state as an 'enterprise association,' with a meaning, a unity of purpose or motivation beyond the containment of civil society. This enterprise state, in Oakeshott's mind, relied necessarily on 'managerial' decision-making.[133] Oakeshott's distinction begins to illuminate where Powell's and Thatcher's commitments to the free market stand in contrast. Powell's 'new patriotism' was a revolt against a liberal, progressive notion of British history as a moral crusade. Within Thatcherism, economics is a method of elevating human nature – the state is, therefore, endowed with moral purpose. Thatcherism may be read, therefore, as a continuation of a postwar liberal belief in human transformation via state economic policy.[134]

For Powell, 'the nation' is an act of faith. In its true form, the nation, like the Church of England, is 'supernatural' in character.[135] This parallel sits at the heart of Powell's understanding of allegiance and consent. 'Men live and die within it and for it by virtue of participating in a

---

[131] Enoch Powell, speech to the Annual Meeting of the Wolverhampton Southwest Conservative Association, 13 December 1963; and Enoch Powell, Speech to Louth Constituency Open Meeting, 8 March 1963. POLL 4.1.1.

[132] 'A Conservative' [J. Enoch Powell], 'Patriotism Based on Reality Not Dreams,' *The Times*, 2 April 1964.

[133] Michael Oakeshott, *On Human Conduct* (Oxford, 1975), p. 137.

[134] Margaret Thatcher, 'Dimensions of Conservatism' (Iain Macleod Memorial Lecture), London, 4 July 1977, in *Let Our Children Grow Tall* (London: Centre for Policy Studies, 1977), pp. 103–113.

[135] Enoch Powell, 'Tradition in Culture and in Politics,' *Confluence: An International Forum*, 2: 3 (September 1953), p. 22.

belief,' explained Powell, 'to which the rational categories of truth and falsehood are inapplicable.'[136] This is not the belief in abstract democracy or the Christian mission but a faith in Church and Parliament; community is made possible via faith in the institutions of the nation. The constitutional forms are, like that of the Church of England, 'valid by reason of evolution and acceptance, not by conforming to some absolute, objective criterion.'[137] Institutional form, then, whether Church ritual or parliamentary process, is the very content of community and basis of authority. As Powell put it, 'forms and content are not separable.'[138]

Powell's vision of political identity, marked by the act of war over the dream of peace, was tied, in this sense, to this picture of the role of the Church. Arguing in 1951 that a 'kind of vague philanthropy' is not Christianity and Christianity is, rather, membership of a Church, he explained his reasoning as follows:

> Only men's acts (which includes words) can be in common. Their thoughts are essentially peculiar and (in the last resort) incommunicable. Whether the community be man and wife, or the men of a battalion, or the Members of the House of Commons, it is what they do together that counts.[139]

Only through institutional or communal *acts* could belief be asserted. Importantly, the willingness to give one's identity entirely to the nation through war was the ultimate or final act of political belief.

Against the 'coercive' state, Powell would focus in these years on what he called the 'doctrine of the market.'[140] However, Powell's 'new patriotism' cannot be read merely as a liberal free market critique. John Locke's assertion of the free and independent individual born equal was, for Powell, 'void of any real meaning' outside the (hierarchical) structures of community. He called Locke his 'litmus paper' for being a true Tory.[141] In a radio interview in 1964, Powell insisted that just because he saw economics 'in the hard light of the two times table of laissez faire. Well that doesn't make me a liberal: it doesn't make me a radical.'[142] As Powell put it when asked if he was perhaps really a 'Gladstone man'

---

[136] Ibid.
[137] Ibid.
[138] Enoch Powell, 'Social Services: Theory and Practice,' *Listener*, 17 April 1952. POLL 6.2.2.
[139] J. Enoch Powell, 'The Church,' part of unpublished One Nation Book, 1951. POLL 3.2.1.1.
[140] Enoch Powell, 'Theory and Practice.' POLL 6.2.2.
[141] J. Enoch Powell, 'Massimo Salvadori, *Locke and Liberty*,' Book review for *Birmingham Post*, 19 January 1960.
[142] J. Enoch Powell, 'Frankly Speaking,' Radio Broadcast, 28 February 1964. POLL 4.1.27.

rather than a Tory (to which his answer was a definitive no): 'a community which makes its economic choices through the market is behaving
instinctively as a Tory believes society best behaves.'[143] He then added
tellingly, 'Perhaps that's a rationalization.'[144] When pressed to explain
what he meant by his assertion that he was 'born a Tory,' rather than a
liberal, Powell made clear the meaning of 'Tory' in his mind:

I simply mean that congenitally I was Tory in that my characteristic attitudes
way back were Tory, were of an instinctive reverence for instance for tradition,
for a hierarchy, a dislike of claims of equality, a disposition to see differences
more than similarities, a belief that things were better justified by what they
were and by their past than by any reasoning.[145]

Elsewhere, he described a Tory as someone who 'believes that inequality is not only natural and inevitable, but within a sound society is of
infinite value.'[146] In June 1964, Powell would write again to the *Sunday
Times* as 'A Conservative'; here he noted that 'money is colour-blind
and economic forces will help the work of integration which must be
done if a homogeneous' – and here it could be added *deferential* – 'community, local and national, is to be restored.'[147]

Powell, linked as he was in these years to the contemporaneous work
of the conservative theorists Maurice Cowling and Oakeshott, echoed
their emphasis on the significance of the market as a moral community.[148]
Morality did not exist outside community – likewise it could not be
expressed by a community and projected outside of itself – rather morality existed in contractual or legal relations *between* individuals *inside* the
structures of habit and expectation. Even more, charity and altruism had
no meaning, according to Powell, when applied to taxation by a public
authority, as the forced redistribution of wealth at home or abroad.[149]
In other words, Commonwealth development aid could not represent a
moral act. This did not exactly mean opposition to social services within
Britain, however. Speaking as Minister of Health in 1963, Powell juxtaposed two visions of social services, the Conservative and the socialist,
in a speech entitled 'Compassion or Domination':

---

[143] Ibid.   [144] Ibid.   [145] Ibid.
[146] J. Enoch Powell, cited in Anna Marie Smith, *New Right Discourse*, p. 138.
[147] 'A Conservative,' *Sunday Times*, 14 June 1964, cited in Brooke, 'India, Post-
Imperialism, and the Origins of Powell's "Rivers of Blood" Speech,' p. 683.
[148] Powell was friends with Maurice Cowling (who even tried to get Powell to agree to
become Master of Peterhouse College after Cowling believed Powell's political career was over). Powell and Oakeshott knew each other through their mutual friend,
the influential conservative writer and activist Diana Spearman.
[149] J. Enoch Powell, 'International Charity,' Draft copy, *New Society*, 5 June 1965.
POLL 6.1.1.

We believe that the social services have the purpose of providing for the members of the community, or for a section of it, those conditions which community action, and only community action, can provide ... Socialism has always seen social services as an engine for dominating the social life of the nation to the State as completely as they would subject its economic life: nationalisation of our society, as the companion piece to nationalisation of our economy.[150]

The 'corporate recognition by the community of its common obligation' was the heart of social services for the true Tory.[151] These services, however, did not promise the transformation of social life and could not be projected outside of the community.

Powell insisted on a divide between the material and the moral – the political and the religious, the 'authority without' and the 'authority within' – to oppose the validity of redistributive taxation and protect the limits of 'the political.' Powell worked, then, to marry a Tory notion of the organic community, structured by the moral expectations and responsibilities of status, with the logic of the market. He describes the market as an organic, evolutionary entity and the theatre of innumerable human interactions. In this schema, the market is not a set of abstractions but is fundamentally contingent and historical – it cannot be planned, controlled or universalized. The market is the expression of the community through which the moral individual can exist. He remained adamantly opposed, in this sense, to the notion that the embrace of free market capitalism could be equated with the embrace of the Americanization of Britain: 'the market' was not the United States, it was a distinct (cultural) community. The market was, then, Powell's post-imperial myth; in other words, it represented for him the 'natural order' or true nature of the (hierarchical) nation.

A new patriotism

The sex scandal of the Profumo affair in 1963 and the later appointment via an antiquated system of the Earl of Home, Alec Douglas-Home, as leader of the Conservatives underlined a growing public anxiety and frustration with the political classes in Britain.[152] After leaving his position as Minister of Health in 1963 due to Douglas-Home's appointment, Powell devoted himself to transforming both the party and the intellectual parameters of Tory politics.[153] Once in opposition in 1964,

---

[150] J. Enoch Powell, 'Compassion, or Domination?' *West Midlands Review*, no. 1, Sept/Oct 1963. POLL 6.1.1E.

[151] Ibid.

[152] Foote, *The Republican Transformation of Modern British Politics*, p. 139.

[153] Ibid., p. 146.

Powell's criticisms became more strident. Twelve years in office, coping with the movements of the outside world and with what he called 'the debts and debris of the past' had left the party without a sense of itself.[154] An era was passing, 'one phase in our party's life yielding to another.'[155] The party, he argued, needed to reassert its basic principles. These were, in Powell's mind, controversially the defence of capitalism and the defence of the nation:

> [We must] seek to re-establish our self-confidence and faith in ourselves upon a new basis and to find, as it were, a new patriotism befitting this changed world, to replace the old, imperial patriotism of the past. To help the nation in this work to express its purpose is uniquely the mission of the Tory Party: to proclaim to ourselves and to our fellow countrymen that the reserves of energy, or resource, of enterprise, from which our past achievements sprang, are not exhausted.[156]

In public speeches and in journalism from 1963 onwards, Powell would stress the need for 'new patriotism' in the party, not based in 'wistful imaginings' of a powerful past nor preoccupied by protecting British society from a return to the hungry thirties through economic planning, but one instead that could be based on present market 'reality' – on the viability and strength of the national economy.

The party had faced in 1962–1963 what Powell called the 'year of disaster.' Common Market negotiations had failed. And the Tory party had '[t]acitly almost … agreed to drop their most distinctive badge,' the Nation: 'you can almost feel them wince when they sing "Land of Hope and Glory" at the Albert Hall. It hurts more than the Union Jack in which the speaker's table at meetings of the faithful always has to be swathed. It hurts – and the pain is a symptom of something still amiss.' The Tories had lost their way: 'In 1964, as in 1945.'[157] Powell's new patriotism was about national survival in a post-imperial age. Against the centralization of the newly formed (and bipartisan) council for economic planning, he called on the party to represent instead the energies of those who thought as the unselfconscious and entrepreneurial imperialist had once thought, individuals who would make Britain a new national economic success.

Only through a loss of national confidence would, Powell argued, the British people be tempted to 'go bankrupt' and pass over the management of their economy to the state.[158] Conservative Quintin Hogg called

---

[154] Enoch Powell, speech to the Bromsgrove Unionist Club, 6 July 1963. POLL 4.1.1
[155] Ibid.
[156] Enoch Powell, speech delivered at the S.W. Norfolk Conservative Fete, 15 June 1963. POLL 4.1.1.
[157] J. Enoch Powell, 8 March 1963, POLL 4.1.1.
[158] Ibid.

Powell at this time 'a sort of Mao Tse-tung of Toryism' for taking the logic of capitalism to its extreme and called his blanket denunciation of economic planning just plain nonsense.[159] This was the early Powellism to which Powell remained committed throughout his life, a Powellism that was no doubt deeply linked to the Powellism of anti-immigration.

During the Profumo scandal, Powell appeared in the papers pedantic but virtuous. The breaking of the scandal had uncovered a seamy mix of upscale prostitution and Cold War secrecy: Britain's Secretary of State for War, John Profumo, and the senior naval attaché at the Soviet Embassy in London were revealed to have been sleeping with the same woman. Profumo had then lied about it. Speculation covered the papers that Powell would (once again[160]) resign because his conscience was so disturbed by the affair and that, as Minister of Health, he would lead a bid to force out Macmillan by a Cabinet revolt, leading the 'revolt of the revolted.'[161] Nothing came of the rumours. Instead, only a few days later, he pledged his support for Macmillan. Still, the Conservative Party's disarray and disunity after the crisis was seen as a distinct advantage for the opposition.[162] *The Spectator* denied the force of the crisis as a moral issue, but emphasized its political potency, claiming, 'This is the truth of it: the man who pulled together not merely a divided party but a deeply divided nation after the shock and shame of Suez must quit because of a weak and prevaricating colleague's minor sexual indiscretion.'[163] The 'submerged anxieties' revealed in the scandal made Macmillan's leadership of the party untenable.[164] Julian Amery likewise wrote to Powell that he believed Macmillan should resign and that the Conservative Party should form a new government, lamenting in the postscript, 'I do hope though we are not going to commit suicide.'[165] The affair had turned the Conservative Party and the government into, what another Conservative MP, William Deedes, called 'a repository for many national sins, real and imaginary.'[166] This was, after all, the party of empire and class status, the party that asserted the moral legitimacy

---

[159] 'Mr. Powell – Tory MA,' *Wolverhampton Express and Star*, 23 April 1964.

[160] In 1957 he resigned as Secretary of the Treasury under Thorneycroft due to Macmillan's refusal to accept their tight national budget.

[161] 'More Characters in the Crisis and Talk of "Background" Man,' *Express and Star*, 14 June 1963, and 'The Inside Story: of Enoch Powell and the Plot that Failed,' *Daily Mail*, 14 June 1963.

[162] James Margach, 'Eve of Eruption,' *Sunday Times*, 16 June 1963.

[163] 'No Moral Issue,' *The Spectator*, 21 June 1963, p. 796.

[164] Ibid.

[165] Julian Amery, 13 June 1963. POLL 3.1.24.

[166] William Deedes, 'Claptrap to Blame Tories for Decay,' *Evening Standard*, 15 June 1963.

of hierarchy. According to this Conservative, the allegations of morally degeneracy were 'claptrap': the affair was not symptomatic of moral decay but rather of a fundamental transformation happening in British politics – 'Change at a speed and of a kind which imposes the severest stresses within society.'[167] Deedes was talking here of a decline in the acceptance of the class structure.

Some would, briefly, see the resolution of this fundamental political transformation represented in the body of Powell. As the *City Press* put it, Powell was their 'new hope' and a 'new spirit.' Unlike the overly indulgent and now morally ambiguous elite, Powell could with his flat Midlands accent, free market beliefs and scrupulous politics stand for a morally upstanding, (politically powerful) middle class: 'He is the kind of man who is badly needed at this point in our history and he could win the next election for the Tory Party.'[168] He received a round of positive letters from the public, supporting his moral stand and the prospects for his leadership of the party.[169] Iain Macleod wrote to Powell during the crisis, indicating that he believed that whatever decision Powell made, it would be the right one: 'this I know and so do thousands of others. This is the measure of the trust and confidence you inspire.'[170] Critics meanwhile regarded Powell during the crisis as dreary and, in the end, politically insignificant and uncompromising.[171] And the polls supported this view. The *Daily Express* and *Daily Telegraph* sponsored polls of Conservative MPs that summer; they found that Powell had only 5 per cent and 6 per cent of the party's support, respectively, if Macmillan were to resign.[172] And the *Daily Express* found in a poll that support for Enoch Powell among the people, as a possible replacement for Macmillan, was at this time only 3 per cent.[173] It would, in the end, be Edward Heath two years later who would come to be a middle-class leader of the Conservatives.

When Macmillan stepped down a few months after the Profumo crisis due to sickness and Douglas-Home took the party leadership, Powell would again take up the role of the conscience of the party by refusing, alongside Macleod, to serve in the Cabinet. Both Macleod and Powell had supported Rab Butler to be the next leader and believed

---

[167] Ibid.
[168] 'New Hope,' *City Press*, 14 June 1963.
[169] See POLL 3.1.24.
[170] Iain Macleod, 14 June 1963. POLL 3.1.24.
[171] 'The Crisis Man,' *Daily Mail*, 19 June 1963.
[172] As cited in Douglas E. Schoen, *Enoch Powell and the Powellites* (Basingstoke: Palgrave Macmillan, 1977), p. 6.
[173] Ibid.

the appointment of a peer irreconcilable with a modern Tory party. Two letters Powell received at this time mark out the parameters of the crisis of confidence in the party – indicating, again, a fundamental shift in the basis of its political legitimacy. On the one hand, we find fear of a party failing to salvage its tradition of honour – the only thing that could essentially legitimate social status. '[Y]ou are now the conscience of the Conservative party,' began a Conservative voter from Hampstead, 'I hope it is true, for it badly needs one.'[174] The man then begged Powell to 'salvage a little of its honour by opposing the latest indefensible ... breach of promises, made only 8 months ago to the minority tribes of Kenya.' Ever since the Suez invasion, he emphasized, the government seemed to have 'lost all sense of honour.' '"The word of an Englishman" must be joked indeed from Cairo to Salisbury compared with these dishonourings of Government and Country.'[175] Profumo was trivial. If the party was to even learn the 'alphabet of morality, they needed – the letter-writer feared – 'a long spell in opposition.'[176] The old boy network had failed. The underhand appointment of Douglas-Home was yet another indication of a party without scruples. On the other hand, Powell received a letter the very next day from the One Nation group, lamenting that for the many who were working to make the Conservative Party 'mildly progressive' the recent appointment of Douglas-Home was a serious defeat. Others wrote of it as a gesture of contempt – from 'a clique of men of aristocratic or semi-aristocratic background' – against those who had worked hard in their local wards to project a modern image.[177] As the letters make clear, the party was falling between two stools – appearing neither ancient and honourable nor modern and transparent.

Powell's refusal to serve in a Douglas-Home government had, then, a 'sociological significance' – and, increasingly, Powell came to represent a challenge to patrician politics.[178] As *The Times* put it, 'the Conservative Gentlemen had taken on the Conservative Players and had won hands down in a day when everybody thought the Conservative Gentlemen had given up.'[179]

In April 1964, a few months before the Conservative Party was to lose control of government for the first time in 13 years, Powell wrote a series of essays for *The Times*. These essays became major national news. They appeared three days running and were, importantly,

---

[174] Letter to Powell, 27 October 1963. POLL 3.1.27.
[175] Ibid.   [176] Ibid.
[177] 'Old Boy Network in New Tory Regime,' *The Times*, 24 October 1963.
[178] Schoen, *Enoch Powell and the Powellites*, p. 7
[179] *The Times*, 21 October 1963.

written anonymously and signed 'A Conservative.' From the moment of their publication, speculation and scandal surrounded them. Powell became the prime suspect of their authorship – discussed on television, in Parliament, and abundantly in the press – though he refused any responsibility. Their anonymity and their damning criticisms of the party combined to incite an angry response from many Conservatives. In the first article, Powell described the Suez Crisis as inducing an 'agony of soul through which the Conservative party passed.'[180] He goes on to imply that the Conservatives' subsequent eschewal of imperial and national pride had led the party to turn to an (unfortunate) 'cult of newness,' to modernization and technocratic planning. The next article, entitled 'Patriotism Based on Reality not on Dreams,' focused on the Commonwealth.[181] Powell called it a 'humbug' and 'a gigantic farce.' He warned that while some humbugs perform a valuable function, enabling slow adaptation to change, 'like the fluid which a snail exudes to mend its broken shell,' they can if not shed at the right time be fatal.[182] Now, 'the wounds have almost healed' it was time that the Conservative Party took stock of Britain's relative power and position in the world. The Commonwealth was a gigantic farce and everyone knew it: both the Old Dominions and new members resented Britain and would be more disposed to Germany or Japan. While it might be profitable for Nehru, Nkrumah or Makarios, as '[t]hey give nothing,' for Britain 'the absurdities it imposes on our laws and thought have already done more harm than enough.'[183]

Powell began with its influence on domestic Britain: the social and political 'damage' of black immigration, two decades of bad economics in Commonwealth preference, and the prostitution of the monarchy to the service of a 'transparent fiction.' At this time, Powell had already begun arguing for the tightening of the Commonwealth Immigrants Act, stressing that integration of immigrants into all sections of British society depended on further limiting the number of newcomers. By 1965, he added the proposal that government provide assistance for voluntary repatriation.[184] As the next section of this chapter will discuss, the presence of the immigrant further compromised for Powell

[180] J. Enoch Powell, 'A Party in Search of a Pattern: From the Years of Protest to the Year of Disaster,' *The Times*, 1 April 1964.
[181] J. Enoch Powell, 'A Party in Search of a Pattern – 2: Patriotism Based on Reality Not on Dreams,' *The Times*, 2 April 1964.
[182] Ibid.
[183] Ibid.
[184] Peter Brooke, 'India, Post-Imperialism and the Origins of Enoch Powell's "Rivers of Blood" Speech,' p. 676.

the 'unique structure of power' of British rule and a social order dependent on the inequalities of the market. In terms of foreign policy, the Commonwealth also failed: Britain's current commitments to the world 'combine the maximum chance of involvement, embarrassment, expense, and humiliation with the minimum effect,' and could only be explained historically, by a fixed determination to remain blind to Britain's altered status.[185] He argued against Britain's role policing the world. He asserted that Britain needed a new defence policy and 'non-Commonwealth policy,' not towards 'little England' and quietism, but towards cultivation of its strength as a European power. Britain had to lose the taint of 'colonialism' in the United Nations. It had to reject its treatment of the developing world 'as an exercise in international charity or political bribery,' because 'neo-colonialism' prejudiced development as much as 'old-style imperialism.'[186]

This article would have the profoundest reverberations of the series Powell published in *The Times*. *The Round Table*, the journal of the Commonwealth think tank, levelled a sustained attack on 'A Conservative.' For weeks the letters to *The Times*' editor were filled with references to the 'gigantic farce.' Powell's last and perhaps most important article, 'The Field Where the Biggest Failures Lie,' caused less of a stir.[187] This focused on the party's political compromise on the economy: i.e. in nationalization, prices and incomes policy, and in the uniform benefits of social security. As he later noted, '[w]ithout economic independence, talk about Suez or Vietnam is meaningless.'[188]

The criticisms against these articles came mostly from Conservatives. One letter to the editor asked, if America were to follow Britain's lead in these ideas, becoming respectively Fortress America and Fortress Britain, what of the rest of the world? '[W]here does the process end? Presumably the world outside the United States, Russia, and western Europe rapidly turning itself into one vast rioting Congo?'[189] The world would turn to revolution. Another wrote that while the Suez invasion was a 'well-nigh irreparable disaster,' Britain still had the chance to recover from the blunder of applying to the Common Market by remaining committed to the Commonwealth.[190] Others agreed with this, that

[185] J. Enoch Powell, 'A Party in Search of a Pattern – 2: Patriotism Based on Reality Not on Dreams,' *The Times*, 2 April 1964.

[186] Ibid.

[187] J. Enoch Powell, 'A Party in Search of a Pattern – 3: The Field Where the Biggest Failures Lie,' *The Times*, 3 April 1964.

[188] J. Enoch Powell, speech at Whitland Primary School, Carmarthenshire, 5 July 1966. POLL 4.1.2.

[189] W. C. S. Corry, 'A Party in Search of a Pattern,' *The Times*, 6 April 1964.

[190] Harry F. Batterbee, 'A Party in Search of a Pattern,' *The Times*, 6 April 1964.

Macmillan's treatment of the Old Dominions in his application to the Common Market was 'shameful.'[191] Meanwhile in government, Arthur Bottomley, Britain's new Secretary of State for Commonwealth Relations, described Labour's Commonwealth policy against the accusations of 'A Conservative': 'It's not wishy-washy. It's not dreamy. It's not living in the past. If I had to put a name to it, it's high-pressure friendship.'[192]

In these years, Powell generated a great deal of controversy for all these views. His name became synonymous with a respectable far-right position – so much so that he ended up running, very unsuccessfully, for the leadership of the party against Edward Heath and Reginald Maudling in 1965. After Heath's win, Powell was named Shadow Minister of Defence. For three years running at the Conservative Party conference Powell spoke out controversially against Britain's obligations 'East of Suez.' In these years, the new Defence Minister, Denis Healey, set in motion a series of studies to review defence – in an effort to reduce government spending – which resulted in the cancellation of the fifth Polaris submarine, followed by the cancellation of the P-1154, HS-681 and TSR-2 aircraft projects.[193] The growing cost of maintaining Britain's uncompetitive aircraft industry meant that the principle of independence in arms manufacture became increasingly untenable.[194] In keeping with US global policy at this time, Labour's 1965 White Paper maintained that the immediate threat to the West came from the Third World rather than Europe.[195] Reflecting in large part Heath's views at this time, Powell would continually emphasize that Britain was now a European economic power, urging that the country break from both its imperial delusions of the Commonwealth and its continued support of the United States East of Suez in Vietnam. Linked to this, he opposed the 'theology' that any outbreak of fighting in Europe would quickly escalate into nuclear fighting – he therefore continually opposed in these years the reduction of conventional armed forces and Britain's dependency on the United States.[196] Crucially, the 'post-colonial problem' – and the Cold War – were expensive. Since 1958, net military spending overseas, predominantly in Asia and Europe, had increased by 90 per cent, and

---

[191] E. L. Higgins, 'A Party in Search of a Pattern,' *The Times*, 6 April 1964.

[192] As cited in 'Labour's Commonwealth Policy,' *The Round Table*, vol. 55, no. 217 (December 1964).

[193] Malcolm Chalmers, *Paying for Defence: Military Spending and British Decline* (London: Pluto Press, 1985), p. 82.

[194] Ibid.   [195] Ibid.

[196] Leadership Consultative Committee Meeting (LCC (67) 149th Meeting), 23 January 1967. See also LCC (67) 153rd Meeting, 6 February 1967, LCC (67) 186th Meeting, 19 July 1967. CPA.

accounted for one-third of the record payments deficit in 1964.[197] For anti-nuclear activists, Britain's economic decline was 'a direct result of Britain's commitment to the trappings of world power.'[198] No longer did Britain have a military financed from the colonial exchequers; no longer did it have a professional Indian Army funded by colonial taxation.

When asked by the BBC for suggestions on radio programmes about the Commonwealth in 1964, the Assistant Head of Talks had trouble identifying any Commonwealth subject that would be suitable for light programming.[199] He wrote: 'The Commonwealth hardly evokes popular passion, except in a form very near the knuckle: coloured immigration.'[200] Powell in these years linked the indignities of the Commonwealth abroad, Britain's national humiliation, to the 'colour problem.' Politicians, he argued, had fallen out of line with the sentiments of the people: they have felt wrongly obliged to 'profess and perform' the consensus line in support of the Commonwealth 'until by now there is an almost complete divorce between the politicians' words and public opinion.'[201] Due to Britain's 'grand national virtue of solidarity' and 'humbugging,' the political convention has been that it is not 'done' to say what one thinks of the Commonwealth – that would be irresponsible.[202] When Peter Griffiths beat Patrick Gordon Walker, once Secretary of State for Commonwealth Relations, for the seat at Smethwick in 1964, with a campaign that included racist slogans, Powell described the defeated Patrick Gordon Walker as 'more like a humbug than a martyr.'[203] The *Birmingham Post* similarly described Gordon Walker in September 1964 in classed terms as a 'pipe-smoking history don turned politician' who had proven himself unable to interpret the public mood on race.[204] Dennis Barker at *The Guardian* went even further on this point of a social divide when he described Smethwick as a 'brutally monosyllabic industrial town' wherein 'there seemed to be something primitive and tribal about the local bafflement and growling at Mr. Gordon Walker.' Walker had remained patrician or 'gentlemanly till the end' by 'closing his ears to the unhappier expressions of human nature.'[205] Powell

[197] Chalmers, *Paying for Defence*, p. 77.
[198] Ibid.
[199] Webster, *Englishness and Empire*, p.149.
[200] As cited ibid., p. 149: 'Memorandum from Assistant Head of Talks,' 12 March 1964, BBC WAC R 51/783/1, Talks, Commonwealth.
[201] J. Enoch Powell, Camborne Speech, 14 January 1966. POLL 4.1.2.
[202] Ibid.
[203] 'Smethwick: Mr. Powell hits out,' *Wolverhampton Express and Star*, 19 October 1964.
[204] Ritscherle, 'Opting out of Utopia,' p. 207.   [205] Ibid.

was shocked by the sounds of 'self-righteous unction' which arose after Griffiths won the seat – especially Wilson's condemnation of Griffiths as a 'parliamentary leper.'[206] Homemade political placards – 'Vote Labour for more nigger-type neighbours' – had been stuck on the walls and public buildings around both Smethwick and Wolverhampton that year.[207] As Alice Ritscherle has explored, though Peter Griffiths did not attract national support to the extent of Powell in 1968, it is possible to see in his assertions of democratic representation and defence against black immigration a reworking of memories of the Second World War that would appear again within Powellism.[208] Griffiths and his supporters continually distinguished themselves from fascist organizations and asserted that their activities were an expression of Britain's democratic culture.[209] Griffiths' self-described 'declaration of independence' from the liberal elite on immigration remarkably echoed the political language of besieged white identity coming from Rhodesia at this time.

Powell related Wilson's response to Griffiths to problematic transformations in the nature of authority and consent within the postwar state. When Labour took office, Powell spoke out in opposition to the managerial or technocratic approach of government and became preoccupied by the use of one word: *responsibility*. Responsibility was, in Powell's mind, the burden of power. He believed, however, that the word had come to mean something wholly negative in public debate in Britain. Reflecting his training in the classics, Powell set out to uncover the relationship between the misuse of this word and Britain's 'assumptions about life, its moral stature.'[210] Most importantly, Powell argued, it had taken precedence over truth. Words and deeds in politics were deemed, he argued, not true or false but 'responsible' or 'irresponsible.' 'The force and the danger of the modern usage of "responsible" and "responsibility,"' he explained, 'is that it is a sectional opinion, (whether majority or minority), masquerading as authoritative … "irresponsible" comes to mean simply what I (the speaker) don't approve of.'[211] Powell and Harold Wilson were in one breath called 'immature, irresponsible' in the newspapers for failing to agree with some sectional opinion.[212]

[206] 'Smethwick M.P. brought Colour issue into the Open,' *Wolverhampton Express and Star*, 6 November 1964.
[207] 'Immigration Control "Essential",' *Wolverhampton Express and Star*, 10 October 1964.
[208] Ritscherle, 'Opting out of Utopia.'
[209] Ibid., p. 214.
[210] J. Enoch Powell, 'Responsibility: A Dangerously Misused Word,' Guild of British Newspaper Editors Annual Conference, 15 April 1967. POLL 4.1.2.
[211] Ibid.   [212] Ibid.

And so, when the Secretary of the National Union of Mineworkers said at the beginning of April 1967 that the high rate of absenteeism in South Wales coalfields indicated 'irresponsible, anti-social behaviour' and that 'the standards of individual responsibility to the interests of the people as a whole had deteriorated,' Powell quickly condemned him. The coal miner is not criticized, Powell noted, for dishonesty, breach of contract, or the failure to care for his dependants at home. Thus as a kind a 'paradoxical inversion,' the word responsible is applied 'precisely where the person described is not answerable, or is not failing to render the account due from him.'[213] Actual accountability is not discussed, and instead 'a spurious or fictitious accountability' reigns.[214] This, he concluded, was symptomatic of the modern trend towards the 'lawless exertion of power, of the modern preference for mob-rule over rational individual freedom within the law.'[215] The collective power of labour was, in Powell's mind, 'mob' rule. Importantly, the same mob rule Powell found in the collective politics of the union, Powell also found governing Macmillan's National Economic Development Council and Wilson's National Board of Prices and Incomes. All represented a breach in the rule of law: economic intervention by the state superseding regulation, commands superseding the processes of law. This was, he insisted, a political revolution: 'We are witnessing today an enormous and exceedingly swift extension of the ownership, power and influence of government. Its dimensions are those of a revolution.'[216] It represented, for Powell, 'the insolence of power without authority' – or power without consent.[217] The growing economic crisis of the 1960s underlined these criticisms. He argued that this 'revolution' fundamentally failed to protect Britain from economic crisis: it was not intervention, the control of wages, that could curtail inflation; inflation was caused, Powell argued, by government expenditure, consequential national debt and the government's tendency to print money to cover up this debt.[218] The government sold government securities to the money market but also produced money for the money market to purchase these securities.[219] All this was, in Powell's mind, a ruse by which politicians sought to 'escape from responsibility for the consequences of their own policies.'[220]

Importantly, in Powell's critique of state power, collectivism and the 'paternal state,' Powell attempted to bring to life the memories of the

---

[213] Ibid.   [214] Ibid.   [215] Ibid.
[216] J. Enoch Powell, Public meeting, Bognor Regis, 18 November 1966. POLL 4.1.2.
[217] J. Enoch Powell, speech to the Annual Dinner of the Birmingham branch of the Institute of Chartered Secretaries, 21 April 1967. POLL 4.1.2.1.
[218] Gamble, *The Conservative Nation*, pp. 117–118.
[219] Ibid., p. 118.   [220] Ibid., p. 117.

Second World War and, through this, worked to destabilize the marrying of the war with the promises of a postwar reconstructed state. He told the Dulwich Conservative Association:

It is no accident that the Labour Party of 1964 should share this craving for autarchy, for economic self-sufficiency, with the prewar Fascist régimes and the present-day Communist states. They are all at heart totalitarian.[221]

Three years later, Powell warned the South Oxfordshire Political Conference:

We are today in imminent danger of slipping unawares into that form of state socialism which is known as fascism, whereby the control of the state over individuals is exercised largely through corporations which purport to represent the various elements of society, and particularly the employers and employees ... There is an ominous ring of the corporate state about the present relations between the Government, the TUC [Trades Union Council] and the CBI [Confederation of British Industry].[222]

And, he explained to the Stratford Young Conservatives:

You cannot [make economic decisions for private citizens] in time of peace and then pretend that you believe in giving people the opportunities of choice – which incidentally, is the reason why socialists are so often heard using military terms, 'Dunkirk', 'the battle for economic survival' and so on. This reflects their need to persuade the country that it is really living under war or siege conditions and therefore ought to surrender choice and decision to the government. Dictators always talk like that.[223]

Powell, in these years, is attempting to disrupt the fusion within social democracy of 'state' and 'people.' The state is drawn, not as a servant of the people, reflecting the habits and expectations of the national community, but as an enemy dramatically reminiscent of that which was fought against in the Second World War. Powell associated the Conservative compromise with state planning, or the economic consensus of the Middle Way of reformed capitalism, with the appeasers of the 1930s. Though Powell's re-imagining of the memory of war here was to have a limited effect, it would develop, in the following year, into a popular critique of anti-racist legislation.

---

[221] J. Enoch Powell, speech to the Dulwich Conservative Association (29 February 1964), cited in *A Nation Not Afraid: The Thinking of Enoch Powell* (B. T. Batsford, 1965), p. 75.

[222] J. Enoch Powell, Extract from speech at the South Oxfordshire Conservative Political Conference, Wheatley Secondary School, 11 March 1967. POLL 4.1.2.

[223] J. Enoch Powell, Extract from speech at the Stratford Young Conservative Political Day School, Stratford-on Avon, 12 March 1967. POLL. 4.1.2.

Again, Powell insisted that economic controls could not be described as, somehow, moral. While the market was the vehicle of the moral individual, economics itself could answer no moral question. When Ray Gunter, then Minister of Labour, blamed Britain's economic ills in the autumn of 1966 on the 'dishonesty' and 'thriftlessness' of the nation at large, Powell himself received a flood of letters for and against the nation. He viewed this as a sign of how much the idea of the state controlling people's lives had affected those writing to him.[224] It was neither his job nor the job of the National Economic Development Council, but a 'job for moralists,' to work on the nation's moral ills. His job was very different:

For the purposes of politics, human nature, including the human nature of the nation concerned, must be treated as constant, something given and assumed, a starting point. The politician's business is with the environment in which human nature is placed.[225]

Like Oakeshott, this was Powell's opposition to 'rationalism' in politics, against the perfectability of man. While politics and the politician may be 'the nation's psychiatrist' when they create and recreate myths that legitimize their authority,[226] they cannot dramatically change that organic evolutionary entity, the habits and expectations of the community. Instead, the politician is employed by society to dramatize the inevitabilities of the world so as to make them 'appear human, explicable, and amenable to management.'[227] This was Powell's essential critique of Keynesian social democracy and the corporate state that attempted to plan, to manage, human society.[228] On the heels of this critique, Powell would give it new form in the guise of a critique of ethnic communalism in Britain – as will be discussed in the next chapter. In this, Powell would be far more successful in his critique of state power. There the corporate identity of the minority group again demanded the same use of the word (collective) 'responsibility.' In this schema, belief in economic redistribution and communal recognition – the politics of equality and the politics of difference – are symptomatic of the same flawed foundation in political thinking.[229]

[224] J. Enoch Powell, Wessex Area Young Conservative Weekend School, Weymouth, 1 October 1966. POLL 4.1.2.

[225] Ibid.

[226] J. Enoch Powell, speech to Manchester Convention Dinner, 6 November 1965. POLL 4.1.2.

[227] J. Enoch Powell, 'Truth, Politics and Persuasion,' *Advertising Quarterly* (Spring 1965), pp. 7–13 (p. 12).

[228] Samuel Beer, *Modern British Politics: A Study of Parties and Pressure Groups* (London: Faber and Faber, 1965).

[229] See Nancy Fraser and Axel Honneth, *Redistribution or Recognition? A Political-Philosophical Exchange* (London: Verso, 2003).

Powell's rejection of the moral potential of economics was the backbone of his denunciation of Commonwealth development aid. Powell – unlike most of his Conservative colleagues – rejected the benefits of a paternal state. It is an 'inherent absurdity,' he argued, to imagine a state behaving charitably, 'it is collective advantage that governs how a state acts.'[230] Both redistributive taxes and international aid were best understood, he believed, as political bribery. But also, perhaps more importantly, the aid in the Commonwealth was not going to work:

[A]id has more serious effects than repressing or wasting indigenous savings. The reasons for the immense gap between the economic achievements of (for instance) the peoples of Europe and those of the Indian subcontinent in the last three centuries are neither superficial nor predominantly physical: they are deeply rooted in history, in belief, in custom, in race – in short, in the profoundest characteristics of men and societies.[231]

That was in the draft, in the published copy Powell took out any ambiguities regarding race, sanitizing it somewhat of its old imperial tone. The reasons are neither 'superficial nor predominantly geographical: they are deeply rooted in the profoundest characteristics of men and societies.'[232] 'Development' would, necessarily, fail. International charity only led both sides to delude themselves into believing that capitalist achievement did not require social, moral and political change.

The Commonwealth at home

On Remembrance Day 1959, Enoch Powell sat as guest of honour of the Wolverhampton Branch of the Association of Jewish Ex-Servicemen at their tenth annual reunion.[233] For years he had served as regular guest and speaker at these annual dinners. That night, he surprised the audience by telling them that he was broadcasting a description of the proceedings to Israel that very evening. He was in two places at once: as he stood praising the 'double loyalty' of Jews in Britain, so too his regular radio broadcast to Israel, translated into Hebrew, described the ceremony and praised the men and women before him that night. In the speech and the broadcast, Powell would reveal his conception of Britishness and its links to the political life of Britain. Marked by its ability to encompass difference, in stark contrast to the political necessities of belonging found in his arguments against

[230] J. Enoch Powell, 'International Charity,' Draft copy, *New Society*, 5 June 1965. POLL 6.1.1.
[231] Ibid.   [232] Ibid.
[233] 'M.P. Broadcasts Report on W'ton Dinner to Israel,' *Wolverhampton Express and Star*, 9 November 1959.

'New Commonwealth' immigration, Powell's conception of Britishness explained on Remembrance Day 1959 is a revealing starting point in Powell's understanding of national belonging.

The successful double loyalty of the Jewish ex-serviceman – to the Queen and to Israel – was, he explained, as much a result of Britishness as of Jewishness: 'Here are people, who, like myself, have worn the King's coat in war and are proud to keep alive in peace the memory of having done so,'[234] yet at the same time they nourish an 'attachment to an international racial community and a warm concern for the nation-state of Israel.' How is this political contradiction possible? Part of the explanation, he found, lies in 'the firmly territorial basis of British subjecthood: once established where a person was born ... our constitution looks no further to decide his citizenship.' British nationality law was, in 1959, blind to race, religion and custom. Powell would, remarkably, contradict this position in 1981 in the context of the first nationality bill since 1948: there, he protested against the move to assign British nationality to children born in Britain of foreign parents and described the bill as 'a charter of dual nationality.'[235] In 1959, Powell noted in contrast that there was something in the British 'habit of mind' which restrained them from pushing political principles to their logical conclusion. Political contradiction is let be and continues to stand up 'sturdily and successfully in practical life.'[236]

Similarly, while Israeli politics fragmented on principle, the two-party system held an unchallenged sway in Britain. This is because, Powell explained, like the nation itself the two parties are extraordinarily comprehensive and tolerate almost irreconcilable difference of opinion and prejudice. The parties can be this way because 'there is no ideological test or theoretical catechism for membership of either party – no more than there is a racial qualification for British citizenship!' The Conservative Party is, rather, 'purely historical.' It has, he argues, no ideological origin. While the Labour Party may claim to put a theory of government into practice, still there are influential non-ideological strands in the Parliamentary Labour Party 'which are no less historic and traditional' than that of the Conservative Party. In both the party and the nation, historical precedent – 'a kind of primeval tree trunk, onto which branches of all kinds have been grafted from time to time' – enabled the illogical, the contradictory, and the different.[237] Critically, 'British,' in this rendition,

---

[234] 'International Commentary 8 November 1959.' POLL 4.1.27.
[235] As quoted in 'Synod Condemns "Racially Divisive and Inequitable" Nationality Bill,' *The Times*, 25 February 1981.
[236] Ibid.
[237] Ibid.

is not something that someone can easily *become*. Britishness is not a missionary project or ideological orientation.

But Powell's explanation of political belonging in 1959 points to an essential issue at stake in the presence of the ex-colonial immigrant and Britain's Commonwealth commitments. Was the present political life of the West Indian, the Indian, the Pakistani, the Rhodesian a branch on the primeval tree trunk of Britain? Nations, Powell would argue in 1965, are experienced by the constant construction of the nation as a subject through time. Again, the people need a history which assists 'personification of the nation.' It is through that life-story of the nation that 'all the conscious members of the nation are ... "involved."'[238] How Britain's political communities told and retold their national 'life-story' would, in Powell's schema, continually redefine national belonging. But was it possible for past colonizer and past colonial subject to tell the same national life-story? Could they, like a Welsh miner, a Presbyterian minister and a City banker, be 'involved' in the same history and form one moral community? The 'collective self-consciousness' of the nation had two aspects: 'one looking inwards, the other outwards' – a politics of unity and difference.[239] Again, the existential moment of war is that point when the nation reveals itself:

The sense of unity implies the relationship of parts to a whole. The inhabitants of Coventry and Plymouth accepted the consequences to themselves of Great Britain at war, because they imagined Coventry and Plymouth only as parts of a whole: if the whole survived and prospered, they could be comparatively indifferent to the fate of the parts.[240]

Powell's failure to imagine a collective self-consciousness in which the black Briton accepted the fate of the whole stemmed from a politics wholly preoccupied by the limits of political legitimacy and the maintenance of 'organic' hierarchy. This was a matter of time and history: 'national consciousness is transmitted from generation to generation by a process analogous to that of inheritance. Even while it is transmitted it changes, yet remains the same.'[241] The postwar black worker, Powell later insisted, had always meant for her stay in Britain to be temporary. Migrant communities remained profoundly linked to their 'home societies' by intricate networks of social ties and financial obligations. Millions of pounds a year in remittances, annual holidays 'back home' and personal correspondence are offered by Powell as a sign not of family networks that do not fit within the borders of a single nation-state

---

[238] J. Enoch Powell, German Service, 17 June 1965. POLL 4.1.27.
[239] Powell and Maude, *Biography of a Nation*, p. 7.
[240] Ibid., pp. 7–8.   [241] Ibid., pp. 8–9.

but as a sign of impermanence. Citing a sociological report on West Indian migrant experiences, Powell argued in 1968 that the migrant who decided to stay permanently in Britain often cut herself off from these networks, such that she – like her children – 'lost one country without gaining another, lost one nationality without acquiring a new one.'[242]

Powell's overt contradiction regarding dual nationality, between 1959 and 1968 or 1981, was rooted, at least in part, in a view of the black Briton as the bearers of a problematic (British) history. As a West Indian nurse living in Slough in these years put it: 'We had *heard* about slavery in Jamaica but we didn't sort of put it together and put ourselves within. We didn't think it happened to people we descended from. We thought it was somebody else or some other people we didn't know about. But, coming to this country, you get to realize that we're part of slavery.'[243] The consequences of the meeting of past colonizer and past colonial subject, found in these words of a nurse in Slough, bore Enoch Powell's politics, as it threatened to disrupt a 'personification' of the nation for both immigrant and non-immigrant. The resolution of the political tension of decolonization – finding again Britain's historical sense of self – required for Powell a turn away from the colonial past: this was 'Britain with the imperial episode in parenthesis.'[244] This was a strategic rejection of historical guilt, a rejection of enduring political responsibility without enduring power, which would significantly, by 1968, become a clear personification of the English nation as the *victim* of a disconnected and disinterested political leadership and ongoing and excessive postcolonial reprisals.[245]

Speaking at a St George's Day banquet, Powell explained that the 'unbroken life' of the *English* nation – the Crown and the supremacy of the Crown in Parliament – could still welcome Powell's generation back 'like one which comes home again from years of distant wandering.'[246] The English nation – because it took as 'an axiom' that the American colonies could not be represented in Parliament and 'had to confess' that even Ireland, not to mention the non-white New Commonwealth, could not be assimilated – underwent 'no organic change as the mistress of world empire.'[247] Though Powell spoke consistently of Britain and remained

---

[242] J. Enoch Powell, 'To the Annual Conference of the Rotary Club of London,' Eastbourne, 16 November 1968, in *Reflections of a Statesman*, pp. 382–393 (p. 392).

[243] Cited in Hiro, *Black British, White British*, p. 86.

[244] Ibid.

[245] Gilroy, *Postcolonial Melancholia*, p. 128.

[246] J. Enoch Powell, 'Speech at the Royal Society of St. George,' 23 April 1961. POLL 4.1.1.

[247] Ibid.

committed politically to Unionism, a conscious return to 'England' offered one way for the English to put the (colonial) past in parenthesis.[248] Here in the St George's Day speech, Powell again used the tree metaphor. This time he likened the English to the Athenians, returning to their city after it had been sacked and burnt by the Persians, finding in the blackened ruins, 'the sacred olive tree, the native symbol of their country.'[249] England herself, 'the sap still rising from her ancient roots to meet the spring,' stood amidst a vanished empire and 'the fragments of demolished glory.' When the connections to distant continents and 'strange races' fell away, the life of England, Powell argued, was unbroken. Thus Powell begged his audience to look back past Macmillan's humble empire-builders, past 'the brash adventurous days of the first Elizabeth and the hard materialism of the Tudors,' into the eyes of the Englishman and woman of the old village church, linked to the audience via a shared land – 'where the same blackthorn showered its petals' – and a shared Crown.[250] Through all the change, political authority and cultural community remained.

Margery Perham's injunction in the 1961 Reith Lectures highlights the problem of history for legitimate authority in the postcolonial era. It is the same ambivalence and tension that Powell, among others, worked to mediate in Australia, in India and in Britain. As Powell spoke of a 'clean break' with Britain's imperial past against the Commonwealth and much of the Labour Party and some Conservatives opted for a transformation in the meaning of the past via the Commonwealth, the political expressions of black communities at this time – as the 'unwitting bearers of the imperial and colonial past'[251] and the 'unofficial front line of decolonization'[252] – likewise reveal a historical reckoning with the present. More so than Pakistani or Indian immigrants, and in large part more so than the British, West Indians arrived into Britain well educated in the lessons of the imperial project. The British educational system in the West Indies had been in these years steeped in the history lessons of the 'Mother Country.'[253] For middle-class Jamaicans especially, British identity and (classed) respectability were 'intimately intertwined.'[254]

[248] Heffer, *Like the Roman*, p. 335.
[249] J. Enoch Powell, 'Speech at the Royal Society of St. George,' 23 April 1961. POLL 4.1.1.
[250] 'Mr. Macmillan Praises the "Humble Empire Builders,"' *The Times*, 24 September 1959.
[251] Gilroy, *Postcolonial Melancholia*, p. 101.
[252] Bill Schwarz, '"Claudia Jones and the *West Indian Gazette*": Reflections on the Emergence of Post-colonial Britain,' *Twentieth Century British History*, 14: 3 (2003), pp. 264–285 (p. 267).
[253] E. J. B. Rose, *Colour and Citizenship*, p. 45.
[254] Rush, *Bonds of Empire*, p. 10.

In Britain, present racism was therefore brought to bear on the *classed* ideals of this imperial project. As Bill Schwarz argues, by 'simply going about their daily lives, navigating their way through the lore of the metropolis [West Indian immigrants] discovered themselves having to interrogate the lived culture of the colonizer, in order to comprehend their own discrepant experiences.'[255] We find a moment such as this in the poem 'Roomseeker in London,' written by Jamaican-born James Berry in the 1950s:

> I saw him rapping her door
> Field man of old empire stood
>   with that era he brought
>
> She knew a man from sunny skies
> She knew a bundle in arms
> That walked with a hopeful mind
>
> This then was the trial
>
> Sugar man sighed
>   on outrage the lady effused
>   and she quickly bolted in ...[256]

Margery Perham's 'colonial reckoning' was there, for James Berry, in the door that closed on the room-seeker: British racism revealed the truth of the imperial project and the nature of Powell's organic community in the market. The man at the door brought 'that era' of 'old empire' to bear on Britain.

Over these years, we see the uses of colonial knowledge in Britain also in the right-wing group, the Monday Club. Here, also, we see the rhetorical juxtaposition of the survival of historic British democracy against any commitment to postwar humanism. The Monday Club was a grassroots political group founded in 1961 in reaction to Harold Macmillan's 'Wind of Change' speech in Cape Town – in reaction to the notion that the growth of national consciousness and the end of white rule was inevitable in Africa. Arguments such as that appearing in G. K. Young's talk to a West London Monday Club function entitled 'Is a Multi-Racial Society Possible?' were a regular occurrence.[257] According to Young, it wasn't. Like many other ex-colonialists, Young claimed the authority of experience to speak on race: 'My years in America as a young man brought home some of the complications of

---

[255] Schwarz, 'Claudia Jones and the *West Indian Gazette*,' pp. 267–268.
[256] James Berry, 'Roomseeker in London,' in James Procter (ed.), *Writing Black Britain, 1948–1998* (Manchester University Press, 2000), p. 21.
[257] G. K. Young, West London Monday Club, 16 April 1970. See Immigration Data, SRO, D4490/2.

race ... Several years in the East African forces, when I got to know most of the peoples and languages from Eritrea to the Zambesi and West to the Congo River, raised further questions ...' In the early 1950s, Young was appointed controller of Secret Intelligence Services in the Middle East. From those experiences, he concluded:

If anything formed on me an agonizing reappraisal of the notion of 'Man' – with a capital 'M' – equal in the sight of God or anyone else, it was the discrepancy between the human reality – usually the stark realities of conflict – and the claptrap of British political oratory or even of Cabinet discussions.[258]

Young argued that the very notion of 'Man' denied the stark realities of conflict. Every multiracial state in the world, he went on, had already become an authoritarian government – 'or was embarked on a course which would require increasingly authoritarian methods.'[259] Here, Young based his arguments on race on the prospects of political democracy and employing the imperial experience as evidence of the impossibility of a multiracial state. Angus Maude MP, who only a few years later would play a key role in Margaret Thatcher's bid for the Conservative Party leadership, put it this way in 1971:

Nigel H. Jones ... tells us that the building of a multi-racial society in Britain 'should be the aim of all who believe in democracy, liberty and justice.' It does not seem to me that the infliction on indigenous majorities of large alien minorities – whether whites in Africa, Chinese in Malaya, Indians in Fiji and Mauritius or Scots in Ireland – has ever had much to do with democracy and justice, and I doubt if it has much advanced the cause of liberty. Surely, in the light of other experiments all over the world, it requires considerable faith to believe that this ever leads to anything but trouble and unhappiness. Mr. Jones clearly has his faith; but is he really entitled to be so contemptuous of those who find it less easy to fly in the face of all the historical evidence?

As evidenced by the later influence of Angus Maude in the Conservative Party, the Monday Club by no means remained on the fringes of British politics. The Monday Club was not the National Front. This was Establishment politics. By 1971, the club had the largest membership of any conservative group, with 10,000 members, 55 different groups in universities and colleges, 35 Members of Parliament and 35 Peers.[260] As we shall see in Chapter 5, these imperial memories of disorder would come to the fore as a means of

---

[258] Ibid.   [259] Ibid.
[260] Robert Copping, *The Story of the Monday Club – The First Decade* (Ilford: Current Affairs Information Service, 1972), p. 14.

comprehending the social uncertainty and 'crisis of the regime' of the 1970s.[261]

History was a central component in negotiating the Commonwealth immigrant's political belonging. But, even more, the presence of the immigrant had the potential to reveal a history of class inequity. The collaborative work of film-maker Philip Donnellan and sound archivist Charles Parker in the Birmingham-based BBC1 documentary titled *The Colony* (1964) gives insight into the views of four typical Caribbean immigrants: a teacher Bernice Smith, a nurse Polly Perkins, a railwayman Stan Crooke and a bus conductor Victor Williams. This work was unusual for its time, when close to all social documentaries focused in these years on the indigenous experience of a 'colour problem.'[262] Recorded and framed by these two white British socialists, only the words of the four immigrants are heard. At the beginning and repeated in the middle – providing the refrain of the work[263] – we hear a man's voice say:

Sometimes we think we shouldn't blame the people because it's we who have come to your country and troubled them. On the other hand, we think if they in the first place had not come to our country and spread the false propaganda, we would never have come to theirs. *If we had not come, we would not be the wiser. We would still have the good image of England, thinking that they are what they are not. And the English would be as ignorant as us.*[264]

If the West Indian had not come, both the Englishman and the West Indian would believe that the English 'are what they are not.' Here, he tells the television viewers that the truth of their history is revealed in their meeting. In the documentary, this is both a critical and a revelatory moment: as the transport worker looks at old machinery, he speaks of the Birmingham engineers who built it, men of 100 and 200 years ago, who 'must have had an open mind.'[265] He explains that England is 'so rich with culture of the past' that there is 'nothing the living can do' to destroy it. The challenge, as he describes it, is 'learning from the dead' and taking 'no notice of the living.'[266] *The Colony* ends with a Caribbean family touring an English stately home, with a tour guide telling them when rooms and furniture around the

---

[261] For a discussion of the 'crisis of the regime,' see Anthony King, 'The Problem of Overload,' in A. King (ed.), *Why is Britain Becoming Harder to Govern?* (London: BBC, 1976), p. 26.

[262] Webster, *Englishness and Empire*, p. 163.

[263] Ibid.

[264] Philip Donnellan, *The Colony*, BBC television documentary, 1964 (my emphasis).

[265] Ibid.

[266] Ibid.

home were constructed, stretching back hundreds of years. As we see them on tour, we hear the mother speak: 'One doesn't put slavery in their minds.' But if they really think about it, 'They've got to look onto it.'[267]

The family walking through the front hall, up the stairs, and into the bedroom of the stately home in *The Colony* certainly held symbolic meaning for the viewers at home. The home, especially in the context of postwar housing scarcities, was both the container of a (racialized) postwar domestic order[268] and, linked to this, the ultimate sign of economic viability and wealth. The Caribbean family walking through the stately home, while the mother speaks of slavery, works in the film to underline the colonials' role in Britain's own nation building. This was no doubt in dialogue with the prevalent conflation of the degradation of the home due to non-white settlement and Britain's national decline.

In that schema, the immigrant through the creation of 'a Calcutta in Birmingham' threatened the investment property of the non-immigrant and therefore the very future of Britain. Elspeth Huxley's (Institute of Race Relations-funded) *Back Streets, New Worlds*, which came out only the previous year as a widely read serial in *Punch*, offers one example among many of this vision. Huxley, herself raised in Kenya, had gained notoriety with fictional and journalistic work from an explicitly colonial perspective. In this book, we find Asian and West Indian people, 'often with broods as ample as their predecessors,' crammed into 'middle-class, nineteenth-century … Victoriana' that were too big for the modern single family.[269] Due to modern transformations in class and family structure, this piece of Britain's history is left to turn – with immigrant settlement – into a slum.

Philip Donnellan's choreography of *The Colony* in the richly decorated stately home exactly confronts this fear: this was not any ordinary home, but one that might remind the audience of their historical exclusion from the nation's wealth. This was, in essence, exactly what Powell feared. The immigrant threatened to disrupt the homogeneous, deferential nation (by revealing economic injustice). Ironically, it was in this recognition of their own exclusion that some working-class voters would deny their economic relationship to colonial exploitation. Their own exploitation – in the factory, in the home, or at war – was not

---

[267] Ibid.
[268] See Wendy Webster, 'Race, Ethnicity and National Identity,' in Ina Zweiniger-Bargielowska (ed.), *Women in Twentieth Century Britain: Economic, Social and Cultural Change* (London: Longman, 2001), pp. 292–306.
[269] Ibid.

what linked them to the immigrant worker but what determined their national belonging and what promised to distinguish them from the immigrant.

The political significance of the home – especially in negotiating the unstable social relationships of gender and class in these years – is a constant refrain in the letters Powell received from the public. A letter from a woman in Luton to Powell is a good example. Luton was home of the Vauxhall factory that built Churchill tanks during the Second World War; it consequently suffered severe war damage and, in the postwar years, extensive slum clearance and then long-term construction of multiple housing projects. The Luton woman began her letter to Powell with her feeling that Indians seemed to have 'the monopoly on houses.'[270] She then told Powell of one occasion when she woke up to see her landlord, an Indian, in her bedroom, while her husband worked the nightshift. The landlord quickly '(fortunately for me) tiptoed out and I was obliged thereafter to put a chair under the door knob. It is not the first time a white woman has been raped under these conditions and could do nothing because of disbelief and fear of eviction!' Whatever the landlord was doing, though he tiptoed out, this was seen by this letter-writer as a sexual violation linked, with his ownership of the house, to some inversion of power. In many ways, this letter – on this point – reads as a historian might expect: the (racial) inversion of power is manifest in the letter as a transgression in the bedroom and dramatically echoes the last two decades of highly gendered media coverage of colonial wars. Wendy Webster has argued convincingly that a letter such as this signifies 'the language of empire' coming home: 'Stories of colonial wars and immigration set "Little England" in opposition to a multiracial Commonwealth, emphasizing a domesticated identity – Englishness, not Britishness – exclusive, intimate, private, and white.'[271] But then, after this near dramatic tale, the letter quickly turns to another complaint found as commonly in the letters Powell received over the years.

The Luton woman, in the very next sentence, tells Powell she would like to make one more point: that 'women (white) in this Country have always done the monotonous tedious and dirty jobs without quibble and very poor pay,' yet new immigrants 'straight away moan about poor pay and poor work!' She then exclaims, 'Were [sic] on earth does charity begin!' The immigrant, on social services, was only going to make her job as a woman harder: 'It's the women in this

[270] Letter to Powell, 21 April 1968. POLL 8.1.8.
[271] Ibid.

country that made it function from the start ... The people are like parasites living off our backs.'[272] She reads non-white immigration as not just an intrusion of white domestic order – the political demands of the immigrant threaten, also, the certainties of class, bringing about what Perham calls the 'escape from authority.' Without quibble, women had worked the dirty jobs. Now, she claims, the immigrant complains and goes on to receive the social benefits that were rightfully hers. As Amy Whipple notes in her analysis of Powell's letters, race and social identities were 'mutually constitutive' in the postwar years.[273] Decline in working-class allegiance to the Labour Party cannot be simply read as 'race' challenging 'class' as the basis of party support. A vote for the Conservative Party was considered, for these letter-writers, a vote for their class – for itself.[274]

Of course, the home – as a site of domestic reconstruction – was in no small way tied to the political meaning of the Second World War in the postwar period. The 'Marshall Street Plan,' in Griffiths' town of Smethwick, is just one example of the entangled politics of race, property, home and neighbourhood at this time. The Marshall Street Plan originated in December 1964 from the lobbying of 'a housewives' deputation' that petitioned Conservatives on the Town Council to prevent the emergence of a 'coloured ghetto' on Marshall Street.[275] It resulted in a plan to use municipal funds to purchase houses on Marshall Street that were up for sale and to sell or rent them exclusively to whites on Smethwick's council housing register.[276] The name was, according to Alice Ritscherle, no accident:

[B]ased primarily upon the street targeted for Council action, the frequent omission of 'Street' in the name 'Marshall Plan' carried powerful suggestions of the widespread destruction wrought by fascist aggression ... By casting the 'Marshall Plan' as part of a larger effort to revitalize Britain in wake of a devastating and destabilizing war, and to repair the damage caused by foreign aggression, Smethwick's leading Conservatives referring to 'Marshall Aid' rhetorically cast immigrants as foreign elements that had brought social and economic hardship to beleaguered Britons.

Here we see an important contour of the emergent politics of a property-owners' democracy.[277] In other words, black immigration

[272] Letter to Powell, 22 April 1968, POLL 8.1.8.
[273] Whipple, 'Revisiting the "Rivers of Blood" Controversy,' p. 728.
[274] Ibid.
[275] Ritscherle, 'Opting out of Utopia,' p. 218.   [276] Ibid.
[277] Foote, 'The Importance of Enoch,' in The Republican Transformation of Modern British Politics, pp. 139–161.

was presented, by some, to exactly threaten the promises of postwar reconstruction.

The idea that the services of the postwar welfare state were a direct political recompense for past *English* sacrifice can be found in a vast number of Powell's letters from the public. Along with the sacrifices of war, perpetual sacrifice to 'the monotonous tedious and dirty jobs' – the willing sacrifice of labour – was, for the Luton woman, the very substance of national belonging. So, too, a widow of an ex-serviceman in South London wrote to Powell: 'Our British working classes have maintained this country all down the years with the toil of our hands and the sweat of our brows, and shed rivers of blood in its defence as you know,' yet '[t]raitor politicians wrenched our birth-right from us and handed it over to immigrants' such that the British working classes are now being treated as a 'slave element' and 'the intruders.'[278] This woman goes so far as to regret that the British people had not the 'guts like the Russian PEOPLE to kick out their brutal oppressors, and seize their own country.'[279] Another writes to Powell after Sir Learie Constantine, the West Indian cricketer and member of the British government's new Race Relations Board, spoke of the need to recognize the significance of slavery in British history: 'Tonight, we have [him] telling us we owe his people a living because of their history – is he referring to past slave labour, let them look up ... at our own beautiful Churches, mute symbols of slave labour.'[280] That was the mute slave labour of the English labourer. She continues, 'Let them read <u>our</u> History, of pregnant woman [sic] working the mines – of children being exploited and made to work long hours – or people being executed for stealing a loaf of bread ... The natives of this country are getting restless, the natives who's [sic] forbears sacrificed so much for the greatness of this Country.'[281] The history of their suffering as a class – their victimization – again and again stood in sharp contrast to the political claims of the ex-colonial. They alone had been the labourers of the British state. Unlike white America or white South Africa, they as a class held no historic obligation to blacks in Britain or the Commonwealth. The working classes, they emphasized (and Powell assured them), shared no history with the colonial worker. Remarkably, the presence of the 'New Commonwealth' immigrant came to be read

[278] Letter to Powell, 22 April 1968. POLL 8.1.1.
[279] Ibid.
[280] Letter to Powell, 22 April 1968. POLL 8.1.8.
[281] Ibid.

as a further extension of (historical) inequities – not in terms of race, but in terms of gender and class.

It was in this schema that the upper classes had a historical relationship and responsibility to the West Indian immigrant. Again, as Huxley put it in *Punch*:

I think it hit me most in Bath; that elegant, essentially European eighteenth-century town with its honey-coloured crescents and its ghosts of fobs and beaux and Jane Austen and the stout, ebony Jamaican in her baggy purple cardigan and red beret and old skirt, pushing a pram over a zebra crossing ... And yet, in Bath's heyday, to see a Negro page in hose and doublet carrying the fan of a pomaded lady ... was a sight as commonplace as gouty gentlemen.[282]

The civility, the pomp and display of class and race difference expressed by the pomaded lady and her 'Negro page' is imagined here against a frumpy 'stout' woman inhabiting streets once walked by Jane Austen. The meaning of the presence of a black person in Bath had transformed from a reinforcement of rank and racial superiority to a disruption of it. 'Oh!' wrote one supporter to Powell, 'If some of those high and mighty know-it-alls would take time away from their detached houses and their country estates and come and live with us for a while!'[283] Living as neighbours, working side by side, immigrant and non-immigrant are indistinguishable. The passing of the second Race Relations Act in 1968 – which will be discussed in further detail in the following chapter – was seen in clear class terms by most of Powell's supporters as the (Labour) government's abandonment of their historic responsibilities to the working classes. With the act, private businesses – most commonly the pub and the boarding house – were liable to anti-discrimination law. As Powell told it, the upper classes passed these laws as recompense for their colonial past. In this view, the Commonwealth – as the moral resolution of British imperialism – was a political necessity with which the working classes were uninvolved. The expansion of the principles of the welfare state beyond Britain's national borders in the guise of Commonwealth aid and Commonwealth immigration – a premise accepted by many in the Conservative Party[284] – only disrupted the welfare state's essential meaning, for Powell's supporters, as a historical resolution of Britain's class war.

Significantly, British Asian and West Indian labour groups similarly came to invest little in the political potential of Commonwealth

[282] Elspeth Huxley, *Back Streets, New Worlds: A Look at Immigrants in Britain* (Toronto: Chatto and Windus, 1964), p.39.
[283] Letter to Powell, 21 April 1968. POLL 8.1.1.
[284] *A Changing Partnership: A Report by the Young Conservatives on Problems of the Commonwealth* (London: Conservative Political Centre No. 248, 1962).

membership after the Commonwealth Immigrants Act of 1962. Prior
to 1962, black activists would more often assert their rights as citizens
of the Commonwealth rather than as permanent members of British
society.[285] Thus Claudia Jones, the editor of the *West Indian Gazette*,
condemned the bill on the ground that it 'knocked down the very foundations of the Commonwealth.'[286] She appealed, then, to 'the British
working class, with its rich tradition of human brotherhood and unity
of working people,' which she was sure would be 'appalled by this dangerous government policy.'[287] The Act belied any equality of British
and Commonwealth citizenship. In the years ahead, in the struggle for
minority labour rights and recognition after 1962, focus would again be
given to a broad working-class internationalism or equality of national
citizenship but with little reference to the Commonwealth. The Indian
Workers' Association came to refer to the Commonwealth as a fundamentally paternalistic entity, representing a distinctly pro-capital, pro-
American international position. The failure of the Commonwealth
ideal with the passing of the 1962 Act and increasing political significance of Vietnam, South Africa and the US Civil Rights and Black
Power movements – all outside the Commonwealth and all essential
catalysts of black political activism in Britain – combined to reveal by
the mid- to late 1960s a shared history and sense of belonging outside
the confines of Britain's imperial political history.[288] With this, African-
American soul music enunciated a compelling vision of black struggle
and liberation. James Brown's 'Say It Loud I'm Black and I'm Proud'
and the Chi-Lites' 'Power To The People' were, at this time, taken to
the heart of black communities in both Britain and the Caribbean.[289]
Here, at least in Britain's Afro-Caribbean communities, emerged a new
politics detached from the promises of an imperial past made good.

The Commonwealth is dead

It was, also, in Britain's dealings with Africa – through protests against
white rule in Rhodesia and South Africa, development aid, as well as
Kenyan Asian immigration – that Britain's relationship with its imperial past was, in large part, put to the test. Powell claimed that the

[285] Rich, *Race and Empire in British Politics*, p. 199.
[286] Claudia Jones, leaflet for the Seventh Afro-Asian-Caribbean Conference, 31 January
1962, as cited in Rich, *Race and Empire in British Politics*, p. 199.
[287] Ibid.
[288] For instance, see 'Anti-imperialism Campaigns, 1961–1979,' IWA, MS
2141/A/4/15.
[289] Gilroy, *There Ain't No Black in the Union Jack*, p. 236.

Commonwealth ideal had inevitably failed in Africa. The notion that Whitehall was the source of lawful government in Rhodesia would, he argued, be as absurd as declaring the same of Outer Mongolia.[290] Rhodesia's white minority rule and Unilateral Declaration of Independence (UDI) was, simply put, a political reality. This broke from the official positions of both the Conservative and Labour Parties, which affirmed Britain's special responsibility in the Rhodesian crisis. Commonwealth leaders, likewise, insisted on Britain's political responsibility to refuse Rhodesian independence and increase pressures against the illegal regime. Powell received letters from Rhodesians, thankful for his unpopular position.

The date 11 November 1965 marks one endpoint in the life of the Commonwealth. On that day Prime Minister Ian Smith signed the Unilateral Declaration of Independence of Rhodesia. The date was significant. It was Britain's day of remembrance for the veterans of the world wars. Rhodesia, Smith reminded Britain, had also sent its men to die for England. 'The streets of Salisbury were silent,' began one journalist's account, 'but not in memory of Armistice Day.'[291] The meaning of the day had dramatically changed. On 14 November, no official representative from Rhodesia was present to lay a wreath at the Cenotaph in the Remembrance Day service. The Rhodesian High Commissioner, Brigadier Andrew Skeen, had been on the list of official wreath bearers for that day but had left the country suddenly only 24 hours before. His absence, one reporter noted, 'tended to show Remembrance Day is very much a Commonwealth occasion.'[292] Proof of this the reporter found in the crowd: 'Apart from the High Commissioners themselves, the vast crowd, 20 deep in places, was liberally interspersed with coloured onlookers.'[293] Smith's declaration on the day of remembrance was less a rejection of the significance of war than a pointed reference to wartime sacrifice.

In the UDI, Smith made explicit use of the American precedent when declaring independence. This was not unusual in Rhodesian nationalist politics. *The Guardian* went so far as to compare the parallel wording of the American and Rhodesian declarations side by side.[294] This was, Smith declared, a 'refusal by Rhodesians to sell their birthright,' a declaration for the 'preservation of justice, civilization, and Christianity' and a declaration of Rhodesia's 'sovereign independence.'[295] He declared that the 220,000 whites in Rhodesia were a nation

[290] J. Enoch Powell, speech in London, 10 January 1969. POLL 3.2.1.20.
[291] Marion Kaplan, 'Their Rhodesia,' *Transition*, no. 23 (1965), p. 32.
[292] 'A Wreath Missing at Cenotaph,' *The Guardian*, 15 November 1965, p. 3.
[293] Ibid.
[294] 'A Difference of Wording,' *The Guardian*, 12 November 1965, p. 13.
[295] *East Africa and Rhodesia Newspaper*, 18 November 1965, pp. 204–205.

unto themselves. Harold Wilson quickly made efforts to differentiate the UDI from the historical political validity of the American Declaration of Independence: unlike the United States, he emphasized, Rhodesia did not have the 'respect for the opinions of mankind.'[296] The Labour government had been negotiating with Smith for a year to secure a plan toward majority rule in Rhodesia. Due to ongoing parliamentary political pressure and protests by groups such as the newly formed Campaign Against Racial Discrimination and the Indian Workers' Association, as well as international pressure from the Commonwealth and the UN, the Labour Cabinet refused to accept Rhodesia's declaration and adopted a policy known as NIBMAR (or No Independence Before Majority African Rule).

In public statements during the Rhodesian crisis, Powell argued that Britain had no power to refuse Rhodesia's independence. There was no arguing with the existence of a state: Rhodesia was a political reality. All Britain had was the influence of a 'kindred country.'[297] Smith rejected the idea that the solution to Rhodesian 'racial problems' would be resolved by the British government succumbing to the 'blackmail' of African nationalists: 'We Rhodesians have rejected the doctrinaire philosophy of appeasement and surrender.'[298] Powell and Angus Maude together noted that, 'the Westminster formula' of one man, one vote 'automatically meant their elimination.'[299]

The same day as Smith's announcement, Wilson replied in the Commons, calling the declaration an act of rebellion and emphasizing Britain's singular political responsibility. The Foreign Secretary in New York emphasized to the UN and to the United States that Rhodesia was a British responsibility, even more so than it had been in the past, 'because now the responsibility lies directly on this country and on this House, because certainly no other country will have any legal right to exercise power in Rhodesia.'[300] This, Wilson declared, was 'our tragedy.'[301] Likewise, Maudling, then Deputy Leader of the Conservative Party, the next day agreed that the problem of Rhodesia was 'essentially one for Britain.' And it had to be kept that way. Britain had to show the world what it had done to solve the situation 'by measures acceptable to the British people both here and in the African continent.'[302] On the left,

---

[296] 'The Conflict of Different Worlds ...' *The Guardian*, 12 November 1965, p. 3.
[297] J. Enoch Powell, 'Land of Hope and Glory Reinterpretation,' *New Horizons*, 10 November 1966.
[298] Ibid.
[299] Powell and Maude, *Biography of a Nation*, p. 234.
[300] 'Mr Wilson Outlines Plans for Sanctions,' *The Guardian*, 12 November 1965, p. 3.
[301] Ibid.
[302] '"Only Britain" has Rhodesia Solution,' *The Guardian*, 13 November 1965, p. 9.

Fenner Brockway, chairman of the Movement for Colonial Freedom, speaking at an anti-UDI meeting in Hyde Park on 14 November, likewise called for the government to accept the 'responsibility of applying direct rule pending the introduction of a democratic Constitution.'[303] This was the spectacle of Britain claiming responsibility, yet – in Angus Maude and Powell's words – 'calling on the rest of the world to help her in the vain attempt to coerce the rebels into obedience.'[304] Here we find 'a weird colophon to end the chapter of Britain in Africa.'[305]

In January 1964, Duncan Sandys, then minister at the Commonwealth Relations Office, received a dispatch from Southern Rhodesia. The report explained that the white Rhodesians saw 'our realistic colonial policies' as a 'dereliction of imperial duty.'[306] Further, these white Rhodesians 'delude themselves that British public opinion is fundamentally on their side: *if it could only find expression.*' Rhodesians, by 1966, believed they had found that public support in Powell. The language of the white settler, particularly that of the Rhodesian, converged after 1956 with opponents of non-white immigration into Britain.[307] As Schwartz argues: 'With immigration, the colonial frontier came "home." When this happened, the language of the colonies was reworked and came with it ... two inter-related sentiments slowly cohered, unevenly and partially. First, whites were coming to imagine themselves as historic victims; and second – commensurably – blacks were believed to be acquiring a status of supremacy.'[308] Crucially, this convergence relied on a remaking of the meaning of the Second World War. Martin Francis's work on Ian Smith has shown that the stories of Smith's heroism in wartime, as an RAF pilot, were a powerful source of support for Smith in both Britain and Rhodesia.[309]

Two months after the UDI, Powell would tell a Conservative rally in Cornwall that he believed 'the great majority of people in this country' saw 'no reality or substance' in the proposition that they belonged to

---

[303] 'Demonstrators Clash with Police,' *The Guardian*, 15 November 1965, p. 3.
[304] Powell and Maude, *Biography of a Nation*, p. 234.
[305] Ibid.
[306] J. B. Johnston dispatch, 'Southern Rhodesia: the political scene,' 17 January 1964, cited in Ronald Hyam and William Roger Lewis (eds.), *The Conservative Government and the End of Empire, 1957–1964: Economics, International Relations and the Commonwealth Pt. 2* (London: The Stationery Office, 2000).
[307] Schwarz, 'The Only White Man In There,' pp. 65–78; Bill Schwarz, 'Black Metropolis, White England,' in Mica Nava and Alan O'Shea (eds.), *Modern Times: Reflections on a Century of English Modernity* (London: Routledge, 1996), pp. 182–207; Schwarz, 'Reveries of Race: The Closing of the Imperial Moment,' in Conekin, Mort and Waters (eds.), *Moments of Modernity*, pp. 189–207.
[308] Schwarz, 'The Only White Man In There,' p. 73.
[309] Francis, *The Flyer: British Culture and the Royal Air Force*, p. 192.

a Commonwealth of twenty-two nations, 'which by colonization, by cession, by conquest, by purchase, by a variety of other means, had come under the domination or protection of the British Crown at the time of the Second World War and are now independent countries.'[310] The myth of the unity and coherence of empire had been replaced by another, less convincing, myth. The great majority of people note the Commonwealth countries' 'antipathy' towards Britain in the United Nations. They note that the manner of their internal affairs is 'repugnant to their own basic ideas of liberty and democracy.'[311] This is no political community.

In the Rhodesian newspaper *The Chronicle*, a report on his speech appeared immediately. He found welcome ears there for his arguments against the 'indignities' of belonging to such an ungrateful group.[312] Since 'it ceased to be an Empire,' it noted, the Commonwealth 'has become the most malleable body in history, twisting, turning and contorting itself to accommodate new ideas and ideologies,' while ungrateful member countries 'twist the lion's tail with impunity.'[313] Again, at this time, *The Economist* would go so far as to call it 'the world's biggest experiment yet in sustained and creative historical humour.'[314] Powell received letters from the public, lamenting that '[t]hings have completely changed since the Commonwealth was first formed,' and that England must put its interests first and 'not be shackled by a lot of members who should not be in the so called Commonwealth.'[315] England was the victim, shackled, now, by historic 'responsibilities' without power. In 1970, Powell wrote that Britain would have been 'fortunate' if it had suffered only the 'transitory' 'embarrassments incident upon the dissolution of Empire' – that is the 'Suez fiasco' and the 'Rhodesian episode.' But 'there was another inheritance' – not from the empire itself, but from the contrivance by which the British had endeavoured to conceal themselves from the realities of its decline.

This sense of victimization to international commitments would serve as the foundation of Powell's arguments on immigration. Just a month after his 'Rivers of Blood' speech, when the reverberations of the speech were already dramatic but their meaning not yet clear, Powell was asked

---

[310] 'Tory: Commonwealth's Finished,' *Toronto Star*, 15 January 1966. SRO, D3123/240; see also 'Mr. Powell Criticizes Hypocrisy over Commonwealth,' *The Times*, 15 January 1966.

[311] 'Mr. Powell Criticizes Hypocrisy over Commonwealth,' *The Times*, 15 January 1966.

[312] 'Kissing in the Club,' *The Chronicle*, 17 January 1966. SRO, D3123/240.

[313] Ibid.

[314] *The Economist*, 6 June 1964.

[315] Letter to Powell, 9 March 1966. SRO, D3123/233.

in a radio interview if Britain had failed to restrict Commonwealth immigration prior to 1962 due to a 'false sense of moral superiority' over, for instance, the United States.[316] To this Powell answered,

... the deeper and political cause was the myth of the Commonwealth. We in this country, and particularly the Conservative Party as the ex-imperial party wanted passionately to go on believing that we had a great Commonwealth of Nations, now nobody else took any notice of this and therefore it was only by our own actions that we could continue to assert that there was any unity at all.[317]

And so Britain asserted an unreal unity, according to Powell, via immigration.

... the sole remaining unity after the destruction even of the unity of the crown was our inability in this country to distinguish between the citizens of one Commonwealth country and another Commonwealth country. Alone of all Commonwealth countries could we do this, and so we claw[ed] desperately to this theoretical shred of reality in this otherwise bogus mythical self-consoling invention of the British Commonwealth.[318]

Finally, Powell agreed with his interviewer that this came close to a problem of moral superiority: the myth of the Commonwealth was a 'peculiarly British humbug,' a 'self-consoling invention,' that had been the cause of 'why this fantastic thing' – unrestricted immigration – had been allowed to happen.[319] As one man wrote to Powell from the Inverness Conservative and Unionist Association: 'To us who have lived in Africa, India and the West Indies, our government at best was guilty of unbelievable stupidity and ignorance.'[320] There will be 'howls of agony at the inevitable result.'[321] The empire had come home, not just in the presence and politics of the 'New Commonwealth' immigrant, but in the political thinking of the white colonial.

By 1967, when Powell was Shadow Minister of Defence, fears about New Commonwealth immigration intensified when thousands of Kenyan Asians attempted to immigrate to Britain within a few short months. Much like the later process of 'Africanization' in Uganda, Kenyan Asians were restricted to certain sectors of the economy and sacked from the civil service. Having been given the option of applying for Kenyan citizenship in the first two years of independence (between 1963 and 1965), the majority of Asians in Kenya had opted

---

[316] 22 May 1968 taping. POLL 4.1.28.
[317] Ibid.   [318] Ibid.
[319] Ibid.
[320] Letters to Powell, 10 August 1972. See 'East African Asians, 1972,' SRO, D3123/185.
[321] Ibid.

to retain their status as British subjects. This amounted to approximately 50,000 United Kingdom citizens according to Kenyan Asian leaders (though the estimates in the political debates in Britain ranged up to 250,000).[322] The Colonial Office under the Conservative politician Duncan Sandys had negotiated Kenya's independence and, with white colonials in mind, had legislated that all subjects in Kenya who did not automatically become Kenyan citizens (those who, in other words, were not indigenous Africans) could retain British citizenship and could apply for a passport issued by the British government. A year before Kenyan independence, the Commonwealth Immigrants Act of 1962 was passed, which was the first legislation to attempt to distinguish the entry rights of United Kingdom and Commonwealth citizens into Britain, or the entry rights of British subjects. It did this based on where a passport had been issued. If the passport had not been issued in Britain, an individual had to apply for one of a limited number of work vouchers. This avoided putting race explicitly into the legislation, but had the effect of limiting Indian, Pakistani and West Indian entry. Yet, importantly, it did not restrict Kenyan Asians since their passports were issued by the British government.

Families of Indian and Pakistani descent who had for decades and generations laboured within the British Empire were by the late 1960s under threat in Kenya and attempting to migrate to the United Kingdom. And so, Duncan Sandys, along with Enoch Powell, began in 1967 to campaign to stop their entry. Powell argued then that Britain could not be condemned to a future like the United States due simply to an 'unforeseen loophole' in the law.[323] With an allusion to Sir John Seely, he warned that Britain, which had absent-mindedly colonized the world, was now absent-mindedly destroying itself with the possibility of racial violence. Powell visited the United States for the first time in October 1967; the following year, he gathered hundreds of regular press cuttings from Detroit papers on Black Power unrest as well as reports about any violence in the black community.[324] Birmingham, he asserted, faced a future like that of Detroit. By early February in Walsall, just before the debates on the Commonwealth Immigrants Bill, he began warning of the threat of communalism due to non-white immigration. 'So far as most people in the British Isles are concerned,' he lamented, 'you and I might as well

---

[322] For a discussion of the controversy over the numbers, see David Steel, *No Entry: The Background and Implications of the Commonwealth Immigrants Act, 1968* (London: C. Huret, 1969), p. 141.

[323] George Clark, 'Immigration Net Loosened: Legal Loophole Revealed,' *The Times*, 19 October 1967.

[324] 'Immigration Data: press cuttings and Detroit press cuttings,' 1968. POLL 8.2.6.

be living in central Africa for all they know about our circumstances.' It was enough, he said, 'to make you weep.' The government had ignored the Midlands. Powell called for further restrictions on the dependants, the wives and children, of immigrants.[325] Along with the ever-increasing restrictions put in place in Kenya, Powell's and Sandys' campaign in Britain contributed significantly to the panic in Kenya among the Asian community and the increased influx of Kenyan Asian immigration. Life under the protection of a British passport was under threat.

Harold Wilson's Labour government was in power at this time. Until this point, and particularly after the Conservative Party's turn to Europe in the early 1960s, Labour claimed that they were the new party of the Commonwealth – supporting international cooperation and development. The Home Secretary, James Callaghan, was, however, heavily swayed by anti-immigration appeals among Labour voters, who would in the following months, after the 'Rivers of Blood' speech, make up the core of Powell's public support. In late February 1968, Callaghan announced that the government would no longer respect the Kenyan Asians' passports. Just over a week later, legislation ending this community's unqualified right to enter Britain went into force.[326] Fully booked planes carrying Asian émigrés were turned away. Though they held United Kingdom passports, these Kenyan Asians were in effect stateless. The 1968 Commonwealth Immigrants Act added the immigration requirement that one's father or one's grandfather had to have been born, adopted or naturalized in the United Kingdom. This was known as the 'patrial clause.' It was soon amended to include maternal connections, but would retain its clear racial character. Powell himself, who argued instead for a revolution in citizenship law, a few years later likened the clause to the law that a Jewish grandparent defined one's status in Nazi Germany.[327] Discussing the entry rights of some white colonials, Powell argued against citizenship through ancestry. A heated debate in Parliament revolved in large part around the question of whether Britain was turning its back on a pledge it had given to Asian communities at Kenya's independence. The bill cut across party lines. Iain Macleod, the Conservative Colonial Secretary before Sandys, was adamant that Britain had given these communities an explicit pledge of protection.[328] Sandys would throughout the crisis

---

[325] 'Mr Powell Urges Immigrant Curb,' *The Times*, 10 February 1968.
[326] Randall Hansen, 'The Kenyan Asians, British Politics, and the Commonwealth Immigrants Act, 1968,' *Historical Journal*, 62: 3 (1999), pp. 809–834 (p. 810).
[327] HC, 8 March 1971, col. 80.
[328] Iain Macleod, 'An Open Letter to Duncan Sandys,' *The Spectator*, 23 February 1968, p. 225.

deny this.[329] Protected by the Official Secrets Act, 1963 was already buried history.

The historical circumstances of Britain's pledge at Kenya's independence opened the larger question of who was responsible for these Asian communities in Kenya. In 1999 Randall Hansen in large part resolved the mystery surrounding the Macleod–Sandys debate.[330] As he has shown, archival evidence makes it clear that in 1963 the British Cabinet, and above all Duncan Sandys, understood the rights that would be granted to Asians in post-independence Kenya. Sandys did, on several occasions, affirm those rights. However, Hansen also notes that the historical contingencies that led to Kenyan Asian immigration – particularly the absence of inclusive local citizenship in Kenya – were not foreseen by those negotiating Kenyan independence in Britain. Though this point is perhaps settled by Hansen, it is still clear that the historical uncertainty of Britain's 1963 pledge was a point of entry into a larger historical negotiation in the late 1960s and 1970s, amidst protests over Vietnam, arms sales to South Africa and the rise of 'Third Worldism,' regarding the political responsibilities of Britain's imperial past. Powell worked to emphasize this by theoretically linking arguments in favour of Britain's withdrawal from East of Suez and acceptance of Rhodesia's Unilateral Declaration of Independence to the rejection of its responsibility to the Kenyan Asians.

In Kenya, the question of the Kenyan Asian was essentially linked to the birth of the nation – to a new national history. Kenyan leaders, against Sandys, made clear their view that Britain had at independence assured the Kenyan Asians protection under their United Kingdom passports. Their willingness to deny Kenyan Asians access to membership of the Kenyan political community was, however, on a deeper level linked to the independence struggle. Throughout the colonial period Kenyan Asians were deemed to be willing practitioners of colonial government, a hindrance rather than a help to the nationalist cause. Kenyan Asians had worked in the lower grades of the civil service and predominated in small urban businesses. Efforts to exclude them from Kenya's economy were deemed by the Kenyan media as fundamentally the Asians' own fault: the harvest of seeds sown by them. They were called both derisively and sympathetically 'the Jews of Africa.'[331] They were said to be exclusive, traditional and inward looking. They had been the middlemen of empire. Kenyatta's radio broadcasts followed

---

[329] 'Mr Sandys Denies Pledge,' *The Times*, 28 February 1968.
[330] Hansen, 'The Kenyan Asians,' pp. 809–834.
[331] Ibid., p. 814.

this line of thinking, stating: 'there are some who, probably out of conceit, could not live as citizens of an African nation. To those people I say that, if they felt themselves to be too big, they should not now come in tears for Kenya Citizenship.'[332] The Asians had had their chance to make amends, Kenyatta argued, and had failed. While this Kenyanization was compared to British Powellism,[333] Kenyan leaders – such as James Gichuru (Kenya's Minister of Finance) – continued to deny the racism of the new business laws.[334] Kenya, as one government spokesman put it in 1969, was 'non-racial.'[335]

Though forty thousand Europeans – including a large number of redundant civil servants and military personnel – did leave Kenya between 1960 and 1966, there was no mass exodus of white settlers at independence. By 1968, the white population was only 25 per cent smaller than it had been in 1961. And it was a staggered process. One historian has asked: 'what then hindered the settlers and administrators from fleeing en masse to Britain ... after independence? What stopped the Kikuyu, the Kenyan African National Union ... and Jomo Kenyatta ... from seeking revenge on their British taskmasters for the crimes committed, as had indeed occurred in Algeria?' His answer was land reform. The British government's 'million acre buyout' scheme provided tens of thousands of African families with land in the former White Highlands.[336] The land that made up the million-acre scheme was, in large part, consolidated small farms that had grown mixed produce for local consumption. The big farms did not go. Poor Afrikaners did. The Kenyan government bought the consolidated land from the Land Board through British and World Bank loans and sold it to wealthy Kenyans, including some white Kenyans. Economic inequity was actually strengthened in this process. On a smaller scale, throughout this period, Britain's Compassionate Land Purchase scheme also bought a limited number of small farms from poor, elderly or crippled white farmers. There were about five hundred cases of compassionate compensation between 1962 and 1968.[337] These schemes both tended to remove poor and middle-class whites from the country.

[332] 'Non-citizens told: pack up and go,' BBC, 27 January 1969 (PRO National Archives, FCO 31/379).
[333] 'Discrimination in Africa,' *Daily Telegraph*, 23 January 1969.
[334] 'Asians: On the Carpet, James Gichuru Talks to Vivienne Barton,' *Sunday Nation*, 26 January 1969.
[335] 'Kenya Government Denies Racialism Charge,' *Financial Times*, 17 January 1969.
[336] Gavin Nardocchio-Jones, 'From Mau Mau to Middlesex? The Fate of Europeans in Independent Kenya,' *Comparative Studies of South Asia, Africa and the Middle East*, 26: 3 (2006), pp. 491–505.
[337] Ibid.

Importantly, by the late 1960s resentment of economic inequity in Kenya was in large part focused on Asians instead of on Europeans. In an effort to remain a business-friendly economy and retain European investment, the Kenyan state turned away from its recent history of bloodshed and distanced itself from the revolutionary struggle of Mau Mau. As one anonymous article put it at the time, the Kenyan masses were 'urged to "forget the past" and to labour in "the spirit of harambee"' because it was thought that Kenya would be 'toppled into an economic abyss [unless a] business alliance formed' between white and black Kenyans. When political independence came, the writer went on, those who had fought for it were 'easily deceived by neo-colonialism' and, consequently, adopted 'the colonial way of life.'[338] The violence of the British in Kenya in the 1950s (described most graphically in Caroline Elkins' book *Britain's Gulag*[339]) was written out of the national story.[340] Perhaps Asians became, in the context of this closure on past violence, the carriers of British colonial exploitation.

Powell was not alone in arguing that Britain needed to shed its burdensome past. The Labour peer Lord Elton sounded much like him and his supporters in a letter entitled 'Burdens of Past' to the editor of *The Times*. Elton wrote of public resentment and hostility against the Commonwealth in Britain. He argued that the notion that Britain had a 'moral obligation to admit great numbers of Commonwealth citizens' was due to the 'strange guilt complex' that 'has been fostered in respect of our imperial record. In the past we did more harm than good to our colonies and dependencies and consequently we owe them some compensation now. Such is the current ideology; it is most unlikely to stand up to the verdict of history.' He took the point further. Again echoing Powell's criticisms of the Whiggish histories of commonwealth/imperial political thought, Elton argued that it was the *imperial* arrogance of the liberal mind to argue in support of the entry of African and Asian immigrants. As he put it, 'the assumption that Britain must eventually prove able to anglicize hundreds of thousands of African and Asian immigrants is a survival of the analogous assumption of our empire-building forefathers that they would somehow be able to anglicize the Asian and African continents.' This was out of touch with the man on the street, Powell's

---

[338] Anon., 'The Asian Exodus: Who's Responsible?,' *East African Journal*, 5: 4 (April 1968), p. 5.
[339] Elkins, *Britain's Gulag*.
[340] For a discussion of the significance of governmental censorship of the memory of Mau Mau, see Wole Soyinka, 'Twice Bitten: The Fate of Africa's Culture Producers,' *Proceedings of the Modern Language Association* (Special Topic: 'African and African American literature') (January 1990), pp. 110–120.

letter-writers. For the ordinary citizen, such 'post-imperial obligations' were part of the 'mad, make-believe world of Whitehall.' For the ordinary citizen, 'the moral obligation of the British taxpayer to continue to provide £270m. a year in overseas aid is as unintelligible as the moral right of thousands of Asians from Kenya and Uganda to permanent residence in Britain.'[341] And those people, he emphasized, were 'Mrs. Jones, Mrs. Brown and Mrs. Robinson' who were 'fellow-citizens' not the unknown Kenyan Asian, the 'newcomer to Birmingham who cannot speak English, and three months ago had never heard of Birmingham or even of England; it is as simple as that.'[342]

While in the House of Lords, the main debate on the Commonwealth Immigrants Bill revolved around the shame and honour of the nation, Britain's failing to uphold a historical pledge, in the Commons the criticisms took another approach. The Liberal Party led the opposition to the bill. In contrast to both Labour and the Conservatives, who, courting the same voters, had in large part reached an agreement on the need for further immigration restrictions, the Liberal Party set the parameters of debate against the bill. 1968 was the official United Nations Year of Human Rights. Denying a citizen the right to enter their own country was a breach of the European Convention on Human Rights, which Britain had signed.[343] Significantly, Liberals such as David Steel used the crisis to argue that Britain was in dire need of its very own Bill of Rights. The Kenyan Asian crisis and the claims of the Kenyan Asians were therefore firmly set in that political movement.

East African Asians both in the United Kingdom and in Kenya began to organize opposition from 1967 onwards against the Commonwealth Immigrants bill. Leaders of the Kenyan Asian community in Kenya sent a telegram to the Queen insisting that, as Head of the Commonwealth, she oppose the bill.[344] Mr M. S. Khimasia, a founding member of the Committee of the British Citizen Merchants, demanded (unsuccessfully) that Britain take responsibility and grant compensation to Asian business owners, as it had done for some white Kenyans.[345] Others took to the streets in non-violent protest, carrying pictures of the Queen and

[341] Ibid.
[342] Lord Elton, 'Burdens of Past,' *The Times*, 8 January 1969.
[343] Sir Anthony Lester eventually took the case to the European Commission of Human Rights as the *East African Asians' case* challenging the compatibility of the partial clause of the Commonwealth Immigrants Act with the Convention. In 1973, the Commission ruled that the clause was in breach of the Convention, though the British government did not argue the ruling and the matter was therefore not brought to court.
[344] Steel, *No Entry*, p. 159.
[345] 'Kenya Asians See British Envoy on Compensation,' *The Times*, 9 January 1969.

Mahatma Gandhi.[346] Meanwhile most opposition in the United Kingdom was wholly set in the language of human rights and highlighted rights of citizenship rather than any notion of service to the British empire and British reparations. Organizers focused on Britain's legal, rather than moral, responsibilities. Early on, David Steel worked closely with the political organizer Praful Patel, an Asian businessman originally from Uganda. Patel founded the Committee of United Kingdom Citizenship that stood at the centre of the East African Asian community's opposition to the bill.[347] Rather than being preoccupied by reminding Britain of the Kenyan Asians' historic place in Britain's wider political community, organizers in the United Kingdom focused on their legal and economic rights – this was in part a consequence of both a wider failure of the politics of the Commonwealth and the rise of the politics of human rights. Neither, in Powell's estimation, represented the natural relationship between history – or a nation's myths – and political power. Powell's pessimism regarding the Commonwealth would consequently find fertile ground. In the very passing of the Commonwealth Immigrants Act, and also in Britain's failure effectively to oppose the racist Smith regime in Rhodesia, the weight of Britain's moral leadership in the Commonwealth was already lost.

Conclusion

By 1971, amidst arms negotiations with South Africa, Sir Alec Douglas-Home again spoke of the break-up of the Commonwealth. Some members had threatened to leave the Commonwealth if Britain's arms deal with South Africa went through. And the government faced accusations that it was 'taking a racialist side.'[348] But Douglas-Home insisted that these accusations were unfounded, and defence interests took precedence. As Howard Winant explains, apartheid's sponsors in the West, in the 'free world,' continued to uphold the South African regime until the fall of the Soviet Union as 'a supposedly distasteful but necessary anti-communist outpost.'[349] Britain had seen Communist power in Europe: 'We know what [it] means,' Douglas-Home insisted. It was spreading to the Mediterranean, and 'without question [is] going to be translated

---

[346] 'Why Asian Families Stayed British to Suffer Distress in Kenya,' *The Times*, 18 February 1970.

[347] Steel, *No Entry*, p. 170.

[348] *The Modern Commonwealth: This Pamphlet is based on a recent talk which Sir Alec Douglas Home gave to the Commonwealth Press Union* (London C.P.C. No. 476, 1971), CCO 150/4/2/80, CPA.

[349] Howard Winant, *The World is a Ghetto: Race and Democracy since World War II* (New York: Basic Books, 2001), p. 138.

at some future time into the Indian Ocean and towards the countries on its shores.' Here, the post-imperial community was fundamentally a defence against Communism. Tellingly, Douglas-Home noted that, if Britain's arms sales brought the break-up of the Commonwealth:

Without the Commonwealth it would be far more difficult for any British government to carry public opinion with it in support of aid efforts on the present scale, especially in times of financial stringency at home. The Commonwealth idea carries with it in the public mind a sense of historic obligation which makes sacrifice justified; and we can do under the Commonwealth 'umbrella' what we could never do for Commonwealth countries if that 'umbrella' was taken down.

As the Research Department warned in a letter to Douglas-Home, this was – in essence – a veiled threat. This was, as Powell warned, economic bribery. For Douglas-Home, Britain's post-imperial community appears to be no moral ideal but, rather, a means to carry public opinion through the Cold War.

As Ian Smith and Enoch Powell's words emphasize, the history of war continued to work to define who belonged and who did not, to whom the state owed a political debt and whom the state could reject – at both the domestic and international level. It was fundamentally tied to the promises of the postwar 'activist' state. This chapter has tracked the 'death' of the British Commonwealth – the death of a liberal racial 'partnership' in a Cold War world and at home.

Powell's realism, his insistence that political belief be wed in some way to a changing material reality and the constancy of 'human nature,' structured his response to controversies surrounding decolonization and the class 'peace' of the postwar years. Powell critiqued political thinking that was afraid of the past (particularly the economic hardships of the 1930s) but that still longed for a return to it (in a return to the 1900s or 1850s).[350] This is not to say that he rejected the value of myth. Rather, he argued that Britain, *like Kenya*, needed to forget. Britain, like Kenya, needed to put the 'the imperial episode in parenthesis' and embrace the myth of the 'free' market. This was, in Powell's mind, a matter of national survival – the survival of mankind as a 'political animal' – against internationalist thinking. Again, when Pakistan withdrew from the Commonwealth in 1972, this was, for Powell, an opportunity for Britain to break free from the imperial past. Powell insisted that Britain must legally deny the permanent residence and electoral rights of both Bangladeshi and Pakistani immigrants, who

[350] 'Encounter with Enoch Powell: from an interview by Erskine Childers and Keith Kyle,' *The Listener*, 29 April 1965.

were now, he argued, no longer of the Commonwealth. Britain owed nothing to the empire and nothing to the colonial subject. Rather, Britain was merely haunted by that postwar moment, by that post-war project of 'sinking national sovereignty in organizations for uniting the world' of which the Commonwealth and the British Nationality Act of 1948 were an unfortunate part.

4   The war within, 1968–1970

Compassion is something individual and voluntary. You cannot compel somebody to be compassionate; nor can you be vicariously compassionate by compelling somebody else. The Good Samaritan would have lost all merit if a Roman soldier were standing by the road with a drawn sword, telling him to get on with it and look after the injured stranger.

J. Enoch Powell, 1969[1]

The 'Rivers of Blood' speech is one of the most famous and most controversial speeches in modern British political history. It was delivered by Enoch Powell to a small group of Conservative activists in an upstairs room of a Birmingham hotel on 20 April 1968. In the speech, Powell warned that, with continued large-scale immigration of non-white people into the country, Britain would face inevitable racial violence and eventual national disintegration. The civil war that was going on in the United States, he argued, would be Britain's future, too, unless something was done. Specifically, on immigration, Powell argued against the rights of dependants to enter the country and called for an entirely new nationality law which would no longer recognize the Commonwealth citizens' special rights of entry. Most controversially of all, he argued for a programme of subsidized voluntary repatriation.

Though his points on immigration reform were within the parameters of Conservative Party policy, the speech sent a shockwave through the country. In many regards, it was not the policy content of the speech but *how* Powell argued his case that generated such controversy. The speech was impassioned, drawing the urban working classes as victims of government blindness and immigrant communities as carriers of future violence and revolution. Powell echoed the racist slurs of his constituents. The British people who had fought to protect the nation from a German invasion now faced what Lord Elton had just

[1] Speech to the Harborough Division Conservative Association Gala, Leicester (27 September 1969), from *Still to Decide* (Kingswood, Surrey: Elliot Right Way Books, 1972), pp. 22–23.

a few years before called an 'unarmed invasion.'[2] Though the speech is remembered, above all else, for its call to halt further immigration, its immediate causation was, in fact, the imminent second reading of the government's 1968 Race Relations Bill. As this chapter will demonstrate, the importance that Powell assigned this pending anti-discrimination law promises to offer new insight into Powell's 'Rivers of Blood' speech. This anti-discrimination law was, Powell believed, a sign of a state at war with the social order – at war with the meanings, the discriminations, the racism of everyday life. It was, most of all, a sign of the continued failures of the postwar consensus.

Prior to delivering the 'Rivers of Blood' speech, Powell had, against usual protocol, purposefully kept the contents of his speech a secret from the Shadow Cabinet. He knew it would have a dramatic effect – he had prepared the local newspapers. He even told one local Wolverhampton news editor: 'I'm going to make a speech this weekend and it's going to go up "fizz" like a rocket; but whereas all rockets fall to earth, this one is going to stay up.'[3] After the speech, Edward Heath, the Conservative leader, quickly fired Powell from his position as Shadow Minister of Defence due to the racist tone of the speech. This would mark the end of Powell's political career in the Cabinet. Within days, hundreds of East End dockers and Smithfield meat porters – traditional Labour supporters – marched to Westminster to protest against Powell's dismissal.[4] On 23 April, 250 unionized workers at the West India Dock voted independently of the union leadership in support of an immediate day-long strike in protest against Powell's dismissal.[5] Within one hour, all but 21 of the 1,300 workers at the West India Docks had gone on strike.[6] By the afternoon, approximately 4,000 dockers and porters across London had walked off their jobs – and between 1,000 and 1,500 travelled by Underground and on foot to demonstrate at Westminster against the Race Relations Bill and against further immigration.[7] In the following two weeks, Powell received an estimated 110,000 letters from the public in support.[8] Remarkably, this far-right politician came to be viewed by many Labour voters as speaking the truth to the wilful silence of the political elite on immigration. As one commentator put it, Powell's

[2] Elton, Baron Godfrey. *The Unarmed Invasion: A Survey of Afro-Asian Immigration* (London: Geoffrey Bles, 1965).
[3] Heffer, *Like the Roman*, p. 449.
[4] 'Enoch Powell,' Confidential Security Service Report, April 1968. PREM 13/2315.
[5] Ritscherle, 'Opting out of Utopia,' p. 285.
[6] Ibid.   [7] Ibid.
[8] For a selection of these letters, see POLL 8.1.8.

speech revealed, 'how far towards civility the Right has moved in the last 20 years ... what Mr. Powell has added is that force of soul which turns an unnoticed majority into a superiority.'[9] Though racism and anti-immigrant sentiment were strong currents in popular conservatism throughout the postwar era, without doubt, Powell's articulation gave a new air of respectability – and a new political reasoning – to popular racism against Britain's black communities.

Critically, Powell's 'Rivers of Blood' speech came at a moment when the moral coherence of the postwar consensus appeared to be in jeopardy. Trade union opposition to prices and incomes policy and government efforts to restrict unions' rights pointed to a fundamental breakdown in the relationship between the state and union power. Sikh immigrants' efforts in the workplace to gain the right to wear a turban and beard further challenged the traditionalism of trade union power. By 1968, the notion of a culturally coherent and politically unified people celebrated in the 'People's War' was increasingly being called into question. As this chapter will demonstrate, this unsettling and dismantling of the consensus required a new vision of British history that would reposition the myth of the Second World War in popular politics.[10] The war, which had served as the foundation for the moral justification of social democracy, state power and Britain's alliance with America's Cold War crusade, would be remade, with Powell's help, into a myth of Britain permanently under siege. Further, the myth of the heroic sacrifice of 'the people' – a sacrifice that worked to resolve the contradictions of a classed society and legitimize the social peace of 1945 – could mature into a myth of sacrifice that revealed the victimization of the people by the political Establishment. The People's War was retold, not as a resolution of the class war of the interwar years, but as an assertion of self-reliance – 'the people' against the liberal state. Powell's populist patriotism has much to tell us about social identities and understandings of legitimate governance in postwar Britain. In this sense, this chapter establishes that it is impossible to understand the making of postcolonial Britain outside the politics of class.

The roots of 'Rivers of Blood'

Since the Second World War, with the postwar economic boom, approximately two million immigrants predominantly from India, Pakistan and

---

[9] 'The People's Enoch,' *The Listener*, vol. 80, no. 2074, 26 December 1968, pp. 841–843 (p. 842).
[10] Eley, 'When Europe Was New,' in Riera and Schaffer (eds.), *The Lasting War*, p. 20.

[handwritten annotation: RRA 1965 – public sphere / RRA 1968 – added private sphere]

the West Indies had settled in the industrial centres around London and the West Midlands. The postwar economic recovery had involved both the super-exploitation of black workers in Britain[11] and – as E. J. B. Rose's official study of race discrimination made clear as early as 1969 – a fundamental failure of the welfare state to take any responsibility for the housing and welfare of these new populations.[12] The 'civility' of both the Conservative and Labour Parties was, in essence, an effort to keep race from becoming a political issue. While the Labour Party, with its commitment to racial equality, regarded the question of immigration and race relations as a political liability,[13] the Tory leadership wished to avoid the charge of racism. This led to an emphasis on language, on avoiding emotionalism, and on bipartisan efforts to steer public perception. It also led to a widespread failure on the part of the labour movement to represent black workers.

In 1967, the first annual report of the government's Race Relations Board and a report by its Chairman, Mark Bonham Carter, on his month-long visit to America, together made a very strong case for extending the powers of the Race Relations Act of 1965.[14] The Race Relations Act had made it illegal to discriminate 'on the ground of colour, race or ethnic or national origin' in a number of places of public resort, including hotels, pubs, public transport and places maintained by a local or any other public authority.[15] It also expanded the Public Order Act of 1936 beyond penalizing 'breach of the peace,' by making it a criminal offence to incite racial hatred through peaceful means – such as through the written word.[16] The extension of the Act with the Race Relations Bill of 1968 was a major advance because it increased the scope of anti-discrimination law to include discrimination in private employment, housing, credit and insurance – areas where racism was, as the Race Relations report made clear, rife. American lawyers, with greater experience in anti-discrimination law, had been brought in to help in its drafting.[17]

Prior to Powell's speech, the Conservative Shadow Cabinet walked a fine line. In 1965, a Shadow Cabinet meeting (which Powell attended)

---

[11] Anna Marie Smith, *New Right Discourse*, p. 137.

[12] E. J. B. Rose, *Colour and Citizenship*, p. 137.

[13] Tony Benn interview with the author, 20 November 2005.

[14] Leader's Consultative Committee (67) 171st Meeting, 1 May 1967. CPA, LCC 1.2.9.

[15] 'Race Relations and the Law,' Advisory Committee on Policy (ACP) (67) 37, CPA Conservative Central Office (CCO) 3.16.2.

[16] Home Affairs Committee, Extract from the minutes of meeting held on 12 February 1965. H (65) 5th Meeting, HO 376.68.

[17] Ibid.

CIA 1968 restricted immigration from Kenyan Asian

set out that, publicly, integration 'should <u>always</u> be talked about at the same time' as stricter control of immigration.[18] This was an effort by the party leadership to appear balanced and unprejudiced in approach. As Quintin Hogg put it in 1967 in response to the policy report, on the issue of the coming Race Relations Bill of 1968, 'My conclusion is that we should play this issue coolly, and cautiously, but liberally. We should not shut the door against extension [of race relations law]. We should take the credit for the conciliation machinery. We should, on the other hand, sound a warning against excessive precipitancy. We must lead public opinion, not drag behind it, or bulldoze it.'[19] Similarly, as a Cabinet report put it, if the law was to be extended, 'it will only make headway against colour prejudice if it is backed up by the moral authority of the whole community. If will not make headway without the support of both major parties.'[20]

The bill of 1968 gained political momentum at the beginning of 1968 as a counterbalance to the recent Commonwealth Immigrants Act discussed in the previous chapter. Due to new laws passed by the Kenyan government in 1967 that restricted the employment of Kenyan Asians, approximately one thousand Kenyan Asians with British passports were immigrating to Britain each month. The Labour government rushed through the Commonwealth Immigrants Act in March 1968, restricting those Kenyan Asians who could enter Britain to only those with a relative who was already a British resident – thereby, effectively introducing race into British immigration law. Whenever either party argued for a stricter immigration policy, the need for successful integration and 'racial harmony' would serve as the rhetorical accompaniment.[21] The Race Relations Bill came on the heels of the racially exclusionary Commonwealth Immigrants Act.

The Conservative Party was, however, split on the new legislation. Attitudes in the party had hardened against the bill – in the Home Affairs and Commonwealth Committees feelings towards it had been, according to Hogg, 'surprisingly hostile.'[22] The Tory right, led by Duncan Sandys, Ronald Bell and Powell, insisted that the party take a stand

---

[18] Leader's Consultative Committee, 9 March 1965, LCC (65) 29th Meeting, CPA LCC 1/2/2.
[19] Quintin Hogg, 'Race Relations and the Law in Britain: A Note from Quintin Hogg,' 4 July 1967, ACP (67) 38, CPA CCO 3/16/2, Conservative Party Papers.
[20] Leader's Consultative Committee, 9 March 1965, LCC (65) 29th Meeting, CPA LCC 1/2/2.
[21] Edward Heath, 'Immigration and Racial Harmony,' 20 September 1968; *Immigration* (London: Conservative Central Office, 1971).
[22] Leader's Consultative Committee (68) 231 Meeting, 10 April 1968. CPA, LCC 1.2.12.

Powell rejected RRB 1968 on the basis of laissez faire economics - the market should regulate itself.

against it: the bill went too far – credit and insurance were economic matters – and individual discrimination was a matter of individual freedom. Bell offered an amendment against a second reading of the bill because it 'deeply encroaches upon the proper sphere of the freedom of the individual.'[23] As discussed in the previous chapter, Powell's faith in the free market – his belief, as he put it, to see the economy 'in the hard light of the two times table of laissez faire'[24] – was represented, by Powell, as the *absence* of ideology, the *absence* of a moral imperative, and the field in which the social order could 'biologically' exist. Racist discrimination in the market was part of this 'natural' order. When debating the bill, Bell insisted that, 'when, after the war, American legislation moved into the social field, the tensions rose. The same thing would happen here for the same reasons.'[25] Still, a liberal minority in the party remained determined to support the Labour government on the issue. Heath and his allies, in an effort to avoid the worsening of these divisions and placate the left and right of the party, drafted a reasoned amendment criticizing the method, rather than the intentions, of the bill.[26] This strategy appeared – according to one reporter – 'vague to the point of evasion.'[27]

To all this, Powell repeated his Tory faith in inequality as social order. Powell emphasized, in his arguments against the 1968 Race Relations Bill, that this was legislation to control the *thoughts* and *emotions* of the individual – this was a denial of the citizen's right 'to discriminate in the management of his own affairs between one fellow citizen and another' without being 'subjected to inquisition as to his reasons and motives for behaving in one lawful manner rather than another.'[28] In other words, in Powell's mind, via political recognition of racism, the basis of the social order – hierarchy and discrimination – fell under a new threat.

Two weeks prior to Powell's 'Rivers of Blood' speech, on 4 April 1968, Martin Luther King Jr was assassinated. This international context contributed to the divides within the Conservative Party. The assassination was major international news. It made headlines across Britain. Powell had visited the United States for the first time in late 1967. In July of that year, Detroit witnessed one of the most deadly riots in US

[23] Ian Trethowan, 'Tory Dilemma over Race Bill,' *The Times*, 18 April 1968.
[24] J. Enoch Powell, 'Frankly Speaking,' Radio Broadcast, 28 February 1964. POLL 4.1.27.
[25] HC, vol. 763, col. 107, 23 April 1968.
[26] Schoen, *Enoch Powell and the Powellites*, p. 31.
[27] Ian Trethowan, 'Tory Dilemma over Race Bill,' *The Times*, 18 April 1968.
[28] Powell, 'To the Annual General Meeting of the West Midlands Area Conservative Political Centre' (Birmingham, 20 April 1968), in *Reflections of a Statesman*, pp. 373–379 (p. 376).

history. At the conclusion of 5 days of rioting, 7,000 people had been arrested, 1,189 injured, and 43 people lay dead. Those killed had been shot by police. Racial violence in the United States was the crucial backdrop of the bill. While for Powell legal recognition of the rights of black immigrants would be equated with a future of internal violence and unrest, for others legislation was the means by which to avoid America's race war in Britain. Powell would, for the following year, receive regular newspaper clippings from a contact in Detroit on the unrest and racial violence going on there.[29] He saw in America's own postwar migration to northern cities an absolute parallel with Britain:

An almost precise arithmetical parallel is afforded by the transformation of the cities of the northern and north-eastern States of America which has taken place since World War II, a process which is an immigration in all but name ... At an interval of twenty or thirty years you can leave out 'Detroit' and insert 'Birmingham.'[30]

Britain's immigration policy and American-style race relations legislation was Britain accepting an American 'model of our future.'[31] This future was racial ghettoization and black alienation from state authority. Paradoxically, Powell believed that the construction of a legally recognized minority – through race relations legislation – only furthered the political alienation of Britain's immigrant communities.

While Powell would regard racism as an undeniable aspect of human nature, Powell refused to define 'race' itself. Analysing race was the business of the anthropologist or physiologist, not the business of the politician. 'Are a Welshman and an Englishman of the same race?' he would ask.[32] Conflict did not occur between races, he insisted, but between 'social organizations' – on political, not biological terms.[33] Here, again, was Powell's Tory rationalization for the consequences of race: race was merely another aspect of the political order. Powell argued, further, that the word 'race' had come into common parlance due to the exaggerated influence of the United States:

It comes from the United States, where 'race' is used to distinguish Negro from non-Negro; but this is clearly a specialised and American acceptance of the term. The importation of American vocabulary into the discussion of circumstance in the United Kingdom is dangerous and misleading.

[29] 'File 2,' POLL 8.2.6. See also: 'Violence,' SRO, D4490/4.
[30] J. Enoch Powell, speech delivered at Longford, Middlesex, Southall Chamber of Commerce, 4 November 1971. POLL 3.2.1.20.
[31] Ibid.
[32] Enoch Powell, 'Beyond Immigration,' *Frontier* (February 1973), in *Reflections of a Statesman*, pp. 152–158 (p. 152).
[33] Ibid., p. 153.

Its use by others, both inside and outside Britain, did not compel Powell to come to terms with it, 'any more than I have to concern myself with it if people are expelled from Soviet Russia or from Nazi Germany.'[34] Rather, he must ask, 'What were the ideas which either actually caused this event or were alleged to be the reason for it?'[35] The British media had become obsessed with the word. The reason for this was political.

The Vietnam War and the British government's immediate support of American bombing campaigns there – as well as the increasingly vocal and angry opposition to that support – threatened a loss in the British state's legitimacy. Powell argued that radical sections of British society – white and black – were encouraging the increase and the politicization of distinct minority communities to break down the congruity of nation and state, of rulers and ruled. According to Powell, 'like so many other subjects neutral in themselves, the so-called "Kenyan-Asians" became an important focus of agitation and brain washing.'[36] This was a vision of liberal progressivism devoid of its utopian principles – with an intent only to disrupt society and redistribute power to a radical minority. Though he regularly argued, as Shadow Minister of Defence, against Britain's military dependence on and unquestioning support for the United States, Powell viewed protests against the war as representative of this larger phenomenon of social disintegration – student unrest was just one symptom in the erosion in 'all forces of authority.'[37]

As the *Christian Science Monitor* tellingly asked, were Britain's New Commonwealth immigrants the 'seedbed for dissent or progress?'[38] Britain had yet to produce an 'indigenous militant civil rights movement' – was this to come?[39] While older immigrants had 'learned to live with discrimination,' the question still remained: 'will first- and second-generation youngsters accept it so passively?'[40] This was a common refrain in official circles, also. The times had changed. The real challenge now was not immigration but the consequences of it. As Home Secretary James Callaghan put it, 'We now have to get away from talking about immigrants and start talking about good community relations.'[41] In Powell's mind, 'good community relations' meant

---

[34] Ibid., p. 152.   [35] Ibid.
[36] Powell to Nall, 20 October 1970. Immigration Data, SRO, D4490/2.
[37] Powell, *Still to Decide*.
[38] 'Britain's Immigrants: Seedbed for Dissent or Progress?,' *Christian Science Monitor*, 22 October 1969.
[39] Ibid.   [40] Ibid.
[41] 'Speech by James Callaghan to the Manchester Council for Community Relations,' 13 June 1970. Immigration Data, SRO, D4490/2.

the further encroachment of the state into, as he put it in 1958, the Church's role as the 'authority within.'[42]

In Wolverhampton at this time, the crucible of race relations in employment was the Sikh turban issue. Powell no doubt saw it through the filter of the American model of the future. By 1967, the city councils of Manchester, Huddersfield, London, Bristol, Birmingham, Glasgow and Newcastle-upon-Tyne all allowed turbans and beards to be worn as bus conductor attire.[43] Four out of five Indians in Britain at this time were Sikh.[44] This had resulted in some violence on the city's buses – with some passengers harassing Sikh conductors. In late July 1967, Tarsem Singh Sandu, a Sikh employee of the Wolverhampton Transport Department, turned up one morning after three weeks' sick leave with a beard.[45] Sandu, inspired by his father's involvement with uniform changes at Wolverhampton's Goodyear factory, had 'regained his Sikh consciousness' and – following Sikh religious law – grown a beard.[46] Sandu was told he could not return to work without shaving.

In the Wolverhampton Transport Department, it had been an unwritten agreement between the union, the Transport and General Workers Union (TGWU), and management that untrimmed beards were banned. Union officials initially refused to get involved in Sandu's case. Their view was that Sandu had agreed to the conditions of the work when he took the job.[47] When Sandu arrived home, he called Mr C. S. Panchi, president of the Sikh organization in Wolverhampton, *Shiromani Akali Dal*.[48] After many meetings between Panchi, the Transport Department and the TGWU, the Transport Department agreed to defer the decision on Sikh beards and turbans until there had been a vote on the issue among union members. In August, Powell took sides as an MP in this local dispute, arguing that no question of discrimination arose if Sikhs were made to dress without turban or beard – like everybody else.[49] In September, the question was put to union members, 'Are you in favour of ex-driver Sandu's request to wear a beard and turban?'[50] Of the 578 who voted, 336 were in favour.[51] There were 150 Sikhs then

[42] J. Enoch Powell, 'Bishops and Kings,' *The Listener*, 16 October 1958.
[43] Editorial, *Sikh Review*, April 1967.
[44] 'A Lancashire lass leads Britain's Sikh revival,' *Sunday Times*, 20 January 1967.
[45] David Beetham, 'Wolverhampton 1967–1969,' in *Transport and Turbans: A Comparative Study in Local Politics* (Oxford University Press, 1970), p. 37.
[46] Ibid., p. 40.
[47] *Express and Star*, 10 August 1967.
[48] Beetham, *Transport and Turbans*, p. 40.
[49] 'In Search of Enoch Powell,' *The Observer*, 28 April 1968.
[50] Beetham, *Transport and Turbans*, p. 42.
[51] Ibid.

working for the Transport Department. The department, however, reconvened in November and, despite the vote, refused to accept any change in regulation. This refusal was in large part due to opposition from union officials and the general manager. The Wolverhampton Transport Department had, over the years, been committed to a certain vision of integration and 'the basic principle of impartiality' – this had meant, they emphasized, the similar firing of a Christian English woman who would not work on Sunday.[52] They argued that it had, so far, been a successful principle.

But the Sikhs' demands had the tide of opinion on 'race relations' behind them. In 1966, Labour Home Secretary Roy Jenkins gave a new working definition of integration. This definition was an attempt to reform the official approach to the integration of immigrants based solely on their assimilation into British culture (assimilation as an approach had increasingly lost favour among race relations experts after the riots between white and ethnic communities in Notting Hill and Nottingham in 1958).[53] Jenkins' definition of integration would remain a working tool for British integration policy for decades to come:

Integration is perhaps a rather loose word. I do not regard it as meaning the loss, by immigrants, of their own national characteristics and culture. I do not think that we need in this country a 'melting pot', which will turn everybody out in a common mould, as one of a series of carbon copies of someone's misplaced vision of the stereotyped Englishman ... It would deprive us of most of the positive benefits of immigration that I believe to be very great indeed. I define integration, therefore, not as a flattening process of assimilation but as equal opportunity, accompanied by cultural diversity, in an atmosphere of mutual tolerance.[54]

Despite the official government position on integration, the Sikh bus conductors in Wolverhampton were unsuccessful in convincing the local TGWU to support their efforts to wear turban and beard. After

---

[52] Beetham, *Transport and Turbans*, p. 45.
[53] Christophe Bertossi, 'French and British Models of Integration: Public Philosophies, Policies and State Institutions,' Working Paper No. 46, *ESRC Centre on Migration, Policy and Society* (University of Oxford, 2007), pp. 19, 20. Remarkably, Jenkins' vision of integration would not be expanded to face the widespread discrimination systemic to Northern Ireland. The Catholic community in Northern Ireland was politically marginalized, due both to long-term discrimination in housing and employment and to the drawing of local electoral boundaries in favour of Unionist candidates. Religion had been purposefully left out of the Race Relations Act of 1965 so as to avoid confronting the historical tension between Catholics and Protestants throughout the United Kingdom. See 'Racial Discrimination and Incitement to Racial Hatred,' Extract from the Minutes of a Meeting held on 12 February 1965, H(65)5th Meeting, Home Affairs Committee, HO 376/68.
[54] Cited ibid., p. 20.

continued negotiations, Panchi and his supporters turned to direct action. They decided to march through Wolverhampton – with the support of the Indian Workers' Association as well as local Sikh temples. The march took place in February 1968, with an estimated 5,000 to 6,000 Sikhs from all over the country taking part.[55] The Sikh campaign got national and international attention, especially after Powell's 'Rivers of Blood' speech. Both the mayor of Wolverhampton as well as Prime Minister Harold Wilson received regular correspondence from the Indian High Commission and international Sikh organizations on the issue of the turban in Wolverhampton.[56] Powell told a crowd in Walsall, soon after the protest march of the Sikhs through Wolverhampton:

> We have been seeing in Wolverhampton the cloud no bigger than a man's hand in the shape of communalism. Communalism has been the curse of India and we need to be able to recognize it when it rears its head here. Large numbers of Sikhs, who had been serving the Wolverhampton Corporative voluntarily and contently, have found themselves against their will made the material of communal agitation. They have the same right as anyone else to decide which if any of the rules of their sect they will keep, and they found no difficulty entering the corporation's employment and complying with the rules as their fellow employees … This issue in this instance is not racial or religious discrimination: it is communalism.[57]

He would later quote John Stonehouse, Labour MP and Minister of Technology, in his Birmingham speech as saying that the Sikh communities' campaign was to be regretted: 'To claim special communal rights (or should I say rites?) leads to a dangerous fragmentation within society. This communalism is a canker … to be strongly condemned.'[58] Immigration, Powell argued, brought with it communalism and communalism threatened to deprive citizens of political and economic will. Powell's Walsall speech lacked the explosive force of his 'Rivers of Blood' speech to come only two months later, but it did draw over 800 letters in reply. Those letters served as Powell's sources for the 'Rivers of Blood' speech. Five days after the Walsall speech, the Labour government accepted that controls on the immigration of Kenyan Asians were necessary – the Commonwealth Immigrants Bill passed. In the press, Powell's Walsall speech took most of the credit and blame for having panicked the Labour government into this concession.

---

[55] Ibid., p. 52.   [56] See FCO 37/440.
[57] J. Enoch Powell, 'Speech delivered to the Walsall South Conservative Association,' 9 February 1968. POLL 3.2.1.20.
[58] John Stonehouse cited by Powell in 'To the Annual General Meeting of the West Midlands Area Conservative Political Centre' (Birmingham, 20 April 1968), *Reflections of a Statesman*, pp. 373–379 (p. 379).

Hence, the West Indian communities in Britain were not the primary focus of Powell's ire. Black Power in America had caught the headlines in Britain and it was, he argued, 'under the shape of the negro that the consequences for Britain of immigration and what is miscalled "race" are popularly depicted.'[59] But, Powell emphasized, 'it is more truly when he looks into the eyes of the Asian that the Englishman comes face to face with those who will dispute with him the possession of his native land.'[60] It was through Asian immigration that towns had been transformed into 'alien territory'[61] – or, as he put it, 'parts of this town' of Wolverhampton had 'ceased to be part of England, except in the sense that they are situated within it geographically.'[62] These immigrant communities, such as the Sikhs in Wolverhampton, threatened the same war as that in Detroit and the same challenge to the legitimacy and authority of the state. The Race Relations Bill, as he famously put it in the 'Rivers of Blood' speech, was 'the very pabulum' that divisive elements needed to flourish – allowing immigrant communities to 'agitate and campaign against their fellow citizens.'[63] The bill was like 'throwing a match on to gunpowder.'[64] Ironically, due in large part to the bad press of Powell's Birmingham speech, the Wolverhampton Town Council would reverse its ban and allow the turban and beard to be worn by transport employees.

In 1967, the Northern Ireland Civil Rights Association (NICRA) formed, modelling itself on the US Civil Rights Movement. The NICRA fought for the abolition of anti-Catholic measures and equality for Catholics in Northern Ireland. By 1968, the fight for civil rights among the Catholic communities of Northern Ireland blossomed into violence that could no longer be ignored by the British state. Civil rights protest marches began in Belfast just a month prior to Powell's Birmingham speech. Labour MP Ben Whitaker offered an amendment to the Race Relations Bill, which called for the title of the bill to be changed to the 'Civil Rights Bill,' for its scope to extend to Northern Ireland, and for discrimination against a person's religion to be added to all the major clauses of the bill affecting housing,

---

[59] J. Enoch Powell, speech delivered at Longford, Middlesex, Southall Chamber of Commerce, 4 November 1971. POLL 3.2.1.20.

[60] Ibid.

[61] J. Enoch Powell, speech delivered at Smethwick, Smethwick Conservative Supper Club, 8 September 1971. POLL 3.2.1.20.

[62] 'Home Secretary Offers Watchdog Committee on Race Relations: Mr Hogg Defines Three Principles of Conservative Policy,' *The Times*, 24 April 1968.

[63] Heffer, *Like the Roman*, p. 454.

[64] Powell, 'To the Annual General Meeting of the West Midlands Area Conservative Political Centre,' *Reflections of a Statesman*, pp. 371–379 (p. 376).

employment and education.[65] The amendment failed. The emerging violence in Northern Ireland confirmed Powell's political fears. Though both parties attempted to avoid making what was viewed as an intractable, unsolvable dilemma into an electoral issue, by the 1970 general election the central problem facing the British government was the strife in Northern Ireland.[66]

The world in 1968 no doubt faced a crisis in political authority. As the Minister of Technology, John Stonehouse, put it in June 1968:

> With upheavals in so many countries in Europe, with the French economy paralysed, the United States in turmoil and with Nigeria's fateful war dragging on, we can be grateful to live in these islands. But let us not be complacent. No one would deny that 'it could happen here.' And 'never' is a word to be used with very great caution.[67]

For the British state, this worldwide crisis manifested itself not in London but in Belfast and Derry. Powell's response to this crisis is the foundation of the 'Rivers of Blood' speech. In April, Powell's eyes were set on Detroit, on Belfast, and on his own town of Wolverhampton. Or, more exactly, Powell imagined the future of Wolverhampton through the events of Detroit and Belfast. What now may be viewed as limited political democratization and the new participatory impulse of the New Left, Powell viewed fundamentally as 'communal agitation' – and the path to anarchy. Importantly, at that moment, revolution – at least in Derry and Detroit – was not out of the question. Powell's role as a statesman, as he imagined it, was to revitalize and protect the legitimacy of the British state. We must now turn to how he chose to do this, with the racist words of his constituents.

Breaking the consensus

Two weeks prior to Powell's speech, Richard Rose in *The Times* wrote that, 'Public confidence in the ability of the leaders of the two major parties to deal with the nation's problems had reached a post-war low.'[68] The decline in working-class representation in Labour's

---

[65] 'Heath Asks Nation to Be Calm, Fair, Responsible, Constructive,' *The Times*, 27 April 1968.

[66] George Gale, 'The 1970 Election Campaign,' in John Wood (ed.), *Powell and the 1970 Election* (Surrey: Elliot Right Way Books, 1970), p. 51.

[67] John Stonehouse speaking in Staffordshire, 8 June 1968. Immigration Data, SRO, D4490/2.

[68] Richard Rose, 'Voters Show Their Scepticism of Politicians,' *The Times*, 9 April 1968.

Parliamentary membership gave many the feeling that Parliament contained only a 'remote and closed circle of like and limited ideas.'[69] The 1970 Nuffield study, in explaining the widespread political alienation of the British populace, similarly pointed to lack of political disagreement and an apparent party convergence.[70] The Conservative Party had, since the Macmillan government, accepted many of the basic tenets of the welfare state and nationalized industry introduced by Labour. Both parties embraced economic planning and what many would later regard as a paternalistic approach to governance. Race and immigration, like other issues, were to be managed rather than politicized. Six days after Powell's 1968 speech, David Watt wrote in the *Financial Times*:

> The isolation of politicians, the ingroupness of Westminster, the blandness of the establishment, the tendency to keep unpleasant facts under the carpet for the best of motives (as well as the worst), the irrelevance of many of the old party divisions to modern problems – these are the main characteristics of the conventional system as the man in the street sees it. The balance and stability of the constitutional machinery – which are protections against revolution and tyranny – often seem less important than its increasing remoteness, irrelevance or incompetence.[71]

This was, by Watt's estimation, a stable state without politics.

The postwar governing philosophy of Keynesian social democracy was in 1968 at the beginning of its end. It would fail to survive the social and economic trials of the late 1960s and 1970s, particularly mass industrial strikes and high inflation, and would largely collapse in the closing years of the 1974 Labour government.[72] Adherents of the New Right have argued that the break-up of the postwar consensus was due to the inherently inflationary nature of Keynesian economic planning and incomes policy. The impact of Powell's Birmingham speech, however, also points to the political limitations of the postwar consensus. John Vincent, a fellow of Peterhouse College, wrote in 1969 that, 'Nobody believing in a democratic rapport between nation and politicians should blame Mr Powell for creating, most hopefully, a model of a possible alternative to managerial government.'[73] Powellism can

---

[69] Schoen, *Enoch Powell and the Powellites*, p. 234.
[70] Ibid.
[71] David Watt, *Financial Times*, 26 April 1968.
[72] David Marquand, 'The Decline of Post-war Consensus,' in Antony Gorst, Lewis Johnman and W. Scott Lucas (eds.), *Post-war Britain, 1945–64: Themes and Perspectives* (London: Pinter Publishers, 1989), p. 1.
[73] Cited in Schoen, *Enoch Powell and the Powellites*, p. 234.

222 The war within, 1968–1970

be viewed – at least in Powell's own terms – as a revolt against this approach to governance.[74] In Powell's view, consensus without choice threatened the very basis of political authority.

After Labour's 1970 election failure, Tony Benn agreed with Powell – at least in terms of Powell's critique of the political process. He argued that Labour had lost contact with the people – the party had 'pulled out the plugs.'[75] 'We seemed,' he said to the conference of the International Association of Political Consultants a few months after the election, 'in the public mind to have crossed the "we-they" frontier.'[76] This was crucially important, because in his view significant changes were taking place in the electorate and Labour had missed the opportunity to gather the new sources of energy and power which were consequently emerging.[77] He was, here, talking about the rise of the New Left. An era in parliamentary democracy that retained 'the arrogance of an elected monarchy' was coming to an end. Benn, much like Powell in 1968, offered a critique of the Establishment:

At its worst, it still keeps the citizen at arm's length from the business of decision-making, bullying him into believing the ballot box is the last word in participation. People will not turn back to Labour unless we have thought through this change which I have been trying to describe and set the political process in wider perspective that takes account of the bigger role people themselves want to play. We shall have to offer ourselves in our new consultative role showing people how it can be done, rather than seeking to convince people that if they vote for us their problems are over.[78]

Benn then argued that Powell understood politics better than the new Prime Minister, Edward Heath. '[Powell] knows that to change the structure you must first change the people. He went round to shopkeepers and others and talked to them in an intellectual way. I believe that he had more influence on more of the British people than many Conservatives who are Ministers.'[79] What divides Benn and Powell here is that Powell's effort to get 'in touch' with the British people was in no way an effort toward social egalitarianism.

Importantly, Powell's insistence that there was a gulf between the political Establishment and the people was not confined to his arguments on black immigration. He repeatedly critiqued Labour power and economic planning in these terms prior to 1968. Citing the swing

---

[74] For a discussion of the problem of mobilizing consent, see Samuel Beer, 'The British Legislature and the Problem of Mobilizing Consent,' in *Essays on Reform, 1967* (Oxford University Press, 1967), p. 81.
[75] 'Tory Tells When Labour Could Have Won,' *The Guardian*, 16 December 1970.
[76] Ibid. [77] Ibid. [78] Ibid. [79] Ibid.

to Conservatives in his own, largely working-class constituency in 1964, he noted that, 'In the end, the Labour Party could cease to represent labour. Stranger historic ironies have happened than that.'[80] By 1966, Powell believed that the Labour Party failed to represent the interests of the worker:

The dream world and aspirations of the Socialist government and the real world and aspirations of the workers have nothing in common. Between them is a great gulf. In that gulf the trade union, that is to say, the organisers, the managers, what are called the 'leaders' of the trade unions, hover uneasily, torn between two worlds, to neither of which they properly belong ... The planned state is death to trade unionism. The events of the past weeks, the pay freeze and the rest, have speeded up something which had already been happening, but more gradually, over most of the time since the war. The Labour Party has ceased to be the party of labour and of trade unionism. What the worker looked for in the Labour Party and in the trade unions he no longer finds there. His security no longer lies, if it ever did, in restriction.[81]

The democratic limits of the postwar consensus, and the emerging political de-alignment of the Labour Party and the British worker, are well drawn out in the early literature on Thatcherism. There, it is explained, the Labour Party, with relative economic decline, increasingly confronted the 'ancient dilemma' of both avowedly representing the interests of labour and, at the same time, acting as a party of government that embraced reformed capitalism. In the effort to control inflation came wage restrictions. Labour as a party had compromised with capital interest; in this sense, it was a party for the state, not for the working classes. As such, 'socialism' had become associated with the (negative) experiences of a disciplinary state.[82] And this contributed to an anti-statism that swung voters to the right.

Remarkably, Powell attempted to tie this disciplinary dimension of social democracy to the memory of fascism. As discussed in Chapter 3, in Powell's critique of state power, collectivism and the 'paternal state,' Powell worked to destabilize the link between the sacrifices of the Second World War and the promises of a postwar reconstructed state. Full employment and welfare services were, at least within the Labour Party, imagined as *found* and *won* in the heat of total war. But the meaning of the victory of the Second World War transformed

---

[80] J. Enoch Powell, *Sunday Telegraph*, 18 October 1965, cited in Heffer, *Like the Roman*, p. 364.

[81] J. Enoch Powell, speech to the Bilston Conservative Association BBQ, Segley, Staffordshire, 10 September 1966.

[82] David Dixon, 'Thatcher's People: The British Nationality Act 1981,' *Journal of Law and Society*, 10: 2 (Winter, 1983), pp. 161–180 (p. 170).

over time, subject to multiple and competing political contexts and ongoing reconstructions throughout the postwar period. In Powell's vision, the Labour Party of 1964 was 'at heart totalitarian' and relations in 1967 between British government, the trade unions and the Confederation of British Industry had 'an ominous ring of the corporate state.'[83] With this, he warned that Britain was in 'imminent danger of slipping unawares into that form of state socialism which is known as fascism.'[84] Welfare services and the state's commitment to full employment were not an extension of the democracy fought for in the war. In Powell's arguments, the state is drawn, not as a servant of the people but as 'the enemy' – an enemy willing to sacrifice the national whole for the maintenance of power. Here, Powell attempted to marry nationalism and anti-Keynesianism. Though Powell's vision of economic planning as essentially fascist was to have a limited impact at the popular level, it would soon reform and return as a populist critique of anti-racist legislation.

Powell's argument in the 'Rivers of Blood' speech was that the British people had been abandoned by a bipartisan approach. The reaction to his speech revealed, he argued, 'a deep and dangerous gulf in the nation.' Not between native and immigrant, but 'between the overwhelming majority of people throughout the country on the one side, and the other side a tiny minority, with almost a monopoly on the channels of communication, who seem determined not to know the facts and not to face the realities and who will resort to any device or extremity to blind both themselves and others.'[85] The outcry over his Birmingham speech 'illuminated like a lightning flash' that gulf between the nation and the Establishment.[86] On the question of immigration and race relations legislation, the majority could no longer patiently wait for the minority to represent their political opinion. This was about democracy, Powell claimed; as US President Nixon claimed only one year later, this was about giving voice to the silent majority. The silent majority believed, Powell contended, that the new immigration restrictions were not enough – tighter controls and mass repatriation were necessary. Powell's populist patriotism questioned the trustworthiness of state

[83] J. Enoch Powell, speech to the Dulwich Conservative Association (29 February 1964), cited in *A Nation Not Afraid*, p. 75, and J. Enoch Powell, Extract from speech at the South Oxfordshire Conservative Political Conference, Wheatley Secondary School, 11 March 1967. POLL 4.1.2.
[84] Ibid.
[85] J. Enoch Powell, 'To the Annual Rotary Club of London,' 16 November 1968, reprinted in *Reflections of a Statesman*, pp. 382–393 (p. 383).
[86] Ibid., p. 384.

bureaucracy. By 1970, the Home Office, charged by Powell with lying about the numbers of New Commonwealth immigrants, became the 'enemy within.' The white working class are redrawn, here, as *victims of a traitorous state*. Even more, race relations legislation would result – this silent majority feared – in the victimization of the native English. Powell was, he believed, reasserting the tie between politics and the people. According to Dennis Kavanagh, Britain's 'liberal' immigration policy was one of the most unpopular aspects of the postwar consensus, such that 'Powell used mass fears to attack elite attitudes – the classic populist strategy – and in so doing he showed that parts of the consensus rested on unsteady foundations.'[87] As Schoen put it, 'To many his message appeared as a legitimation of their sentiments, an appeal to feel no guilt or embarrassment ... a summons to stand up and be counted.'[88]

Echoing his insistence that the state no longer represented the best interests of the people in economic affairs, Powell argued in Birmingham that the will of the British people was being ignored on questions of race – that their fears about the future were 'being swept under the carpet.'[89] Those in power were blinding themselves to an inevitable problem. This was a failure in leadership, not unlike that seen in the 1930s. As he put it that day, on 20 April 1968:

There could be no grosser misconception of the realities than is entertained by those who vociferously demand legislation as they call it 'against discrimination,' whether they be leader-writers of the same kidney and sometimes on the same newspapers which year after year in the 1930s tried to blind this country to the rising peril which confronted it, or archbishops who live in palaces, faring delicately with the bedclothes pulled right up over their heads.[90]

This was, therefore, a story of abandonment and political alienation from a failing leadership. Within minutes of referencing the failure of the 1930s, Powell revealed the consequences of this new era of liberal appeasement:

[The English have] found themselves made strangers in their own country. They found their wives unable to obtain hospital beds in childbirth, their children unable to obtain school places, their homes and neighbourhoods

---

[87] Dennis Kavanagh, *Thatcherism and British Politics: The End of Consensus?* (Oxford University Press, 1987), p. 57.
[88] Schoen, *Enoch Powell and the Powellites*, p. 237.
[89] J. Enoch Powell, 'Panorama: The Man Enoch Powell BBC 1,' 2 December 1968. POLL 4.1.28.
[90] J. Enoch Powell, Annual General Meeting of the West Midlands Area Conservative Political Centre, Birmingham, 20 April 1968, reprinted in *Reflections of a Statesman*, pp. 373–379 (p. 376).

Letters linked immigration to appeasement by Establishment

changed beyond recognition, their plans and prospects for the future defeated.[91]

In other words, the hard-earned gains of the Second World War were being given away. This was Lord Elton's 'unarmed invasion.'[92] Perhaps more than any other reference, this oblique reference to appeasement and war is echoed throughout the thousands of letters Powell received directly after the 'Rivers of Blood' speech:

I beg you to remember what happened to the late Sir Winston Churchill once. He was thrown out, but recalled to lead Britain in a time of fearful danger. I am sure that history will repeat itself.[93]

One man said you reminded him of Winston Churchill, trying to tell Britain during [between] the two wars that Germany was rising again, but Britain, or the ones that were supposed to look after Britain, would not hear him, until it was too late.[94]

[M]ay you continue to fight for our rights and heritage, to let us lead our own life and not be dictated to. As that other great Englishman Churchill said 'What kind of people do they think we are?' There is still plenty of spirit in us, and I'm afraid one day there must come plenty of trouble.[95]

Like Churchill, Powell had to speak a prophetic truth to the wilful blindness of the Establishment. The notion that Britain knew itself at war is a running theme in the letters:

Letters saw immigration as a state of war

How can you talk of racial discrimination, when there is already discrimination between white populating in this OUR Country which we fought to hold as OUR own in two world wars. The spirits of those who gave their lives for Gt. Britain will rise from the past, believe you me!![96]

You were correct in everything you stated, as this is not the England I fought for [woman writing] in the last war! Where I exist in Southall when you walk through the town you dont realise you are in England, its like Bombay believe me.[97]

Is this what my Brother died for? On H.M.S Inglefield (aged 20) on Feb. 25 1943. Gave his life for a bright and better Britain. If it is, God help us. You must send them back.[98]

Hitler taught us fear, but we also had a terrific pride, so we got up, shook ourselves, and with our heads held high, we carried on, all his might could not quell us, but the dregs of humanity that the short sighted politicians have let

[91] Ibid., p. 377.
[92] Elton, *The Unarmed Invasion.*
[93] Letter to Powell, 23 April 1968. POLL 8.1.8.
[94] Letter to Powell, 23 April 1958. POLL 8.1.8.
[95] Letter to Powell, 23 April 1968. POLL 8.1.8.
[96] '80 and not gutless,' Letter to Harold Wilson, cc-ed to Powell, 23 April 1968. POLL 8.1.8.
[97] Letter to Powell, 23 April 1968. POLL 8.1.8.
[98] Letter to Powell, 23 April 1968. POLL 8.1.8.

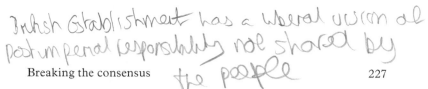
British Establishment has a liberal vision of post imperial responsibility not shared by the people

into <u>our</u> land, have ... Please keep it up Mr. Powell, we are tired of being called 'white trash' being elbowed out of our places in ques [sic]; tired of their insolence – and cunning ways.[99]

Importantly, for many, the failures of the postwar consensus were due to the British leadership's liberal vision of international (post-imperial) responsibility. This is enunciated again and again in the letters Powell received. One long example sums up the sentiment best:

Any adult Britain, with a spark of intelligence, knows that the old British Empire is dead, and has been for many years. And the present Queen is head of a quarrelsome, pestilential, now nearly disintegrated Commonwealth in name only. Our British working classes have maintained this country all down the years with the toil of our hand and the sweat of our brows, and shed rivers of blood in its defence, as you know. We have bled for it, fought for it, worked for it and paid for it. And now, two packs of the dirtiest traitors on Gods earth [British politicians], for the sake of a rotten, old tradition of a dead Empire (which by the way was acquired by the sacrifice of millions of British lives, mostly the workers) have wrenched our birth-right from us and handed our country over on a silver plate to millions of immigrants from all over the world ... We don't owe these people a living as some of the dirty traitors in this country seem to think. Our British people took civilization to their countries many years ago, at a great cost of British lives and money ... *Our British working classes have been sacrificed on the altar of a dead colonialism.*[100]

No doubt conceptions of race from the empire left a deep imprint on British postwar racism – the colonial experience among members of the right-wing group, the Monday Club, is just one important example of its political influence. For members of the Monday Club, multiracial society was synonymous with disorder. The Monday Club attempted to protect a vision of the moral and political superiority of the 'white man' in the context of anti-colonial nationalism and South African brutality. However, especially in Powell's letters, the empire had another meaning too. The complicated transaction of losing an empire and gaining a welfare state haunts these letters. This was a social contract grounded in recent history. Liberal internationalism, it seems, threatened to reverse the transaction.

Individual and collective acts of remembrance have the power to democratize political truth, whether for progressive or reactionary purposes. In many ways, the letters Powell received from the public were acts of remembrance. It is rarely noted that the infamous letter that Powell quoted in his 'Rivers of Blood' speech – through which he enunciated the racist slur 'wide-grinning piccaninnies' and spoke of black

conceptions of race from empire remained

Saw whites as morally + politically superior

---

[99] Letter to Powell, 23 April 1968. POLL 8.1.8.
[100] 'Anonymous' to Powell, 22 April 1968. POLL 8.1.1 (my emphasis).

men pushing excrement through the letterbox of an old besieged white woman – began its description of the old white woman as follows: 'She lost her husband and both her sons in the war. So she turned her seven-roomed house, her only asset, into a boarding house.'[101] Throughout Powell's letters, individual memories of war service, the promise of postwar homeownership, and the 'invasion' of immigration are bundled tightly together. Again, this is the class peace of the Second World War revealed as a forgery: the working classes treated as 'the slave element,'[102] 'their roots torn from them,'[103] victims of the 'never-ending humbug of wealthy and privileged pundits.'[104]

During the war, citizenship had a distinctly moral connotation, as civic obligations and sacrifice were increasingly emphasized.[105] One can see in the wartime rhetoric on female sexuality, volunteerism and civic virtue that a significant feature of 'the World War II discursive framework of citizenship' was a focus on issues of morality and ethical behaviour.[106] But as is less noted in the histories – and as Powell's supporters emphasize in their words – the relationship between state and citizen was also informed by traditional notions of class obligation. In other words, in the late 1960s, we can see in Powell's supporters a conception of the welfare state reinforced by a belief in upper-class obligation or paternalism.[107] At very least, the moral value of leadership, which worked to legitimize class hierarchy, still informed understandings of state power and good governance.[108] The continued purchase of this social deference in 1968 does not contradict the research of those who have argued that the Second World War brought about a popular transformation in British political thinking towards social equality and republicanism (nor does it necessarily support the 'apathy school' on the 1945

[101] Powell, *Reflections of a Statesman*, p. 378.
[102] 'Anonymous' to Powell, 22 April 1968. POLL 8.1.1.
[103] Ibid.   [104] Ibid.
[105] Richard Weight and Abigail Beach (eds.), *The Right to Belong: Citizenship and National Identity in Britain, 1930–1960* (New York: I. B. Tauris, 1998).
[106] Sonya Rose, *Which People's War?*, pp. 85, 18. See also, Abigail Beach, 'Forging a "nation of participants": Political and Economic Planning in Labour's Britain,' in Richard Weight and Abigail Beach (eds.), *The Right to Belong*, pp. 89–115.
[107] See Beer, *Modern British Politics*, for the argument that the welfare state was possible in Britain, unlike in the United States, because of the presence of right-wing paternalism, or a belief in the moral value of class hierarchy, in the Conservative Party. According to Beer, this provided an ideological common ground with Labour on which to build the welfare state.
[108] For a discussion of moral leadership as that which legitimates class, see David Cannadine, *The Rise and Fall of Class in Britain* (New York: Columbia University Press, 1999). Cannadine also discusses here one imagined model of Britain's class structure (among three models) as two-tiered, as a dichotomy between the haves and the have-nots, the rulers and the ruled.

The allowing of immigration perceived as a moral failure of the paternalistic upper classes

general election). Rather, it points to the way in which political positions within Britain's classed society could contain seemingly contradictory political ideas – containing, for instance, both radicalism and a traditional notion of a 'moral' organic society. Despite working-class, trade union leadership in the Labour Party and wartime growth in articulated resentment against class inequalities, still Britain remained a classed society – both materially and ideologically. Still, the notion of the divide between 'the people' and the state – or, more precisely, 'the people' and 'the Establishment' – was largely drawn out in class terms.[109] As such, the failure of the state to protect 'the people' was, for some, a *moral* failure of the upper classes. With all this, we see in the letters to Powell a sort of 'populist respectability': a deference both to Powell and 'the weight of English history' and, in the same breath, a condemnation of the political classes.[110] Here we see that expressions of deference are not synonymous with passivity; deference can, in other words, breed its own 'violent passions' and 'dreams of recompense.'[111] The political scientist Douglas Schoen called it assertive traditionalism.[112] Class solidarity and this populist respectability do not, then, stand in simple opposition to each other. The letters indicate, at least, that a complex vision of state power and class politics must inform our understanding of the limits of postwar social democracy or, as Jose Harris has put it, that 'curious alliance' between the British working classes and the upper-class reformist administrative elite who, after the war, both committed to a public service model of government and society.[113]

Non-white, New Commonwealth immigrants were not only, as theorist Paul Gilroy has noted, the 'unwitting bearers of the colonial past,'[114] they were also the unwitting bearers of a wartime past – in that, for Powell's supporters, their presence seemed to belie the integrity of that 'curious alliance.' According to a Butler-Stokes survey in

---

[109] For the debate over whether the Second World War was about a radical transformation in British politics, see: Addison, *The Road to 1945*; Steven Fielding, 'What Did "The People" Want?: The Meaning of the 1945 General Election,' *Historical Journal*, 35 (1992), pp. 623–639; Fielding, Thompson and Tiratsoo, *'England Arise!'*; Harold Smith (ed.), *War and Social Change: British Society in the Second World War* (Manchester University Press, 1986); and Brian Brivati and Harriet Jones (eds.), *What Difference Did the War Make?* (London: Leicester University Press, 1993).

[110] Schwarz, *The White Man's World*, p. 45.

[111] Ibid.

[112] Schoen, *Enoch Powell and the Powellites*, p. 208.

[113] Jose Harris, 'Tradition and Transformation: Society and Civil Society in Britain, 1945–2001,' in Kathleen Burk (ed.), *The British Isles since 1945* (Oxford University Press, 2003), p. 120.

[114] Gilroy, *Postcolonial Melancholia*, p. 128.

[handwritten margin note: M/c economic insecurities helped Powell gain support - belief immigrants taking out of society]

1969, for instance, respondents showing the most extreme degrees of 'downward mobility' (comparing subjective measures of present class identity to memories of childhood) were the most prone to give support to Enoch Powell.[115] Even more, later surveys found a correlation between Powellite support and feelings of economic insecurity, particularly middle-class economic insecurity, up to at least 1974.[116] One supporter wrote that immigrants were 'like parasites living off our backs,' another likewise insisted that 'white people are getting fed up paying through the nose to try and keep this country solvent' when immigrants 'are doing their best to sink it.'[117] 'It would seem that we spent years fighting for our freedom,' wrote another, 'only to find the Govt making us into the serfs of the "late comed" uns.'[118] Black immigrants were referred to as culturally different, but even more than that they were seen as 'bad citizens,' scamming social services,[119] using 'cunning' to take houses, hospital beds and unemployment benefits.[120] The immigrant was drawn, in these terms, as a scrounger, an embodiment of all that is wrong with an (undemocratic and authoritarian) state.

Powell's letters in favour of greater immigration restrictions are steeped in racism, yet they also reveal the experience of profound social and economic uncertainty and serve as testaments to social changes unrelated to immigration. Especially after the 'Rivers of Blood' speech, historical injustice reverberates throughout the letters to Powell. Here is one typical example:

How disgraceful that [my father] who has served in two world wars and worked damn'd hard all his life should be forced out of his neighbourhood by foreigners. I'm sure that our boys who died from 1939–1945 to preserve our wonderful country … would turn in their graves if they could see the hordes of invaders we are now getting.[121]

Erroneously linking the housing shortage of the 1960s with immigration, another wrote to Powell that Christianity died 'en masse' when the 'Homes fit for Heroes' failed: 'many lived, begat, and died in one or two rooms, Christianity en masse died then, + has never been resurrected. The Archbishop should wake up to reality or it will be much blood.'[122]

[115] Schoen, *Enoch Powell and the Powellites*, pp. 216–217.
[116] Ibid., p. 231.
[117] Letters to Powell, 23 April 1968. POLL 8.1.8.
[118] 'Anonymous' to Powell, 21 April 1968. POLL 8.1.8.
[119] Letter to Powell, 21 April 1968. POLL 8.1.8.
[120] Letter to Powell, 21 April 1968. POLL 8.1.8.
[121] 'Anonymous' to Powell, 21 April 1968. POLL 8.1.1.
[122] 'Anonymous' to Powell, 8 May 1968. POLL 8.1.1.

Powell's letters bring together old stories with experiences of postwar scarcity. As discussed in the previous chapter, the housing shortage and the (racial) politics of housing remained a key source of complaint. Many of the letters to Powell are highly personal. They often involve a story of personal injustice. They read like offerings to Powell – sources to be quoted in his next speech. In these letters, in the thousands of acts of writing to Powell and in Powell's uses of them, we see the translation of private memories into political meaning.

Powell's place in enunciating fear in the failure of Britain's social services due to immigration is ironic, as he was a well-known opponent of nationalized industry, economic planning and government housing. In all Powell's previous arguments against the gains of the postwar consensus, however, Powell did not argue against Britain's need for the National Health Service. He had successfully served as Minister for Health only a few years before, overseeing the introduction of a ten-year plan to modernize hospitals in the country. Powell made clear that immigration threatened the National Health Service – immigrant women were taking hospital beds. The Commonwealth immigrant came to Britain 'as a full citizen' and 'entered instantly into the possession of the rights over every citizen, from the vote to free treatment under the National Health Service.'[123] This was the common ground he held with many of those who wrote to him. The letters made little of Powell's reference in the speech to the vote and to Powell's overriding argument regarding the future political consequences of minority cultures, or the threat of communalism. But concern that immigration could destroy the National Health Service and public housing ran throughout.

Crucially, Powell made it clear that something could be done, that Britain was not like the United States – the problem was not historically predetermined: 'Nothing is more misleading than comparison between the Commonwealth immigrant in Britain and the American Negro. The Negro population of the United States, which was already in existence before the United States became a nation, started literally as slaves and were later given the franchise and other citizenship.'[124] The Commonwealth immigrant came to Britain by choice as a full citizen. The history of British imperialism, again, had no bearing on the Commonwealth immigrant's place in Britain. In Britain, at least according to Powell, mass repatriation was possible. Even before Martin Luther

---

[123] J. Enoch Powell, 20 April 1968. Speech reprinted in *Reflections of a Statesman*, pp. 376–377.
[124] Ibid., p. 376.

King's death, the American analogy was a preoccupation. In response to his Walsall speech, one man wrote to Powell from London:

With regard to the forthcoming legislation against 'racial discrimination', I understand that to a certain extent this legislation is going to be based on American experience. I do feel this analogy is absolutely false. The white American feels a sense of obligation to the American Negro because the latter are descended from slaves forcibly dragged to America. We Anglo-Celts here have no such obligation. Why should we?[125]

It was essential to distance Britain from what were regarded as the moral dilemmas of white America. As one woman put it to Powell after his Birmingham speech:

When the situation here is compared with America, there is no parallel. That is the only place the Negros [sic] have for hundreds of years, but all these people here have there [sic] own independent countries from which they were more or less thrown out. Why don't they stay there and make something of it instead of coming here demanding special treatment … They should be made to contribute to these things for years, as I have had to.[126]

Instead of any such obligation, Powell's supporters saw themselves as victims of liberals in government. Another supporter wrote that immigration threatened to turn Britain into 'some sort of overcrowded international island' – which was an 'idiotic social experiment to satisfy the combined requirements of nurserymen for cheap labour and the lunatic desire of "Liberals" who think that all the world's troubles will end if people are forced to live with foreigners.'[127] Ronald Bell, speaking at a Monday Club meeting, would call this Britain's 'muddled idea of the nobility of being overwhelmed.'[128] This made Britain, as another letter to Powell put it, 'the laughing stock of the world' – the immigrant was no longer a loyal subject of Britain: 'We are under no (well some are) delusion as to what these immigrants think of us even though they are only too glad to take everything there is to be had. They despise us and have no respect for us.'[129]

The English were, then, victims. He recounted in the Birmingham speech that he had been 'surprised and alarmed' by the 'ordinary, decent, sensible people writing rational and often well-educated letters' who write anonymously for fear of persecution:

The sense of being a persecuted minority which is growing among ordinary English people in the areas of the country which are affected is something that

[125] 'Anonymous' to Powell, no date. SRO, D3123/255.
[126] Letter to Powell, 23 April 1968. POLL 8.1.8.
[127] Letter to Powell, 23 April 1968. POLL 8.1.8.
[128] Ronald M. Bell, speaking at York University Monday Club, 12 February 1971. 'Immigration Data,' SRO, D4490/2.
[129] Letter to Powell, 23 April 1968. POLL 8.1.8.

those without direct experience can hardly imagine. I am going to allow just one of those hundreds of people to speak for me.[130]

The letter that Powell then cited included the infamous lines which described the persecution of one old woman: 'She finds excreta pushed through her letterbox. When she goes to the shops, she is followed by children, charming, wide-grinning piccaninnies. They cannot speak English, but one word they know. "Racialist," they chant.'[131] Powell received this letter, which told of the old pensioner intimidated by black neighbours, from a woman in March 1968. It began with the line: 'I am writing to you on behalf of the poor and inarticulate white people whose whole lives have been disrupted.'[132] The Conservative Party was, according to this woman, 'the last (and fading) hope of these people.'[133] Never in history, she noted, had any but a 'conquered people' been settled by such great numbers of aliens.[134] She warned of an 'explosion [from] the kindest and most tolerant people in the world' that would be 'frightful.'[135] She argued for voluntary repatriation, as Powell would echo a month later. After Powell's Birmingham speech, she told Powell then that 90 per cent of the British people supported him, that it was as though the Conservative Establishment thought that 'the volcano can be pushed back underground,' and that the effort of both parties to 'take Race out of politics' was merely an attempt to pervert the British people.[136]

Two months after Powell's speech, this woman wrote again to Powell. She asked him to burn the original letter.[137] He replied, 'I can assure you that I have taken, and shall continue to take, all possible steps to conceal your identity.'[138] When questions arose about the validity of the story, Powell would refuse to reveal his source. Her story of the old pensioner – both the racist words and the imagery of the imperilled old woman – became something of a hallmark in Britain's immigration debate. As Jonathan Rutherford notes, it was the 'the imperial "black peril" of the black male brought home' – the 'white mother … besieged by black males, persecuted, her life slowly extinguished.'[139] Roy Jenkins, Chancellor of the Exchequer, commented soon after the speech: 'the story could not be checked, although, possibly without existing, she has achieved a national fame and impact.'[140] Another story from that infamous letter not included

---

[130] Powell, *Reflections of a Statesman*, p. 377.
[131] Ibid., p. 378.
[132] Letter to Powell, 'Immigration Data,' SRO, D4490/2.
[133] Ibid.   [134] Ibid.   [135] Ibid.
[136] Letter to Powell, 9 June 1968. 'Immigration Data,' SRO, D4490/2.
[137] Ibid.
[138] Letter from Powell, 27 June 1968. 'Immigration Data,' SRO, D4490/2.
[139] Jonathan Rutherford, 'Enoch Powell's Island Story,' in *Forever England*, p. 134.
[140] *Sunday Times*, 5 May 1968.

in Powell's speech – one that informs that of the old pensioner – tells of three men in a YMCA bathroom with the door ajar: 'One negro sat on the toilet. One was urinating in the hand basin and a third was awaiting his turn with his trousers down.'[141] This vision of black men was perhaps too profane for Powell's speech. However, its presence next to the story of the embattled pensioner underlines the letter-writer's perspective. This was a portrait of the black immigrant – and, fundamentally, black male sexuality – as obscene, threatening and taboo.

Powell, like this letter-writer, wished to give voice to the embattled Englishman – the archetypical 'man on the street.' As Powell recounts in the speech, a man told Powell that if he had money to go, he would leave Britain, because, 'In this country in fifteen or twenty years' time the black man will have the whip hand over the white man.'[142] Again, a letter warns of violence and imagines a world turned upside down. Powell knew repeating these words would draw some criticisms, saying in the next line: 'I can already hear the chorus of execration. How dare I say such a horrible thing? How dare I stir up trouble and inflame feelings ...? The answer is that I do not have the right not to do so ... I simply do not have the right to shrug my shoulders and think about something else. What he is saying, thousands and hundreds of thousands are saying and thinking.'[143] As he put it in a speech later that year:

My judgment then is this: the people of England will not endure it. If so, it is idle to argue whether they ought to or ought not to. I do not believe it is in human nature that a country, and a country such as ours, should passively watch the transformation of whole areas which lie at the heart of it into alien territory.[144]

After his dismissal, Powell insisted that he was not a racist and that the speech did not rely on any racist argument.[145] Powell denied that recounting the fear of the black 'whip hand' relied on racist sentiments; it merely relied on the recognition that racism among the British people could not be denied. Powell's acceptance of racism as an aspect of human nature that could not be reformed (for it was a *sin* rather than a social problem) opened the way for his use of racist language. He insisted at the very opening of his speech: 'people are disposed to mistake predicting troubles for causing troubles ... Perhaps this goes back

[141] Letter to Powell, 'Immigration Data,' SRO D4490/2.
[142] Powell, *Reflections of a Statesman*, p. 374.
[143] Ibid.
[144] Powell, 'To the Annual Conference of the Rotary Club of London,' Eastbourne, 16 November 1978, in *Reflections of a Statesman*, pp. 382–393 (p. 390).
[145] '"Am I a Racialist? NO!" says Enoch Powell,' *The Post*. MS2141/A/7/15.

to the primitive belief that the word and the thing, the name and the object, are identical.'[146] He named it; he did not, he insisted, create it.

However, in a September 1968 interview with the *Sunday Times*, Powell explained that he viewed his role as being a representative in the Burkean sense, rather than as merely a delegate whose job it was to voice the people's sentiments. The politician at his best gave voice and meaning to an unarticulated feeling.[147] To name it – to act as the prophet of the 'the River Tiber flowing with much blood' – was itself a creative act.[148] In this sense, the 'Rivers of Blood' speech was an *event* to be remembered. It was, for one of Powell's openly fascist supporters, 'as important as Dunkirk.'[149] The ensuing debates about whether Powell was a 'demagogue or a democrat' ultimately hinged on whether Powell spoke for 'popular experience' or whether, in fact, he 'distorted and manipulated reality.'[150] Powell knowingly endowed the social experiences of his supporters and opponents with political content. The unarticulated feelings of resentment against immigrants were given meaning via Powell's Churchillian language of war, appeasement and invasion. Powell's metaphors in his speeches on immigration were highly violent and militaristic: with phrases such as an 'invasion of our body politic,' 'alien territory,' 'whole areas, towns … occupied,' 'detachments from … the West Indies or India or Pakistan encamped in certain areas in England,' 'whip hand,' 'throwing a match on to gunpowder,' 'much blood' and 'impending disaster.'[151] This is not just Powell the politician speaking – this is Powell the brigadier. As will be discussed in the next chapter, Powell's notion of war as a moral process of self-knowledge and identification infiltrated his political thinking.

Despite his rejection of any definition of race, Powell's understanding of racism as a reality outside the parameters of his influence haunted his political career after 'Rivers of Blood.' He consistently refused to publicly condemn it among his supporters – refusing to argue over what 'they ought to or ought not to do.'[152] As such, whether it was integral to his arguments or not, much of the energy behind his support emanated from a clearly articulated racism.[153] As a *Sunday Times* reporter noted, Powell 'found peace in the race issue … discovering a kind of mystical

[146] Ibid., p. 161.
[147] *Sunday Times*, 3 September 1968.
[148] Powell, *Reflections of a Statesman*, p. 379.
[149] Dennis Herbert Harmston quoted in 'Callaghan Orders Airport Race Inquiry,' *Daily Mail*, 25 April 1968.
[150] Ritscherle, 'Opting out of Utopia,' p. 297.
[151] Labour Research Department, *Powell and His Allies* (London, 1969), p. 10.
[152] Powell, *Reflections of a Statesman*, p. 390.
[153] See POLL 8.1.8.

contentment in the sacks of letters supporting him.'[154] The conservative philosopher Maurice Cowling's critique of the politics of liberalism is important here – especially as it surely influenced Powell's thinking on race relations legislation. Cowling offered a conservative critique of the dominance of secular liberalism in British contemporary political life and asserted an argument about the nature of political authority and community itself. As Cowling put it, 'To live [by instinct and habitual action] is to live in no condition of amorality, but to live in as close proximity to the moral law as possible. To think (or live) otherwise, if it is possible at all, is to be guilty of moralistic irrelevance.'[155] The academic and political Establishment had become, since the rise of liberalism and the decline of the Church, Cowling believed, insidiously dogmatic and moralistic. As such, Cowling held contempt for the pretence of public morality.[156] Liberalism worked to police the interior of man; it wrongly assumed the perfectability of man's soul as a universal goal. Cowling critiqued British socialism in so far as it was liberal – his was a critique of the 'party of virtue.'[157] Likewise, in Powell's arguments, racism – and evil in general – could not be policed by the state. All liberal efforts to mitigate racism in British society could not erase it. A speech Powell delivered in 1980 in Dorking – in what the local Conservative Association called Powell's 'old style' – best emphasizes Powell's pessimism towards social democracy's efforts to transform society through social and economic equality:

[T]hose who sit in the seats of authority are determined to stop their ears. They are abetted in doing so by the drug-pushers of fantasy, who tell the fairy-tale that all the instincts and antagonisms, all the fears, the envies and the ambitions of humankind, can be dissolved and washed away by the application of sufficient money, extracted from the nation and spent by the state. In that nirvana where everyone has a lucrative and satisfying job, where every family is well and cheaply housed, where all complaints and wants have been attended to, the little details of who we think we are and by whom we are ruled will escape attention. When all are happy and all have enough, nobody will discriminate against anybody and no section will differentiate itself from any other section. It is the same old falsehood as was told to our fathers and the generations before them – that crime and violence would vanish as the standard of living rose. It was not true, and it is not true. The causes of evil and the

[154] 'Profile: Enoch Powell,' *Sunday Times*, 28 April 1968.
[155] Cited in Peter Ghosh, 'Towards the verdict of history: Mr Cowling's doctrine,' in *Public and Private Doctrine: Essays in British History presented to Maurice Cowling* (Cambridge University Press, 1993), p. 286.
[156] Geoffrey Wheatcroft, 'Maurice Cowling,' *The Guardian*, 6 September 2005.
[157] Ghosh, 'Towards the verdict of history: Mr Cowling's doctrine,' in *Public and Private Doctrine*, p. 299.

sources of danger lies elsewhere and deeper than in material production and consumption: experience and the face of the world are witnesses to that.[158]

The 'little details of who we think we are and by whom we are ruled' would not go away with prosperity and equality. To Cowling, only Enoch Powell approximated his conception of what a real Tory politician should be – in his understanding of the need for 'spiritual glue,' in a need for a sense of community with shared morals, without moralizing.[159] Powell's commitment to the rule of law and his continued rejection of the validity of race relations legislation, as well as his acceptance of racism as a social reality, stem from this conservative critique of the basic tenets of liberalism. Powell's 'republicanism' – his commitment to the representation of his constituents' thoughts and feelings (whether racist or not) – was not an effort to distribute political power, but an effort to cement the 'spiritual glue' of political community.

The shockwave

Despite all the intellectualism of Powell's speech, it sounded definitively fascist – the subtext of invasion and war resonated, for many, with recent memories of fascism's cult of violence. Heath telephoned Powell the day after the speech and dismissed him from the Shadow Cabinet. He told the papers that he had done this because the speech had been 'racialist in tone, and liable to exacerbate racial tensions.'[160] Quintin Hogg, Shadow Home Secretary and spokesman for Conservative policy on home affairs, had threatened resignation if Powell was not dismissed. Immediately, the Director of Public Prosecutions was called in to ascertain if Powell could be prosecuted for 'racial incitement' under the Race Relations Act of 1965 – he was not.[161] Strikes and marches sprang up all over England in protest against Powell's dismissal. The placards and signs spoke of British free speech. Controversially, thirty-eight immigration officers at Heathrow airport signed a public letter supporting the speech.[162] The Home Office held a full-scale inquiry into those who signed the letter and suspended one immigration officer for writing it.[163] The following week, in an effort

---

[158] J. Enoch Powell, 'Speech to the Surrey Branch Monday Club, Dorking,' 11 July 1980. CPA, CRD 4.9.20.

[159] Cited in Ghosh, 'Towards the Verdict of History: Mr Cowling's Doctrine,' in *Public and Private Doctrine*, pp. 288, 290.

[160] 'Tory leader clamps down on Mr. Powell,' *Birmingham Post*, 22 April 1968.

[161] 'Powell barred by the Tories,' *Daily Sketch*, 22 April 1968.

[162] 'Mr Brown "Horrified" by Powell: Dockers to March,' *The Times*, 26 April 1968.

[163] Ibid.

to reassert party unity, the 'Conservative big guns were out in force' – Heath, Maudling, Sir Alec Douglas-Home, and the party chairman, Anthony Barber, spoke publicly on the issue of race relations.[164]

In response to his dismissal, Powell wrote to Heath:

I believe you will be Prime Minister of this country, and that you will be an outstandingly able Prime Minister, perhaps even a great one. There is one cause for anxiety which I hope that time will dispel. It is the impression you often give of playing down and even unsaying policies and views which you hold and believe to be right, for fear of clamour from some section of the press or public. I cannot help seeing in this light the fact that you took occasion to stigmatize my speech at Birmingham as 'racialist' when you surely must realize that it was nothing of the kind.[165]

In Powell's short letter to Heath, he distinguished himself from the Conservative Party leader in political approach rather than in belief: where Heath was strategic, Powell stayed true to principle. The official policy response to Powell came via Hogg's address to Parliament during the second reading of the Race Relations Bill on Tuesday, 23 April.[166] Hogg echoed Heath, insisting that the controversy be discussed in a 'civilized way,' and that 'one should think in the more immediate future whether one's words are more likely to make [racial violence] happen or less likely to make it happen.'[167] It was between Hogg's approach and Powell's, 'because I attach every bit as much importance in this sphere to the way things are said as to what is said in them.'[168] Powell had embarrassed the party and the Establishment as a whole. According to the press, during the speech, Hogg aroused as much or more support from Labour as his own side.[169] Even if many of their arguments rested on the same acceptance of inequality, Powell had violated the central premise of the political consensus – the rule of polite opinion.

Hogg insisted that Powell had been disloyal to the Shadow Cabinet – that he had broken from the political process – by not informing the cabinet of the contents of his controversial speech. Later in the year, Powell gave a direct reply to this condemnation:

It has been freely alleged that I was somehow guilty of a breach of discipline or of disloyalty, either to my colleagues generally or to the party's spokesman on

[164] 'Race: Heath Calls for Calm – and Spending,' *Sunday Times*, 28 April 1968.
[165] Quoted in 'Tories Plan Positive Line Over Bill,' *The Times*, 23 April 1968.
[166] 'Home Secretary Offers Watchdog Committee on Race Relations: Mr Hogg Defines Three Principles of Conservative Policy,' *The Times*, 24 April 1968.
[167] Ibid.   [168] Ibid.
[169] 'Mr Callaghan Appeals for All-Party Unity,' *The Times*, 24 April 1968.

home affairs in particular, in speaking as I did. There is no substance to this charge. No rule or convention forbids front-benchers to advocate or defend, even before parliamentary debate, the line which the leadership of the party has publicly decided to take ... it was not suggested that I had [recommended a divergent policy]. It was to the 'tone' of my speech that objection was taken.[170]

Powell accepted 'tone' as a matter of personal choice and accepted that the Conservative leader should be entitled to be guided by his own taste when choosing his colleagues. However, on the matter of 'tone,' Powell was unequivocal on what he thought had motivated Heath: 'He was frightened out of his wits ... and scenting danger, ran for cover.'[171]

Directly after the speech, criticisms against Powell within the Conservative Party primarily focused, then, on his language. Douglas-Home came to Powell's defence, noting that 'Mr. Powell's language may have been ill-chosen and extravagant but he is not and never has been a racialist.'[172] His language was 'regrettable' because 'people's emotions could be easily aroused.'[173] Tellingly, this criticism appeared on the far right also. Peter Griffiths, known for winning a seat in Parliament with an anti-immigration platform in the 1964 general election – and for the campaign slogan 'If you want a nigger for a neighbour, vote Labour' – argued that the content of the speech was respectable but thought that 'the language of the speech was exaggerated.'[174] The small (and far from influential) fascist Union Movement of Oswald Mosley officially noted, 'Our policy is clear and firm [against Britain's immigration policy] but at no time have we used language offensive to the immigrants.'[175]

The Labour Party's official response criticized the contents of Powell's speech, specifically Powell's predictions regarding future population figures of non-whites living in Britain. Powell maintained that in the year 2000, one-tenth of the British population, or five to seven million, would be descended from non-white immigrants.[176] They charged that Powell's statistics had been shown by the Institute of Race Relations to be 'wildly high.'[177] The official number was 3.5 million.[178] But, again, Labour also focused on Powell's use of language. One Labour Research

---

[170] J. Enoch Powell, 'Speech To the Annual Conference of the Rotary Club of London, Eastbourne,' 16 November 1968. Reprinted in *Reflections of a Statesman*, p. 383.
[171] Cited in Heffer, *Like the Roman*, p. 457.
[172] Quoted in 'Heath Asks Nation to Be Calm, Fair, Responsible, Constructive,' *The Times*, 27 April 1968.
[173] Quoted ibid.
[174] 'Mr Brown "Horrified" by Powell: Dockers to March,' *The Times*, 26 April 1968.
[175] Ibid.
[176] Powell, *Reflections of a Statesman*, p. 374. The 2001 Census indicated that approximately 4.3 million individuals in Britain defined themselves as black, Asian or mixed race.
[177] Labour Research Department, *Powell and His Allies*, p. 7.
[178] Ibid.

Department report noted that Powell's use of 'metaphors and adjectives' was almost exclusively 'ugly and cruel.'[179] Between 1968 and 1969, his speeches on immigration used words such as 'evil,' 'insane,' 'mad,' 'lunacy,' 'conspiracy' and 'filthy.'[180]

Fenner Brockway, president of the Movement for Colonial Freedom and Labour MP, took the criticism of the speech further, but echoed the same Tory argument that Powell's speech was distinct mainly in presentation:

> It is a shocking speech – the most reactionary I can remember since the war. It is a reversion to the Tory philosophy before Disraeli which believed in a superior class and a superior race. It is indicative of the extreme racialists who have led to the Tory Party deciding to vote against the Race Relations Bill. It should awaken liberal-minded people to the true meaning of Toryism in the same way as did the Suez adventure.[181]

The Communist Party general secretary, John Gollan, likewise said the day after Powell's speech that it had only 'spelt out the essential fascist credo of the majority of the Tory Party.'[182] The left-wing daily paper, *Morning Star*, held that Powell's speech was an embarrassment to the Conservative Party because it revealed their policies in an 'open way.'[183] This had consequences. President Kaunda of Zambia warned Heath that if Powell's policy on the Race Relations Bill was officially supported by the Conservative Party, it would mean an end to the Commonwealth if the Conservatives came to power.[184] He condemned the notion that, 'while Zambians had fought with Britain against the Nazis,' they could not go to Britain because they were black.[185] Kaunda called the Conservative campaign against the bill 'a shocking madness, un-Christian, and uncivilized.'[186] Powell had internationally shamed the party – the Commonwealth countries, especially, were listening.

As Alice Ritscherle's work has emphasized, many critics of Powell tended to condemn his supporters' racism in classed terms.[187] Racism was, they argued, a product of ignorance and working-class culture. This criticism, Ritscherle argues, was an attempt to 'resolve the contradictions between racist politics and democracy.'[188] James Crawford, secretary of

---

[179] Ibid., p. 9.   [180] Ibid., pp. 9–10.
[181] 'A Shocking Speech, Says Brockway,' *Morning Star*, 22 April 1968.
[182] 'It's an Icy Incitement to Race War,' *Morning Star*, 22 April 1968.
[183] 'Out of the Shadow Cabinet,' *Morning Star*, 22 April 1968.
[184] 'Zambia Issues Warning,' *The Guardian*, 22 April 1968.
[185] Quoted ibid.   [186] Quoted ibid.
[187] Ritscherle, 'Democracy and Demagoguery: Representing an "Enlightened" Society in 1968,' in 'Opting out of Utopia,' pp. 280–316.
[188] Ibid., p. 299.

the West Indian Standing Conference, wrote a letter to *The Times* arguing that Powell had offered 'mythical figments of imagination' in his story of 'the old lady who lives in fear of violence.' As such, Powell manipulated ignorant people incapable of distinguishing truth from imagination. Crawford argued that the thousands of letters of support that Powell received after the speech could not have been written by 'ordinary, decent, rational, and well-educated people.'[189] Powellism was, then, a function of social disadvantage. Powell himself was condemned for failing to guide public opinion. Elchon Hinden wrote in the *Socialist Commentary* that politicians needed to work 'in advance of public opinion, leading it and changing it.'[190] The statesman, he argued, must transform the man on the street. Despite Powell's middle- and upper-class support, ignorance and the vulgarities of working-class culture remained the explanatory framework for understanding opposition to black immigration.

Still, there were politicians who came out in support of Powell directly after the speech. Powell was strongly supported by the far-right Monday Club – which included twenty-five members of Parliament at that time.[191] The Monday Club had formed under the patronage of Lord Salisbury in 1961 as a revolt against what was called 'the neo-socialist betrayal of Harold Macmillan' – specifically, the Macmillan government's economic policy and the 'Wind of Change' approach in British colonial Africa.[192] After his Birmingham speech, Powell received a telegram from the Monday Club stating, 'You are not alone: the majority of the people inside and outside the Tory Party support you on this issue ... Your absence from the Conservative front bench can only be a short one.'[193] A number of other MPs also came out with unconditional support for Powell. Among them was John Jennings, Conservative MP for Burton, who called Powell's dismissal from the Shadow Cabinet 'a tragedy.'[194] Angus Maude, Conservative MP for Stratford-upon-Avon and someone who had worked closely with Powell after the war in the One Nation group, insisted that Powell was helping to have the 'dangers' of immigration 'exorcised now.'[195] Also noteworthy is Captain Henry Kerby, Conservative MP for Arundel and Shoreham, who called Powell's speech 'truthful and courageous,' adding, 'At last the nation has

[189] *The Times* (27 April 1968), as cited in Ritscherle, 'Opting out of Utopia,' p. 299.
[190] *Socialist Commentary* (July 1968), as cited in Ritscherle, 'Opting out of Utopia,' p. 299.
[191] Labour Research Department, *Powell and His Allies*, p. 11.
[192] Lord Critchley, *The Times*, 23 November 1968.
[193] *Daily Telegraph*, 23 April 1968.
[194] *The Times*, 22 April 1968.
[195] *Daily Telegraph*, 27 April 1968.

found a leader brave enough to break the all-party conspiracy of silence which has for too long shrouded this sinister and festering issue.'[196] Similarly, in letters to Powell from the public, he is consistently thanked for this 'courage.' In some, again, this would be directly linked to Powell's own history as a soldier: 'When we ... read of your War Record in the News of the World last Sunday, we both knew of the amount of courage you must have had.'[197]

According to the press, the speech caused an 'emotional scene' in the Commons when Andrew Faulds, Labour MP for Smethwick, fiercely attacked Powell – insisting that the Birmingham speech be repeated in Parliament so that it could be challenged.[198] According to witnesses, Faulds' voice rose to a 'shriek' as he cried out, pointing to Powell, 'un-Christian, unprincipled, undemocratic and racialist.'[199] David Winnick, Labour MP for Croydon South, during questions on Rhodesia, referred to 'the type of race poison we had from the dishonourable Member for Wolverhampton South West last night.'[200] The Speaker of the House, Horace King, insisted that Winnick withdraw his reference to Powell as 'dishonourable' and told Faulds to 'restrain himself.'[201] The Liberal Party leader Jeremy Thorpe noted that the 'tragedy' of Powell's speech was that by 'inflaming emotions' he was making it more difficult to resolve the problem of race relations.[202] Much of the discussion immediately after Powell's speech similarly focused on the country's 'emotional upsurge.'[203] Powell had 'uncovered' suppressed feelings and attitudes.[204] In the press and in political speeches, the politicization of race and immigration was seen to threaten to make its management impossible. Both front benches were, according to _The Times_, 'anxious to drift no further apart than was absolutely necessary for internal party harmony.'[205] Callaghan called for 'all-party unity' on the issue.[206]

On 23 April, Hogg offered the Tory compromise amendment that, though supporting the intentions of the Race Relations Bill, declined to give it a second reading (due, Hogg explained, to Conservative opposition to the use of anti-discrimination law in credit and insurance and due to the need for 'vastly greater exemptions' for owner-occupiers in

[196] _Daily Telegraph_, 23 April 1968.
[197] Letter to Powell, 1 May 1968, D3123/6.
[198] 'MP for Smethwick Attacks Mr Powell,' _Birmingham Post_, 22 April 1968.
[199] Quoted ibid.   [200] Quoted ibid.   [201] Quoted ibid.
[202] Quoted in 'Heath Asks Nation to Be Calm, Fair, Responsible, Constructive,' _The Times_, 27 April 1968.
[203] 'Wilson to Ease Race Tension?' _Evening Mail_, 29 April 1968.
[204] 'In Search of Enoch Powell,' _The Observer_, 30 April 1968.
[205] 'Mr Callaghan Appeals for All-Party Unity,' _The Times_, 24 April 1968.
[206] Ibid.

housing).[207] Despite efforts to shore up party discipline after Powell's speech, the amendment did not pass. The government carried the second reading with a majority of over one hundred votes – twenty-five Conservative MPs had abstained, many due to the conviction that the reasoned amendment did not make it clear enough that the opposition was in favour of some form of legislation to combat racism. The revolt of backbenchers who shared Powell's views and 'spoke militantly' of mounting a vote against the intentions of the bill did not, in the end, materialize.

Still, it is clear that public support for the tone and the policies of Powell's speech was hard for both parties to ignore. Overall, within a Gallop poll, 97 per cent of 'middle class' and 95 per cent of 'working class' respondents had heard about the speech, with 70 per cent and 78 per cent agreeing with the views expressed within the speech respectively.[208] The party immediately recognized that Powell had found widespread support from across the socio-economic spectrum. On Thursday, 25 April, all but 21 of approximately 3,000 West India Dock workers came out on strike in protest at Powell's dismissal.[209] Nearly 1,000 signed a petition asking the government 'to seriously consider their continuous threat to our living standards by this blind policy of unlimited immigrants being imposed on us.'[210] There were no official ring-leaders of the strike, though Harry Pearman, who was active in the Labour Party and a regular organizer for elderly and disabled dockers, came out in the front of the 1,000-man march to the Commons.[211] Butler-Stokes survey data found, the following year, that working-class Powellites had higher levels of trade union membership and activity and, at the same time, were more likely than non-Powellites to say that unions had too much power in society.[212] When asked if the dock workers had any misgivings about coming out in support of a leading Conservative, one explained to the press that it did not matter who it was that said what Powell said: 'If it had been that good lady Scottish Nationalist MP [Winifred Ewing], the men would have acted in the same way.'[213] One of the most vocal of the dock workers in the march referred to his father, who had also been a docker and had

---

[207] 'Home Secretary Offers Watchdog Committee on Race Relations: Mr Hogg Defines Three Principles of Conservative Policy,' *The Times*, 24 April 1968.
[208] Schoen, *Enoch Powell and the Powellites*, p. 69.
[209] 'Backlash: Why Dockers Marched,' *The Observer*, 28 April 1968.
[210] 'Dockers March for Powell,' *The Times*, 24 April 1968.
[211] Ibid.
[212] Schoen, *Enoch Powell and the Powellites*, pp. 209–211.
[213] Quoted in 'Backlash: Why Dockers Marched,' *The Observer*, 28 April 1968.

violently protested *against* a fascist demonstration in the 1930s, saying of his father, 'But he agrees with what I'm doing today. We think there are too many bloody coons coming into the country. They ought to be stopped or sent home.'[214]

Racist arguments and racist slurs were there, then, in the march. One reporter summarily recounted the dockers' views gathered during the protest:

Blacks are monkeys that ought to be trampled out. They bring VD and TB into the country. They proliferate. They smell. They suck the welfare services dry, getting something for nothing. They choke the hospitals and flood the schools. They ought to be sent home.[215]

As one dock worker put it, 'We won't be able to say "boo" to a nigger now without getting reported.'[216] But hardly any of the home-made banners revealed racist sentiments; instead, they emphasized Powell's right to free speech and right to say 'What Britain thinks.'[217] Echoing Powell, dockers also talked of a press conspiracy in support of the immigrant which prevented 'the decent working man getting his voice heard.'[218] They called the pending Race Relations Bill 'dictatorship.'[219] This was a march, like other marches, with many perspectives and many intentions behind it, but most were energized by racism.

The porters of London's Smithfield meat market also marched after the 'Rivers of Blood' speech in opposition to Powell's dismissal. Dennis Herbert 'Big Dan' Harmston, who had during the 1966 general election stood as Oswald Mosley's British Union Movement candidate in South-West Islington, led the march. At a meeting beside Smithfield, he told the porters:

At last the Englishman has had some guts. This is as important as Dunkirk. We are becoming second-class citizens in our own country. Immigrants have been brought here to undercut our wages in time of crisis. When there is vast unemployment in this country immigrants will compete with you for your jobs.[220]

The porters then marched from Smithfield to Westminster – singing such songs as *White Christmas, There'll always be an England*, and *Ten little niggers*. After meeting with Powell, Harmston again addressed marchers outside the House of Commons:

---

[214] Quoted ibid.   [215] Ibid.   [216] Quoted ibid.
[217] 'Dockers March for Powell,' *The Times*, 24 April 1968.
[218] Quoted in 'Backlash: Why Dockers Marched,' *The Observer*, 28 April 1968.
[219] Quoted ibid.
[220] Quoted in 'Callaghan Orders Airport Race Inquiry,' *Daily Mail*, 25 April 1968.

This is a colour issue. All immigrants should return home even if it means giving them repatriation grants. They are an embarrassment to our society. We are not racialists – but realists.

The porters cheered Harmston. Perhaps due to the greater influence of the British Union Movement among them, the meat packers' march was more overtly xenophobic.

On a smaller scale, workers came out in support of Powell across the country, affecting breweries, car factories and engineering works of all kinds.[221] For example, five hundred workers at the Dunlop Rubber Company factory at Gateshead staged a token demonstration in support of Powell and against the Race Relations Bill – there shop stewards did not support the demonstration and 'washed their hands of it.'[222] These small-scale strikes were especially widespread in the Midlands. Many workers were supported by their employers, such as those at an agricultural machinery factory at Huntingdon, whose managing director Karl Brooks came out in support of his employees' show of solidarity with Powell and 'free speech.'[223]

The Transport and General Workers' Union, to which both the dockers and Sikh bus drivers belonged, opposed the protests in support of Powell. Frank Cousins, general secretary of TGWU, spoke on the issue publicly:

I have been very saddened during the week that some of my own members, and members of other unions, have been so foolish as to be emotionally influenced into thinking that the solution to our economic problems can be reached by taking action about racial integration.[224]

Union officials were particularly concerned that the workers' expressions of racism would force immigrant workers to start all-immigrant unions of their own. One union official wrote to a Midlands paper criticizing Powell's speech and subsequently received a string of hostile calls from his union members, with one asking, 'Why doesn't the union look after people like us instead of those nig-nogs?'[225] Kafiat Ali, general secretary of the Pakistani Workers' Association, which had a membership in 1968 of approximately 10,000 Pakistani-British workers, said after the dock workers' protest and march that, 'We have lost faith in the British trade union movement. The dockers have confirmed our

---

[221] 'Backlash: Why Dockers Marched,' *The Observer*, 28 April 1968.
[222] 'Mr Brown "Horrified" by Powell: Dockers to March,' *The Times*, 26 April 1968.
[223] 'Backlash: Why Dockers Marched,' *The Observer*, 28 April 1968.
[224] Quoted in 'Heath Asks Nation to be Calm, Fair, Responsible, Constructive,' *The Times*, 27 April 1968.
[225] Quoted in 'Backlash: Why Dockers Marched,' *The Observer*, 28 April 1968.

suspicions.'[226] Similarly, Jagmohan Joshi, general secretary of the Indian Workers' Association (IWA), contended that trends in industry and employment showed that separate unions were a possibility in the near future 'and this will be bad for the principle of trade unionism.'[227] One IWA member told the press, 'We are not satisfied with the TUC – particularly not with the Transport and General.'[228] In remembering this period before and after Powell's 1968 speech, Shirley Joshi – Jagmohan Joshi's partner and fellow political activist – pointed to the fundamental failure of Britain's labour movement to confront racism as *the* essential precursor of the Powell phenomenon.[229] As an editorial in the *Morning Star* put it on the Monday after Powell's Saturday speech, when arguing that Powell should be prosecuted for incitement to racial hatred, 'the Labour Government's attitude to immigration and racialism has prepared the way for the backwoodsmen to come out with their blatant incitement.'[230] John Gollan of the Communist Party said the day after Powell's speech that the growing belligerence of the Conservative Party stemmed from Wilson's policies: it was, after all, 'the logical outcome of the betrayal of the Kenyan Asians.'[231]

The Trades Union Council had just a year before effectively boycotted talks with the government on legislation against racial discrimination in employment.[232] In February 1967, the government-sponsored National Committee for Commonwealth Immigrants – whose chairman was the Archbishop of Canterbury – had organized a two-day conference in London to discuss the possibility of legislation with an aim to 'persuade leaders of both sides of British industry to avoid American mistakes and act before the problem hurts.'[233] As the Race Relations Board Chairman Mark Bonham Carter asserted, such legislation was Britain's chance to show that democracies can act at the right time and learn from others rather than be driven, where the ballot is sovereign, solely by political necessity. For the conference, they brought to London seven leading trade unionists, employers and civil rights workers from the United States and Canada to speak to their British counterparts. Victor Reuther of the United Auto Workers, Ben Segal of the Equal Opportunities Commission, and the African-American leader and organizer of the 1963 'March on Washington' for civil rights, Bayard Rustin, were among them. George Woodcock, general secretary of the

[226] Quoted ibid.   [227] Quoted ibid.   [228] Quoted ibid.
[229] Shirley Joshi interview with the author, September 2005.
[230] 'Put Powell in the Dock,' *Morning Star*, 22 April 1968.
[231] 'It's an Icy Incitement to Race War,' *Morning Star*, 22 April 1968.
[232] 'Unions Boycott Race Law Talks,' *The Observer*, 26 February 1967.
[233] Ibid.

TUC, refused to attend. Of the fifty places for industry, only eighteen union representatives eventually agreed to attend – ten of them from white-collar unions.[234] The *only* major industrial union to be represented was in fact the Transport and General Workers, which sent two of its top men, Frank Cousins and Jack Jones, as speakers.[235]

The TUC joined with the employers' organization, the Confederation of British Industry, to issue a joint statement of opposition to possible race relations legislation. It maintained that discrimination was best dealt with in employment through 'voluntary action, preceded by a joint statement of opposition to racial discrimination.'[236] Race relations legislation could enable the government to issue a non-discrimination clause in official contracts – it was a basic issue, for the TUC, of the Race Relations lobby 'meddling in its territory.'[237] Their opposition bears the mark of the conservatism and political inertia of many in the TUC leadership at the time. Their North American counterparts at the conference stressed that voluntary action had been tried and failed in America and Canada. Bayard Rustin warned that if British industry failed to represent black workers via this legislation, the result would be immigrant unions and immigrant strikebreakers – resulting in 'a tremendous effect on the wages that white people in this country will be able to command.'[238] In this first major debate in Britain on race relations legislation, those that did attend accepted the findings of the PEP report[239] that discrimination was widespread in Britain in housing and employment. Home Secretary Roy Jenkins issued a statement at the conference that, whatever the protests of the TUC or employer organizations, the government would soon pass anti-discrimination law. The marches were, in many regards, born out of this unresolved tension between the unions and the government's approach to the question of discrimination in employment.

Difficulties after the 'Rivers of Blood' speech were felt most, however, on city streets. A week after the speech and only a couple of days after the big protest marches, on 28 April, fourteen young men disrupted an Afro-Caribbean family's christening party in Wolverhampton chanting 'Powell.'[240] They punched Wade Crooks, a fifty-one-year-old British-West Indian, as he sat in his car, and slashed above his eye with a razor blade. They also punched his son, Albert Crooks, the father of the child

[234] Ibid.   [235] Ibid.   [236] Ibid.   [237] Ibid.
[238] Quoted ibid.
[239] Political and Economic Planning (PEP) was a British policy think tank formed in 1931. It would be influential in the formation of the National Health Service, postwar planning, African development, and the shaping of the 1968 Race Relations Act.
[240] 'Coloured Family Attacked,' *The Times*, 1 May 1968.

christened.[241] As Wade Crooks put it, 'I heard my son shout that he had been hit ... the crowd were shouting "Powell, Powell" and "Why don't you go back to your own country?"'[242] It was the first attack in Wolverhampton since the speech. James Woodward, a Wolverhampton Labour councillor, insisted that Powell was responsible.[243] Wade Crooks told the press, 'I have been here since 1955 and nothing like this has happened before. I am shattered.'[244] Similarly, Paul Boateng, a former Labour MP, remembered the fear he experienced as a child after the 'Rivers of Blood' speech:

I was one of those 'wide-eyed, grinning piccaninnies' that [Powell] saw fit to quote in a letter ... For the first time in the country of my birth, [on the day following the speech] I was shouted at and spat at and abused in the street.[245]

After Powell's Birmingham speech, tension between immigrants and the native British population dramatically increased. In fact, following each speech on immigration by Powell, the Wolverhampton Council for Racial Harmony found that there were increased incidents of provocation and threats to black people on the streets.[246] Members of the West Midlands Caribbean Association coined a new notation on time – BE and AE, 'Before Enoch' and 'After Enoch.'[247] As one member who had moved from Jamaica to Wolverhampton put it, before Powell's speech things seemed to be improving, but then the 'sky fell in.' 'People we thought had no option but to accept us suddenly became hostile. It is obvious that 90 per cent of the population support Powell.'[248]

The Indian Workers' Association kept records and received regular reports of incidences of violence against immigrants both before and after the speech. What is clear in their records is that after April 1968, ethnic communities no longer viewed the mugging or violent attack of a black person as an isolated incident. For instance, in the Euston area of London, appeals had been made throughout 1967 and early 1968 to the police, local councillors and MPs to increase police patrols of the area and stop attacks against the black community. No arrests were made. In May 1968, though, the WPPE (Working People's Party of England) and PWU (Pakistani Workers' Union) organized a public meeting at the Student Movement House in Camden where Pakistani, West Indian and native English people agreed to organize patrols to

---

[241] Ibid.   [242] Ibid.   [243] Ibid.   [244] Ibid.
[245] Quoted in Shepherd, *Enoch Powell*, p. 126.
[246] Labour Research Department, *Powell and His Allies*, p. 3.
[247] 'From Calypsos to Catcalls,' *Wolverhampton Express and Star*, 5 August 1968.
[248] Ibid.

provide self-defence for the people in the area.[249] In the context of the pro-Powell marches, violence against Britain's ethnic group had taken on a clearer political meaning.

Soon after Powell's Birmingham speech, West Indian, Pakistani and Indian labour organizations came together to form the Black People's Alliance. In total, more than fifty separate organizations joined forces under its banner as an explicit response to the speech. This led, in 1969, to thousands participating in a 'March for Dignity' against racism in British society and against the 1968 Commonwealth Immigrants Act. This was, in 1969, the largest demonstration against racial inequality yet seen in Britain. In light of the failure of international pressure to move Rhodesia towards a political system that recognized the rights of the African majority, the march involved a 'funeral' for the British Commonwealth, replete with an effigy of Powell carried aloft in a coffin, as described in the previous chapter, painted black on one side – labelled *Common* – and white on the other – labelled *wealth*. At the end of the procession, Powell's effigy was set alight outside No. 10.

As is signalled by the birth of the Black People's Alliance, anti-racism activists increasingly borrowed from the militant US Black Power movement to critique the limits of postwar liberalism and reformed capitalism. The words 'wide-grinning piccaninnies' had come from the very heart of the political order. Liberal anti-racism had failed. Out of Powell's 'Rivers of Blood' speech and its popular support emerged a radical critique of the progressive potential of Britain's postwar state. The Black People's Alliance was soon followed, in 1970, by more militant black power groups, such as Black Unity, the Croydon Collective and the Black Workers' Co-ordinating Committee. The shared experience of prejudice and poor conditions, the failures of the trade union movement to confront racism in the workplace and the dramatic expressions of support for Powell evident in the spring of 1968, helped produce a new collective politics of black British identity that was aligned to anti-capitalism and that traversed the borders of cultural, religious or ethnic difference. 'Black' was embraced as a position of protest. Importantly, at this moment, British black power politics tended to be male-dominated, emphasising traditional commitments to (male) equality within the labour movement and working to reconstruct public masculinity in Britain's political culture. 'Black power' was not yet effectively informed by the political agency of women of colour in Britain nor by emergent feminist criticism. Black feminist groups, such as the Brixton

---

[249] 'Memorandum Concerning Attacks on Pakistani People in London.' 26/3/1970, MS 2141.

Black Women's Group of 1973, quickly developed however, in part due to the stimulus of women's involvement in revolutionary struggles in Zimbabwe (Rhodesia), Angola and Eritrea.[250] These 'black power' groups variously campaigned, then, against racism in British society and provided a significant training ground for the black activism of the later 1970s and 1980s. Undoubtedly, the 'Rivers of Blood' speech was a critical turning point in these developments. Activists quickly recognised that Powell could be used to galvanise popular opposition to racism; the 'Rivers of Blood' speech helped to politicise the issue of racism and racial inequality in Britain. By 1968, 'race' had taken on a wider meaning, linked as it was to liberation struggles in the United States and Africa especially. Again, at this moment, the 'liberal race relations settlement' appeared a failure;[251] 'race' was not merely a 'social problem' to be managed but the basis of an unjust social order with deep historical roots.

Importantly, not all of Powell's supporters took to the streets. Powell's most active supporters were, in fact, distinctly middle and upper-middle class – their influence was felt, instead, within local political and civil institutions, in local government, on school boards, in housing associations. The activities of the Young Conservatives, the Monday Club and the association and newsletter *Powellight* served as hubs of this middle-class base. *Powellight* – whose name was a play on the anti-fascist magazine *Searchlight* – began in 1970 due, in part, to the initiative of one activist in particular. Beryl 'Bee' Carthew served as its honorary secretary and provided the energy behind its publication. Carthew's activities tell us a great deal about the attempt to construct 'Powellism' as a politically viable movement between 1968 and 1974. Her detailed descriptions of the right-wing revolt that was going on in the London suburbs and Powell's written responses reveal something of Powellism's fraught relationship with extra-parliamentary politics. They also reveal a clear overlap, at the local political level, between Powellism and the overtly racist National Front party. Significantly, Powell's departure from the Conservative Party in 1974 resulted in Carthew's turn, in 1975, to the National Front.[252] Carthew's apartment – which had once been the headquarters of the Powellight association – would by 1976 become the address of a West London branch of the National Front.

[250] Susan Kingsley Kent, *Gender and Power in Britain, 1640–1990* (London: Routledge, 1999), p. 342.
[251] Shamit Saggar, 'The Politics of "Race Policy" in Britain,' *Critical Social Policy*, 13: 37 (July 1993), pp. 32–51.
[252] Letter to Powell, 28 October 1975. POLL 1.1.23A.

Post Nazism, Britain found it difficult
to address the taboo subject
of its own racism past

The responses to Powell's speech and his sacking from the Shadow Cabinet produced what one editorial in *The Observer* called a 'deep sense of shock' in Britain.[253] As biographer Simon Heffer put it, 'the press furore was unstoppable, and fed on itself and on the reflex hysteria of polite opinion.'[254] The problem was, the editorial explained, that the experience of Nazism made 'clear thought in this field ... exceedingly difficult. We are nervous of the subject.'[255] This nervousness had, in Powell's mind, caused Britain to bury its head in the sand. It was, according to the editorial, the 'European experience' which 'made the British aware of the enormity of their past dealings with coloured people.'[256] As the editorial put it, due to the 'European experience,' the 'accepted "colour bar" relationships of the Colonial Empire became matters of uneasy shame and regret ... But because "race" had become a taboo subject, there was almost no public discussion of the possibilities of tension that were being created' by immigration.[257] The accidental arrival of black people 'at this time in our history' had confused 'the problem of colour' with the unrelated grievances and uncertainties surrounding housing problems, wage standstills, unemployment, rising living costs and 'Britain's future place in Europe and in the rest of the world.'[258]

In late April and early May 1968, representatives of the National Federation of Pakistani Associations, the Birmingham Co-ordinating Committee Against Racial Discrimination, the West Indian Standing Conference, Jeremy Thorpe of the Liberal Party and Jagmohan Joshi of the Indian Workers' Association petitioned the Attorney General, Sir Frederick Elwyn Jones, to begin the prosecution of Powell under the terms of the Race Relations Act of 1965. Powell had, they argued, publicly used language 'with the intent to stir up hatred' against blacks in Britain.[259] In private correspondence, the Attorney General, members of the Law Officers' Department and the General Secretary of the National Council for Civil Liberties (NCCL) expressed concern that prosecuting Powell would turn him into a martyr. As Tony Smythe, General Secretary of the NCCL, put it: 'I do not think isolated prosecutions against white racialists are going to change the minds of the many thousands of people in this country who are consciously or unconsciously addicted to a racialist approach.'[260] The Race Relations

---

[253] 'Facing the Hard Facts,' *The Observer*, 28 April 1968.
[254] Heffer, *Like the Roman*, p. 457.
[255] 'Facing the Hard Facts,' *The Observer*, 28 April 1968.
[256] Ibid.   [257] Ibid.   [258] Ibid.
[259] Correspondence about Enoch Powell's speech, Form Letter by Fredrick Elwyn Jones, PREM 13/2875, as cited in Ritscherle, 'Opting out of Utopia,' p. 291.
[260] 'Freedom of Speech and Enoch Powell, 1968–1969,' Tony Smyth to Mr Smithe, 26 November, 1968, Brynmor Jones Library (BJL), DCL 585/11 as cited in Ritscherle, 'Opting out of Utopia,' p. 295.

Act of 1965 outlawed public expressions of racism which carried
the intent to incite racial hatred; this was regardless of whether that
expression of racism actually advocated the breach of the peace. In
this sense, it was a radical legal break from the 1936 Public Order Act.
The legal question remained: did Powell truly foment racism or merely
(democratically) reflect it? Such legal uncertainty produced renewed
criticism of the 1965 Act. For instance, the editor of *The Times* wrote:
'Parliament should confine the class of criminal utterances to those
which threaten public order, and allow the expression of views judged
good or bad, liberal or illiberal, constructive or destructive, to compete unmolested for the minds of men.'[261] Meanwhile, some pundits
went so far as to assert that, without an airing of Powellite grievances,
Britain could turn to outright fascism. The suppression of popular
resentment would 'inspire support for the Ku Klux Klan activities,
rather than Mr. Powell's.'[262] The legal question of the representative
nature of Powell's words resulted in Powell putting together files of
letters from the public in support. In many ways, Powell's official
papers concerning his pronouncements on race and immigration at
the Churchill Archives Centre (as opposed to his research, writing and
constituency letters left at the Staffordshire Record Office) reflect that
deliberate effort to construct an image of Powell as a democrat and
parliamentarian.

Critics called Powell a demagogue. Again, the presence of the
'European experience' was there in the protests for and against Powell.
James Callaghan, Labour Home Secretary, said that Powell's proposal
to send a million people home through a voluntary repatriation scheme
would be comparable to what Hitler did to Jews in Poland.[263] David
Ennals, Minister with special responsibility for immigration policy, similarly declared that Powell's speech was 'reminiscent of the early growth
of anti-Semitism in Germany.'[264] The Labour MP for Kelvingrove said
the speech was a call to arms to 'every racialist nazi or fascist element
in our society.'[265] Powell was, therefore, both dangerous and anachronistic – as one senior officer lamented, the liberal media had worked to
preserve 'the Colonel Blimp image' to discredit their concerns.[266]

Anti-racist demonstrators would commonly call Powell a Nazi or
fascist. During the May Day marches, just eleven days after Powell's

---

[261] *The Times*, 4 May 1968.
[262] *The Times*, 26 April 1968.
[263] 'Hitler's Method,' *The Observer*, 28 April 1968.
[264] Labour Research Department, *Powell and His Allies*, p. 5.
[265] 'A Shocking Speech, Says Brockway,' *Morning Star*, 22 April 1968.
[266] 'Senior Officer Concerned About "Subversive Forces",' *The Times*, 23 May 1972.

speech, dockers and students clashed outside the House of Commons.[267] According to *The Times*, the trouble started when 'three long-haired youths held up a picture of a uniformed nazi and baited the dockers.'[268] The May Day march began as an 'uneasy alliance' between trade unionists and a large number of banner-bearing students.[269] Pro-Powell and anti-Powell groups soon began to yell at each other.[270] Violence followed:

A boot goes into a man's kidney, another comes crashing down on his skull. He was a casualty in a clash over immigration outside the House of Commons yesterday. The boots belong to dockers who support Mr. Enoch Powell's views. The man on the ground: one of the students who demonstrated against Mr. Powell.[271]

While France experienced a watershed moment in May 1968 – when students and workers joined in a general strike against postwar Gaullism – members of the Old and New Left in Britain clashed on the question of immigration. According to one reporter, the trade unionists' chant at the head of the march – 'May Day is workers' day' – sounded 'lonely and irrelevant' against the roaring student cries of 'Enoch Powell, we want you – dead.'[272]

The overwhelming presence of the war experience in the letters Powell received from his supporters and the ongoing use of the charge 'Nazi' against Powell no doubt indicates that, in 1968, memories of the Second World War were still highly determinative in setting the parameters of the debate on racism and immigration. On the issue of the Kenyan Asians' right to enter Britain, Shivabhai G. Amin, an influential lawyer and former President of the Kenya Indian Congress, insisted that the question of immigration was 'really a test for Great Britain and is not the first test she has faced. She has taken much greater risks before. These Asians are not like the Nazis.'[273] The immigrants could represent both an 'unarmed invasion' and a test of liberal political belief – in essence, this was a test of the legacy of the war.

Importantly, according to Powell, Britain would soon face its 'finest hour' again. In 1967, Powell wrote for the *Daily Telegraph* that Commonwealth immigration had transformed entire areas of England like a 'bulldozer.'[274] It had altered the appearance and life of towns and

---

[267] 'Dockers and Students in Angry Scenes,' *The Times*, 2 May 1968.
[268] Ibid.   [269] Ibid.   [270] Ibid.
[271] 'Putting the Boot in ...' *Daily Mail*, 2 May 1968.
[272] 'Dockers and Students in Angry Scenes,' *The Times*, 2 May 1968.
[273] 'Lawyers Briefed to Fight Britain's New Bill on Immigration,' *Birmingham Post* (No. 34,105).
[274] J. Enoch Powell in John Wood (ed.) *Freedom and Reality*, p. 223.

'had shattering effects on the lives of many families.'[275] But the long-suffering British had responded without antipathy. 'This speaks volumes for the steadiness and tolerance of the natives,' he insisted. There was a limit, however, to British tolerance. 'Acts of an enemy, bombs from the sky, they could understand,' he explained, 'but now, for reasons quite inexplicable, they might be driven out of their homes and their property deprived of value by an invasion which the Government apparently approved and their fellow-citizens – elsewhere – viewed with complacency.'[276]

Exactly a week after Powell's speech, Heath spoke at the Town Hall of Dudley in the West Midlands. He entered in the rear as a crowd outside of approximately one thousand chanted 'Heath out, Enoch in' and sang a selection of racist songs.[277] When he spoke, Heath made little direct reference to Powell but appealed to Britain to remain calm:

These problems must be discussed in Parliament and Press, in the pubs and in the home. But they must be discussed calmly and reasonably. The more directly you are involved, the more necessary it is to keep calm. The more responsible those who speak out in discussion, the more necessary it is for them to be reasonable.[278]

Powell had made reasonable relations between blacks and whites in Britain 'infinitely more difficult' according to Heath.[279] David Ennals, Labour spokesman, similarly criticized Powell for being 'irresponsible.'[280] The use of the word 'irresponsible' and the focus on Powell's failure to be reasonable or civilized surely aggravated Powell. Powell had spent the last few years speaking regularly on the misuse of the word 'responsible' in contemporary Britain. According to Powell, due to the public appeals of the political consensus, the word had lost its meaning as contractual obligation and represented efforts to silence critical perspective and force citizens to conform to a planned economy – he called this mob rule. After the 'Rivers of Blood' speech, Powell only became more adamant that this was a sign of a larger phenomenon: 'One of the most alarming phenomena of our time is the breakdown of the rule of law, and a significant symptom of that breakdown is, once again, the

[275] Ibid.   [276] Ibid.
[277] 'Heath Asks Nation to Be Calm, Fair, Responsible, Constructive,' *The Times*, 27 April 1968.
[278] Quoted in 'Race: Heath Calls for Calm – and Spending,' *Sunday Times*, 28 April 1968.
[279] Quoted in 'Heath Hits out at Enoch Powell – and the Government,' *The Observer*, 28 April 1968.
[280] Quoted in 'Put Powell in the Dock,' *Morning Star*, 22 April 1968.

metaphorical use of "responsibility" and inversion of its proper meaning.'[281] Language itself hid the 'bullying' of consensual politics.[282] It
was this mob rule that caused him, he believed, to suffer 'endless abuse'
and 'vilification' after his Birmingham speech, where 'no imputation
or innuendo has been too vile or scurrilous.'[283]

As well as politically distancing himself from Powell's words, Heath
used the Dudley speech to attack the Labour government – using the
event of Powell's speech and the support that it gained to level his
attack. It would, in the end, be a successful strategy. He attacked the
government's failure to meet 'or perhaps even to understand' the 'natural
fears' among those who have a high proportion of black immigrants.[284]
He cited the fears that appeared in Powell's speech: overcrowding in
schools and shortages in housing, inadequate teaching facilities and a
breakdown in health and social services.[285] It was, according to one
reporter, obvious by the applause and questions that the audience was
in sympathy with Powell.[286] One woman from the audience announced
that she was from Wolverhampton and that Powell's constituents
had been imploring him to speak out to 'save our children and our
schools' and claimed, 'He was the only one who had the guts to do
it.'[287] Heath vigorously defended the sacking of Powell, yet attempted
to use the phenomenon of Powellism to critique Labour and garner the
movement's support.

By the beginning of May 1968, Hogg had introduced over thirty
amendments to the Race Relations Bill; most were aimed at widening
the terms of discrimination and limiting the scope of the bill to employment and housing.[288] One amendment would bring the bill into line
with Article 2 of the Declaration of Human Rights, making discrimination apply also to 'sex, language, religion, political or other opinion, national or social origin, property, birth, or other status' – thereby,
undoing its focus on anti-racism. Others limited the bill so that it
would not apply to employers with fewer than twenty-five employees
and would exempt owner-occupiers and owners of not more than five
dwellings. Another attempted to remove insurance and credit from the
bill entirely. At the third reading of the bill in July, MPs on the far right

---

[281] J. Enoch Powell, 'Speech to the Annual Conference of Commerce, Lanchester
Polytechnic Coventry,' 25 April 1970. POLL 4.1.6.
[282] Ibid.
[283] J. Enoch Powell, 'Address to the Rotary Club of London,' 16 November 1968.
Reprinted in *Reflections of a Statesman*, p. 384.
[284] Quoted in 'Heath Hits out at Enoch Powell – and the Government,' *The Observer*, 28
April 1968.
[285] Ibid.   [286] Ibid.   [287] Ibid.
[288] 'Tories Seek to Widen Race Relations Bill's Scope,' *The Times*, 1 May 1968.

of the party stood against it. The bill still passed, though, with many of the Tory amendments.

The coming years, prior to the 1970 general election, were precarious for Heath. Powell had substantial public backing. By the beginning of 1969, in a speech in Walsall, Heath came to echo Powell's argument that Britain was in a state of emergency on the question of immigration and race, though he continued to differentiate himself in tone. He insisted: 'I want, so far as is possible, to strip the issue of its emotional overtones. Because that is what those who have to deal with schools and hospitals and housing are doing every day of their lives. They are getting on with their job.'[289] Powell became mildly obsessed with Heath's Walsall speech. There, in Heath's call for the need for mass repatriation of black immigrants and even stricter controls on the immigration, was proof for Powell that he had been right all along. Many of Powell's supporters also noticed the similarity of Heath's words and Powell's ongoing arguments. One man wrote to Powell, 'you must be amused by statements from Renee Short and Heath, etc., re-saying exactly what you said but at the same time denouncing you as the personification of evil.'[290]

The authority within

Just two months after the 'Rivers of Blood' speech, one of Powell's supporters wrote to the BBC about its lack of impartiality in its reporting of Powell. Powell was, after the speech, predominantly represented as a xenophobe in the mainstream press. This supporter had heard in a report that the corporation no longer acknowledged its duty to give impartial and unbiased accounts of certain matters. He wrote, 'This seems very strange to me.'[291] He received this in reply, from the Head of Secretariat of the BBC:

I think what you must have heard was a report of a speech made by the BBC's chairman, Lord Hill, to the Guild of British Newspaper Editors ... Lord Hill was quoting a remark made by Sir George Greene before the Race Relations Bill came into being. It was that: 'A man who speaks in favour of racial intolerance cannot have the same rights as a man who condemns it.' Lord Hill prefaced this by saying that there were two very important exceptions to the BBC's obligations to be impartial. One was crime and the other race hatred.[292]

---

[289] Edward Heath, 'Walsall Speech,' 25 January 1969. See 'Conference '72 Speech Material,' SRO, D4490/4.
[290] 'Anonymous' to Powell, 28 January 1969. POLL 8.1.6.
[291] Letter to the Director General of the BBC, 19 June 1968. SRO, D3123/344.
[292] R. D. Pendlebury, Head of Secretariat of the BBC, 4 July 1968. SRO, D31234/344.

When the letter-writer sent Powell this reply from the BBC, they began a correspondence. The following year, Powell would give a speech to the Institute of Journalists which focused on Lord Hill's words. Powell argued that the way that 'race hatred' and 'crime' are linked in Hill's statement is highly revealing:

'Crime' denotes something perfectly objective. To ascertain what is and is not crime one resorts to the law, to its definition by statute and its interpretation and application by the courts ... With this perfectly objective thing, 'crime,' the Chairman of the BBC places on the same plane what he calls 'race hatred,' which is perfectly subjective. 'Hatred,' though a sin, is not a crime ... How wide this charter is, may be gauged if, for 'hatred,' we substitute other, equally reprehensible sins, such as 'greed' or 'envy,' and reflect what a range of subjects would be withdrawn from impartiality if the BBC were declared not impartial about these.[293]

While the BBC would remain impartial about the hatred of other things, where race emerges they would reject impartiality.

Powell's refusal to condemn the racism of his constituents remained a sticking point throughout his career. In order to understand Powell's approach to racism and the nation, it is necessary to look again at this question of evil – and the politics of moral responsibility. In 1969, the day after Enoch Powell gave a speech on immigration and race relations at Wolverhampton, Reverend Trevor Huddleston, then the Bishop of Stepney, publicly referred to Powell's speech as 'evil.'[294] After Huddleston's public utterance, a correspondence ensued which finally led to a televised debate between Powell and the bishop.[295] They stood across from each other awkwardly at their podiums and debated the relationship between religious responsibility and their respective stands on race in Britain. Huddleston urged Powell that, as Christians, they must recognize the universal brotherhood of man: 'The fact is that God became man. He did not become an Englishman, he did not become a Palestinian, he did not become an Irishman.'[296] Powell's speeches were 'evil' because they were bound to increase racial tension and violence. They, therefore, threatened to 'undermine the real dignity of man.'[297]

[293] J. Enoch Powell, 'To the Institute of Journalists,' 9 December 1969. Reprinted in *Still to Decide*, pp. 43–44.
[294] Trevor Huddleston, *The Times*, 30 June 1969.
[295] J. Enoch Powell, *No Easy Answers* (London: Sheldon Press, 1973), p. 95.
[296] 'Dialogue with Trevor Huddleston,' in *No Easy Answers* (London: Sheldon Press, 1973), p. 97. See also: 'The Great Debate: Enoch Powell and Trevor Huddleston' (1969) National Film Archive Catalogue. NFA.
[297] Ibid., p. 95.

Huddleston, an Anglican monk, had spent from 1943 to 1956 working in a mission school in the South African township of Sophiatown. In 1956, he published *Naught for Your Comfort*, in an effort to make the world aware of apartheid and its 'consequences for mankind.'[298] Not unlike Powell's persistent nostalgia for India, Huddleston claimed his 'heart' was in South Africa. On his return to Britain, Huddleston became a long-time leader of Britain's Anti-Apartheid Movement.

Powell was at this time a practising Anglican. He viewed, he said, a 'distinct connection between the religious forms … and the political forms' of his thinking.[299] To Huddleston, Powell insisted that as a politician his most pressing duty was a social duty to represent his community and that Christianity did not and could not describe political reality. If we were to follow Huddleston's argument, Powell maintained, 'We shall throw open all frontiers, we shall say that all men are literally brothers, and that nations have been abolished. This I can see. But as long as we retain frontiers, and national identification, and as long as people do in fact feel as national communities (a thing easier to say than define), this is something of which I feel I am duty bound to take account.'[300] Further, he argued, only 'a glance at the world' would show how easily tensions leading to violence arise when there is an ethnic minority and a majority and 'sharp differences, recognisable differences, and mutual fears' between them.[301] For Powell, Christianity conflicted with the essentials of national identity, human nature and therefore politics itself.

Huddleston, however, did not shy away from the political argument. He had spent most of his life in South Africa. He knew the effect Powell's speeches could have on millions of Africans in the newly independent countries of Africa. The question of race was not a local conflict, he insisted, it was international. He could not believe 'we are a nation that is so dim and stupid that we cannot see this national purpose in terms of our place in the world community.' The new political influence of internationalism could not be denied; the new international system was a moral community.

Powell would not budge, replying 'those for whom I am responsible are not the whole of the world.'[302] The parable of the Good Samaritan tells us 'your neighbour is everyone,' but then, Powell argued, we are

[298] Trevor Huddleston, *Naught for Your Comfort* (London: William Collins, 1956), p. 11.
[299] J. Enoch Powell, 'Frankly Speaking,' Radio Broadcast, 28 February 1964. POLL 4.1.27.
[300] Powell, *No Easy Answers*, p. 99.
[301] Ibid., pp. 98–99.   [302] Ibid., p. 110.

confronted with a religion that 'denies certain profound characteristics of actual human life.'[303] His duty, still, was to represent his constituency. The two men could not agree. The Social Gospel and Powell's politics were irreconcilable. Powell closed the debate on television with a quick conclusion, 'it seems to me ... that what we have been doing, Bishop, is analysing our respective functions in society.'[304] In their disagreements, Powell and Huddleston revealed profound differences in what they imagined to be the parameters of the political. Though certainly speaking from opposing ends of the political spectrum, even the parameters of the debate concerning New Commonwealth immigration and race relations diverged. For Huddleston, this was a 'world issue,' the newly independent nations of Africa were listening. For Powell, this was about the nation, or more precisely, about Wolverhampton. As Powell maintained elsewhere: 'There can only be rights ... which flow from the constitution and nature of a particular society. Human rights in the abstract, in abstraction from a given society, are an absurdity, a collection of sounds without meaning.'[305] Powell's critique of Huddleston's Christian humanism was a critique of the notion of politics detached from sovereignty and the nation.

Huddleston would remain a symbol for Powell. When in May 1970, right before the general election, Huddleston appeared with Labour Prime Minister Wilson at a student rally for a Labour victory in Manchester, Powell attacked the bishop.[306] Powell said that Anglicans should be outraged by it: 'He is a party politician who is prepared to prostitute the authority of his sacred office for political ends.'[307] Huddleston replied, 'I have never, ever, hidden the fact that I am a Socialist. I have always made it perfectly clear that a Christian has a right to take part in the political life of his country.'[308] Tellingly, the epitome of the problems of the liberal consensus Powell found in the left wing of the Anglican Church. The postwar transformation in the Church toward social/political practice was, Powell contended, due to the historical contingencies of the moment – particularly secularization and the closing of the imperial 'mission field.' In an essay entitled, 'How the church militant is fighting the wrong fight,' Powell made his criticism of the Church clear.[309] In the face of a dwindling membership

---

[303] Ibid.   [304] Ibid., p. 112.

[305] Powell, *Wrestling with the Angel*, p. 27.

[306] 'Hard Treatment by Students,' *The Times*, 9 May 1970); 'Powell Attacks Bishop,' *Sunday Telegraph*, 10 May 1970.

[307] 'Powell Attacks Bishop,' *Sunday Telegraph*, 10 May 1970.

[308] Ibid.

[309] J. Enoch Powell, 'How the Church Militant Is Fighting the Wrong Fight,' *The Times*, 25 November 1970.

both at home and overseas, the Anglican Church was attempting to gain relevance through political action. As Powell put it, 'More and more the Church – and so far as I see, only in England – has tried to be heard by saying and doing anything and everything but what it alone can say and do. Not surprising, it is heard less and less.'[310] It no longer, through its actions, asserts 'the unique truth and indispensability of the Christian revelation and of the sacraments of the Church.'[311]

Instead, Powell finds the Rector of Wolverhampton at a celebration of the Hindu Durga Puja, participating in the activities of 'community relations' with the Mayor of Wolverhampton.[312] The Anglican Church, Powell argued, was by nature missionary: consequently, in the past, 'those who said the Creed and received the sacraments in English towns and villages were told, and accepted, that they were obliged, so far as in them lay, to support and further the preaching of the gospel and the extension of the Church in "heathen lands afar."'[313] But since then, a large proportion of the population of England had ceased to be practising members of the Church, the mission field was folding up overseas, and 'England was in the early stages of a revolutionary change in the composition of her population.' Why then, Powell asks, did the 'mission field' not come home?

The Christian Church, on which Asia and Africa were closing their doors as being the cultural badge of the west, was now confronted in England by the religious and cultural badges of large and growing communities transplanted from the very lands where, if 'thick darkness' brooded when the hymn was written, no less 'thick darkness broodeth yet.'[314]

For Powell the irony was that the Church was failing in its mission to profess the unique truth of Christianity, and was instead taking on the role of politics – offering 'homilies on trade unions, on housing, on economics and productivity, on politics and trade.'[315] Powell levelled these criticisms against the very top of the Church hierarchy. The Archbishop of Canterbury, Dr Michael Ramsey, as a member of the House of Lords, had voted against the immigration restrictions of the Commonwealth Immigrants Act. Until June 1968, he had been an active chairman of the National Committee for Commonwealth Immigrants.

Linked to this, against those preaching the social gospel and the importance of Christian duty in the political field, Powell held that Christianity was, above all, an 'intellectual religion.' As a Christian, one could not deny the creed, 'Quicunque Vult,' or 'whosoever will (be

---

[310] Ibid.   [311] Ibid.   [312] Ibid.   [313] Ibid.
[314] Ibid.   [315] Ibid.

saved).'[316] It showed – as Powell put it in 1965 in a lecture to Great St Mary's Church in Cambridge – the 'problematic assertion about faith, salvation and damnation as not a threat but a statement' that 'ignorance of the holy trinity lead[s] to eternal damnation.'[317] Importantly, the creed revealed that Christianity 'makes demands on peoples [sic] minds.' It revealed the 'possibility, indeed the probability, the prevalence of failure' to be saved, in which failure can be 'final, absolute and irrevocable.'[318] This, he noted, 'we are extremely reluctant to recognise, and to which the prevalent mood of our age and society renders us particularly allergic.'[319] The notion of Christianity as an 'intellectual religion' above all else ran counter to the contemporary social justice movements gaining ground within Britain's churches. Against these movements, Powell insisted on institutional practice:

There is a common custom, by no means new, of laying claim to a kind of vague philanthropy and calling it 'Christianity.' This is based on a delusion. No social or political effects flow from mild approval of some or all of the Sermon on the Mount. 'Christian' means a member of the Church, or it means nothing ... Only men's acts (which includes words) can be in common. Their thoughts are essentially peculiar and (in the last resort) incommunicable. Whether the community be man and wife, or the men of a battalion, or the Members of the House of Commons, it is what they do together that counts.[320]

This vision of the Church, of the saved and the unsaved, is the key to understanding Powell's vision of (political) community.

Conclusion

Powell's insistence on the divide between the moral and the material is so important for any analysis of Powell's critique of race relations legislation and liberal immigration policy because the question of the moral imperative runs throughout – both in Powell's arguments and elsewhere. As the well-known interviewer David Frost put it to Prime Minister Harold Wilson in 1969: 'But – do you, in fact, believe – can a government do anything about the moral state of the nation, this nation, any nation?'[321] Wilson did not offer an answer. But replied:

Yes, I think the whole world is facing this crisis. You've seen probably so much of it in the United States while you've been there. The problem now of violence,

[316] Enoch Powell, 'The Heart of the Matter "Quicunque Vult,"' 7 November 1965. POLL 4.1.2.
[317] Ibid.   [318] Ibid.   [319] Ibid.
[320] Enoch Powell, 'The Church' (part of unpublished One Nation Book), 1951. POLL 3.2.1.1.
[321] David Frost, 25 July 1969. SRO, D4490/2.

the problem, above all, I think the most odious thing of our time, the development of racial politics ... I can feel anger – but the only thing that gets me really
blazing mad is this question of race and colour. And people exploiting it. And
then I do lash out, perhaps a bit immoderately.[322]

Powell called the efforts to legislate with such a moral imperative
'compassionate humbug.'[323] Powell argued that 'Compassion is something individual and voluntary. You cannot compel somebody to be
compassionate; nor can you be vicariously compassionate by compelling
somebody else. The Good Samaritan would have lost all merit if a Roman
soldier were standing by the road with a drawn sword, telling him to get
on with it and look after the injured stranger.'[324] It was, according to
Powell, impossible to translate Wilson's moral reaction to racist politics,
in Africa and at home, into a moral consensus of the nation.

Above the challenge of 'race relations,' Powell argued, came political
representation and the public expression of self in 'self-representation.'
The British leadership's refusal to stem the flow of immigration was a
moral failure as it was a failure to enable the populace to identify itself.
It was, further, a failure in the proper relationship between ruler and
ruled. As he put it:

[N]o government has the moral right to alter, or permit to be altered, the character and the identity of a nation without that nation's knowledge and without
that nation's will. It is a moral issue, and it is a supreme issue. Whatever this
government is destined to achieve elsewhere with all its hopes, its determination and its courage, if it fails in this, it fails in all; and its epitaph will be the
verdict of our children: 'They betrayed our inheritance while there was still
time to save it.'[325]

Approaches toward European membership and liberal immigration
policy were, Powell believed, symptoms of the same phenomenon –
a liberal consensus that applied a moralistic policy before seeking a
moral mandate. It was not, in 1972, the thousands of Ugandan refugees that were the problem, Powell noted, 'It was that the conduct
of the whole operation from the start was seen as a cruel and cal-
culated gesture of contempt for the feelings and forebodings of that
large number of people in all parties and walks of life who, wisely
or unwisely, had expected a Conservative Government to show
itself alive to the consequences and dangers of past and continuing

---

[322] Ibid.
[323] J. Enoch Powell, 'To the Harborough Division Conservative Association Gala,
Leicester,' 27 September 1969. Reprinted in *Still to Decide*, p. 22.
[324] Ibid.
[325] J. Enoch Powell, 'Speech to Carshalton and Banstead Young Conservatives at
Carshalton Hall, Surrey,' 15 February 1971. POLL 3.2.1.20.

Commonwealth immigration.'[326] It was all the same, 'from Ulster to Rhodesia, from the Industries Act to incomes policy,' all could have been made intelligible and even agreeable to the public, but none were. Resulting, Powell emphasized, in a 'widespread public sense of being despised.'[327] Powell's critique of British consensus politics was two-edged: it was both republican, in its assertion of the primacy of representation, and anti-liberal in its vision of governance as best limited to material, rather than moral, power – or 'authority without' rather than 'authority within.'[328] What had once been an argument primarily levelled against a managed economy and a managed society, had come to life for Powell when confronted with the demanding and dominant question of civil rights. In 1968, Powell called the split between the government and the nation 'a dangerous gulf.' By 1970 he called it war.

[326] Ibid.   [327] Ibid.
[328] J. Enoch Powell, 'Bishops and Kings,' *The Listener*, 16 October 1958.

5   Naming the crisis

> Without war the sovereign nation is not conceivable.
>
> Enoch Powell on the 25th Anniversary of the United Nations

In 1974, Powell advised his constituency to vote Labour and that year, too, left the Conservative Party because of its pro-Common Market stance. Months later, in the second general election of that year, he ran for a seat as a Unionist member for South Down in Northern Ireland. This chapter follows Powell's turn to Ulster Unionism away from the party to which he had dedicated more than twenty-five years. The fact that Powell found a home in the politics of Ulster, wherein communalism and ethnic hatred determined the political scene, is far from accidental. Powell did not view the violence and unrest in Ulster as distinct in kind from labour disputes, student protests or Black Power politics in Britain. Rather, the breakdown of civil society in Northern Ireland was part of a larger whole. In other words, in Powell's mind, his turn to Protestant communalism did not contradict his fear and rejection of communal rights. Instead, Powell viewed Ulster as the frontline of a war with which the entire United Kingdom was engaged. For Powell, this was a war for the survival of the British state.

As discussed in the previous chapter, Britain at this time faced what Stuart Hall has persuasively called an 'organic crisis.'[1] The postwar promises of affluence, consensus and an ever-enlarging middle class were exposed in the 1960s and 1970s as unemployment rose, wages did not, and the patriarchal norms underpinning Britain's postwar settlement appeared increasingly tenuous and unstable. In 1978, Hall and others insisted that the moral panics surrounding crime in the 1970s were largely produced by this crisis in the postwar settlement. 'Law and order' campaigns at this time were, they argued, the ideological axis around which the struggle over social and political authority was fought and a crucial means by which state hegemony was reasserted. At the local and national level, 'law and order' campaigns served as the

[1] Stuart Hall et al., *Policing the Crisis*.

264

basis for a cross-class alliance in support of state authority and police power;[2] they enabled the development of rational forms of direct state control when indirect forms of social control lost their strength.[3] At very least, through Hall's analysis, it becomes clear that political consent, or the hegemony of state power, was not a given at this time, but was a site of intense and continuous struggle. In Gramscian terms, Hall et al. explained, hegemony of the state 'has to be *won*, worked for, reproduced, sustained.'[4]

Recent historical work is now just beginning to disentangle the pervading vision of a crisis of sovereignty in this period and its political consequences.[5] As Colin Hay has noted, crises 'are above all public constructions,' which 'need bear no direct correspondence with the symptoms they narrate.' The events or 'raw materials' are real but require a process of narration to give them meaning.[6] Powell himself recognized the significance of the public construction of 'crisis.' As he put it in 1981:

Between a nation's perception of its situation and the actual outcomes, the relationship of cause and effect is complex and doubtful. Did the words and imagination of Winston Churchill in 1940 alter the course of events? Was the resolve of the British people and the physical defensibility of this island home enhanced because they were provided with an expression of their own convictions, which drew a response from their hearts and hands? Every politician is obliged, by the nature of his calling to give the answer Yes to those and similar questions. He must speak what he thinks he sees, like it or not, come what may. He has no other business. The spectacle which I cannot help seeing, and therefore cannot help relating, is that of a Britain which has lost, quite suddenly, in the space of less than a generation, all consciousness and conviction of being a nation: the web which binds it to its past has been torn asunder.[7]

Powell's particular contribution to the public construction of a national crisis is one key building block in the radicalization of British politics in the 1980s. Even more, the notion of a nation constantly on the verge of being 'torn asunder' remains a critical feature of Britain's postcolonial

[2] Ibid., p. 177.
[3] Centre for Contemporary Cultural Studies, *The Empire Strikes Back*, p. 14.
[4] Stuart Hall and Tony Jefferson (eds.), *Resistance Through Rituals: Youth Subcultures in Post-war Britain* (London: Routledge, 1993), p. 40.
[5] Robert Saunders, 'Crisis? What Crisis? Thatcherism and the Seventies,' in Ben Jackson and Robert Saunders (eds.), *Making Thatcher's Britain* (Cambridge University Press, 2012).
[6] Colin Hay, 'Chronicles of a Death Foretold: The Winter of Discontent and Construction of the Crisis of British Keynesianism,' *Parliamentary Affairs*, 63 (2010), pp. 464–466.
[7] J. Enoch Powell, 1981, Thurrock Conservative Association, 30 October 1981. POLL 4.1.12.

identity. Despite Powell's pessimism, he offered a vision at this time of a 'new politics of the nation' and demonstrated the possibility of a populist assault against some of the central aspects of postwar social democracy and the 'intrusive state.'[8] Into the 1970s, we see increasing concern among conservative activist groups that the 'cherished freedoms' fought for in the Second World War were under threat. Importantly, as we shall see, Powell tied the expansion of the welfare state to the above spectacle of national dissolution. As he put it in 1969, the translation of 'a want or need into a right'[9] within social democracy had led to untenable expectations demanded of the postwar state. Powell believed that social democracy was, in this sense, the real root of political violence, race politics and the declining authority of state power. Critically, his particular vision of Britain's existential crisis – and the mass support that this vision at times produced – worked to endow some British people's experiences of unrest and uncertainty in these years with radical political meaning. As one political analyst put it, Powellism played an essential 'preparatory role' in making the electorate more receptive to radical politics.[10] Powellism made Britain ready, in other words, for Thatcher's crusade.

Naming the crisis

Among political scientists, Powell's mass following in the late 1960s and 1970s has come to be read as a precursor to the 'decade of dealignment,' or the loosening of postwar political loyalties based on traditional class divisions, and the emerging influence of issue voting.[11] It is, in essence, read as a pre-history to the radical conservatism of the 1980s and the ability of Thatcher's governments to capture the popular vote. E. H. H. Green's seminal account of the history of British conservatism convincingly emphasizes the political consequences of social transformations in postwar Britain: growth demographically and economically in the south and south-east, towards 'embourgeoisement,' towards 'non-unionised' 'service-sector activity' and towards 'a greater degree of "economic instrumentalism" in … voting allegiance.'[12] In this view, Powell's construction of a nation in crisis is side-lined as a less

---

[8] Andrew Gamble, *The Free Economy and the Strong State*, p. 71, as cited in Anna Marie Smith, *New Right Discourse*, pp. 7–8.
[9] Powell, 27 September 1969, *Still to Decide*, p. 21.
[10] Schoen, *Enoch Powell and the Powellites*, p. 240.
[11] Bo Särlvik and Ivor Crewe, *Decade of Dealignment: The Conservative Victory of 1979 and Electoral Trends in the 1970s* (Cambridge University Press, 2010).
[12] Green, *Ideologies of Conservatism*, pp. 216, 236–237.

significant moment in a rather 'neat story' of the New Right 'riding the wave of independent socio-economic change.'[13] Here Thatcherism appears to represent an inevitable transformation and Powell happens to be along for the ride. Though without doubt various structural changes transformed the make-up of the Conservative Party, critical analysis of the political discourse of the 1960s and 1970s reveals that the 'decade of dealignment' was not a simple, uniform process. The historical work of Florence Sutcliffe-Braithwaite and Jon Lawrence, for instance, highlights that, in fact, the decline of class politics was by no means inevitable.[14] In fact, the mid-1970s saw the quickening of classed identities: at that time, two-thirds of Britons believed there to be 'a class struggle in this country,' which was double the level recorded at the beginning of the decade.[15] Alongside a classed language within the militant union ranks, middle-class groups such as small business organizations, ratepayers groups, middle-class unions and the National Association of Freedom embraced activism and political militancy on behalf of their specific class interests. Meanwhile, conservatism came to be widely recognized as in a state of ideological confusion and crisis. As Paul Rich explains:

The downfall of the Heath government in February 1974 in the wake of the miners' strike and the three-day week led to a state of growing unease in dominant Conservative circles at the possibility of nationalism – divorced as it was from the former grandeur and mystique of empire – to provide adequate ideological continuity and stability in what was seen as a period of rapid economic and industrial change.[16]

Or, as the New Right journal the *Salisbury Review* put it, 'never before had it seemed so hard to recreate the verbal symbols, the images and axioms, through which the concept of authority could be renewed.'[17] The Conservative Party had, by 1975, suffered four defeats in the previous five elections.[18] It had slipped into third place among first-time voters and, even more, its share of the vote was at its lowest since 1918, losing votes in all parts of the United Kingdom.[19] Thatcherism was, then, not simply an inevitable outgrowth of the break-up of class but

---

[13] Jon Lawrence and Florence Sutcliffe-Braithwaite, 'Margaret Thatcher and the decline of class politics,' in Jackson and Saunders (eds.), *Making Thatcher's Britain*.
[14] Ibid., p. 132.   [15] Ibid., p. 133.
[16] Paul B. Rich, 'Conservative Ideology and Race in Modern British Politics,' in Layton-Henry and Rich (eds.), *Race, Government and Politics in Britain*, pp. 57–58.
[17] Gilroy, *There Ain't No Black in the Union Jack*, p. 48.
[18] Saunders, 'Crisis? What Crisis? Thatcherism and the Seventies,' in Jackson and Saunders (eds.), *The Making of Thatcher's Britain*, pp. 25–42 (p. 27).
[19] Ibid.

required a concerted effort to challenge the politics of class and recast 'the dominant social discourses of British public politics.'[20] To this end, by the mid-1970s, Thatcher attempted to ditch her own class baggage and proclaimed that her words represented the spirit of the 'ordinary working family.' In this sense, the decline of class was, at least to some extent, a *political* rather than *sociological* transformation: a matter of language at least as much as economics. It is here that we can begin to see more clearly Powell's broader political contribution. As Andrew Gamble put it in 1974, Powell aired new grievances, new alliances and a new 'politics of power,'[21] which would eventually be harnessed in support of Margaret Thatcher. Powellism was not merely a *sign*, then, of things to come, but contributed to the reconstruction of social and political discourse in this period.

Powell was not alone in his concerns about the survival of British sovereignty. In 1976, Anthony King argued that Britain was facing 'the sort of "crisis of the regime"' not seen 'since 1832, possibly not since the seventeenth century.'[22] That year, too, 65 per cent of those questioned in a National Opinion Poll thought that there was a 'serious threat' or 'some threat' to the survival of British democracy.[23] By that point, it was common parlance to speak of the 'ungovernability' of Britain. Indeed, constitutional authority was ceded, to some extent, to the unions in these years, which at certain points in the decade held almost veto power over budgetary policy.[24] But, alongside this well-recognized uncertainty surrounding the limits of union power, ran beliefs about the deeper roots of 'crisis': beliefs, in particular, that framed this political crisis as a symptom of a decline in national values and demise of the moral order. As Lord Chancellor, Quintin Hogg, claimed in 1976, 'We are living in the City of Destruction, a dying country in a dying civilization.'[25] The fact that the National Viewers' and Listeners' Association (NVLA) and the Nationwide Festival of Light submitted a petition of 1,350,000 signatures to No. 10 in 1973 against indecency

[20] Lawrence and Sutcliffe-Braithwaite, 'Margaret Thatcher and the decline of class politics,' in Jackson and Saunders (eds.), *Making Thatcher's Britain*, p. 135.
[21] Gamble, *The Conservative Nation*, p. 218.
[22] Anthony King, 'The Problem of Overload,' in A. King (ed.), *Why is Britain Becoming Harder to Govern?*, p. 26, as cited in Jackson and Saunders (eds.), *Making Thatcher's Britain*, p. 30.
[23] Ibid.
[24] Ross McKibbin, 'Thatcherism in Historical Perspective,' Oxford Thatcherism Conference (September 2010).
[25] Lord Hailsham, *The Dilemma of Democracy: Diagnosis and Prescription* (London: Collins, 1978), pp. 15, 22, as cited in Jackson and Saunders (eds.), *Making Thatcher's Britain*, p. 30.

in the media is not insignificant and, in many ways, it is not a separate story from Powell's narrative of the nation. Here, again, we see increasing concern that indirect forms of social control and cohesion had lost their strength.[26] As the NVLA petition explained: 'moral issues cannot be separated from the other problems which vex the government and the country. The truth, as we see it, is that our ability as a nation to accept limitations in human desire in the economic sphere is inseparable from our willingness to set limits on "freedom" in the realm of personal morality.'[27] Mary Whitehouse, the leader of the NVLA, called on women particularly to vote for candidates who would work to 'revitalise those moral and spiritual values which has [sic] made Britain great in the past.' There was, she argued, 'a far greater danger to the future of our country than the much discussed economic state of the nation': namely, 'the drift towards moral anarchy which is seen in so many areas of our society.'[28] As Second Wave feminism gathered momentum and sought to liberate women from stifling conceptions of femininity, an 'assertive traditionalism' among some female activists also took hold. For many of Powell's female supporters, the fight against moral anarchy explicitly required women's activism to shore up a (gendered) moral order. 'I would like to be able to stand at factory gates,' one woman wrote to Powell in 1970, 'and bellow at the men to stop acting like sheep and become men and stop following the Communists.'[29]

Via Powell's vision of national disintegration, the crisis of authority – the apparent threat of moral, economic and political 'anarchy' – could take on radical political meaning. The threat of 'moral anarchy' would be linked by Powell and others to questions of national survival and to a racially coded language of British order, civility and 'responsible values.' In other words, for many the crisis of authority became 'thematised through race.' In the face of economic and moral decline, race became 'the prism through which the British people are called upon to live through, then to understand, and then to deal with the growing crisis.'[30] Importantly, this relied on a notion of black people in Britain as consummate outsiders. Through 'ideas of externality and criminality,' Powellism constructed a view of black people as a definitively 'outside'

---

[26] Centre for Contemporary Cultural Studies, *The Empire Strikes Back*, p. 14.

[27] As cited in Matthew Grimley, 'Thatcherism, Morality and Religion,' in Jackson and Saunders (eds.), *Making Thatcher's Britain*, pp. 85–86.

[28] Ibid., p. 81.

[29] Letter to Powell, 5 December 1970, D4490/49. Though she had for years worked on Powell's political campaigns, Pamela Powell, Powell's wife, became more deeply involved in political activism through these networks of women activists.

[30] Stuart Hall, *Race and Resistance*, p. 30, as cited in Procter, *Stuart Hall*, p. 83.

force, 'an alien *malaise* afflicting society.'[31] The crisis was not intrinsic to British society; Britain could reassert itself. Or, as Anna Marie Smith put it, Powell's campaign 'used racial antagonism as a framework which could account for virtually every aspect of the national crisis ... racial antagonism operated as the key which made the disintegration of the nation – and the inevitability of national recovery – intelligible.'[32] With this, Powell's archive contains files filled with evidence of grassroots efforts to organize the mass repatriation of black people from Britain.[33] The Send Them Back (STB) campaign, which was started in 1971, for instance, sought to win public support for 'the compulsory repatriation of immigrants' and, remarkably, explicitly based its campaign strategy on the 'great success' of left-wing organizations.[34] The approach and three-letter logo of 'STB' was modelled on the 'CND,' the Campaign for Nuclear Disarmament.[35]

In 1983, against these visions of national decline, the Centre for Contemporary Cultural Studies at the University of Birmingham worked to show that the weakness of the British state and the 'moral panic' of the 1970s were inherent or internal to Britain and were largely a consequence of 'an advanced industrial capitalist nation, seeking to stabilise itself in rapidly changing conditions on an extremely weak, post-imperial economic base.'[36] Likewise, 'race' was not an external problem arriving on British shores after the war, but constitutive of Britishness: 'It is the sugar you stir; it is in the sinews of the famous British "sweet tooth"; it is in the tea-leaves at the bottom of the next "British" cuppa.'[37] Postwar racism relied on a denial of 'this (internal) overseas history' by turning what is inside out.[38] While the Centre maintained the centrality of 'race' and racial oppression as that which has historically constituted Britishness and the British state – arguing that the black immigrant is therefore internal or intrinsic to the history of Britain – it is crucial to add to this that black Britons at this time were leading new political thinking and action that traversed the border between inside and outside. Many immigrant groups were agents of transnational political action beyond the borders of the nation-state. Tariq Ali's leadership in the Vietnam Solidarity Committee, the Indian

---

[31] Centre for Contemporary Cultural Studies, *The Empire Strikes Back*, p. 26.
[32] Anna Marie Smith, *New Right Discourses*, p. 8.
[33] See POLL 8.1.2, POLL 8.1.4, POLL 8.1.5, POLL 8.1.14.
[34] STB Campaign Manifesto, POLL 8.1.4.
[35] Ibid.
[36] Stuart Hall et al., *Policing the Crisis*, p. 317.
[37] Stuart Hall, *Race and Resistance*, p. 25, as cited in Procter, *Stuart Hall*, p. 82.
[38] Procter, *Stuart Hall*, p. 82.

Workers' Association's vocal opposition to the denial of civil liberties by Indira Gandhi's government, and the Black People's Alliance's marches against the 'butchering of black militants'[39] by the US government are just a few examples of the alliances made between the international New Left and black activists in Britain.

With this in mind, Powell's preoccupations – and the significance he assigned the postcolonial immigrant – point to a central problem of 'Britishness.' Due to the imperial experience, the inside/outside distinction is more ambiguous and problematic in the constitution of the British nation than in many other nation-states. It is both a nation and not a nation; a collection of nations that were made one, to some extent, through the turning outward to the shared imperial project. In many respects, the 'Britishness' that looked outward, that failed to hold the distinction between inside and outside, found a foothold in postwar internationalism. As discussed in Chapter 2, the Universal Declaration of Human Rights (1948) was perceived by some influential British politicians as a genuine extension of Britain's imperial mission, despite possible 'embarrassments' on the ground. Similarly, British protesters against white-minority rule in Rhodesia would, in 1969, tear down the Rhodesian flag and hoist the Union Jack over Rhodesia House in London in an effort to represent 'freedom.'[40] From the marketing of the BBC around the globe to the centrality of the postcolonial experience in modern British literature, 'Britishness' has retained this distinct '(internal) overseas' perspective.

While the breakdown of social norms and the economic crisis of the postwar consensus were, in many respects, internal to Britain, Hall's effort to situate the 'crisis' of authority within the borders of Britain downplays the unique global challenge to national sovereignty and social democracy evident in the post-1968 era. As we shall see, on both left and right, the British political imagination could not be contained by the nation. This chapter is, then, an effort to give a name to the 'alien *malaise*' that Powellism assigned to the black population of Britain. It situates Britain's 'crisis' of (national) authority in the context of the increasing strength of transnational protest and supranational political bodies. In the face of these forces, beliefs about British imperial and domestic governance – and, particularly, the juxtaposition of British order and civility against foreign subversion and violence – prove significant.

---

[39] 'U.S. Imperialism Stop Butchering Black Militants,' 15 March 1970. Demonstration in front of the US Embassy. MS 2141 Box 4. Indian Workers' Association, Birmingham Library.

[40] *Wolverhampton Express and Star*, 13 January 1969.

The story begins prior to the general election of 1970, when Powell was, arguably, the most popular or at least the most widely recognized politician in England. In the lead-up to that election, Powell travelled widely around the country expounding the Powellite faith. Ironically, the Conservative victory of that year, which Powell believed was his win, secured Powell's place outside the party leadership for the rest of his career. Powell's turn to Ulster is, therefore, also the story of political alienation. It was in these years, in the political wilderness, that Powell became absolutely preoccupied by the global 'anarcho-student' movement and its fundamental challenge to the structures of authority in Britain. This obsession, which manifested itself in a file of thousands of newspaper clippings and letters documenting signs of the destruction of society, took root when universities and institutions began cancelling his speaking engagements due to fear of an outbreak of violence. From this moment on, Powell imagined himself as an embattled political figure, speaking the truth to the 'mob mentality' of anti-racist protest.

The forces of anarchy

When Professor Harry Ferns, head of the Department of Political Science at the University of Birmingham, cancelled Powell's speaking engagement two months after the 'Rivers of Blood' speech, Powell took offence. By this point, Powell had already had some universities cancel his visits but not the way Ferns had done it. Rather than writing to Powell in private, Ferns sent a letter first to the *Birmingham Post*. Ferns maintained in the letter that it would be impossible to ensure Powell's safety from attack. In the following few weeks, Powell caused a huge public relations problem for the university, claiming that it was failing to maintain free speech – which was, he argued, fundamental to its very purpose. Powell created a file of evidence on the incident which is now tucked away, not in the collection of Powell's official papers at Cambridge University, but in his constituency papers at the Staffordshire Record Office. It is no coincidence that there together with the Ferns file is a file – created shortly after the Ferns incident – with the ominous title 'The Thing.' 'The Thing' is a file filled with thousands of pieces of evidence collected by Powell between 1968 and 1971 of social and political unrest: evidence of industrial militancy, student protest, violence in Northern Ireland and even Black Power politics in Detroit.[41] There, for instance, we see a confidential report

---

[41] 'The Thing,' Papers of Enoch Powell. SRO D4490/49.

leaked to Powell on the involvement of leaders of the National Union of Students in the Anti-Apartheid Movement and, locally, a secret report sent to Powell describing the political activities of students and lecturers at Birmingham University, as well as newspaper clippings of anti-racist protest and a published academic paper investigating the psycho-social causes of political violence and radicalism.[42] The file was, he later explained, primarily concerned with the forces of 'anarchy' and the breakdown of law and order in Britain. Ferns' public letter was a sign, he believed, of the institutional consequences of a profound transformation. This was the *absence* of institutional order. Unlike many of his far right contemporaries, Powell did not merely read all this as evidence of a rising red tide of communism in Britain. 'It did not have to have a name,' Powell explained.[43] When reading this vast collection of reports, letters and newspaper clippings, the political world of these years momentarily comes to life. But, even more, it becomes clear in this file that Powell's vision of national dissolution became the abiding, even inescapable, logic of his political imagination.

In the years that followed, Powell warned that the forces of disorder – in the guise of liberal media, student demonstrations or anti-racist protest – were winning. They had 'mastered the art of establishing a moral ascendancy over [their] victims and destroying their good conscience' with race politics and guilt over the plight of the Third World.[44] They were purposefully misleading the country. This was the beginning of an 'anarchist brainwashing' that insisted that the public 'literally ... say that black is white.'[45] They were successfully professing 'nonsense' and a world turned upside down, wherein the victims of violence are guilty and law is to blame for lawlessness.[46] As he put it, 'When in 1942 the *Repulse* and the *Prince of Wales* disappeared beneath the waters of the Gulf of Siam, at least we knew that Britain had suffered a defeat,' when the Home Secretary capitulated to anti-apartheid demonstrators who stopped the South Africans' cricket tour in the summer of 1970, 'we suffered no less decisive a defeat.'[47]

[42] Brian Crozier, 'The Study of Conflict,' *Conflict Studies* No. 7 (October 1970), found in SRO D4490/49.
[43] J. Enoch Powell, 'The Role of the Individual.' Address to 'The Challenge of Crime' Police Federation Seminar, Cambridge, April 1976; in *Reflections of a Statesman*, pp. 560–569 (p. 566).
[44] Powell, *Still to Decide*, p. 38.
[45] Ibid., pp. 38. 36.
[46] J. Enoch Powell, 'The Enemy Within,' 13 June 1970, *Reflections of a Statesman*, pp. 244–248 (p. 246).
[47] *Daily Telegraph*, 15 June 1970; ibid., p 245.

In keeping with his conservative philosophical outlook, Powell recognized disorder as an endemic aspect of human society.[48] As he put it to a seminar of policemen in 1976, this was because 'the heart of man is incurably evil.'[49] But this endemic aspect of society, Powell argued, could become an epidemic. The use of hijacking as a political tool was, for example, contagious: 'as a disease it is communicated from one country to another and one continent to another, like the importation of smallpox from India into London.'[50] It spread across borders. The choice of analogy is telling: anarchy and terrorism are presented as a (post)colonial disease.[51] As he later described in a revealing interview in the 1990s, an epidemic began *internationally* in the 1960s with a discovery:

It was discovered, the discovery was made that you could destroy institutions by certain forms of defiance of convention, that you break through. And if you break through that web of conventions, authority was helpless in the face of anarchy ... There are certain laws of political mechanics, which were brought into action, which were discovered as a political force in the middle of the 1960s and utilized and explored, not dissimilar to the discovery of the consequences of combining sulfur, saltpeter and charcoal. I was fascinated by this engine for the destruction of authority and its beautiful simplicity and its effectiveness.[52]

The essence of the 'The Thing' was, Powell argued, 'that violence is used in order to subjugate the will of the majority by destroying its good conscience.'[53] Crucially, it 'learnt how to make authority apologetic.'[54] It was 'one of the great discoveries of mankind' which would be looked back upon in history as a 'remarkable achievement.'[55]

Significantly, Powell believed that this 'Thing' had no purpose other than destruction: this was not the revolt of the hungry against those hoarding food or the revolt of those denied the franchise against those monopolizing political power. While the 'bastilles, the aristocracy, the rich – these were the natural and intelligible targets of incipient revolution,' the protester now required no concrete grievance.[56] Again, this

---

[48] Enoch Powell, April 1976, in *Reflections of a Statesman*, p. 564.
[49] Ibid.   [50] Ibid., p. 564.
[51] Powell is, here, also echoing the language of the conservative political establishment in the United States. US President Nixon told Kansas State University in 1970 that the 'same cancerous disease' of political violence that prompted the hijacking of airliners by Arab guerrillas had spread to universities in the United States. 'Nixon on Disease of Violence,' 17 September 1970, *The Times*, in 'The Thing' SRO D4990/49.
[52] J. Enoch Powell, Bill Schwarz interview, 26 April 1988.
[53] Powell, April 1976, in *Reflections of a Statesman*, p. 566.
[54] Ibid.   [55] Ibid.
[56] J. Enoch Powell, Bexley Political Forum, Welling Kent (4 October 1977). POLL 4.1.12.

represented a shift in the history of violence. In essence, Powell did not recognize that the challenge to state hegemony and the creation of new political loyalties across state borders could, in itself, be a valid political motivation, on a par with enfranchisement. Nor could Powell accept the politicization of private life and social norms; he remained profoundly committed to white patriarchy, opposing the 1975 Sex Discrimination Act as he did race relations law. For Powell, 'anarchy' was the absence of (national) law and convention. Transnationalism, among other forces, threatened to disturb the 'natural' order of convention and thereby corrode the imagined community of the nation.[57]

But Powell's analysis went further than this simple rejection of the politics of protest; he insisted, even more, that 'The Thing' was born of the modern, liberal state. The state, due to the enlargement of state-funded social services, had become the servant of the individual. Powell argued that the reason for the increasing use of the politics of 'civil rights' lay, in other words, with the welfare state and the consequential translation of a 'want or need into a right.'[58]

The modern state is characteristically the welfare state; but that popular term covers two utterly different, and indeed opposite, meanings. It can mean that the state is the agency by which the community discharges its responsibility to ensure a tolerable livelihood. It can also mean that the state undertakes on behalf of its members the responsibility for meeting whatever needs of theirs it chooses to recognise. In the last quarter century there has been a rapid and accelerating transition, here and elsewhere, from the first to the second meaning, of the welfare state.[59]

British promises of welfare and development in Africa had, it seems, borne the same consequences. This transformation in governance lay at the root of social unrest:

The state which undertakes, and is accepted as undertaking, the obligation to meet the general needs of the citizens is particularly vulnerable to violent agitation, for one simple reason – the obligation it has accepted is by its nature unlimited … the unlimited role of the state provides unlimited fuel for dissatisfaction.

In 1968, Margaret Thatcher similarly claimed that it was the expansion of state power – with 'a complete new generation' knowing life only under the postwar welfare state – which produced widespread public

---

[57] Benedict Anderson, *Imagined Communities: Reflections on the Origin and Spread of Nationalism* (London: Verso, 1991).

[58] Powell, 27 September 1969, *Still to Decide*, p. 21.

[59] J. Enoch Powell, Extract from speech to the Annual Meeting of the Armagh Unionist Association, Co. Armagh, NI, 7 February 1970. POLL 4.1.6.

dissatisfaction with the political process as well as individual irresponsibility in British society.[60] But Powell pushed the criticism further: in 1972, he insisted that with increasing violent agitation, people in 'their apprehension' turn 'to government and to authority itself.'[61] And they say to the government: 'Something must be done; you must act.'[62] There, however, the unanimity ends: 'about what must be done, what actions are needed, is dark. That is why government and authority speak in platitudes: at all times they condemn violence, but refused to *fight* it.'[63] The British state's failure of nerve, for Powell, got to the very heart of the problem:

The reason is that the cause of violence sits enthroned in the heart of authority itself. Authority has lost its good conscience, that conviction of its own rightness which is the very lifeblood of authority. Today authority, in the same moment, the same sentence in which it 'condemns violence,' goes on to accuse itself as the true culprit and don a penitent's garb over the chain and mantle of the ruler.[64]

Violence in Northern Ireland, student protest and Black Power politics were, according to Powell, symptoms of the same problem – namely, the failing (moral) authority of the nation-state. As Powell saw it, the 'secret weapon' of these movements was 'the assumption that violence and disorder imply grievance.'[65] When 'violence is purposeless, everybody's bound to set to work at once on discoveries lying ready to be made … with the speed of an explosion,' he explains, 'the roles are reversed: the blame of violence is discovered to lie with authority; government, law, society itself, are put in the dock by the criminal; the simple fact of the violent aggression becomes proof that those attacked are the guilty.'[66] This was only possible due to a humiliated and apologetic political authority. Echoing Powell, the political scientist Anthony King claimed that the loss of public confidence in the state was due to the expansion of its responsibilities: 'Once upon a time man looked to God to order the world. Then he looked to the market. Now he looks to government.' Such that, when things go wrong, people blame 'not "Him" or "it" but "them."'[67]

[60] Margaret Thatcher, 'What's Wrong with Politics?' Conservative Political Centre Lecture, 11 October 1968, MTFW 101632.
[61] Enoch Powell, 18 March 1972, Newham North East Conservative Association, cited in *Powellight*, March 1972. SRO D4490/51.
[62] Ibid.   [63] Ibid.   [64] Ibid.
[65] Enoch Powell, To the Northern Universities Dinner, Federation of Conservative Students, York, 7 March 1970, reproduced in full in *Still to Decide*, p. 28
[66] Ibid., p. 18.
[67] King, 'The Problem of Overload,' in King (ed.), *Why is Britain Becoming Harder to Govern?*

Throughout the 1970s, Powell would continue to bemoan the 'apologetic' state; he called for a reassertion of political authority against 'artificial' grievances, against historical injustices, against – in other words – identity politics. Powell would equate 'social responsibility' or 'collective guilt' with state encroachment, 'mob rule' and national decline. As he explained:

We are told that the economic achievement of the Western countries has been at the expense of the rest of the world and has impoverished them, so that what are called the 'developed' countries owe a duty to hand over tax-produced 'aid' to the governments of the underdeveloped countries. It is nonsense – manifest, arrant nonsense, but it is nonsense with which the people of the Western countries, clergy and laity – but clergy especially – have been so deluged and saturated that in the end they feel ashamed of what the brain and energy of Western mankind have done, and sink on their knees to apologise for being civilised and ask to be insulted and humiliated.[68]

This points us, again, to Powell's wider intellectual challenge to postwar social democracy and its links to the making of a postcolonial Britain. The Australian conservative theorist Kenneth Minogue argued in 1988 that the key ideological achievement of the New Right was its rejection of the 'culture of guilt': in regard to the developing world, minority and women's rights, union power and social inequality.[69] By 1984, Minogue believed that the Conservative Party had finally shaken off the 'guilt complex' of the postwar years via Thatcher's leadership style. During the 1984 miners' strike, for instance, despite a 'a guilt-driven chorus led by churchmen' insisting that the government make a symbolic compromise with the National Union of Mineworkers, Thatcher remained 'entirely unmoved.'[70]

Ferns had not been dishonest in his claim that he believed that Powell might be physically threatened. He had heard that someone 'outside this University' was planning to attack him. The university paper printed a piece on a leading political organizer at the university. Pete Gowan, who would go on to become an influential activist, academic and editor of the *New Left Review*, was, in 1968, a first year graduate student at Birmingham University, studying the Russian peasantry. He was also the chairman of the university's Socialist Union. The university newspaper described him as 'bearded and quietly spoken,' with close alliances to Tariq Ali's Vietnam Solidarity Committee and leading

---

[68] J. Enoch Powell, 'The Enemy Within,' 13 June 1970, in *Reflections of a Statesman*, pp. 244–248 (pp. 247–248).
[69] Kenneth Minogue, 'The Emergence of the New Right,' in Robert Skidelsky (ed.) *Thatcherism* (London: Chatto & Windus, 1988), pp. 133, 135 and 141.
[70] Ibid., p. 141.

the Socialist Union 'very strongly on certain issues, particularly race.'
The paper highlighted most of all that Gowan was 'sympathetic with
the aims of coloured militant groups.'[71] A senior lecturer in Political
Science at the university attempted to make amends with Powell. He
explained that the 'worrying factor in the situation' was that they had
no way of preventing 'outside elements joining in the demonstrations.'
He had been informed by a student that someone may 'try to assault
you' who was 'a former activist in the Algerian Revolution.'

> The danger from outside elements seemed to us real, since we knew that the
> extremists were in touch with certain immigrant organizations ... The serious-
> ness of the situation was impressed on Ferns by a high official of the University
> (not the V.C.) whose advice he sought as a friend. The official, an ex-colonial
> civil servant with experience of civil disturbances, opined that Ferns, if any-
> thing, was <u>under</u>estimating the gravity of the developing situation.[72]

The very concept of social order and civility in postwar Britain was,
as Schwarz has highlighted, 'driven by a powerful, if displaced, recollection of forms of authority which had been deeply shaped by the
experiences of empire.'[73] Likewise, domestic 'disorder' in Britain in
these years was explicitly informed by those with the very recent experiences of the dissolution of British sovereignty in the colonial world.
The unrest in Birmingham, it is implied, could take on the character
of 'civil disturbances' in the colonies. For these men, at least, the 'disorder' of imperial dissolution represented the clearest insight into the
possible impact of a former activist of the Algerian Revolution on 'certain immigrant organisations.' Despite his protestations, Powell himself
was also concerned about his safety. The police had him, his home and
his family under constant surveillance. He later confessed to Simon
Heffer that, like Ferns, he believed the main threat to his safety was
not British but foreign extremists: principally, he feared the American
Black Power movement.[74] In fact, he would confess to Heffer that he
had been surprised that Black Power did not emerge in greater strength
in Britain, but he felt sure it would.[75] Still, Powell argued that the university's refusal to allow him to speak was a mark against civil society,
the tradition of free speech and academic exchange. The Birmingham
lecturer turned Powell's protests on their head, however. He replied to
Powell on the question of free speech:

[71] Who is Pete Gowan?' *Redbrick*, June 18 1968. D3123/349.
[72] Letter to Powell from Geoffrey Ostergaard, 23 June 1968. Papers of Enoch Powell.
     SRO D3123/349.
[73] Schwarz, *The White Man's World*, p. 9.
[74] Heffer, *Like the Roman*, p. 537.
[75] Ibid.

I can appreciate what I take to be your attitude … [But] I do not think the attitude is the appropriate one to adopt towards a meeting whose purpose is academic rather than political. As a political science department, we have to draw
as sharp a distinction as we can between an academic and a political occasion:
we cannot do our job unless we make this distinction … As a department, we
must be politically uncommitted, whatever our personal political views.[76]

Powell claimed that in order to maintain academic exchange and 'civilized' debate, he should be allowed to speak. But this lecturer had highlighted a problem: Powell, the name, the political figure, had become
synonymous with a political position. In the years ahead, Powell could
not dissociate himself from that single position, from that effigy burnt
in front of No. 10. He was not a free, rational thinker in an open, academic debate. His very presence at the university was political.

This exchange between Powell and the political science lecturer represents a broad contestation that was going on at this time in Britain
and elsewhere over the meaning and purpose of the university. This
was a contestation that reflected, to some extent, a crisis of legitimacy for the bourgeois public realm as a whole. As in other countries
across Western Europe, the postwar years in Britain saw the dramatic
expansion of the national student body. The 'Black Papers' against the
excesses of progressive education, popular opposition to arbitration
with students in the running of university programmes and the adverse
reaction to student disturbances in towns and cities across England
indicate that, indeed, Powell's views on the student 'protest industry'
were not altogether unusual.[77] Notably, however, neither the Home
Office nor university officials ran into many problems with regard to
student unrest. Over one hundred thousand protesters marched across
London in support of the Anti-Vietnam campaign without an incidence
of police violence in October 1970, dozens of sit-ins across the country peacefully attempted to democratize the university administration
throughout the next few years, and the National Union of Students
eventually emerged as a working pressure group, representing hundreds
of thousands of British citizens. Still, we see in Powell's files an anxious

---

[76] Letter to Powell from Geoffrey Ostergaard, 23 June 1968. Papers of Enoch Powell.
SRO D3123/349.

[77] A 'Black Paper' pamphlet arguing against the excesses of progressive education
was published in the spring of 1969 with contributions from, among others, the
Conservative MP Angus Maude, the writer Kingsley Amis, and the warden of All
Souls College Oxford, John Sparrow. The aim of the pamphlet was to criticize the
use of equality as a rationale for educational reform, lamenting that 'competition has
given way to self-expression' (David Linden, 'The Black Papers and the Debate about
Standards,' *The Conservative History Journal* (September 2011), http://conservative-
history2.blogspot.co.uk/2011/09/black-papers-and-debate-about-standards.html).

concern over the political future and function of the university. We see, for instance, the director of a major car manufacturer in Coventry and member of the University Council at Warwick supporting covert efforts to listen in on particular meetings of the Coventry Labour Party in 1969, due to concerns that students were being exposed to 'undesirable indoctrination.'[78] And, similarly, we see a report written by a union insider (and sent to Powell) about the American labour historian David Montgomery – then working at the University of Warwick – and his history lessons to a local union in the area.[79] Here, 'education' – as Powell defined it 1939 – was breaking down: it was not an expression of 'one society under one cultural tradition,' it was not 'the transference of the *whole* experience, modes of thought and knowledge of one generation to the next,' but had become, he feared, a space of revolutionary indoctrination and failing institutional authority.[80] The now popular study of sociology, for instance, potentially untethered aesthetic traditions and social norms. By 1972, Powell even found that the teaching of the Welsh language in primary and secondary schools in Wales had become, in some cases, 'a means of oppression and even subversion.'[81] Meanwhile, the values of indoctrination in some universities appeared definitively multidisciplinary and – if we look especially to the Centre of Cultural Studies at Birmingham University – increasingly interested in subcultures and identity politics. This is not to say, of course, that Powell saw academic work in stasis or separated from the influences of other intellectual traditions.[82] In Nietzsche's words – and this is Powell's 1939 translation – the university had become that 'city called "bunte kuh," the cow of many colours.'[83] Or, in Powell's mind, a British

---

[78] Anonymous report, 1969, 'The Thing,' SRO D4490/49.

[79] Report on the activities of historian David Montgomery, 1969, 'The Thing,' SRO D4490/49.

[80] Enoch Powell, 'The Case for Greek in Education,' 1939. POLL 1.1.12 (emphasis in original).

[81] Letter from Powell, 3 March 1972, 'Correspondence on "The Thing,"' SRO D4490/49.

[82] See 'On Translation,' Folio Society Literary Dinner and Debate, 1987, in *Reflections of a Statesman*, pp. 123–125. 'Write Latin, and you think with a particular kind of logic and severity. Write German, and, if you write German well, you *become* half German yourself. Write French, and you enter into a unique inheritance of pride and confidence. Whatever is said, written or poetized in any of these languages, is inseparably coloured by the *nature* of those languages … We *say* – and it is arguable that we *think* – only what we are able to say … What I am asking you to accept is that translation at its best is always the creation of something different, something new, something fine – something of importance for the future. For a translation is directed to those to whom the original was not spoken or written: to a different age, a different generation, to men in societies with different thoughts, different assumptions. And the translation has to absorb something of those assumptions, of those thoughts' (pp. 124–125).

[83] Enoch Powell, 'Nietzsche on Education,' 1939. POLL 1.1.12.

university education was becoming – at best – a modern, incoherent pastiche increasingly unable to defend 'national values.'

Powell would, after much debate, come to speak at Birmingham University in June 1968 despite Ferns' concerns. The audience was closed; he spoke only to the members of the local Young Conservatives student organization. There was no incidence of violence. At Powell's departure, Ferns was quoted as saying, 'In this age of instant communication when a senator of the United States can became a casualty of the war in the Middle East' there was no assurance that 'a conspicuous and controversial British politician cannot become a casualty of war on the banks of the Niger or a war on the banks of the Seine.'[84] That same month, John Stonehouse, Labour Minister of Technology and the man who had recently spoken out against the 'canker' of communalism of the Sikh community, like Ferns, saw the assassination of Senator Robert Kennedy as an indication that Britain could not keep violence outside its political borders:

The fatal shots, according to the reports so far available, seem to have been fired not in the context of the endemic violence in America itself, but as a result of the overflow of the intense racial bitterness in the Middle East. This is indeed 'one world' when the tensions of one area can erupt in insane violence 10,000 miles away. It behoves all of us to search for lasting solutions to racial conflicts wherever they may be, before they engulf us and destroy civilized humanities.[85]

The 'outside' influence that threatened civilized humanity, in this case Birmingham University, was a former activist of the Algerian Revolution. The unrest in Birmingham, as the ex-colonial civil servant warned, could be worse than you could even imagine. Colonial violence, both Ferns and Stonehouse insisted, could come home.

A month after Powell spoke at Birmingham University, there was a 'minor rumpus' in the Commons when a number of Conservative MPs pushed the Labour government to clamp down on 'foreign agitators.'[86] Debates continued throughout that year in the Commons regarding the control and deportation of politically active foreign students. The debate would culminate in October 1968 with the Conservative MP Tom Iremonger calling for an amendment to the Public Order Act of 1936 that would provide for 'the identification, imprisonment and subsequent deportation of persons other than Her Majesty's subjects and of alien militant agitators taking part in, or conspiring in the preparation

---

[84] 'Powell Visit Goes Calmly' *The Times*, 20 June 1968. SRO D3123/349.
[85] John Stonehouse, 8 June 1968, Staffordshire, 'Immigration Data,' Papers of Enoch Powell. SRO D4490/2.
[86] HC, vol. 767, cols. 1680–1681, 4 July 1968.

of, lawful public demonstrations.'[87] Remarkably, deportation under this proposed amendment would require no illegal activity. Labour MP Eric Lubbock described the amendment as a 'monstrous proposition' that would contravene the European Convention of Human Rights, and which had more in keeping with 'the Communist or Fascist dictatorships.'[88] The 1968 amendment did not pass, but it did find the support of sixty-two members, such as Angus Maude, Quintin Hogg and Airey Neave. The Conservative Party's official line on the issue of student unrest can be found in a party pamphlet, published in March 1969, which insisted that universities 'should be neither "ivory towers" for academics, not "sausage-machines" for producing graduates. They must pay regard to the needs of society for skilled manpower, but they are also guardians of certain values and traditions which must be protected from outside influence.'[89] It was not unique to Britain that civil society appeared, in the context of the 'epidemic' of global, transnational protest, perpetually threatened from the outside. Still, we see in this the making of a postcolonial politics. Though only approximately five percent of Powell's letters after his 'Rivers of Blood' speech mentioned the empire explicitly, this proportion increased dramatically in the years ahead, in the context of anti-war demonstrations, political violence in Northern Ireland and trade union militancy. For instance, one man wrote in support of Powell's call for repatriation and denunciation of the student movement. He agreed, 'for I saw it all happen in India 1927–35 when all the Universities were throwing up thousands of "Wallpaper" degrees … Demonstrations started a train of disruption of Law & Order which culminated in Riots & finally in Anarchy which the troops had to quell with the use of batton [sic] charges and rifle fire with huge death tolls. As I see it we are fast approaching the same position here.'[90] Like many others, the memory of imperial disorder sprang to life for this man in the face of political conflict at home.

The enemy within

Of course, the student movement was significant not only for its international concerns and connections. As we saw in Chapter 4, it is impossible to tell the story of Enoch Powell in these years without recognition of the experience of political generations. Critically, for Powell, the

---

[87] HC, vol. 770, col. 1290, 23 October 1968.
[88] HC, vol. 770, cols. 1293–1294, 23 October 1968.
[89] 'Masterbrief 23: Universities and Students' Conservative Party Pamphlet. Papers of Enoch Powell. SRO D4490/47.
[90] Letter to Powell. SRO D4490/1.

student movement was symptomatic of a generation that seen no national war. As one man put it to Powell in 1970, 'Our greatest danger comes from a generation who have never know war-or-slump!'[91] The breakdown of 'British' values was, in Powell's mind, linked to forgetting the true nature of politics. It was linked to forgetting the war – when the British knew themselves through what they would die for. A sit-in of Welsh students in Aberystwyth against an increase in places for English students signalled, in Powell's mind, a failure to comprehend the borders of political unity.[92] The revolutionary socialist politics of the New Left represented only a tiny minority of the British population but it signalled, to Powell and his supporters, a broader, generational crisis of British values and national commitment. When Iremonger called for the amendment against 'militant alien agitators,' he tellingly recalled only one moment from a police report of a demonstration. The report read as follows:

The German contingent were particularly militant ... and occasionally halted in the roadway until there was a clear space ahead, then, holding their banner poles horizontally with each man in the front rank gripping a pole with both hands, they ran forward in step chanting 'Sieg heil'.[93]

Remarkably, for Iremonger, it was not Tariq Ali – then Chairman of the Ad Hoc Committee against the war in Vietnam – nor the communist-sympathizing Indian Workers' Association that served as singular proof of an 'enemy within' Britain, but German students willing to parody the Nazi victory salute.

As was common at this time, when Powell appeared to speak in Wolverhampton on 8 June 1970, police had to keep apart those demonstrating for and against him.[94] At this point in his campaign work, the chant 'Sieg heil!' was common among the demonstrators against Powell.[95] Powell was rattled, however, when one demonstrator against him gave him the Nazi salute. Over chanting, Powell shouted across the police line:

You may think what you are seeing here is an exhibition of youthful exuberance and bad manners. It is not. You may think it is harmless. It is not. You may think it is aimed at me. It is not. It is aimed at all of you. They are after you. All of you are their target. Its aim is to see the day to day way of life, the

[91] Leslie Russell to Enoch Powell, 7 December 1970, 'Correspondence on "The Thing."' SRO D4490/49.
[92] Letter to Powell, 5 December 1970, 'Correspondence on "The Thing"' SRO D4490/49.
[93] HC, vol. 762, col. 748, 4 April 1968.
[94] Heffer, *Like the Roman*, p. 558.   [95] Ibid., p. 563

decent things of life, that the majority want, demolished and destroyed. It is a movement that is in its infancy in this country. It is world wide but no mistake about it, it is spreading.[96]

He then turned and pointed to the man who have given the Nazi salute and said, 'Some of us personally witnessed what was done on the continent under that sign and it is a symbol we will never forget.'[97]

Five days before this, on 3 June 1970, Tony Benn, then Minister of Technology, spoke to a meeting of Students for a Labour Victory:

The flag of racialism which has been hoisted in Wolverhampton is beginning to look like the one that fluttered 25 years ago over Dachau and Belsen. If we do not speak up now against the filthy and obscene racialist propaganda still ... issued under the imprint of Conservative Central Office, the forces of hatred will mark up their first success and mobilize for their next offensive.[98]

Benn called Powell's comments on immigration, 'evil, filthy, and obscene.'[99] They stirred up hatred and threatened disorder. Powell had spoken out against Irish rights of entry due, he argued, to the threat of the free movement of Republican radicals in and out of the United Kingdom. Tellingly, Powell first became concerned about the Ireland Act of 1949 and the border between the Republic and Ulster when two students, one French and one German, were arrested for throwing petrol bombs in Londonderry.[100] These two students with petrol bombs were, he argued in 1969, just the 'tip of the iceberg' of future danger.[101] But this 'speaking out against the Irish' Benn saw as a sign that 'Anti-semitism is waiting to be exploited as Mosley exploited it before.'[102] Benn was at the time frustrated with the Labour Party's electoral strategy of being silent on the race issue. He justified his remarks by saying that, as a child, he had witnessed events in the East End of London, he had seen Mosley in action before the war.[103] The speech was, at the time, believed to be politically damaging for the party – with a general election coming later in the month.[104] 'Wilson was absolutely furious,' Benn later recounted, 'and thought I had lost

[96] Ibid., p. 558.   [97] Ibid.
[98] George Gale, 'The 1970 Election Campaign,' in Wood (ed.), *Powell and the 1970 Election*, pp. 66–67.
[99] Schoen, *Enoch Powell and the Powellites*, p. 52.
[100] Heffer, *Like the Roman*, p. 528.
[101] J. Enoch Powell, 'Powell Raises Question of Republic Citizens in Britain,' *The Times*, 28 August 1969.
[102] Gale, 'The 1970 Election Campaign,' in Wood (ed.), *Powell and the 1970 Election*, p. 67.
[103] Heffer, *Like the Roman*, p. 556.
[104] Tony Benn, Camilla Schofield interview, 20 November 2005.

the election.'[105] Heath positioned himself as the moderate voice between Powell and Benn and was applauded for saying at a rally in Bristol that Benn had 'impugned the patriotism of the whole of the Conservative Party, in addition to that of Enoch Powell, with whom I have differences of view but whose patriotism cannot be doubted.'[106] The Labour Campaign Committee had issued a directive to avoid making Powell an issue; Benn was told by Wilson to keep off the race issue.[107] Yet, despite Wilson's reprimand, the analogy that Benn drew in his Belsen speech would be repeated by trade unionists and Labour politicians well into the 1980s. In fact, the expansion and consolidation of extreme, racist organizations would spark even greater emphasis on these particular memories of fascism. For instance, in 1974, the year the National Front enjoyed its first party political broadcast and obtained 113,844 votes in the October general election, a trade union pamphlet would echo Benn by calling the National Front 'the modern version of the Fascism of Hitler, Mussolini and Mosley.'[108] Here, patriotism is associated with anti-racism. The Second World War remained the dominant source with which to mobilize British people against the dangers of contemporary racism, with the National Front drawn as intrinsically un-British.[109] Again, with this emphasis on wartime fascism, the history of British patriotism is distanced from its complex associations with racial oppression in the British Empire.

Speaking at a recreational centre in Smethwick on the evening of Benn's speech, Powell denied Benn's assertions with the counter, 'For myself, in 1939 I voluntarily returned from Australia to this country to serve as a private soldier against Germany and Nazism. I am the same man today.'[110] As discussed in Chapter 1, the war that Powell experienced and to which he referred was drastically different in kind from the war that so many experienced at home in Britain or on the European front.[111]

---

[105] Tony Benn, Simon Heffer interview, cited in Heffer, *Like the Roman*, p. 557.
[106] *The Times*, 9 June 1970.
[107] Heffer, *Like the Roman*, p. 557.
[108] As cited in Gilroy, *There Ain't No Black in the Union Jack*, pp. 152–153.
[109] Ibid.
[110] Gale, 'The 1970 Election Campaign,' in Wood (ed.), *Powell and the 1970 Election*, p. 68.
[111] Powell's war was the highly regimented and homo-social world of the Middle East HQ and Dehra Dun. At his desk in these imperial outposts, Powell felt no loss of will to die for King and Country. He was, as he put it in 1987, 'estranged' from the European theatre of 'total war,' his mind 'totally unaffected by the gigantic struggle in which Germany was destroyed by the Allies in Europe.' For the copies of the audio, see POLL 5.1. For transcripts, see POLL 1.6.26.

Two days after Benn's speech, Powell responded forcefully to Benn's attack with what is now called the 'Enemies Within' speech. He began with the line: 'Britain at this moment is under attack.'[112] A minute or two later, 'I assert, then, that this country is today under attack by forces which aim at the actual destruction of our nation and society as we know or can imagine them.'[113] Britain was at war and did not know it. Powell explained:

The future of Britain is as much at risk now as in the years when Imperial Germany was building dreadnoughts, or Nazism rearming. Indeed the danger is greater today, just because the enemy is invisible or disguised, so that his preparations and advances go on hardly observed. When Czechoslovakia was dismembered or Austria annexed or Poland invaded, at least one could see that a shift of power had taken place; but in the last three years events every whit as pregnant with peril have given no such physical sign.[114]

It is unclear whether Benn's words were what inspired Powell to stress the analogy of the world wars. What is clear is that the charge of fascism profoundly disturbed him.

Though the 'Rivers of Blood' speech is without doubt the most famous of Powell's speeches, Powell best articulated his political vision in this later speech. This was, in many ways, Powell's public articulation of 'The Thing.' By 1970, a considerable portion of the British Army was in Northern Ireland. The unrest there was, according to Powell, not due to substantive political issues – such as republicanism or ethnic discrimination – but due to the fact that 'disorder, deliberately fomented *for its own sake* as an instrument of power,' had almost successfully destroyed the authority of civil government there.[115] The fact that the enemy had 'utilized the materials of religious division,' was just as fortuitous as 'a mob us[ing] missiles from a near-by building site.'[116] Again, Powell emptied militant republicanism of its constructive content; it was all the same, this was the loss of sovereignty.

But importantly, Powell offered a new picture of the 'enemies' of the British people – they were the liberal media, the liberal clergy, student protesters, union militants, the 'mob' on the streets, as well as a great deal of the political Establishment. These were the forces of 'organised disorder.'[117] They controlled knowledge, particularly in the Church and in media, and thereby destabilized the norms of society. Race – like

---

[112] Powell, *Still to Decide*, p. 33.
[113] Ibid., pp. 33–34.   [114] Ibid., p. 33.
[115] Ibid., pp. 34–35.   [116] Ibid., p. 34.
[117] Ibid., p. 38.

religion – was, for this 'enemy,' a means to an end. Powell argued that 'race' *in itself* carried the seed of disorder:

The exploitation of 'race' is a common factor which links the operations of the enemy on several different fronts. In the last three or four years we have seen one city after another in the United States engulfed in fire and fighting, as the material for strife provided by the influx of Negroes into the Northern States, and their increase there, was flung into the furnace of anarchy. 'Race' is billed to play a major, perhaps a decisive, part in the battle of Britain, whose enemies must have been unable to believe their good fortune as they watched the numbers of West Indians, Africans, and Asians concentrated in her major cities mount towards the two million mark.

Why are crime rates amongst those of West Indian origin higher? Six years later, while describing 'The Thing' to a group of policemen in Cambridge, Powell attempted to answer this question. It was not due to higher unemployment rates, it was a matter of self-identification:

Here then is a criminal phenomenon that is associated with social disintegration – the fact that a society, the inhabitants of these areas of the great cities, who once regarded themselves as one, are not one, were one in the past but are not one now, and are still growing apart.[118]

It was, again, explicitly the presence of ethnic communities that served as the corrosive agent which broke down the certainties of old forms of social life. Black people are by their very presence causing social disintegration and crime. Whether they executed the crime or not, with this they can become its cause. To this challenge, 'Society is increasingly helpless to deal with it because it has ceased to be society.'[119]

Powell refused to recognize that identity politics had any democratic content; it represented merely the disassociation of 'nation' and state. As noted in Chapter 3, George Kennedy Young, once a director of the Secret Intelligence Service in charge of Middle East operations during the Suez Crisis, similarly used his experiences in the United States and East Africa as evidence to argue to a Monday Club meeting two months prior to Powell's 'enemies within' speech that a peaceful multiracial society was a proven impossibility. In the ex-colonies, British order and civility had been lost due to the 'weapon' of race. Every multiracial state in the world, Young argued, had already become an authoritarian government – 'or was embarked on a course which would require increasingly authoritarian methods.'[120] Integration had been revealed as a fallacy due to growing racial tensions worldwide – produced, again,

---

[118] Enoch Powell, April 1976, in *Reflections of a Statesman*, p. 563.
[119] Ibid.
[120] G. K. Young, West London Monday Club, 16 April 1970. SRO, D4490/2.

not by the realities of racial inequality but by the inherent tendencies of 'communalism.'

According to Powell, the 'deepest and strongest' instinct of mankind, the instinct of race, was undeniable. As his speech emphasized, what had once constituted the outside threat of colonial war was now within. But, 'fortunately,' the threat could be defeated – this immigration was 'reversible.' With this, Powell meant that Britain needed to repatriate large segments of its black community. Powell stressed that this repatriation would be voluntary. After 1970, over the following few years, an ongoing debate between Powell and those in the Conservative government would develop regarding the impact that subsidizing voluntary repatriation could have on the size of Britain's non-white population – and on the changing and unknowable question of how many immigrants wished to return to their countries of birth.[121] In 1971 – after the passing of the 1971 Immigrants Act, which further restricted immigration and formalised the concept of 'patriality' in UK immigration law – the Conservative government put repatriation on the backburner. The repatriation scheme was handed over to the small International Security Service. Powell would continue to insist on large-scale investment and would harangue Home Secretary Reginald Maudling for refusing to accept letters he had personally received asking for assisted repatriation.

Though he espoused similar arguments regarding the liberal 'enemy' and the prospect of repatriation elsewhere prior to June 1970, the 'enemies within' speech is particularly important because it was Powell's clearest articulation of a new 'enemy' in British society – at a crucial point in the lead-up to the general election. There was little overtone of partisan politics in the speech; in fact, the implication throughout was that politicians on both sides had failed to recognize the dangers that Britain faced.[122] Still, according to Powell and according to many of his supporters, this speech was a major reason for the Conservative Party's surprise general election win. At very least, Powell in the lead-up to the election drew dramatic crowds and incited large demonstrations for and against his speeches. Powell was constantly in the news. In 1971 he told a constituency dinner: 'It is the cause of permanent, indeed historic, pride for us in Wolverhampton to know that without what was done and said here a year ago, Edward Heath would not be Prime Minister and there would still be a socialist government in office.'[123] According

---

[121] For evidence of this debate, see Repatriation, 1968–1972.' POLL 8.1.4.
[122] Schoen, *Enoch Powell and the Powellites*, p. 53.
[123] *Daily Telegraph*, 8 May 1971.

to a Conservative Party private poll, 48 per cent of the British electorate heard about Powell's 'enemies within' speech, and 67 per cent of those who had heard it said that it had 'made sense.'[124]

The reasons behind the Conservatives' surprise win are unclear. At the time, commentators believed that an unexpectedly bad set of balance of payments figures released in polling week, as well as the English football team's defeat in the World Cup, contributed to the Labour defeat. Douglas Schoen and R. W. Johnson, however, have argued that it is 'beyond dispute' that Powell attracted 2.5 million votes to the Conservatives. Johnson later wrote that 'It became clear that Powell had won the 1970 election for the Tories ... of all those who had switched their vote from one party to another in the election, 50 per cent were working class Powellites.'[125] Significantly, Powell had managed to tie a number of disparate political issues into a single line of attack, under the banner of (racial) disorder. Remarkably, by 1970, trade union members who supported Powell were about 50 per cent more likely than those who did not support him to believe that trade unions had too much power in Britain.[126] As will be discussed in the Postscript, Thatcher herself would return to the text of the 'Enemy Within' speech in the lead-up to the 1979 election. Critically, the speech contributed to a particular narrative of national 'crisis' that, in the years to come, underlay populist opposition to the postwar social democratic state.

Powell received a wave of letters in support of the June 1970 speech. One man offered Powell his own story of the 'enemy' and, thinking it would be useful for Powell's arguments, offered to repeat it 'anywhere at anytime I would be prepared to do so on oath.'[127] The man had gone to Ruskin College, Oxford, 'to talk to someone about my concern as an ordinary shop floor factory worker about industrial unrest in the motor car industry.'[128] 'Imagine my reaction,' he wrote, when admitted into the room of a white north country union official, 'I saw, decorating one of his walls, a large poster of Michael X and decorating another the tattered remnants of a Union Jack!'[129] Here was quite a clear moment of confrontation between Old and New Left. He was, he told Powell,

[124] Ibid.
[125] Heffer, *Like the Roman*, p. 568.
[126] The Butler-Skokes Panel Study of 1968–1970 found in 1970 that 64 per cent of 'working class' Powellites agreed with the assertion that 'trade unions have too much power' while only 43 per cent of non-Powellites agreed. As cited in Schoen, *Enoch Powell and the Powellites*, p. 211.
[127] Letter to Powell, 24 June 1970, 'Correspondence on "The Thing."' SRO D4490/49.
[128] Ibid.   [129] Ibid.

'deeply disturbed.'[130] Again, race became a means to understand New Left internationalism. He closed the letter to Powell: 'Judging by the number of coloured men in Ruskin it made me wonder whether we are not paying for the education of people dedicated to destroy us.'

Two months after Powell's 'Enemies Within' speech, an explicitly middle-class activist group, with a membership that overlapped with both the Young Conservatives and the Monday Club, also formed, in West London. The group organized talks, maintained a lending library of Powellite publications and produced stickers, pamphlets and a monthly newsletter, entitled *Powellight*, which contained reports on Powell's activities and copies of both contemporary and past speeches. Among its six founding members was a business efficiency expert and a young, 'diligent' man who was described as still 'struggling to grow a moustache' and living in 'a black homburg [felt hat].'[131] Fortunately, one of its members, Bee Carthew, who was also a member of the West London Monday Club, was fastidious in including Powell in all her political work and Powell was equally fastidious in keeping a file on Carthew and *Powellight*. Their correspondence began in January 1969. In this correspondence, we see close friendships develop between Carthew and both Enoch and Pamela Powell[132] – so much so that, by March 1970, they all attended the Ideal Homes Exhibition together in Olympia, London. In her letters over the next five years, Carthew's focus is explicitly on creating a 'professional' middle-class platform for Powell's views. She recounts names and occupations of those who have attended meetings and offers a picture of the tensions and uncertainties of radical activism on the ground. Here, in these letters, we see the beginnings of right-wing revolts in Dorking, Surbiton, Kingston and Malden against local Conservative councillors and candidates who had spoken out against Powell in the lead-up to the 1970 election. Importantly, with this, we see also the limits of Powell's commitment to a new populist politics: Powell remained clear throughout their correspondence that he would not support the efforts of 'independent' candidates to launch, as Carthew put it, 'a public movement to make [Powell] King-Emperor.'[133] Still, in Carthew's accounts, we see something of the as

---

[130] Ibid.

[131] Letter to Powell's secretary, 2 September 1970, SRO DA4490/51.

[132] Unfortunately, copies of Pamela Powell's letters are not held in either Enoch Powell's official or unofficial archives. Though she was clearly incredibly active in Powell's campaigns, she remains largely silent in his papers.

[133] As Enoch Powell wrote: 'On the subject of your letter [regarding a right wing revolt in the London suburbs], the principle is clear: not only must I (of course) in no way connivance any more to displace a conservative member or adopted candidate, but so far as possible there must be no ground for even the malicious to allege that I have

yet undefined parameters and alliances of far right nationalism both before and after 1970. There, for instance, we see efforts of 'independent candidates' to establish relations with Scottish, Cornish and Welsh nationalists along Powellite lines. There, too, we see efforts to align with certain 'nationality minorities,' such as those of Italian or Cypriot origin, by suggesting 'how benign were Englishman's feelings to their minorities in the good old days,' and '[h]ow all this has changed and wouldn't it be splendid to get back to things as they were.'[134] The implication is, of course, that 'to get back to things as they were' required an end to any non-white immigration and, even more, large government investment in repatriation. In 1970 and in the following four years, *Powellight* remained acutely conscious of its public profile; it purposefully foregrounded Powell's economic, anti-socialist arguments before issues of race relations and immigration.[135] Still, racism ran throughout. Via these publications and Carthew's revealing letters, we find an inside picture of disputes and uncertainties within popular conservatism at this time. As one activist put it to Carthew, 'The days of blind allegiance to the Party are, I believe, gone.'[136]

The Conservative win of 1970 did not, therefore, quiet Powell's criticisms and his popular support. In fact, the economic crisis and industrial militancy that ensued during the Heath government came to be blamed, by these conservative radicals, on Heath's 'pseudo-socialism.' Powell had found, by this point, fellow travellers on the far right. But, again, Powell insisted that the troubles in Britain went deeper than economics. He continued to argue that Britain was suffering from a 'moral epidemic' due to its loss of faith in state power and law and order,[137] and called for greater faith and investment in the police force. He spoke to the Institution of Industrial Security, whose primary purpose was to investigate security measures that might prevent corporate loss. Perhaps unsurprisingly, Powell's arguments at this time sound most like a group of senior Army officers who made controversial claims, that same year, about the strength of police power in Britain. 1972 was the year of a major miners' strike and a year before the Provisional IRA conducted its

done so. Those therefore who identify themselves with what I do and say because they believe it right, should hold completely aloof from any such moves.' Letter from Powell, 18 June 1969, 'Powellight,' SRO D4490/51.
[134] Letter to Powell, 6 September 1969, 'Powellight,' SRO D4490/51.
[135] Letter to Powell, 23 August 1970, 'Powellight,' SRO D4490/51.
[136] Letter to Powell, 9 August 1970, 'Powellight,' SRO DA4490/51.
[137] Enoch Powell, speech to the Institution of Industrial Security in London (20 October 1972), quoted in *Powellight* (November 1972), 'Powellight.' SRO D4490/51.

first bombing campaign in England. In May 1972, Brigadier Brian Watkins, Brigadier Frank Kitson, Major-General Ronald Buckland and other officers voiced concerns about the 'subversive forces' in British society:

The whole period of the miners' strike made us realise that the present size of the police force is too small. It is based on the philosophy that we are a law-abiding country, but things have now got to the stage where there are not enough resources to deal with the increasing numbers who are not prepared to respect the law.[138]

According to the *Daily Mail*, 'any officer who has served in Ulster' will say at one time or another: 'We are desperately afraid that we are learning a job here that we may have to do in ten or 15 years time in Leeds or Wolverhampton or even London.'[139] 'The more discerning of us,' Major-General Buckland told *The Times*, 'are extremely depressed about the way things are going. We seem nearer and nearer anarchy all the time.'[140] Brigadier Frank Kitson, who won 'striking victories against guerillas in Kenya, Malaya and Cyprus,' told the *Daily Mail* that he was 'prepared to envisage ... urban guerilla warfare in British cities.'[141] And, at least according to the *Daily Mail*, this again came down to 'race': 'Any intelligent Army officer is quite capable of constructing a "scenario" for Ulster-type trouble in Britain. They don't talk about them a great deal because they mainly involve the black community whose parallels with the Catholics in Ulster are in some ways frighteningly close.'[142]

Frank Kitson had been a mid-ranking officer involved in the suppression of the Mau Mau uprising. Tellingly, in 1971, using his experiences of colonial counter-insurgency and under the auspices of the Ministry of Defence, he wrote what was soon to become an influential text in intelligence and security circles, the book *Low Intensity Operations: Subversion, Insurgency and Peacekeeping*.[143] Kitson's arguments on the need to control the political unrest of non-state actors with military force and counter-intelligence would inform British military conduct in subsequent years, particularly in Northern Ireland. But perhaps the most bizarre historical consequence of this revolt among ex-colonial army officers was the founding of a non-governmental 'patriotic', 'civil defence' group by the retired General Sir Walter Walker

---

[138] 'Senior Officers Concerned about "Subversive Forces,"' *The Times*, 23 May 1972.
[139] Angus MacPherson, 'After Ulster ... Leeds or even London? That's the Disturbing Question Some Army Officers Are Already Asking,' *Daily Mail*, 26 May 1972.
[140] 'Senior Officers Concerned about "Subversive Forces,"' *The Times*, 23 May 1972.
[141] Ibid.   [142] Ibid.
[143] Frank Kitson, *Low Intensity Operations: Subversion, Insurgency and Peacekeeping* (London: Faber & Faber, 1971).

(who himself was Commander-in-Chief of NATO forces in northern Europe between 1969 and 1972). The Monday Club's George Kennedy Young recommended, early in 1973, that a private, voluntary force be formed to counter strikers in Britain. But it was Walker who would go on to organize the explicitly anti-communist Civil Assistance campaign, claiming over 100,000 volunteers by 1974.[144] In late 1973, miners voted to take industrial action if their pay demands were not met; Heath's Conservative government refused. The government's strategy of putting the question of union power to a national vote in February 1974 failed. Labour won the general election. Walker, who drove the recruitment campaign out of the City of London Corporation's office church, St Lawrence Jewry, called for the 'remoralizing' of the British public against these 'subversive' forces. Both Conservative and Labour leaders condemned Civil Assistance as an incredibly dangerous idea; it was, of course, never put to use. In 1975, it soon faded from view, but not before one public appearance of some of those disgruntled 100,000 volunteers, who were, a reporter noted, mostly middle-aged men and women, some of them bankers.[145]

As Powell and these army officers make clear, 'naming the crisis' of the nation involved the conflation of a vast array of political initiatives under the banner of 'disorder' and 'subversion.' It is in this context, in the context of revolutionary activity in Northern Ireland, student protest and militant labour activism across Britain, that memories of colonial 'disorder' truly came to the fore and a vision of race as a *weapon* of subversion took root.

Surrender to Europe

When Heath gave his first speech as Prime Minister outside of Britain in 1970, Powell highlighted large sections of the speech. Powell was, he believed, vindicated by the echoes of the 'enemies within' speech in Heath's words. It was a speech to the General Assembly of the United Nations on the twenty-fifth anniversary session of the UN. Heath spoke of 'the growth of a cult of political violence' and the increasing use of violence for the 'simple unconstructive aim [of] anarchy.'[146] Heath warned that the threat was not of violence between states, but within them: 'It is a sombre thought but it may be that in the 1970s

[144] 'Leaders of Civil Assistance Now Selecting over 50 'Controllers,' *The Times*, 5 September 1974.
[145] 'General Warns Britons of Subversion,' *The Times*, 26 February 1975.
[146] Speech by Heath to the General Assembly of the United Nations, 25th Anniversary Session, New York, October 23 1970. SRO D4490/49.

civil war, not war between nations, will be the main danger we will face.'[147] He then referred specifically to Northern Ireland. Like Powell, the line was drawn not between political beliefs, but between political means: 'The crucial division in Northern Ireland is not between Protestant and Catholic or between Left and Right. It is between those who believe that constructive change is the only sound basis for peace, justice and progress, and those who reach at the first opportunity for the rifle and the bomb.'[148] Powell highlighted all of these words, though what he did not mark on the page is just as significant. After speaking of the forces of 'anarchy,' Heath claimed that 'The truth is that the possibilities of peaceful change have never been so great throughout the world.'[149] He spoke of working to 'harmonise' national interest with 'the pursuit of peace, justice and progress. And I would add, happiness' and the importance of UN peacekeepers in holding the ring when violence occurs.[150]

Like Heath, Powell also responded to the anniversary of the United Nations. He wrote in the *Daily Telegraph* that he, like other politicians, was 'living out their lives with a bad conscience about the United Nations.'[151] He, like others, had not attacked the UN because it was about peace. The UN embodied the dream – or 'superstition' – of peace, which protected it from political attack. But this, according to Powell, denied the reality of human experience. The UN, in Powell's mind, denied political reality:

The United Nations is, always has been, and always will be, an absurdity and a monstrosity, which no lapse of time and no application of ingenuity and effort can remedy. It is so because it embodies a contradiction. The United Nations, as its very name declares, adopts as its basis the nation, the sovereign, independent, self-conscious nation. If anything, this basis has become more pronounced over the past 25 years, during which no sooner has the tiniest group been recognised as a nation than it has been enrolled in the company of the elect. As between these entities the United Nations purports either to maintain … the *status quo*, or to regulate its alteration without the use of force (which must of necessity include the prospect of the use of force).

Here lies the fatal contradiction; for the very nature and existence of the nation itself are inseparable from force, which is why the rise and growth and disappearance of nations is mediated by force. A nation is unthinkable without the prospect and the intention of defending itself and its territory, and this necessarily implies the prospect and possibility of being attacked. Without war the sovereign nation is not conceivable.[152]

---

[147] Ibid.   [148] Ibid.   [149] Ibid.   [150] Ibid.
[151] *Daily Telegraph*, 19 October 1970.
[152] Ibid.

If sovereignty was the ultimate endpoint, the internationalism of the postwar period was, as Powell put it, a monstrosity.

After the Conservative win in 1970, the Labour Party – out of office and standing in opposition to entry – began to insist on a consultative referendum to put the question of entry into Europe to the British people. As early as 15 June 1970, just prior to the Conservatives' surprise election victory, Powell agreed.[153] Edward Heath enjoyed the reputation at this time as the man of Europe. Between 1970 and 1974, pro-marketeers held sway in the Conservative Party; federation was framed as pro-business and a means to expand into the European market. This would be Britain's answer to the economic contractions associated with imperial decline. Over the next few years, the economic fragility of the country was made abundantly clear to the British public. Extreme inflation and a decline in real wages contributed to feelings of economic vulnerability in everyday life. By 1972, the television offered viewers a vision of industrial chaos with thousands of miners out on strike over the demand for a nationwide wage increase; with this, 135 coal pits closed in South Wales alone. The next year, OPEC's oil embargo rocked the international economic system and led to an energy crisis in Britain and the temporary institution of a three-day working week to ration the use of electricity. This was indeed an 'alien *malaise*' that threatened the foundations of Britain's postwar settlement. The Conservative Party presented membership of the EEC as a possible economic solution.

But this was not, Powell insisted, about 'the cost of butter'; this was about the continuance of British parliamentary democracy.[154] He lamented that the electors, though able to choose between socialism and capitalism, more nationalization or less, were not being given any choice on the most important political questions – what he called Britain's 'national decisions.'[155] Immigration was one of these, but the question of joining the Common Market was, according to Powell, the 'most fundamental of all' national decisions.[156] It was the question, 'not merely of what *sort* of a nation are we to be, but *what* nation are we to be?' It was a question of 'who is the "self" about whose self-government we speak, or the "we" who will fight to the death for "our" freedom.'[157]

[153] J. Enoch Powell, Election Address, Tamworth, 15 June 1970, in *Reflections of a Statesman*, pp. 467–470.

[154] Richard Crossman, 'Power to the People, via Enoch Powell,' *The Times*, 13 June 1973.

[155] 15 June 1970, in *Reflections of a Statesman*, p. 467.

[156] Ibid.

[157] J. Enoch Powell, excerpt from *Freedom and Stability in World Economy*, in *Reflections of a Statesman*, pp. 474–480 (p. 476).

Powell's argument against European membership turned, then, on identity: on the interdependent relationship between self-identification and self-government. This self-identification could not 'be blown up like a balloon ... nor does it grow and grow like an amoeba.'[158] Again, this had been proven by history. The empires had failed:

> The salient feature of this century both in Europe and in the world at large has been the break-up of former giant states and imperial structures into smaller and sometimes very small self-governing and independent units. Modern Europe itself is the product of this process. The experiment of the dying British colonial empire with quite modest schemes of federation proved an almost total failure, from Africa to the Caribbean.[159]

He had, himself, argued after the war that the only way to save the British Empire was via the construction of a new 'we' – a super-state, rather than a Commonwealth.[160] But nationalism had prevailed in Africa and Asia, as in Europe. In a speech on 8 June 1973 – in which Powell famously supported voting Labour against European membership – Powell insisted that Britain, like the newly independent nations, had to again assert its independence.

> Independence, the freedom of a self-governing nation, is in my estimation the highest political good, for which any disadvantage, if need be, and any sacrifice are a cheap price. There is not a state in Africa or Asia, hewn out of some administrative unit of Western colonial rule, which would not scorn to bargain away its independence. It is not for us to judge what others may think it right to do with their own. It is for us, and us alone, to determine if we will continue to be a free, self-governing people. I refuse to imagine that we shall answer no.[161]

Criticisms against nationalism within Britain, with the derisive term 'Little Englandism' for instance, merely revealed a double standard. Why – while 'there is no limit to the fissiparous states that are sure of a welcome to the ever-widening ranks of the United Nations'[162] – is Britain, 'one of the oldest nation states in the world, who themselves have played the liberators to so many other nations ... berated for the anachronism of desiring to retain their parliamentary self-governing independence?'[163] Why, after all its history, should Britain now embrace a federation of Europe?

---

[158] Ibid., p. 479.
[159] Ibid., p. 479.
[160] J. Enoch Powell, speech to Penn Fields, 16 February 1950, 'Constituency Special Subjects.' SRO D3123/223.
[161] Powell cited in Heffer, *Like the Roman*, p. 669.
[162] Powell, *Freedom and Stability*, 1976, in *Reflections of a Statesman*, p. 480.
[163] Ibid.

Powell insisted that those who sought federation did not understand Europe. As he put in 1972, 'I often think that those are least European, have least understanding of what Europe is and what is great and imperishable about Europe, who have appropriated to the European Community, which in many respects is a caricature and even a denial of what is essentially European, the title of "Europe."'[164] In Powell's mind, Europe had never and would never offer a viable 'we.' As Britain's imperial history showed, power can be pooled, but national sovereignty, or 'we-ness' as Powell put it, could not so easily. While some Continental nations, such as Germany and Italy, were the products of a revolutionary 'pooling' of sovereignty, this was an anathema in Britain's political history. Powell asserted the power of the mythology of piecemeal evolutionary change. A United Kingdom had taken time and history. Europe, he argued, would not by a Treaty of Brussels or by a Treaty of Rome become a political unit that could generate representative consent: 'Nine "we's" do not become one "we" by dint of their government undertaking the obligations' of these treaties. With Europe, self-government – and representative consent – would be surrendered without anything taking its place but 'bureaucracy or the irresponsibility of national governments exercising collective authority.'[165]

Importantly, as a part of a common Europe, the British people would no longer have control over their identity – grassroots efforts to reform immigration policy and finance mass repatriation of immigrants would, for instance, be politically powerless in a federation of Europe. Members of Parliament responsible for the representation of Britain's towns and cities would be drowned out. Instead, by entering the European community, these towns and cities would become, Powell warned, 'the ghettoes of Europe.'[166] Administrators in Europe would 'send over an ever swelling stream of study groups; more and more dissertations will be written in Continental universities on the inexhaustible theme of "Britain's race problem."'[167] Europe would not 'export our folly.' A joint Declaration signed before the Treaty of Brussels enabled members, Powell explained, to avoid Britain's 'problem': 'I can assure you that it is not the prospect of a sudden inrush of Irish or Norwegians which fills the Europeans with anxiety for their "social situation". The Declaration refers to one thing and one thing only –the present and future coloured population of England.'[168] The Continental countries were going to be 'spectators, not participants, in the tragedy of our

---

[164] Powell, 19 April 1972, cited in Heffer, *Like the Roman*, p. 630.
[165] Powell, *Freedom and Stability*, 1976, in *Reflections of a Statesman*, p. 477–478.
[166] J. Enoch Powell quoted in *Powellight*, July 1972. SRO D4490/51.
[167] Ibid.   [168] Ibid.

cities.'[169] The tragedy to which Powell referred was black and white ghettoization, civil war and the break-up of a collective British 'we.'

In 1972, Powell told the Commons during the second reading of the European Communities Bill (which was one of the first major parliamentary debates focused on British membership of the EEC) that entry would sacrifice their legislative sovereignty and that the power of the House over the executive would therefore progressively diminish – resulting in the decline in the self-government of the electorate.[170] This would be, Powell argued, an 'unthinkable act.'[171] Both Sir Alec Douglas-Home and Heath emphasized that the supreme reason for the EEC and Britain's membership in it was to prevent a future civil war in Europe. Heath's was an attack, Powell believed, on the survival of the British nation:

Heath's advocacy of British membership of the E.E.C. has always been frankly based on the view that the day of the nation state, at any rate for a nation like Britain, is over and that the best future of its inhabitants lies in Britain becoming a province of a European super-state, that is, of a non-nation state. It was on that ground that he made his final, and in the event successful, appeal in the referendum debate. As part of the E.E.C. Britain is not a state at all, 'civilized' or otherwise.[172]

For Powell, the question of identity – the self-identification of the nation – stood as the foundation of sovereignty. This is by no means an unusual political argument. What marks Powell out, though, is that for him the basis of this identity was the act of war. This had profound consequences. The 'essential element in forming a single electorate,' Powell explained to an association of French businessmen in Lyon, 'is the sense that in the last resort all parts of it stand or fall, survive or perish, together.'[173] This sense Britain did not share with the inhabitants of Western Europe. In fact, Britain and Russia had this in common. Russia, due to its enormous size, and Britain, due to its 'ditch,' could be defeated in the 'decisive land battle' in Europe and still survive.[174] Britain's ditch would, according to Powell, continue to be as important as it had proven to be in the era of Napoleon or Philip II. And so, Powell explained to his French audience, Britain could never feel entirely one with Europe.

[169] Ibid.
[170] Powell, 'European Communities Bill,' 17 February 1972, in *Reflections of a Statesman*, pp. 218–225.
[171] Powell, *Reflections of a Statesman*, p. 225.
[172] Powell, Extract from speech to public meeting of the Hampshire Monday Club in the Avenue Hall, Southampton, 9 April 1976. POLL 4.1.11.
[173] 'Enoch Powell's Dissent on Europe,' *The Times*, 13 February 1971.
[174] Ibid.

As has been emphasized in the proceeding pages of this book, war and political identity could not be disentangled in Powell's political thinking. As he explained it to a rally organized by the Ulster Young Unionists Council in 1970 in Enniskillen, Northern Ireland, only a few miles from the border with the Republic:

Politics is in the last resort about the life and death of nations, about what nations are, about how they change, how they grow, how they perish or are destroyed. It is for this that the individuals who compose the nations live and die; it is with this that their strongest and deepest emotions and passions are intertwined.[175]

The citizens' willingness to live and die for the nation is the very foundation of its existence. To these young Unionists, Powell made the inevitable Second World War parallel:

For Britain this moment of truth last came a third of a century ago, when we realized that our existence as a nation was menaced by the armed resurgence of Germany and shook ourselves out of sloth to defend it. Such a period is perhaps coming upon us again after all these years; but, as is the way with these periods, in new forms.[176]

The speech was an attack on the Ireland Act of 1949, which enabled citizens of the Irish Republic to enter Britain without control. This was not hostile to the Irish, he insisted, it was respectful of the people of Ireland's deepest held beliefs – that they were not part of the United Kingdom. Due perhaps to Ulster loyalists' relatively limited cultural production of legitimizing national myths,[177] Powell's florid language of bravely fighting, like in the world wars, for the survival of the United Kingdom found a welcome audience among Protestants in the North.

Again, Powell told the Commons during the debates on the European Communities Bill that nationhood was, 'the thing for which men, if necessary, fight and, if necessary, die, and to preserve which men think no sacrifice is too great.'[178] Britain might be culturally, religiously and racially European, but that could not define whether British nationhood should be subsumed by Europe. Rather, echoing both Tom Nairn's arguments on English nationalism and Linda Colley's thesis in

[175] Enoch Powell, speech organized by the Armagh Branch of the Ulster Young Unionists Council, at Enniskillen, 7 February 1970. POLL 4.1.6.
[176] Ibid.
[177] Ronan Bennet, 'Don't Mention the War: Culture in Northern Ireland,' in David Miller (ed.), *Rethinking Northern Ireland: Culture, Ideology and Colonialism* (London: Longman, 1998), pp. 199–210.
[178] HC, vol. 809, col. 1374, 25 January 1972.

Britons, Powell claimed that the very basis of Britain's national identity had been 'antithetical' to the Continent of Europe:

In our history, both recent and earlier, the principal events which have placed their stamp upon our consciousness of who we are, were the very moments in which we have been alone, confronting a Europe which was lost or hostile. That is the picture, that is the folk memory, by which our nation has been formed.[179]

Powell's reputation remained defined by the 'Rivers of Blood' speech; criticism against these views on Europe tended to reflect this. The Conservative MP Cranley Onslow, for instance, directly spoke out against Powell and his 'appeals to instinct' on the question of European membership:

Most of us, as children, were instinctively afraid of the dark. We feared strangers, we believed in ghosts. Most of us, as we have grown older, have ceased to be ruled by instinct, and rely instead on reason. It may be that in the end reason will lead us to reject the terms that come out of the Common Market talks. But we should be very careful not to allow ourselves to be swayed or our judgment clouded by emotive appeals to instinct.[180]

Still, Powell was undeterred. When the European Communities Bill of 1972 reached committee stage, Powell called it a moment of 'life and death struggle' for the independence of Parliament.[181] He went on that 'with other weapons and in other ways, the contention is as surely about the future of Britain's nationhood as were the combats which raged in the skies over southern England in the autumn of 1940. The gladiators are few; there are but words; and yet their fight is everyman's.'[182]

On the passing of the European Communities Act of 1972, Powell argued:

A victorious continental enemy, determined to absorb this United Kingdom into its dominions, could not have dictated at Westminster a more comprehensively humiliating surrender than the Act which Parliament passed in 1972 in order that this country should become part of the European Community ... Wilhelm II could not have demanded so much; I doubt if Hitler would have demanded more. I can still only half believe that I was myself an unwilling witness to my country's abnegation of its own national independence.

Britain had given over power to nations which were 'better acquainted than ourselves with tyranny and inhumanity.'[183] This was the long

[179] Ibid.
[180] Extract from speech by Mr. Cranley Onslow, MP at Woking, 23 April 1971, POLL 1.1.17.
[181] Heffer, *Like the Roman,* p. 622.
[182] Ibid., pp. 622–623.
[183] Enoch Powell, 'Giving Away the Rod,' *The Spectator,* 21 January 1978; *Reflections of Statesman,* pp. 248–251 (p. 248).

feared destruction of Britain's Common Law tradition by Europe's (volatile and revolutionary) republicanism. Years later, he would continue to remind listeners of that recent folk memory that defined Britain against the Continent:

We are taunted – by the French, by the Italians, by the Spaniards – for refusing to worship at the shrine of a common government superimposed upon them all ... where were the European unity merchants in 1940? I will tell you. They were either writhing under a hideous oppression or they were aiding and abetting that oppression. Lucky for Europe that Britain was alone in 1940.[184]

Whatever the leadership did, this folk memory (of war) would not change. Powell responded to the signing of the Treaty of Accession by Heath and his senior colleagues in January 1972 with the assertion that, 'They can sign, and they did sign, the treaty; but they cannot secure for it that consent of the British people which is necessary to validity.'[185] Powell likened the British ministers who signed the treaty to Napoleon in front of Paris after the Battle of Leipzig, when he continued to give orders to his marshals as if they still commanded an army which, in fact, no longer existed.[186] Britain was not behind Heath. He insisted that the British knew that they did not belong in Europe, and 'they have always known that they did not belong to it.'[187]

According to Powell, European unity or the United Nations could not represent the resolution of the political and economic tensions of the wartime era. For many, as well as involving the economic possibilities and the realpolitik of European defence in the Cold War, European unity represented a historical step forward from the world wars. The wars had, in a sense, provided the common experience that could serve as the foundation of community. Self-recognition of others across the national borders of Europe was made possible by the shared experience of war. In Powell's mind, European unification was not any historical step forward from the logic of the European wars, but represented Britain's surrender. The notion that the experience of war – or empire – could constitute a civil society across the borders of state authority did not hold for Powell. Rather, Powell held the 'realist' position that state sovereignty was an absolute. With such thinking, civil society is 'state-contained,' and 'relations between societies [are] subordinate to, and dependent on, political relations between states.'[188] Powell's 'civil

[184] J. Enoch Powell, speech to the Merseyside Conservatives Ladies' Luncheon Club (5 January 1990), as cited in Heffer, *Like the Roman*, p. 928.
[185] J. Enoch Powell, 'Mr. Powell Says Entry Still Unacceptable to the British,' *The Times*, 25 January 1972.
[186] Ibid.   [187] Ibid.
[188] James Anderson, "Rethinking National Problems in a Transnational Context," in Miller (ed.), *Rethinking Northern Ireland: Culture, Ideology and Colonialism*, p. 129.

society' was synonymous with a peaceful community at war – with a community able to wage war outside of itself. For this reason, Powell refused to accept the existence of a 'web of understood relationships' – a cultural and political community – outside the confines of the British state.[189] Importantly, this positions Powell as fundamentally opposed to the rising 'functionalist' perspective on international relations and European integration which developed as realism's mirror-image – a perspective that posits that states are created by civil society, to further the needs of society, not the other way around. While functionalists argue that Europe itself could represent a civil society – that the transnational movement of people, ideas, and markets worked to the make the nation-state redundant – realists insist that the loss of the nation-state, and in this case the loss of the 'high politics' of the British Parliament, brings with it the loss of civil society. (In this way, Powell has more in common with neo-Marxists who insist that civil societies and states are deeply interconnected and co-dependent sites of struggle and negotiation.)

Occasionally, the logic of Powell's political thinking would sit at odds with neoliberal activism. For instance, in 1972, Powell was a member of an influential, international anti-socialist think tank, founded by Friedrich Hayek, called the Mont Perelin Society. In 1975, Hayek got in the British newspapers for calling Powell 'emotionally unstable' due to an outburst at a meeting in 1972. At that meeting, a member of the group had proposed a minute of silence in memory of the Israeli athletes who had been killed by pro-Palestinian terrorists at the Munich Olympics. As Hayek remembers, Powell denounced the idea. As we have seen, Powell saw political violence as an international 'epidemic.' Yet a political stand on the Arab–Israeli conflict could not be treated as an extension of neoliberal belief. He seemed to argue, Hayek recalled, that it was not part of the group's function to make a judgment about the event. 'I was shocked by that,' said Hayek. 'What he said may have been literally correct, but his attitude to what was a well-meant gesture was unreasonable. Ever since, I have thought that there may be this emotional instability about him.'[190] After this hit the papers, Hayek soon wrote a personal apology to Powell. 'I hope you will forgive me,' for this 'appalling indiscretion.'[191] He had not yet learnt, he explained,

---

[189] J. Enoch Powell, Bill Schwarz interview, 26 April 1988. For Powell, then, transnationalism was synonymous only with disorder. This goes far in explaining Powell's absolute rejection of the emerging politics of civil rights at this time, both in Northern Ireland and Britain.

[190] *Daily Telegraph*, 26 September, 1975, POLL 1/1/23B

[191] Letter from Friedrich Hayek to Powell, 6 October 1975, POLL 1/1/23B

how to be interviewed. Powell's response to Hayek a few days later was measured:

Only two things surprise me. One is that you should have imagined anything about myself if it was derogatory would not be greedily reported. The second is that you should associate 'emotion' with my protest, whether justified or not, against the Mont Perelin Society presuming to single out for commemoration a particular group amongst all those done to death by violence throughout the world in a particular period of time.[192]

That minute of silence was, in Powell's mind, a political act.

Powell's political views did not just create some awkward moments. Powell broke away not only from his party but also from alliances on the far right through his insistent opposition to membership in the EEC. In July 1971, George Kennedy Young, Jonathan Guinness, Geoffrey Baber and Geoffrey Stewart-Smith set up the first Monday Club Market promotions group and, in September, a Monday Club Common Market conference. By 1972, Jonathan Guinness became the new chairman of the Club. At this time, Bee Carthew wrote to Powell: 'Jonathan Guinness is not my cup of tea; charming (too charming) rather slick, middle-aged *jeunesse doree*, not Powellite, very pro-Market.'[193] But, tellingly, Carthew continued: 'All this is really leading up to one admission – that I feel things are so far gone that if there were a choice of in the Market with you in charge of the country or out without you in charge, I would canvas day and night for British entry; nobody but you can mould elements of left and right with nothing but nationalistic sentiments in common into a whole.'[194] Here, we see Powell's most loyal activist, Bee Carthew, unlikely to follow him down a path of political isolation against the EEC. There would be, she implies, no populist revolt against Europe.

Fighting for the Union

Though, for Powell, Britain's federation with Europe represented the clearest international challenge to national sovereignty and political survival, it was again the troubles of Northern Ireland that most clearly dramatized the 'crisis' of national dissolution and the consequences of the destruction of the 'good conscience' of the British state. Again, the vision of 'race' as a source of insurmountable division and disorder borrowed much from displaced memories of empire, but – perhaps even

[192] Letter from Powell to Friedrich Hayek, 10 October 1075, POLL 1/1/23B.
[193] Letter to Pamela Powell, 1 August 1972, in 'Powellight' SRO D4490/51.
[194] Letter to Powell, 19 September 1971, in 'Powellight' SRO D4490/51.

more – it borrowed from the events of ethnic violence and revolutionary politics evident in Belfast and Londonderry. By 1969, the situation in Ulster had deteriorated. The Unionist-dominated Stormont was closed and Ulster had been placed under martial law. In 1971, the British Army began internment without trial of suspected IRA members. Internment further polarized communities in Northern Ireland. In opposition to Labour Party calls to oppose internment, Labour leader James Callaghan noted that, when two MPs visited a camp of internees, the men 'drew themselves up in military formation with an officer in front, acting and behaving as if they were prisoners of war.'[195] He then asked, 'do we release these men?'[196] Britain was, he implied, at war.

In August 1971, Amnesty International sent a senior officer, Dr Zbynek Zeman, to Belfast to observe Britain's policy of internment of suspected IRA members.[197] It was the first international body to send an observer to Northern Ireland. In September, *The Times* reported that Zeman would report his observations to representatives of the Council of Europe in Luxembourg later that month.[198] That year, Enoch Powell had begun travelling regularly to Ulster to critique Conservative government policy there. The very day that *The Times* reported that Zeman's visit could result in Britain finding itself in the 'embarrassing position' of having its internment policy in Ulster brought before the European Commission on Human Rights,[199] Powell spoke to nine hundred Unionists at a rally in Omagh, County Tyrone. On that day, Powell explained that Heath was failing to lead during a time of war. 'The fact remains,' he told the Unionist rally, 'that the people of Northern Ireland are in the front line. An assault upon the United Kingdom is in progress, and the men and women of Ulster have for months been the forward troops in an exposed position under increasingly heavy attack … front-line troops have a right to expect from time to time the presence and encouragement of their commander in chief.'[200] Heath had not visited Ulster as Prime Minister. The juxtaposition of Zeman and Powell, travelling through Ulster within weeks of each other, offers a point of entry into understanding competing visions of a postcolonial Europe.

---

[195] 'Call to End Internment in Ulster Fails,' *The Times*, 8 October 1971.
[196] Ibid.
[197] 'The Times Diary: Amnesty Send Observer to Ulster,' *The Times*, 16 August 1971.
[198] 'The Times Diary: Ulster for Human Rights Court?' *The Times*, 11 September 1971.
[199] Ibid.
[200] *Daily Telegraph*, 12 September 1971.

Dr Zbynek Zeman and Dr Enoch Powell in many ways embody two perspectives on the legacy of the Second World War and on the place of nationalism in postwar Europe. They are in a sense tied together, too, by the significance of the break-up of empires in their political formation. Like Powell, Zeman was an academic. Born in Prague in 1928, Zeman would become a professor of Modern History at Oxford University and write several books on the world wars, particularly on the break-up of the Habsburg Empire, on the propaganda of Nazi Germany and on the 'making' of Eastern Europe.[201] He travelled to Prague in the spring of 1968 – while Powell spoke of 'Rivers of Blood' – and would go on to write a sympathetic account for Penguin Press on the mood of rebellion there.[202] Zeman brought European eyes to Ulster. He also brought a distinctly postwar perspective – one that embraced the necessity of transnational bodies and one that was highly cynical of the uses of nationalism. Dr Zbynek Zeman's visit to the internment camps in Ulster represents, in this respect, the world to which Powell remained blind. In December 1971, Britain would be accused by the Republic of Ireland of a breach of the terms of the European Convention on Human Rights for actions in Ulster, for the torture and internment of Irish nationalists. In the coming years, Ugandan Asians – following the political path taken by Kenyan Asians and Catholics in Northern Ireland – would also turn to human rights law to claim the rights of British citizenship.

Against any notion of civil rights, Powell believed that the root of the problem in Ulster was, again, a failure in authority. Speaking in 1972, he noted:

The history of the last three and a half years has been the story of authority pleading guilty and begging the forgiveness of the criminal and of the devastating consequences for the men, women and children whom authority exists to defend. No sooner did terrorism and murder advance behind the banner of 'civil rights', than government – both at Westminster and Northern Ireland – made haste to worship and bow down and confess their faults. The whole

[201] Z. A. B. Zeman, *Break-up of the Habsburg Empire, 1914–1918: A Study of National and Social Revolution* (London: Oxford University Press, 1961); Z. A. B. Zeman, *Twilight of the Habsburgs: The Collapse of the Austro-Hungarian Empire* (American Heritage Press, 1971); Z. A. B. Zeman, *Heckling Hitler: Caricatures of the Third Reich* (Hanover, NH: University Press of New England, 1987); Z. A. B. Zeman, *Nazi Propaganda* (London: Oxford University Press, 1964); Z. A. B. Zeman, *Masaryks: The Making of Czechoslovakia* (London: Weidenfeld & Nicolson, 1976); Z. A. B. Zeman, *Pursued by a Bear: The Making of Eastern Europe* (London: Chatto & Windus, 1989); Z. A. B. Zeman, *The Making and Breaking of Communist Europe* (Oxford: B. Blackwell, 1991).
[202] Z. A. B. Zeman, *Prague Spring* (London: Penguin Press, 1968).

civil rights ramp was a tissue of trivialities and untruths; and authority at Stormont knew it to be so, and authority at Westminster ought to have known it to be so.[203]

Sometimes, Powell would admit, oppression provokes rebellion – 'or so the history books tell us, though even in the past the appearance of this was probably more common than the reality' – but today, 'violence and mob law are organized and spreading for their own sake.'[204] And so, the words ' "grievance", "reform", "discrimination", "civil rights"' have 'passed into the orthodox Westminster vocabulary [and] turned reality on its head, first by re-interpreting deliberate acts of war as violence provoked by injustice, and then by importing ready-made the whole paraphernalia of the "oppressed minority."'[205] Civil government trembled under the pressure of these forces.[206] Elsewhere, he noted:

It is very human to search high and low for the remedy to our fears and troubles, and not to seek it in the most obvious and nearest place. So it is when people call for this measure and for that measure to counteract violence, and when governments are reduced to empty moralizing, while daily the words and deeds of those set in authority are an implicit accusation of society and condonation of the assaults upon it. Let government look within itself; it is there that the failing, and there that the remedy, will be found.[207]

Only from a realist perspective could the civil rights movement of Northern Ireland be reduced to *only* a power struggle between state and anti-state forces – wherein the reassertion of the legitimacy of the state came from the reassertion of its monopoly on power and violence.

Much like his rejection of the civilizing principles of the Commonwealth and Trevor Huddleston's Christian socialist activism against apartheid in South Africa, on Ulster, Powell continually criticized the translation of Christian teaching into radical political practice. In the early 1970s, a Catholic priest from Liverpool – a city with a large Irish community – started keeping Powell regularly informed of radical Irish priests' activities in the United Kingdom. Their correspondence began when the priest sent Powell a newspaper cutting from the *Catholic Pictorial* entitled, 'Why I, a priest, will risk prison,'[208] which

[203] J. Enoch Powell, 18 March 1972, Newham North East Conservative Association, cited in *Powellight*, March 1972. SRO D4490/51.
[204] Powell, *Still to Decide*, p. 19.
[205] Powell, *Reflections*, p. 182.
[206] Powell, *Still to Decide*, p. 34.
[207] J. Enoch Powell, 18 March 1972, Newham North East Conservative Association, cited in *Powellight*, March 1972. SRO D4490/51.
[208] 'Why I, a Priest, Will Risk Prison,' *Catholic Pictorial*, no date; Douglas Brice, Letter to Powell, 25 July 1971, 'Immigration Cases open at Feb 1974.' SRO D4490/4.

included an interview with a young radical priest named Father Sean McManus. Powell's informer wrote to Powell in the accompanying letter, 'This man Sean McManus has all the qualities of skilfulness that go to make an outstanding troublemaker, and there are many of his kind about.'[209] Powell quickly replied. The interview had touched a nerve: when asked, 'Does the division of Ireland, in your opinion then, contravene Christian rights?,' McManus had answered, 'Very definitely. The basic right of any country is to freedom and independence. It is a grave act of immorality that any country should be artificially divided, like Ireland, against the vast majority of the people.'[210] To this, Powell wrote to Brice, 'I was particularly struck by the expression, used in one of the questions, "Christian rights". The more one reflects upon it, the more profound and significant is the contradiction in terms.'[211]

Over the next two years, Powell's informer would continue to send information to Powell regarding radicalism in Britain's Irish Catholic community.[212] 'Let me make it perfectly clear,' he told Powell, 'an Irish Catholic clergyman would not think twice about giving active material assistance to the IRA. I have lived with the IRA for years.'[213] In 1972, less than a month after Bloody Sunday, Powell's informer wrote:

The hatred of these men is implacable, and as they do not appreciate being allowed to come to England and permitted to live here, I think – with I am sure, a lot of others – that the 'ever-open door' for which this country is well known, should now be closed, and that trouble-makers should either be sent home or issued with Passports ... At the moment they are like fleas in the mattress.[214]

Powell forwarded the priest's reports to a Detective Inspector Waller and, by 1973, the priest had become a police informant.

Again, Powell associated the problem of political violence with the enlargement of state-funded social services and the consequential translation of 'a want or need into a right.'[215] This was, in Powell's mind, the critical predicament of Britain's modern, liberal state: 'the unlimited role of the state provides unlimited fuel for dissatisfaction.' Again,

[209] Letter to Powell, 25 July 1971, 'Immigration Cases open at Feb 1974.' SRO D4490/4.
[210] 'Why I, a Priest, Will Risk Prison.' SRO D4490/4.
[211] Letter from Powell, 28 July 1971, 'Immigration Cases open at Feb 1974.' SRO D4490/4.
[212] Letter from Powell, 16 May 1972, 'Immigration Cases open at Feb 1974.' SRO D4490/4.
[213] Letter to Powell, 22 February 1972, 'Immigration Cases open at Feb 1974.' SRO D4490/4.
[214] Ibid.
[215] Powell, 27 September 1969, *Still to Decide*, p. 21.

authority had lost its good conscience; it has lost 'that conviction of its own rightness which is the very lifeblood of authority.'[216] Instead of compromises, negotiations or any apologetic approach, Ulster needed to be drawn ever more tightly into the very centre of the United Kingdom's political life. He opposed the continuation of the Stormont Parliament. Unlike many Unionists, he argued for the full participation of Ulster at Westminster. As he put it in 1972:

> I have for years advocated the genuine embodiment and parliamentary reunification of the six counties of Northern Ireland with Great Britain, believing that the separate administration and parliament which was forced upon the majority in Northern Ireland over fifty years ago, but which over the years they have come to see as a symbol not so much of their independence as of their union with the rest of the United Kingdom [Stormont] ... has nevertheless, in the last three or four years, turned to the opposite effect and become for them a cause of danger and a source of division. I believe, too, that such true reunification must eventually be the means of healing many of the underlying divisions in the six counties.[217]

By 1974, Powell had spent years speaking about the central importance of Ulster. In February 1974, he told his closest Ulster Unionist associate, Jim Molyneaux, that he would be prepared to consider the role of leader of the Ulster Unionists in Westminster.[218] Though Powell was not picked (Molyneaux himself took the role), he committed himself as a Unionist to the complete integration of Ulster into Westminster. But, in the years that followed, Powell found that the Unionist movement and Ulster identity could not so easily be harnessed towards these political ends. In this sense, the corollary of the white populism that he was able to momentarily channel in England in 1968 would not, in Ulster, produce popular support for complete parliamentary reunification. As Graham Walker put it, Powell 'could not fathom the ethno-nationalism' within Ulster Loyalism; his insistence on the need for unconditional allegiance and integration was, David Miller argues, 'a characteristically English formulation.'[219] Critically, as Paul Corthorn has convincingly revealed, Powell explicitly interpreted Ulster Loyalism as evidence of *British* nationalism: it was, as Powell put it, 'the assertion ... of British nationality, the claim to be party of a whole ... the

[216] Ibid.
[217] As quoted in Alistair Cooke, 'Enoch Powell and Ulster,' in Lord Howard of Rising (ed.), *Enoch at 100: A Re-evaluation of the Life, Politics and Philosophy of Enoch Powell* (London: Biteback Publishing, 2012), p. 257.
[218] Ibid., p. 261.
[219] As cited in Paul Corthorn, 'Enoch Powell, Ulster Unionism, and the British Nation,' *Journal of British Studies*, 51: 4 (October 2012), pp. 967–997 (p. 970).

British nation.'[220] When, in 1972 and 1973, a pressure group within the Unionist Party called the Vanguard Movement started calling for the semi-independence of Ulster and produced a publication entitled *Ulster – a Nation*, Powell emphatically rejected there was such a thing as 'an Ulster nationality' and argued that this would mean 'turning unionism into that denial of itself, isolationism.'[221] Similarly, in 1981, when James Callaghan proposed that Northern Ireland become 'a broadly independent state,' Powell discarded the idea as 'fantastic and wildly unreal.'[222]

The issue of devolution in Ulster, Scotland and Wales were symptoms, Powell believed, of a dying nation-state.[223] The devolution of power and the willingness to turn to the economic protection of Europe were signs of deep-seated political failure, much like the quiet apathy that marked Britain's response to the loss of the British Empire. As Powell put it to the Bromley Chamber of Commerce in 1976:

It is the nation that is dying, it is dying politically – or rather, perhaps, it is committing suicide politically – and the mark of death upon it is that it has lost the will to live. Wherever one looks, near or far, in small or great, one sees the same morphology: the nation is abdicating. Two thirds of the voters confirmed at a referendum the embodiment of this country in the EEC, which its principal advocates openly recommended on the ground that this country was no longer capable of being a nation state and that, indeed, for such countries as this the day of the nation state is over. It is too easy to pretend that the electorate 'knew not what they did.' The fact remains that to be a nation self-governed and self-taxed, living under its own laws and accepting no external authority, meant nothing to the majority of them. What their fathers and their remote ancestors had lived and died for they waved aside with less than a perfunctory sigh. The mirror-image of external abdication is internal abdication. As we no longer believe in the independence of the nation, we no longer believe in the unity of the nation.

And there it was. Powell named the crisis: this was a crisis of identity, a 'crisis of the nation's belief in its own existence.'[224] Despite the challenges of marshalling Ulster Unionism behind his cause, still it offered him, as he put it in 1977, 'living protest against the prevalent self-abasement of the British nation.'[225]

[220] Enoch Powell, speech at the Kelly Hall, Montpottinger, Belfast. POLL 9.1.20; Corthorn, 'Enoch Powell, Ulster Unionism, and the British Nation,' p. 972.
[221] As cited in Corthorn, 'Enoch Powell, Ulster Unionism, and the British Nation,' p. 975.
[222] Ibid.
[223] Andrew Roberts, 'Powell and the Nation State,' in Lord Howard of Rising (ed.), *Enoch at 100*, p. 138.
[224] As cited in Corthorn, 'Enoch Powell, Ulster Unionism, and the British Nation,' p. 977.
[225] Ibid.

A patron saint

In 1975, after winning the Conservative Party leadership election, Margaret Thatcher refused to offer Powell a seat in the Shadow Cabinet, because, she said, 'he turned his back on his own people' by leaving the party.[226] In June 1975, when Powell's campaign for a 'no' vote in the referendum on joining the European Community failed, one of Powell's long-time supporters, Bee Carthew, wrote to him. In the context of this moment of transition, the political trajectory of this long-time, middle-class supporter and editor of the *Powellight* newspaper is perhaps a telling indicator of the roots of Powell's popular support in England. She wrote:

> It seems very right and proper that I should be writing to you on the day of the Patron Saint of Lost Causes, for Pam told me you said it was 'terrible' for me to join the [National Front] ... Pam said you referred to democracy and said the Front was 'dangerous' (Boy, I wish it were!); well, as to democracy, has any party since the war included in an election manifesto the fact that they proposed to turn the United Kingdom into a multi-racial society? Not on your life! 'Democracy' appears to be one of those fair-weather friends.[227]

Carthew blames 'democracy' but keeps it in quotations:

> Chilean Marxists, unlimited Pakistani wives and dependents, the riff-raff of Europe, openly admitting to coming in straightway to squat and live on social security – boasting about it to journalists ... The other night, television showed the inside of the block of condemned houses where the recently sentenced Irish bombers were living before their arrest – 'squatting,' of course. Those houses are still full of other Irish labourers, squatting in the filth and peering suspiciously into the cameras. I suppose it's 'democracy' that allows them to stay there till they're ready to bomb someone else. It seems to me that 'democracy' has turned this country into the dustbin in Europe's backyard.

The careful use of quotations implies that Britain's 'democracy' was corrupted. It is perhaps a nod to Powell and to six years of work promoting his arguments. Still, though, at the end of the letter, we see her less concerned with the prospects of democracy and entirely embracing the racialization of politics:

> The so-called Right Wingers ... are so taken up with their economic theories that they wouldn't notice if the whole country became khaki-coloured so long as everybody worshipped Hayek, whether in or out of the Common Market. Well, in my early teens I was an overseas member of the Fascist League and

---

[226] Heffer, *Like the Roman*, p. 747.
[227] Letter to Powell, 28 October 1975. POLL 1.1.23A.

a member of the Croix de Feu. I suppose it's something like malaria, once in your blood stream it cannot be removed.

In 1973, Carthew had been expelled from the Monday Club.[228] That year, the Monday Club executive became concerned that members of the National Front were taking over branches of the Club; bad publicity led to a crisis that culminated in a series of purges of Club branches. Already, by 1973, divisions within the radical right were cementing. In 1975, Bee Carthew found her political home with the National Front. Again, Carthew's apartment– what had once been the headquarters of the Powellight association – would by 1976 become the address of a West London branch of the National Front. We can assume from this that Carthew became active, at least for a short while, in National Front activism, perhaps attending for instance London's 'March Against Mugging' in September 1975 which carried the slogan 'Stop The Muggers. 80% of muggers are black. 85% of victims are white.'[229]

Powell's reply to Carthew's confession a few days after her letter was written was diplomatic. He would never describe anything she had done as 'terrible,' he protested. Nor did he think that the National Front was dangerous. 'My point,' he explained, 'has always been that by abandoning the attempt or the hope of influencing those who form or might form a majority in the House of Commons and joining an organisation which has no present representation, there is little prospect of it; one is by implication rejecting parliamentary government itself in favour of some other kind. As you know, I am obstinately – perhaps thickly – parliamentarian.'[230] He did not expect her to feel the same: 'Politically and legally speaking, the sovereign to whom I consider myself as owing allegiance is the Crown in Parliament. It is a prejudice in which I have lived + intend to die; but the thing about a prejudice is that one has no right to expect one's friends to share it!'[231] The implication here is perhaps that he, also, did not share her prejudices. At no point, however, in Powell's two huge archives have I come across a moment when Powell, in any letter, reprimands or even critiques someone's blatantly racist views. There were many opportunities to do so.

For all the protestations that Powell's arguments were about saving democracy and not about race, racism was without doubt the energetic source of Powell's support. His supporters' concerns about social disorder and 'national decline' would continue to be inflected by

[228] Letter to Powell, 17 July 1973
[229] Gilroy, *There Ain't No Black in the Union Jack*, p. 155.
[230] Letter from Powell, 2 November 1975. POLL 1.1.23A.
[231] Ibid.

the memories of war and empire, replete with visions of a lost white, male authority, well into the 1980s. One extreme example of the way in which the memories of war, British imperial power, and 'law and order' were entwined is in the revealing hobby of one prison officer, M. G. Crosby.[232] Crosby worked at Brixton prison as a dog handler. He had made his home, which was close to the prison, into something of a mini-museum: it contained a special collection of 9,500 items, containing caps and badges from prison services in Europe, the United States and Japan, 600 military insignias, and 'top brass' from Lord Carrington, Auchinleck, Montgomery, and others. Crosby's mini-museum was an expression, he explained, of his pride 'in our military history, they built the Empire.'[233] After his collection appeared in a couple of issues of a national prison journal, he told Powell in 1972 that he hoped to add Powell to the VIP collection, with a tunic button or an insignia.[234] Crosby insisted that, 'even in this day and age, there are still many who take great pride in this heritage, history and military traditions.'[235] A few years later in 1975, after Powell agreed to donate to the collection, Crosby wrote: 'You are no doubt fully aware that 99.9% of us Prison Officers and Police Constables regard you as our "Patron Saint." Our voices are gagged through the Official Secrets Acts and Codes of Conduct, but you say what we think and feel and we all hope you will continue to do so.'[236] Powell sent Crosby his tunic buttons and became a member of Crosby's VIP 'Rogues Gallery.'[237] That year, when the Metropolitan Police reported to the Select Committee on Race Relations and Immigration that: 'Experience has taught us the fallibility of the assertion that crime rates amongst those of West Indian origin are no higher than those of the population at large,' Powell enthused: 'Splendidly expressed! Beautifully expressed!'[238]

Remarkably, as is well documented in the archive of the Staffordshire Record Office, Powell remained a 'patron saint' for many individuals in Britain well into the 1980s. Despite his turn to Ulster Unionism and even after the Conservative Party took power in 1979, the motto 'Enoch was right' continued to serve as a means to express social and political discontent. When 'race' hit the headlines in 1981, we see, again, something of the character of Powell's popular support.

[232] M. G. Crosby's name has been changed to maintain anonymity.
[233] Letter to Powell, 11 March 1972. POLL 1.1.23A.
[234] Ibid.
[235] Letter to Powell, 6 October 1971. POLL 1.1.23A.
[236] Letter to Powell, 28 June 1975. POLL 1.1.23A.
[237] Ibid.
[238] J. Enoch Powell, April 1976, in *Reflections of a Statesman*, p. 562.

In January of that year, thirteen black teenagers died in a house fire in New Cross, South London; the local black community was dismayed by the seeming indifference of the police and the press towards these deaths and, consequently, 15,000 people marched in London demanding further investigation into the case and against the embedded racism of the Metropolitan Police Force. This was the largest protest Britain had yet seen on the issue of racial equality. That month, too, saw the opening of parliamentary debates on the first British Nationality Bill since 1948; the consequence of a Conservative Party promise 'to end immigration as we have known it in the post-war years.'[239] As tension mounted in the subsequent weeks, Powell argued that a racial 'civil war' was imminent and warned a group of Young Conservatives: 'We have seen nothing yet.'[240] In April 1981, riots against the police broke out in the largely Afro-Caribbean community of Brixton. The whole of Britain was, in 1981, affected by a recession, but Brixton suffered particularly from high unemployment, poor housing, drug abuse and a higher than average crime rate. True to its word as the party of 'law and order,' the Conservative government had instituted new powers for the police under the Vagrancy Act of 1824, which allowed them to stop, search and potentially arrest any person under suspicion of criminal activity. In the lead-up to the riot, there was therefore growing unease between the police and the people of Brixton; many felt that they were being unfairly targeted by this 'sus' law. What emerged was not, then, a 'race riot' between black and white communities, but a riot against the police and a rejection of the moral legitimacy of 'law and order.'

As the days of rioting wore on, Ted Knight, Lambeth's Labour council leader, referred to the police as 'almost an army of occupation within the borough.'[241] Apocalyptic visions dominated the news. On the main day of rioting, 11 April, there were 280 injuries to police and 45 to members of the public, hundreds of vehicles burned and 150 buildings damaged. Reports would later suggest that up to 5,000 people in the area were involved. Labour MPs, such as Shadow Home Secretary Roy Hattersley, insisted that the root of the riots was not race but the conditions of deprivation and despair in the city: the problem was poor housing, education and unemployment. Still, the riots of 1981, in London, as well as Birmingham, Liverpool and Leeds, are definitively remembered as 'racial events.' [242] As Gilroy notes, given that in

[239] Zig Layton-Henry, 'Race and the Thatcher Government,' in Layton-Henry and Rich (eds.), *Race, Government and Politics in Britain*, pp. 73–99 (p. 91).
[240] 'Brixton Streets Boil for Fourth Night,' *The Times*, 14 April 1981.
[241] Ibid.
[242] Gilroy, *There Ain't No Black in the Union Jack*, p. 26.

fact a minority (between 29 per cent and 33 per cent) of those arrested in the 1981 riots were non-white, it is essential to consider the wider purchase of this vision of black social disorder.[243] In the Postscript, we will look to government policies that emerged in response to these conflicts. Unsurprisingly, Powell immediately called for a massive campaign of voluntary repatriation. For our purposes here, it is important to note that Thatcher's government did not roll out any such campaign. Instead, at the party political level, the 'racial threat' had come to be viewed as both an internal 'social problem' and, as Paul Rich argues, in more 'generalised international terms' with parallels drawn from both the United States and the postcolonial world.[244] Again, as Powell insisted in 1970, ethnic difference was presented as a threatening source of 'disorder' and a weapon that could be harnessed in support of socialist revolution. Still, Powell argued that it was not too late, repatriation was still possible. With this, Powell could endure as the 'patron saint' or martyr for those who remained committed to repatriation, committed to the illusory certainty and stability of an England without difference. By 1981, we see the words of an ageing generation in the letters Powell received. We also see loss, fear and bigotry.

One woman speaks of her isolation as an older woman in what she calls the present 'grab and shove society.'[245] She speaks of a feeling of 'unbelonging,' of being 'clutter' and of having to 'get the hell out of the way' in the 'perfected and engineered melting pot.'[246] She links 'race' to what she perceives as the atomization of British society. The black Briton here is no longer just the scapegoat of an undemocratic and authoritarian state, as we saw in 1968, he is now the *cause* of rampant individualism and declining social cohesion: 'It seems to have all gone to a free for all attitude,' in which people assume that, 'if we can't ... beat 'em. and must accept 'em,' then we must be 'allowed to TURN on each OTHER!!' Her experience of loneliness is present throughout: 'Relative to relative or friend to friend or neighbour to neighbour or parent to child may well take out the feeling not allowed to surface as "racial."' Again, 'race' serves as a means to understand the breakdown of social networks and, in this woman's case, increasing isolation.

This letter-writer makes no mention of an exact economic or social policy but insists that the state had, over the years, placed 'coloured

[243] Ibid.
[244] Rich, 'Conservative Ideology and Race in Modern British Politics,' in Layton-Henry and Rich (eds.), *Race, Government and Politics in Britain*, p. 60.
[245] Letter to Powell, 1 April 1981, Surrey SRO D4490/10.
[246] Ibid.

priorities' before training young people as 'plumbers or carpenters or vital electricians,' such that the 'young' had become the unemployed and alienated 'punks.' Economic individualism had come before the nation: consequently, the black 'immigrant' 'will beat an ex-service ailing man' in 'market status.' Again, a distant memory of warfare and social equity is offered to Powell: the '[r]eal truth of the 30s and war is ever more silenced.' Britain has witnessed 'the loss of hospitality, warmth, trust, sincerity which kept our SPIRITS up in WAR.' Compared with those who wrote to Powell in 1968, her recollections of war certainly appear more nostalgic and solidified as a moment of 'happier times.' But, alongside this, she insists: 'It was BIGOT feeling which led my father and uncles and grandfather to be the troops [of the Boer War] and dream ... of their cottage garden [and] markets.' This spirit of warfare and that nostalgia for home is hidden from the 'punks,' she argues, 'KILLED OFF VIA A RACE RELATIONS BOARD!' As in 1968, patriotism and racism are envisioned as one and the same. And the meaning of war service is again rewritten.

Rather than merely representing a threat to declining welfare provisions, the 'immigrant' had become the cause of social atomization, an alienated youth and her own feelings of physical and economic vulnerability. This woman's words, thirteen years after the 'Rivers of Blood' speech, speak to the remarkable persistence of race as a way of understanding social change, as a means of living through economic crisis. After the outbreak of the Brixton riots, Powell again received a stream of letters much as he had done in 1968, though by no means of the same quantity. Here, alongside the expected references to those threatened 'freedoms' fought for in the Second World War, we see explicit parallels drawn between Britain and apartheid in South Africa and the racial order of Australia – again, perhaps indicating that the 'racial threat,' as Rich argues, was now viewed in 'generalised international terms.'[247] But, remarkably, in these letters it appears that the 'disorder' of racial difference is imagined as somehow absent from the once colonial terrain. One seventy-seven-year-old man wrote of his fear in the streets and, offering a picture of racial order in the colonial world against the disorder of race at home, noted that a 'multi-racial society is a fine idea in Penrith [Australia] where the tribes come in from the fells with their sheep. It is quite different in parts of London where white people cannot go out alone by day or night.'[248] Another retired writer offered

---

[247] Rich, 'Conservative Ideology and Race in Modern British Politics,' in Layton-Henry and Rich (eds.), *Race, Government and Politics in Britain*, p. 60.
[248] Letter to Powell, 17 April 1981. SRO D4490/10.

a suggestion: evacuation. Echoing that 'man on the street' quoted in the 'Rivers of Blood' speech who spoke of leaving Britain to escape the 'whip hand' of the black man, this writer insists that the British Government should ask 'our English speaking white Commonwealth countries to accept us as vaccuees [sic] until our country [has] been ridden of its undesirable people and [is] safe for us to return.'[249] Certainty and stability can be found, these men imply, in the racial orders of the colonies; whiteness could be retrieved there in the Australian suburbs.

Conclusion

The war that Powell waged in the 1970s was in essence a war to assert the political primacy and legitimate authority of the sovereign nation-state. Powell employed the language of war because, there in war, civil society's dependency on state power could be revealed – wherein internal peace is codependent and coterminous with the ability to wield external violence. As T. E. Utley put it in an early study, Powell espoused, 'the inevitability of conflict between nations and men and, in certain fields, the positive fruitfulness of such conflict.'[250] Above all, Powell believed that through war a people could know themselves. The Second World War served as the central symbolic referent of this truth throughout Powell's political life.

As Powell's arguments on the international New Left and diaspora politics reveal, Powell failed to recognize a fundamental transformation in the postwar era. He denied the validity of an international community or civil society, beyond the nation-state. For all of Powell's preoccupation with the Second World War, he failed, in this sense, to recognize one of the most profound legacies of the war. In 1948, Britain signed the United Nations Universal Declaration of Human Rights. Two years later, Britain became the first signatory state of the European Convention on Human Rights. Crucially, Powell argued that the acceptance of international human rights or European law requires the threat of enforcement – or imperialistic force against a sovereign state. For Powell, sovereignty came before all else despite the fact that the genocide of war had brought to the forefront the central problem of the 'realist' perspective: the refugee denied sovereignty.

Powell's 'realism' in the face of transnational social and political movements can be drawn as an adamant post-imperialism. Simon Heffer

---

[249] Letter to Powell, 27 April 1981. SRO D4490/10.
[250] T. E. Utley, *Enoch Powell, the Man and His Thinking* (London: William Kimber, 1968), p. 53.

explains that Powell's opposition to British sanctions against Rhodesia, for instance, was not Powell the 'white supremacist defending a racialist regime; this was Powell the vigorous post-imperialist.'[251] Again, for Powell, political action that appealed to any form of internationalism, whether a protest on the ground or in the General Assembly of the UN, always involved an imperialistic paternalism and always involved the threat of force. These views were no doubt marked by a cynical view of the relationship between internationalism and American power. However, Powell's rejection of human rights and his assertion that there must be no compromise on the sovereignty of the nation-state left him incapable of envisaging protests against the Vietnam War, the activities of Ulster Republicans or the international vision of black British radicals as anything other than seeds of destruction. International law and European unification, likewise, could only make sense to Powell as weaponless acts of war.

At the height of Powell's popularity in the early 1970s, Powell drew a mass following from across the social spectrum. He offered an enduring picture of a nation in crisis. In 1974, Powell sought national political revival, another 'populist moment,' in opposition to membership in the European Community. He insisted that the Conservative Party must represent the sovereign nation before business or economic interests. On this subject, however, the people and his party were a disappointment: in 1975, the first referendum of the twentieth century supported Britain's continued membership. In many ways, in Ulster, Powell found what he believed he had been looking for. There, he found the nation and the question of sovereignty taken 'daily, almost hourly – with Ulster and its interest and its future, its safety and its place within the Union, never absent an instant from our minds.'[252] Powell's service in Northern Ireland was marked by a commitment to bringing Ulster into complete integration with the British Parliament. Unfortunately for Powell, the Unionist cause could not so easily be harnessed in support of the British state.

Ironically, despite Powell's wholesale rejection of diaspora politics, his words on the 'nation' became part of a further globalization of race politics after 1968. Just as anti-racist demonstrators turned to the language of the American Black Power movement, Powell's status as a man who stood against the 'oppression' of white people resulted in multiple tours to South Africa, Australia and the American South. Powell gained

---

[251] Heffer, *Like the Roman*, p. 535.
[252] J. Enoch Powell, Meeting of the Banbridge Branch of the South Down Unionist Association, Banbridge, Co. Down, 22 April 1976. POLL 4.1.12.

notoriety as a vocal far-right politician and an intellectual heavyweight for the cause of white racism. For instance, in 1971, Dr Roger Pearson, a former British Indian Army officer and an ethnographer in the anthropology department at the University of Southern Mississippi, helped arrange a speaking tour for Powell of New Orleans, Louisiana and Jackson, Mississippi.[253] The tour was subsidized by the White Citizens' Council, which had in the previous decade worked to maintain racial segregation in Mississippi. In Jackson, Powell met 'leading personalities' including some Superior Court judges. The timing of the visit was not coincidental: the state desegregated its schools in 1970–1971. This meeting was, however, kept quiet, because – Pearson warned – the national press might attempt to 'misinterpret' Powell's visit to the state capital of Mississippi. Avoiding controversy was essential: campaigners had just won a US Supreme Court verdict that entitled the city to close down swimming pools rather than integrate them.[254] Further emphasizing the explicit connections drawn across the national boundaries of white racism, Pearson sent Powell a year-long subscription to the white South African paper *Behind the News*, in thanks for his tour of the American South.

Powell's 'Rivers of Blood' speech has been defined as Britain's first 'postcolonial moment' when 'decolonization and its ethnic consequences were first publicly recognized as a popular issue, of historical significance for white as well as black.'[255] But Britain's postcolonial character was not solely – or, one could argue, predominantly – defined by the presence and activities of ethnic communities in Britain. Critically, by the mid-1970s, the consequences of immigration were widely read through the lens of global protest, the miners' strike and – most of all – through the lens of Ulster. It was in this context that memories of empire were most clearly articulated.

Even though the dust eventually settled on Brixton, and no civil war exploded in its wake, Powell's warnings of national dissolution have continued to serve as a way of understanding social unrest and political violence in Britain. Whether it be in the context of the London bombings of 2007 or the urban riots of 2012, Powell's racialized picture of a lost nation is never far from the television analyst's lips. In this sense, he remains the patron saint of lost causes.

---

[253] For files relating to Powell's speaking tour of the American South, see 'United States Tour, 1971–72.' POLL 10.6 A.

[254] Letter to Powell from Roger Pearson, 20 June 1971. POLL 10.6 A.

[255] Bill Schwarz, 'Decolonizing England,' paper delivered at University of Michigan, 10 February 2000, as cited in Ritscherle, 'Opting out of Utopia,' p. 286.

Conclusion: postcolonial Britain

> If the nation into which I was born is what I believe it to be, nothing
> can prevent it from sooner or later re-asserting itself. I was wrong
> when I despaired of this in 1938. I will not make the same mistake at
> the end of my life as I made at the beginning.
>
> Enoch Powell, 1992[1]

The slogan 'Enoch was Right' still today carries considerable political
weight. In November 2007, Nigel Hastilow, a Tory candidate for a seat
in the West Midlands, was forced to resign after invoking the slogan
in an article in a local newspaper. Former Deputy Labour Leader Roy
Hattersley noted in 2008 that one cannot speak of immigration control after 1968 without fearing the 'ghost of Powell.'[2] Historian David
Starkey's startling assertion after the English summer riots of 2011 that
Enoch Powell was 'absolutely right' seems to indicate that Powell's particular apocalyptic vision still informs understandings of social change
and uncertainty in Britain.[3]

In 2008 two BBC broadcasts were aired to commemorate the forti-
eth anniversary of the 'Rivers of Blood' speech. One was on Radio 4;
the other, an hour-long documentary, was on BBC2. In contrast to the
media reception of Powell's arguments in 1968, both were remarkably
sympathetic to Powell. Denys Blakeway's BBC2 documentary was a
part of the 'White' season on BBC2 – the season's aim was to uncover
Britain's white working-class culture. Its trailer is itself remarkable. It
shows a series of brown hands scrawling messages in foreign languages
upon the face of a white man. In the background Billy Bragg sings out
a call for the building of a New Jerusalem. Eventually the man's face
is covered in so much ink that he can no longer be seen against the

---

[1] Enoch Powell on Britain joining the European Union. Enoch Powell, 'Preface,' *Enoch Powell on 1992*, p. xiii.

[2] As cited in Denys Blakeway, *Rivers of Blood* (BBC television documentary, 2008).

[3] As cited in Chris Hastings, '"White Chavs Have Become Black": David Starkey TV Outburst Provokes Race Row as He Claims Enoch Powell Was Right,' *Daily Mail*, 11 August 2011.

black background – the trailer then asks, 'Is the white working class becoming invisible?'[4] The clear implication here is that it is immigrants who are to blame for white working-class invisibility. Even more, the utopian promises of social democracy (that postwar New Jerusalem) appear to be marred by their presence. Britain's existential crisis, that postwar transformation in social values, continues to be understood as the encroachment of black culture.

The *Rivers of Blood* documentary begins and ends with imagery of the bombed London bus, attacked on 7 July 2005, with the pending question, was Enoch Powell right to predict disaster? We are presented, in this documentary, with Powell as Britain's very own Samuel Huntington – a brilliant, though flawed, prophet of the so-called clash of civilizations. He is described as a man who dared to speak up, a man who, according to Lord Hurd, had the 'gift of prophet utterance.'[5] Conservative philosopher Roger Scruton describes Powell as a man who was above all interested in truth over political strategy – and in taking truth to its logical conclusion. The Brixton riots in the early 1980s as well as the riots in Bradford in 2001 are taken – alongside current Islamic radicalism in Britain – as indicating that, indeed, Enoch Powell was right. As Powell's official biographer Simon Heffer actually put it, the current political tensions in Britain 'validate' Powell's argument in 1968.[6] There was widespread criticism of Blakeway's BBC2 documentary – much of which argued that it failed to account for the successes of multicultural Britain.[7] The documentary gave the impression that Britain was on the brink of apocalypse. Clearly, though, to accept that there has been racism and division in Britain is not the same as accepting them, like Powell did, as the logic by which to live. Forty years after the 'Rivers of Blood' speech, we must do more than simply call Powell a Nazi or argue over the accuracy of Powell's predictions. Rather, we must work to understand Powell's place in the long historical relationship between liberal democracy, war and racism.

Robert Shepherd's Radio 4 broadcast, which promised to reveal the 'real tributaries' of Powell's 'Rivers of Blood' speech, took as its foundation the academic work of Peter Brooke.[8] The real source of

---

[4] 'BBC's White Season is Founded on Racist Lies,' *Socialist Worker*, vol. 2091, 8 March 2008.

[5] Quoted in Blakeway, *Rivers of Blood*.

[6] Ibid.

[7] Martin O'Neill, 'Echoes of Enoch,' *New Statesman*, 10 March 2008.

[8] Robert Shepherd, 'The Real Tributaries of Enoch's "Rivers of Blood,"' *The Spectator*, 27 February 2008.

Enoch Powell's 'Rivers of Blood' speech was the bloodshed of post-independence India. According to Shepherd, Powell was forever scarred by the nightmare of post-independence violence in the Punjab. Brooke's characterization of Powell as forever the liberal – and one-time liberal imperialist – has been distilled for public consumption by Shepherd into Powell as a scarred and pathetic figure, a casualty of empire. It is Powell's love for India and sympathy for Indians that explains his desire to keep Britain white. He does not want history to repeat itself; even more, he would not disrespect Indian cultures by assuming that they could become *part* of a wider British culture. We are reminded here of Slavoj Zizek's warning that today the word 'immigrant' has replaced the term 'worker' and that this transition has taken place within a 'reflected racism' that 'is paradoxically able to articulate itself in terms of direct *respect* for the other's culture ... I know very well that the Other's culture is worthy of the same respect as my own: nevertheless ... [I] despise them passionately.'[9]

Shepherd's construction echoes a particularly telling epitaph that appeared in 1998, on the occasion of Powell's death, in Australia's national daily newspaper *The Australian*:

[Powell] argued that humans are tribal, maybe not actually using that word ... Powell went back to a childhood in India where his parents were part of the British Raj. He spoke with moving affection of the Indian servants who were his companions – and the nearest thing he had to friends. Those piercing eyes misted over ever so slightly as he looked back on a loneliness by his own admission made bearable by the sort of people he wanted to expel from England. He acknowledged the irony of it all and it troubled him deeply. He said he loved India. He admired and respected the Indian people. And I believed him. This was no 'some of my best friends' routine. The ice man had a heart, after all, and he was speaking from it.[10]

Television writer Graham Coddington's portrayal here is, of course, entirely untrue. Powell spent no childhood in India. He was a Birmingham boy. However, in Coddington's fabricated universe we see an echo of the same pathetic imperial figure that appeared in Shepherd's Radio 4 broadcast. Powell's eyes mist over: his only friends were his Indian servants. He was a child of imperialism. Like a TV drama, Powell becomes an innocent and abandoned English schoolboy alone in the empire. The drama of Powell's loss of those Indian servants re-enacts the drama of Britain's loss of the imperial family. No doubt, we

[9] Slavoj Zizek, *The Fragile Absolute, Or, Why the Christian Heritage is Worth Fighting For* (London: Verso, 2000), pp. 6–10.
[10] Graham Coddington, 'Getting to Know Mr. Right,' *The Australian*, 25 February 1998.

are led to believe that Powell's psychological damage and Powell's ironic position are Britain's too. Shepherd's discussion of Powell, though historically more accurate, threatens to leave us with the same uncritical and self-consoling vision of Powell's views on race.

Coddington met Powell during Powell's first visit to Australia since the Second World War. At this time, in December 1973, Powell was flush with public attention. In a matter of weeks, on his return from Australia, Powell would tell his constituency to vote Labour due to the Conservative Party's EEC policy. A recent opinion poll in Britain had shown him to be well ahead of Heath in public popularity.[11] He was a regular on British television, speaking out against inflationary economic policy, Britain's nationality law and entry into the EEC. On this short visit to Australia, Powell was to give a series of television interviews in Sydney on the political situation in the United Kingdom. As a television writer, Coddington arranged a television debate on immigration between Enoch Powell and Australia's Minister for Immigration, Albert Grassby. That year, the racially discriminatory aspects of Australia's Migration Act 1958 had been officially overturned. Albert Grassby initiated these reforms and introduced national 'multicultural' policy in Australia. While Australia certainly has its own homegrown racial politics, the meaning of race and belonging in Australia has no doubt been informed by a British imperial past.[12] 'White Australia Policy,' the legislation and policy in place between 1901 and 1973 that was intended to restrict non-white immigration into Australia and promote European immigration, was – as Deborah Gare notes – 'associated and constructed by [a] sense of Britishness.'[13] After the Second World War, and paralleling Australia's political separation from the United Kingdom, this avowed Britishness of Australia was gradually 'contested, questioned, challenged, and eroded, until by [Prime Minister] Gough Whitlam's term in office in the 1970s it was publicly denounced and dethroned.'[14]

---

[11] Heffer, *Like the Roman*, p. 690.
[12] See, for instance, the presence of the Union Jack (alongside the Confederate flag) among anti-immigrant rioters in the 2005 Cronulla race riots in suburban Sydney and the subsequent call to take the Union Jack out of the Australian flag. 'In the Calm of Day, a Little Contemplation on the Beach,' *The Age* (Melbourne: 13 December 2005); 'Aussie Flag Ban Hits the Political Fan,' *Northern Territory News* (25 January 2007); 'Letters,' *Sydney Morning Herald*' (15 December 2005): 'In the aftermath of the battle of Cronulla, is it time to have another look at changing our national flag? The de facto symbol used by the 'yobbos' was the current Australian flag. One has to admit it is a pretty Anglo symbol. Does it really represent Australia anymore?'
[13] Deborah Gare, 'Britishness in Recent Australian Historiography,' *Historical Journal*, 43: 4 (2000), pp. 1145–1155 (p. 1146).
[14] Ibid.

While in Sydney in late 1973 and early 1974, Powell in television interviews discussed his prospects for the leadership of the Conservative Party and attacked Prime Minister Gough Whitlam (a student of his while in Sydney), for comparing the regime in South Africa to Hitler's Germany.[15] In that political climate, Coddington remembers:

> Grassby was colourful, eloquent, persuasive, emotional and on the side of the angels. Powell, on the other hand, argued the indefensible with paralyzing word power. He was on the side of the Right and the righteous, picking every word with seamless precision to make a case for retaining a society that, in reality, never existed ... He yearned for the mythical Anglo-Saxon England of days gone by.[16]

The debate left Coddington 'feeling uneasy, even angry.'[17] He was relieved, after Powell asked him and his wife to dinner, to meet the softer side of Enoch Powell. Powell had, it seemed, 'unbuckled the granite exterior with which he faced an often hostile world. He talked for hours. We sat around a small table in his hotel room and just listened.[18] And there, so Coddington's story goes, did Powell's eyes mist over at the thought of the Indian servants of his childhood. This was, of course, merely a slip in Coddington's memory. Powell's eyes may have misted over for the India he knew while there in the British Army during the war. He may have recalled the tall, solemn Poonchi servant in Dehra Dun who, Powell noted in 1983, 'on the day I left India for home burst ... into tears which trickled slowly down his long henna-dyed beard'; he may have remembered the sadness of saying goodbye to his Urdu teacher, a man of Panipat, a poet himself and nephew of one of the greatest Urdu poets.[19] All these are part of the myth Powell created for himself, a myth of his empire, which he bore with him for the rest of his life.

Despite their differences, the saccharine sentimentalism of both stories – Coddington's and Powell's – surely has a political meaning. The loved and loving servant or the grateful colonial figure serve to humanize his master. The impulse to soften Powell's image in 1998, at his death, was not unique to Coddington. The sad and unthreatening, the morally redeemable, ageing conservative politician is a recurring political figure.[20] Humanizing Powell and those who made up his

---

[15] Heffer, *Like the Roman*, p. 691.
[16] Graham Coddington, 'Getting to Know Mr. Right,' *The Australian*, 25 February 1998.
[17] Ibid.   [18] Ibid.
[19] Enoch Powell, 'A Passage to India,' *Folio* (Summer 1983), pp. 15–22 (p. 17), in POLL 6.2.2.
[20] See, for instance, Dan T. Carter, *The Politics of Rage: George Wallace, the Origins of New Conservatism and the Transformation of American Politics* (New York: Simon and Schuster, 1995).

324   Conclusion: postcolonial Britain

public support is indeed a necessary and productive step on the road to understanding the roots of his political power. But the way in which these narratives have increasingly been used to transform Powell into a flawed idealist and tireless defender of the purity of representative democracy have worked to empty actually existing Powellism of much of its vital historical content – content that for Powell himself was far more central than abstractions such as equality, or even democracy.

For all the pleasure of new insight into the 'real tributaries' of Powell's 'Rivers of Blood' speech, we cannot, decades on, resurrect Powell as a well-meaning, though scarred, liberal imperialist and blind ourselves to the unmistakable racist consequences of his political beliefs. Nor can we stick to the argument that Powell's racism was a consequence of a romantic essentialism of England, due again to the trauma of the loss of empire. If Powell's politics is to inform us of anything, it is that it leaves us with the image of a man taking sides with Sharpeville's police force in 1960 or the landlord's 'whites only' sign – for the sake of the rule of law above all else. In other words, Powell's support for repatriation, his inability to view the black immigrant as anything other than a foreign 'disease' that threatened 'British civilization,' his use of intensely violent and militaristic imagery and language must be confronted. Finally his refusal to clearly distance himself from directly racist supporters and groupings was not peripheral to or an unfortunate consequence of Powell's thinking. Rather, these notions stand at the centre of Powell's vision of a world in a state of perpetual war.

Defence of Powell as 'right' cannot be separated from the acceptance of his vision of 'colour as a uniform' and blackness as *the* root cause of civil disturbance within British society. Powell and, even more, the violence against black Britons that his words inspired is a 'ghost' that casts a shadow over policy discussions about immigration. He is someone to be avoided. But he is still, importantly, seen by many as an intellectual heavyweight. He, among others, offered Britons a new myth: that their society was in a state of perpetual existential crisis. Like Powell, David Starkey's words do not rely on a biologically determined view of race but certainly on the belief that a particular culture of black masculinity stands as the cause of the 2011 English summer riots: one which is and forever will be, essentially, foreign. There appears in Starkey's eyes to be no cosmopolitanism, no hybridity, no exchange. Rather, the riotous city of 2011 has fallen. Englishness has surrendered; whites have become black.[21] The 'alien malaise' of global capitalism seems to

[21] As cited in Chris Hastings, '"White Chavs Have Become Black": David Starkey TV Outburst Provokes Race Row as He Claims Enoch Powell Was Right,' *Daily Mail*, 11 August 2011.

be manifest in the looting for African-American styles by the British-born boy and girl. The real threat to England is, as he described it, the 'violent, destructive, nihilistic, "gangsta" culture' of the African and West Indian black male.[22] The word 'nihilistic' is perhaps most significant in this description as it implies a culture without culture, a threat without promises, a nation without a future. Again, what is not white is anarchy.

Perhaps memories of empire inform such views; at very least, for Powell, the *experience* of empire underlined the essential fragility of any political order. Prior to and during the Second World War, Powell was marked by a belief in Britain's imperial role. It was at this time that the 'inevitability' of the empire, of British rule, was 'strongly borne in upon' him.[23] Powell found his role as an Englishman, in India at least, sanctioned by history and the social order. But, as this book has suggested, the limits of Powell's vision of legitimate imperial rule were there from the start. As is clear in the hundreds of letters Powell sent home while abroad in the empire, Powell's imperial belief was tempered by a deep cynicism towards the new world. The 'web of understood relationships which sustains society'[24] could not be so easily constructed. In many ways, it was through the empire that Powell developed a Tory perspective on the interdependent relationship between culture and power and the fragility of the nation.

Through Powell, we see in British decolonization the unravelling of imperial rationalizations. The (Tory) belief in divinely ordained natural order and the (liberal) ideal of a world remade in the likeness of Europe could no longer be held in productive tension. Powell's revolt against the direction of the Conservative Party in the era of British decolonization makes clear that it is impossible to understand the ending of the British Empire outside of the context of the Cold War and new international pressures within this 'moral' war. Here, the New Commonwealth, in Powell's mind, represented an effort to reconstruct what was once an ordered system of rule into a Cold War project. He argued against the notion that British decolonization could be rewritten as a liberal, Cold War crusade. Echoing a religious divide – that of a community rooted in ritual versus a community of belief – Powell opposed those who argued that a shared commitment to human rights or democratic governance could constitute a political community.

---

[22] David Starkey, 'The 2011 English Summer Riots Revisited,' *The Telegraph*, 5 August 2012.
[23] 'JEP War Memories.' POLL 5.1.
[24] J. Enoch Powell, Bill Schwarz interview, 26 April 1988.

Many of Powell's postwar arguments concerning sovereignty and the limits of the state and nation can, then, be viewed as a product of the Cold War. It was not only communism – or what he preferred to call the 'Soviet empire'[25] – that threatened Britain. As Powell put it in 1965:

This generation which now has twice narrowly escaped destruction at the hands of a [German] military empire which possessed only a private, nationalistic creed. We cannot take lightly the danger of military empires armed with an ideology that claims appeal to all mankind.[26]

This applied to both Soviet and American imperialism. In later years, he would go so far as to argue that the unrest in Northern Ireland was, at root, a consequence of American interests. The American political order, Powell insisted, contained no concept of the nation. According to Powell, 'the flag had followed trade' in the British Empire, but under the American Empire there was no flag – or sovereign authority – there was only ideology. Connected to this, Powell believed that race riots in the United States stemmed, in large part, from the intrinsic failure of the United States as an organic community – a social order must be based in hierarchy rather than ideals. With his eye to the civil rights movement in the United States, Powell viewed Britain's 1968 anti-discrimination law, which did in fact borrow from recent anti-discrimination laws in the United States, as a totalitarian infiltration and regulation of everyday life.

When questioned about race, Powell insisted that it was historical consciousness, more than race, language or geography, that constituted a political community. It was a shared past and the expectation of a shared future – rather than shared belief – that constituted the nation. But, crucially, 'race' carries history. The black Briton made visible the violence and failures of the British past and promised to further contribute to what Worsthorne called, the 'kill[ing] of the class system.'[27] Transnational memories and the consequent suspicion which surrounded the loyalties of those who carried them threatened to disrupt the narrative of Britain as a peaceable kingdom. Further, the presence of black British communities in the metropole, in Powell's mind, disordered the hierarchical whole by putting at the centre of British identity the 'hubris' of British (liberal) imperialism. Immigration from the New Commonwealth represented to Powell and his supporters a continued

[25] J. Enoch Powell, 'To the Brighton Conference,' October 1965, in *Reflections of a Statesman*, pp. 624–627 (p. 626).
[26] Ibid.
[27] Peregrine Worsthorne, 'Class and Conflict in British Foreign Policy,' *Foreign Affairs*, 37: 3 (April 1959), pp. 419–431 (p. 426).

effort to see Britishness as a liberal project. Powell's insistence that to assume an Indian or West Indian immigrant *became* British was offensive (not only to Britons but even more to the immigrants themselves) again has much in common with Zizek's notion of 'reflected racism.'

All of this was important for Powell for one reason. Powell would, throughout his political career, continue to view the health of British society in terms of its ability to turn itself outward, to defence, or to its ability to wage war. As he put it in 1965, 'the ultimate reason and ultimate justification' for the Tory's commitments to the nation is 'that we hold them to be necessary or advantageous for the defence of the United Kingdom.'[28] The myth of the Second World War, and even more the myth of Dunkirk, would remain a potent metaphor in Powell's rhetoric for a number of reasons. Here was the moment when the white Briton could be imagined standing alone, protected by the English Channel, shorn of imperial troops and without American-made guns. Here, too, was the moment when society was engaged in total war, when society itself was at war.

This book has found that it is possible to view Powell's postwar conservative revolt as representative of the disjuncture between British and American forms of imperial hegemony – or, in Powell's mind, an empire that could recognize the multiplicity of cultural difference and one that divided the world into 'goodies' and 'baddies.' With such a perspective it is possible to see more clearly the meaning of race in Powellism. It was not that Powell was committed to humanitarian, egalitarian or democratic ideals and that these ideals had to be curtailed by the realities of racial violence. Powell's understanding of race was Tory in character. Race was a uniform, which ordered the hierarchical whole and served as a sign of political allegiance. In this sense, class and race were inextricably entwined. As noted in the Introduction, the use of this term 'uniform' is significantly ambiguous: it suggests both an acceptance of the historical constructedness of racial categorization while at the same time posing it as an untranscendable boundary. Race, in essence, is a political reality. Racism represented for Powell the impossibility – or, even, undesirability – of constructing an ahistorical, abstract space for democracy.

Thus the use of the term 'liberal' to describe Powell and the emphasis on his concern for 'democracy' obscures the heart of Powell's political revolt. It is, in fact, an inversion of his political thinking. Albert O. Hirschman's explanation of the 'jeopardy thesis' of reactionary rhetoric is useful here.[29] Powell's insistence that British parliamentary

[28] J. Enoch Powell, 'To the Brighton Conference,' October 1965, in *Reflections of a Statesman*, p. 624.
[29] Albert O. Hirschman, *The Rhetoric of Reaction: Perversity, Futility, Jeopardy* (Cambridge, MA: Belknap Press of Harvard University Press, 1991).

democracy was under threat by new political demands – by social rights and by transnational commitments – does not mean that it was democracy that inspired him. As Powell would often note, the life of a nation was 'biological,' 'evolutionary,' its progress was *slow*. Powell argued for the status quo; he argued that the status quo – the sovereignty of British parliamentary democracy and the social order that recognized its sovereignty – was in jeopardy due to the new political claims and new political expectations of the Cold War world. Ironically, Powell failed to view his commitment to the free market as, essentially, a commitment to a revolutionary force that would, with Margaret Thatcher's government, raze the web of understood relationship far more effectively than transnationalism or any recognition of social rights.

Conservatism is a house of many mansions. This book has tried to inhabit one of them, that constructed by Enoch Powell out of his war experience between 1939 and 1945. It was a space he inhabited throughout his life. War was his home, and by staying there, he was unable to see or to understand those who came from a different time and place. Returning to the besieged Protestants of Ulster was one way of turning away from reality, the reality of a multicultural and multiracial Britain. When the present is too harsh to tolerate, reactionary ideas come to the rescue, and clothe prejudice in the language of a tradition under siege. That is Powell's legacy, one which endures to this day.

Postscript: Enoch Powell and Thatcherism

> [The Conservative] is more conscious than anyone else of the delicacy
> and vulnerability of that which sustains society ... That the web of
> understood relationships which sustains society is an object, to a
> degree, of veneration as something which cannot be without danger
> tampered with, which arguably once injured may not be capable of
> being restored.
>
> Enoch Powell, 1988[1]

If one looks at Thatcherism through the prism of Enoch Powell, it
becomes clear what Thatcherism is not: it is not a conservative philosophy of the nation. For Powell, the nation-state was the 'ultimate
political reality.' There was 'no political reality beyond it.'[2] In an effort
to salvage that reality, Powell in 1963 argued for what he called a 'new
patriotism' – oriented towards entrepreneurship and a post-imperial
national pride.[3] Five years later, it was again 'the nation' that took precedence, when he spoke of future national disintegration due to the
supposedly unbreachable divide of racism. For Powell, civil society
once 'lost' could not be found. In contrast, for Margaret Thatcher,
Britain's 'reawakening' was beyond itself, a reawakening of 'the values
and traditions on which Western civilization, and prosperity, are
based.'[4] Britain or Britishness came to be synonymous not with that
fragile 'web of understood relationships' but with a set of values – with

---

[1] Bill Schwarz interview with Enoch Powell, 26 April 1988 (private recording).

[2] Heffer, *Like the Roman*, p. 153.

[3] See, for instance: J. Enoch Powell, speech at the S.W. Norfolk Conservative Fete, 15
June 1963, POLL 4.1.1: '[We must] seek to re-establish our self-confidence and faith
in ourselves upon a new basis and to find, as it were, a new patriotism befitting this
changed world, to replace the old, imperial patriotism of the past. To help the nation in
this work to express its purpose is uniquely the mission of the Tory Party: to proclaim
to ourselves and to our fellow countrymen that the reserves of energy, of resource, of
enterprise, from which our past achievements sprang, are not exhausted.'

[4] Margaret Thatcher, 'Britain Awake,' speech at Kensington Town Hall, 19 January
1976. Margaret Thatcher Foundation website (MTFW) 102939.

the 'spirit of trade' and self-reliance.[5] Yet Thatcherism was a situational, strategic ideology. The question still unanswered in the 1970s for the ideological makers of Thatcherism was, *who* would commit to this 'enterprise culture' – the Asian and West Indian middle classes or Powell's disillusioned working-class supporters (who tended, some polls found, to have 'weak class identifiers'[6])?

There is no doubt that Powellism helped to produce Thatcherism, or that Powell contributed both to the New Right's political and economic thinking and to Thatcher's rhetorical style. Powell aired new grievances, new alliances and a new 'politics of support'[7] that could be harnessed in support of Thatcher. But this coherence between Powell and Thatcherism was contingent and incomplete. Powell himself replied, when it was remarked that Thatcher was a convert to Powell's monetarist policies, that it was, 'A pity she did not understand them!'[8] For Powell, monetarism was not a moral endeavour; it was a necessity of national economic independence. Powell's insistence on the need to release market relations in British society from the constraints of economic planning was less an effort to remake the social order than a sign of his overriding concerns about sovereignty in the context of American global power. Fiscal conservatism was, like an independent military and a loyal and unified 'people,' an essential component of national independence. Thatcher and Powell were, in a sense, fighting different wars – with the same weapons but against different enemies. For Powell, this was a struggle, like the Second World War, to preserve the 'unique structure of power' of British rule.[9] For Thatcher, this was a larger war, an ideological and moral war. Thatcher's war, both inside and outside Britain, was the Cold War.[10] While Powellism gave political meaning to the 'crisis' of the late 1960s and 1970s, with apocalyptic visions of racial violence and national disintegration, Thatcherism offered a solution: the world remade in her own likeness.

In 1988, David Marquand, a former Labour MP and founding member of the Social Democratic Party, claimed that, for the Conservative,

---

[5] *The Right Approach*, Conservative Policy Document, 4 October 1976, MTFW 109439.

[6] Rich, 'Conservative Ideology and Race in Modern British Politics,' in Layton-Henry and Rich (eds.), *Race, Government and Politics in Britain*, p. 54.

[7] Gamble, *The Conservative Nation*, p. 218.

[8] Powell in 'Odd man out,' BBC TV profile by Michael Cockerell, transmitted 11 November 1995. POLL 5.69.

[9] Powell to Ellen and Albert Powell, 9 March 1943. POLL 1.1.5.

[10] Richard Vinen, 'Thatcherism and the Cold War,' in Jackson and Saunders (eds.), *Making Thatcher's Britain*, pp. 199–217.

'[b]etween the state and the citizen there lies, and there ought to lie, a mass of intermediate institutions which protect the individual from arbitrary power.' Wider society is a 'mosaic of small collectivities' in which civility, order, deference and political responsibility and freedom are learnt. He cites, here, Edmund Burke's famous line: 'To be attached to the subdivision, to love the little platoon we belong to in society, is the first principle (the germ as it were) of public affection.'[11] Critically, Thatcherism as a political project lacked a sensitivity to what Powell called 'the delicacy and vulnerability of that which sustains society'; it proved to have little reluctance to transform or 'tamper with' and 'injure' British communities and institutions.[12] In fact, Thatcherism launched a fervent attack on these 'nurseries of civility' in the 1980s – on local authorities, on the trade unions, on the BBC, on universities, and, at times even, on the Church of England.[13] A 'Healthy Society' is counterposed in the Thatcherite project to a society of encroaching socialism and collectivism.[14] As will be discussed in this chapter, economics is treated as instrumental in the speeches and policy papers of the New Right on the remaking of a conservative moral order. In Thatcher's speeches, Britishness appears as an antidote. Britain and 'true' Britishness appear, then, as Cold War belief.

Powell had, for decader, refused the dominant logic of pro-capitalist government spending, maintaining a 'far right' commitment to 'sound money.' Some of Powell's economic disciples – such as Geoffrey Howe, John Biffen, Nicholas Ridley, John Nott and Ian Gow – would go on to serve as Thatcher's ministers.[15] With this, Powell was self-consciously an anachronism, who held dear to his heart the old truths of prewar conservatism. This was a language that Thatcherites, also, sometimes deployed. Nigel Lawson, for example, told an audience in 1980 that Britain had to find a prior, truer self, unlearning the false lessons inculcated during and after the Second World War. Calling for the return of an 'old consensus,' to the 'golden age' of Disraeli and Gladstone, Lawson proclaimed the 'reversion to an older tradition' of sound money. New conservatism was, therefore, truly conservative.[16] However, through Powell, we see in Thatcherism not such a clear disavowal of postwar 'moral' economics. Thatcherism's effort to morally transform Britain

---

[11] David Marquand, 'The Paradoxes of Thatcherism,' in Skidelsky (ed.), *Thatcherism*, p. 171.

[12] Powell, Bill Schwarz interview, 26 April 1988 (private recordings).

[13] Marquand, 'The Paradoxes of Thatcherism,' in Skidelsky (ed.), *Thatcherism*, p. 172.

[14] See 'Stepping Stones' Report, 14 November 1977, MTFW 111771.

[15] Vinen, *Thatcher's Britain*, p. 16.

[16] See Nigel Lawson, 'The New Conservatism' (Lecture to the Bow Group), 4 August 1980, MTFW 109505.

via economic policy appears, rather, as a continuation and development of liberal postwar ideas of social and economic planning.

But Powell was anachronistic in another way, too. Despite the Second World War, a war that proved to many that ideas or values were the real substance of war and politics, Powell retained another unpopular truth. Shared values and shared belief, such as those within the New Commonwealth, could not produce a political community – that was, rather, the function of war and patriotic allegiance. Similarly, 'Britishness' was not a liberal project but a definition of allegiance. Powell refused the political logic, then, of the postwar world: the new internationalism of the United Nations, human rights and nuclear defence remained for Powell throughout his career infringements on national sovereignty, on the truly 'political.' By 1980, Powell had spent his life refusing to join what he regarded as America's liberal war. In this way, Powell serves as a peculiar link in the history of popular conservatism.

Clearly, Thatcherism was not one discourse but 'a field of discourses' at work on the terrain of popular ideology in the 1970s.[17] Powell's historic role in the making of Thatcherism is, likewise, multi-faceted. One frame by which to understand Thatcher, at least, is via the strength of her anti-Communist convictions. For Thatcher, it was in many ways Communism, both within and without Britain – as terrorism, in the unions, in popular culture, within the state bureaucracy, in local government, and also, simply, as Soviet military aggression – that stood against 'the Survival of our way of life.'[18] A revival of the 'Anglo-Saxon heritage' and 'the remarkable qualities of the British people' promised, in Thatcher's schema, to save Britain from state collectivism and consequential moral decay. Though at times explicitly racial, the concept of Britain found here is less a fragile entity facing an existential crisis than it is an ideological orientation. 'Britain' is, for Thatcher, less the divinely ordained and ritualized order of Tory tradition than the exportable, missionary nation. Still, as we have seen, Enoch Powell's particular vision of Britain's existential crisis worked to endow some British people's experiences of unrest and uncertainty in these years with radical political meaning. With this, Powellism played an important 'preparatory role' in making the electorate more receptive to radical politics, 'to positions outside the mainstream of British politics.'[19] Again, Powell's vision of a nation in crisis helped clear the way for Thatcher's crusade.

[17] Nairn, *The Break-Up of Britain*, p. 384.
[18] Thatcher, 'Britain Awake,' MTFW 102939.
[19] Schoen, *Enoch Powell and the Powellites*, p. 240.

Powell externalized, or politicized, social violence.[20] He explained West Indian 'mugging' in the 1970s and, later, the Brixton and Liverpool riots of 1981 as signs of political alienation. The black Briton did not and could not, in Powell's mind, identify with the political order. British citizens were, in this way, placed outside the nation. The same went for those who sought to break the government with labour unrest and those who violently opposed Unionist domination in Northern Ireland. As a Unionist MP for South Down from 1974 to 1987, Powell sought complete integration of Northern Ireland into the British Parliament. He regarded Republican prisoners as enemies of the British state and believed that the difficulties in Northern Ireland were exacerbated by US defence interests. Strikes against nationalized industries, similarly, were not economic, but political: 'The railwaymen, like the miners, are not negotiating with the Railways Board – that is merely a façade – but with the Government. Nor are the railwaymen and the Government negotiating about things economic. They are negotiating about things political.'[21] In other words, for Powell, this was political opposition intimately linked to questions of state sovereignty and its declining authority. Thatcher deployed a similar language, but annexed to it an ideological component that was, by the 1970s, quite absent from Powell's thought. Within Thatcherite circles, there was an 'enemy within' but that enemy was consistently socialist. Anti-racism, for instance, was most threatening, for Thatcher, when wedded to a critique of capitalism.[22] Though Powell at times associated the Labour Party with encroaching fascism and vociferously opposed the extension of economic planning in the postwar years, by the 1970s the threats to the moral authority of the state were, as we have seen, multifarious. Powell's enemy was socialist when it threatened the nation, but he would vote for the Labour Party before supporting entry into the European Community. As he learned in the empire, political community was a fragile construction; it could (perhaps) not survive. On the other hand, within Thatcherism, authority promised to whip the body-politic into the right shape. Black

---

[20] Enoch Powell held the 'realist' position that state sovereignty was an absolute. With such thinking, civil society is 'state-contained,' and 'relations between societies [are] subordinate to, and dependent on, political relations between states.' Powell's 'civil society' was synonymous with a peaceful community at war – with a community able to wage war outside of itself. James Anderson, 'Rethinking National Problems in a Transnational Context,' in Miller (ed.), *Rethinking Northern Ireland*, p. 129.
[21] J. Enoch Powell, *A Nation or No Nation?: Six Years in British Politics*, ed. Richard Ritchie (London: Batsford, 1978), p. 19.
[22] For a discussion of black and anti-racist cultural forms as a critique of capitalism, see Gilroy, 'Diaspora, Utopia and the Critique of Capitalism,' in *'There Ain't No Black in the Union Jack,'* pp. 200–302.

criminality is not political but a consequence of family structure and environment; a strong police force is therefore offered as one component in a 'total system of social control.'[23] Likewise, the IRA prisoner is 'criminalized,' and thereby (unsuccessfully) made non-political and invisible.

The Powellism of the late 1960s has been read as an early sign of the coming social dislocation of the 1970s, the loosening of postwar political loyalties based on class status and the emerging influence of issue voting.[24] According to electoral studies, Powellism initially found its support with the alienated voter. But soon, according to political analyst Douglas Schoen, Powellism became more diffuse. By the mid-1970s, it had evolved into a wider coalition of those dissatisfied with the political system, serving as a major catalyst in the growth of support for extreme right-wing groups, such as the National Front and the Immigration Control Association.[25] Despite the preponderance of working-class letter-writers, Powell's most active supporters were distinctly middle and upper-middle class – their influence was felt on school boards, in neighbourhood groups and in local politics.

Heath sacked Powell from his position as Shadow Minister of Defence just days after his 'Rivers of Blood' speech, and Powell would never again return to the centre of political power. Still, the party's relatively tough stand on immigration contributed to the Conservatives' surprise election victory in 1970. The next year, Heath's Conservative government passed an Immigration Act that formally introduced 'patriality' into British immigration law; this resulted in the further restriction of black immigration into Britain. This did not, however, erase Powellism. Powell left the Conservative Party in 1974 over Britain's continued membership of the EEC, only to join the Ulster Unionists that same year. Race hardly surfaced as an issue in the two general elections of 1974. The miners' strike and Powell's defection to the Unionists focused attention away from immigration. The Conservative loss did, however, seem to have a racial dimension. The Community Relations Commission produced a report showing that thirteen of the seventeen seats Labour gained in the October 1974 election were won with a majority that was smaller than the non-white population of that constituency.[26] Meanwhile, Conservatives

---

[23] Report of Sir Kenneth Newman, Met. Commissioner, October 1984 as cited ibid., p. 137.
[24] Särlvik and Crewe, *Decade of Dealignment*.
[25] Rich, 'Conservative Ideology and Race in Modern British Politics,' in Layton-Henry and Rich (eds.), *Race, Government and Politics in Britain*, pp. 55–57.
[26] Zig Layton-Henry, *The Politics of Race in Britain* (London: Allen and Unwin, 1984), pp. 145–146.

collected just 19 per cent of the Asian vote, to Labour's 73 per cent.[27] The party alienated the non-white voter at its peril.

Keith Joseph joined Powell in warning of social decay in 1974, asking 'Are we to move towards moral decline reflected and intensified by economic decline, by the corrosive effects of inflation? Or can we remoralise our national life, of which the economy is an integral part?'[28] Joseph's answer, then, was social engineering – not solely in terms of class but in terms of reconstructing a conservative moral order. Degeneration was not just economic: he claimed, 'our human stock is threatened,' and called for greater access to birth control for unfit mothers. This eugenic line lost him the leadership of the party. It also begged the question, who would be included in this remoralized Britain? Crucially, for Thatcher and her ministers, 'transformism' was accepted as necessary because British society had taken a wrong historical turn.[29] The 'corrosive effects' of inflation had set in: saving and prudence were under threat. Likewise, the bastions of 'civility' – such as the Church, the voluntary sector and the press – no longer offered lessons in economic and political self-reliance. Thanks to postwar corporatism, 'the people' did not know the moral rules of the game. 'Socialist encouragement of class hatred of the existing order,' as one policy discussion paper explained, 'is easily translated into exemption from obeying society's laws.'[30] For Powell, it was not the politician's role, but the role of the 'moralist' to work against public sins, like lack of prudence – or, even, explicit racism. In response to Joseph's speech, Powell warned that politicians should not preach, as they had little effect on public morals.[31] But it was 'beliefs, not the people,' argued Joseph, that were 'the poison on our economic life. We are trapped by them.'[32] As John Casey put it in 1978, conservative philosophy required 'the largest imaginative leap' in order to grasp the 'decay in customs and patterns of behaviour,' which signalled 'a profound change in the consciousness of the age.'[33]

---

[27] Report to Lord Thorneycroft, June 1976, THCR 2/6/1/140, Churchill Archives Centre.

[28] Keith Joseph, 'Speech at Edgbaston,' 19 October 1974, MTFW 101830.

[29] Tom Nairn, *Pariah: Misfortunes of the British Kingdom* (London: Verso, 2002), p. 22; John Casey, 'Tradition and Authority,' in Maurice Cowling (ed.), *Conservative Essays* (London: Cassell, 1978), p. 87.

[30] Keith Joseph, Shadow Cabinet: Circulated Paper ('Our Tone of Voice and Our Tasks'), 12 July 1976, MTFW 110178.

[31] Ronald Butt, 'The Link Between Public Money and Public Morality,' *The Times* (24 October 1974), p. 18.

[32] Keith Joseph, 'Economy: Sir Keith Joseph to MT' (encloses draft speech on unions), MTFW 111880.

[33] Casey, 'Tradition and Authority,' in Cowling (ed.), *Conservative Essays*, p. 87.

In the autumn of 1977, the ex-army officer and businessman John Hoskyns and another businessman named Norman Strauss prepared a Centre for Policy Studies document entitled 'Stepping Stones.' This now legendary document was distributed and discussed in the Shadow Cabinet, and Hoskyns later became the head of Thatcher's Policy Unit from 1979 to 1981. 'Stepping Stones' viewed the unions as the key stumbling block to economic recovery, and recommended modifying, rather than confronting, the beliefs of union members. Here we see something of the intellectual work involved in producing a new moral hegemony. Hoskyns and Strauss discuss the social introduction of 'discontinuity' – 'breaking constraints which we had assumed were unbreakable.' These constraints had previously been considered 'unalterable "facts of life"' – in other words, the stuff of common sense and culture. The report called for a special working party on the 'Mind Set' of union members. There we see the recognition that union life is a major aspect of a union member's identity – in other words, the nationalized industries and the unions are part of Britain's 'little platoons.' The 'individual worker and his union are closely linked' such that 'Exile would be like banishment to Siberia.'

> Between him and the terrors of being on his own in a society which, as yet, offers fairly unequal opportunity, stands his union – that is, his tribe, his clan, his own small society. Inside it he is warm, and to a large extent, safe. Outside, he is nothing. If he is to desert Labour – and thus by close connection, qualify his loyalty to his union– it must be for something better and equally reassuring.

This is an extreme vision – outside, the union member is nothing, not parishioner, not father, not hobbyist, not consumer. The appendix 'Union Behaviour Change Strategy' offered this as its strategy: 'we realise that we cannot ask the unions, or their members, to give up their current feelings of comradeship, protectiveness and group strength if we do not guarantee them similar feelings of strength, togetherness and security under any new arrangement.' This is true 'transformism': the unionist must be stripped down to 'the terrors of being on his own' and then remade as a non-union man with, they propose, 'a minority stake on the Board of a company, share-owning, or a controlling role in a local authority.'[34]

Powell's response to efforts to produce a 'national revival' with economic policy is particularly revealing. As discussed in Chapter 3, when

---

[34] 'Stepping Stones' Report, 14 November 1977, THCR 2/6/1/248, MTFW 111771, pp. 9, 27, 36, A-9.

the Minister of Labour blamed Britain's economic ills in the autumn of 1966 on the 'dishonesty' and 'thriftlessness' of the nation at large, on a collective irresponsibility, Powell received letters for and against the nation. He believed that this was a sign of how much the idea of the state controlling people's lives had affected Britain. It was neither his job as a politician nor the job of the National Economic Development Council, but a 'job for moralists,' to work on the nation's moral ills.

> For the purposes of politics, human nature, including the human nature of the nation concerned, must be treated as constant, something given and assumed, a starting point. The politician's business is with the environment in which human nature is placed.[35]

Powell insisted that, while politics and the politician may be 'the nation's psychiatrist' when they create and recreate myths that legitimize political authority,[36] they cannot dramatically change that organic evolutionary entity, the habits and expectations of a community. Rather, the politician's role in society is to dramatize the inevitabilities of the world so as to make them 'appear human, explicable, and amenable to management.'[37] This was, again, Powell's essential critique of the *liberalism* of Keynesian social democracy and the corporate state.[38]

Importantly, we see the same criticism appearing again against Thatcherism. In response to Chancellor Geoffrey Howe's first Budget in 1979, Powell spoke out against the notion that economic policy could transform the moral order. The 1979 Budget shifted £2.5 billion onto indirect taxation. As he had done in the past, Powell argued in support of income tax, against indirect taxation.[39] He rejected the argument that income tax cuts motivated individuals to work harder. It is worth quoting Powell at length, for in this we see the fundamental divide between Powell and Thatcherism on economics and the nation:

> [I]t is necessary not to treat people of any walk of life as automata, nor the economy as a kind of marionette, which Governments and Chancellors of

---

[35] J. Enoch Powell, Wessex Area Young Conservative Weekend School, Weymouth, 1 October 1966. POLL 4.1.2.

[36] J. Enoch Powell, speech to Manchester Convention Dinner, 6 November 1965. POLL 4.1.2.

[37] J. Enoch Powell, 'Truth, Politics and Persuasion,' *Advertising Quarterly* (Spring 1965), pp. 7–13 (p. 12).

[38] Beer, *Modern British Politics*.

[39] Heffer, *Like the Roman*, p. 825.

the Exchequer can operate by lifting a leg here and depressing an arm there, through the alterations in the tax system ... The proposition that people will work harder or longer for 3p off the standard rate of income tax, let alone that they will work more effectively – which is what we are talking about – betrays a crass misunderstanding of human nature, individual and social. The reasons why people address themselves collectively and individually to their activities, and the reasons why at one phase of a nation's history they direct them in one way rather than another, are far deeper, more complex and more subtle than can be reached by a remission of income tax.

Powell then went on to critique (Thatcherism's) historical mission:

I profoundly reject that conception and modes of thought which assert that there has been either a relative – if we are compared to our Continental neighbours – or an absolute decline in the quality of life in this country. If it has occurred – and a case could be made that in certain aspects of our life there has been a deterioration – it would be in aspects which are not measured or measurable by GNP ... If we are failing, if the sum total of our pride and satisfaction and achievement is diminishing, I do not believe that it is in the power of Governments, through Budgets, to alter that course of events. Some say that this is a secular decline which has been going on for a century. If it has been going on for a century, so much the more profound, so much the more fated, must be the causes that lie behind it. What certainly will not turn a nation again is to be told to measure itself, to measure what it achieves, against an objective, mechanical, material standard by which its [European] neighbours are also measured; nor to inform it that it will be given opportunity for renewed and wider achievement by a minor adjustment of the relationship between gross and net income. If a Government were to tell a nation that and the nation were indeed in a state of moral and physical decline, it would only encourage it upon that course. I do not believe that the nation reacts to the sort of stimuli in which the Government apparently believe; and if the Government address the nation in the terms in which this Budget speaks, so much the less will the nation listen.[40]

The consistency of Powell's critique, against both Keynesian and Thatcherite economics, offers another perspective on the New Right. Thatcher and Powell both spoke in the late 1960s and 1970s against the notion that redistributive taxes could be 'moral.' Charity and altruism had no meaning when applied to taxation by a public authority, either for the welfare state or for international development aid. They agreed that morality was individual: the Good Samaritan cannot be forced to be good. As Powell put it in 1965, it was an 'inherent absurdity' to imagine a state behaving charitably, for 'it is collective advantage that governs how a state acts.'[41] However, through Powell, we see in Thatcherism a

---

[40] HC, vol. 968, cols. 955–957, 18 June 1979.
[41] Powell, 'International Charity,' Draft copy, *New Society*, 5 June 1965. POLL 6.1.1.

less stark disavowal of postwar 'moral' economics. Rather, Thatcherism may be read in this way as a continuation and development of liberal ideas on social and economic planning. Economics remained the method: the object was to police the heart and soul.[42]

Powell's insistence that politics, both at the domestic and international level, had no logical bridge to 'the assertions of Christianity' stands in contrast, then, to Thatcherism.[43] By 1977, Thatcher had made clear that her party was Christian (as opposed to a party of the Established Church).[44] It was, under Thatcher, a party concerned not with ritual obedience, but individual salvation. As Paul Rich explains, this neo-liberal concern for the individual 'acted as a considerable brake on the emergence of a full-blown Tory organicism which, allied [to] a theory of racial nationalism, would have taken the party's intellectual right a good way towards British fascist ideology.'[45] Instead, on race and immigration, Thatcherism remained ambiguous.

Immigration was, according to Thatcher's assistant in 1976, 'always' the most popular subject in Margaret Thatcher's postbag. In the first six months of 1976, for instance, it was the focus of 25 per cent of all mail that Thatcher received from the public.[46] The Malawi Asian crisis of that year and the passing of the Race Relations Act (which the Conservative Party did not oppose) had produced a renewed opposition to black immigration both at the party and popular level. Enoch Powell's release of details of a secret document which alleged widespread evasion of immigration restrictions and fraud in 1976 further heated the public debate. In the lead-up to the Race Relations Bill, the Party Chairman Airey Neave wrote that 'strong comments' were made within the Party Chairman's management committee of the need for new 'party policy' on immigration. Neave explained that Willie

---

[42] Interview for *Sunday Times*, 1 May 1981, MTFW 104475.
[43] Cowling, 'The Present Position,' in *Conservative Essays*, p. 4.
[44] Thatcher, 'Dimensions of Conservatism' (Iain Macleod Memorial Lecture), London, 4 July 1977 in *Let Our Children Grow Tall*, pp. 103–113.
[45] Rich, 'Conservative Ideology and Race in Modern British Politics,' in Layton-Henry and Rich (eds.), *Race, Government and Politics in Britain*, p. 61.
[46] Letters Report, July 1976, Immigration File, THCR 2/6/1/140. Churchill Archives Centre. I would like to thank Andrew Riley, archivist for the Margaret Thatcher Papers at the Churchill Archives Centre, for kindly opening previously closed files for this research, including letters from the public to Margaret Thatcher on immigration. Those who wrote to her, like Powell's letter-writers, were predominantly of the working classes. Many noted concern that 'Britain is over-populated, under housed and under employed' (Thatcher's underline). Thatcher's assistant believed that the main motivation of writing the letters seemed to be, 'undoubtedly much more fear of the unknown [Thatcher's underline] and of being swamped in the future, than dislike of those immigrants already here.'

Whitelaw's statements seem to be 'adopting an "elitist" attitude which ignored the opinions of reasonable residents of the reception areas for immigrants, who found their neighbourhoods literally taken over.'[47] At the Party conference, Whitelaw promised an end to 'immigration as we have seen it in the post-war years.' That same year, however, with recognition that Asian and West Indian voters were electorally significant in marginal seats, in the Midlands, Greater London, Yorkshire and Lancashire, the Central Office set up a new Central Office Department of Community Affairs, which in turn funded two new national organizations: the Anglo-Asian Conservative Society and the Anglo-West Indian Conservative Society.[48] These attempted to recruit businessmen, doctors, accountants and other middle-class professionals into their ranks. Thatcher was made honorary president of the Anglo-Asian Conservative Society. Still, there were limits to this (classed) anti-racism. When party members were invited to participate in the Joint Committee Against Racialism in 1977 (together with the Labour and Liberal Parties, the British Council of Churches, the Board of Deputies of British Jews, the National Union of Students, the British Youth Council and leading immigrant groups, such as the Indian Workers' Association), Thatcher vetoed the appointment of John Moore MP as joint chairman. She was apparently 'appalled' when she discovered that the party might be involved in activities with far left groups.[49] Instead, Mrs Shelagh Roberts, who was not a Member of Parliament, took up the post.

Thatcher's remark on television in 1978 that the people are afraid that 'this country might be rather swamped by people with a different culture' was a political calculation. Thatcher recognized the impact of Powellism on the 1970 general election. Her files on immigration from early 1978 include an excerpt from a book edited by John Wood, *Powell and the 1970 Election*, with a note attached. The book itself quotes letters from Powell's supporters across the country asserting that they voted Conservative thanks to his work in the election campaign. It includes speeches by Powell and Heath and a discussion of the electoral significance of anti-immigration, all of which are used to assert that it was Enoch Powell who won the 1970 general election for the Conservative Party. The excerpt included in Thatcher's personal file on immigration is a speech by Heath in 1970, which called for strict control of immigration and subsidized voluntary repatriation. The book describes this

---

[47] Airey Neave, report on Race Relations Bill HAC(76)1, 16 July 1976, THCR 2/6/1/140. Churchill Archives Centre.

[48] Layton-Henry, *The Politics of Race*, pp. 104, 148.

[49] Ibid., p. 149 and C/10, Papers of the Indian Workers' Association, MS2141, Birmingham City Archives.

speech as a virtual copy of Powell's arguments. Powell's 'enemies within' speech of June 1970 is also copied for Thatcher, which begins: 'Britain at this moment is under attack.' The note attached to the excerpt reads that Norman Tebbit had 'come across some interesting pronouncements by Ted Heath and Enoch Powell.' Thatcher noted and underlined the text and had the whole thing copied for Willie Whitelaw.

The popular presence of the National Front was at its peak in these years, gaining 120,000 votes in the Greater London Council in the election of May 1977. Just days after her 'swamped' comment, Thatcher spoke, too, of Britain's sick society: 'a state that is responsible for just about everything' and 'a society in which the individual feels responsible for nothing' was a reason why 'prisons are full to bursting; vandalism is growing; in some areas people are afraid to answer their doors at night.' Not only was the state producing discord, it could not be trusted. Here, like Powell, race came in. Thatcher spoke of 'Smokescreen Socialism,' a 'cloud of excuses, explanations and justification' – and here, at this point, she linked the state, socialism and the unknown 'numbers' of immigrants. She promised to remove 'the doubts on numbers' and 'the doubts on commitments' and respect 'the genuine fears and concerns of many of our citizens.'[50] Thatcher's people, here, are white *victims* of state bureaucracy. Thatcher promised to hear and speak for the fears of 'the people.' Like Powell, she received a deluge of letters in support. The *Daily Telegraph* maintained that Thatcher's 'swamped' remark had struck a popular chord, claiming that 58 per cent of Labour supporters, 71 per cent of Liberals and 84 per cent of Conservatives endorsed Thatcher's words.[51] These words all but destroyed the National Front in the 1979 general election. Though immigration was not a big election issue in 1979, still we find massive swings to the Conservatives in Islington through to the East End, to Dagenham: in areas where the National Front had been most active. As Powell described Thatcher's populism, after the Conservatives won the general election: 'People hearing her are convinced that she shares the same frustrations and nurtures the same ambition,' which was, 'in a single word ... "nation."'[52]

Powell refused to believe that indirect taxation could transform Britain, but war was another thing entirely. After the Falklands War in June 1982, Powell experienced a changed Britain: 'A change has come

---

[50] Margaret Thatcher, 'Speech to Young Conservatives Conference,' 12 February 1978, MTFW 103487.
[51] Brendan Evans, 'Thatcherism and the British People,' in Stuart Ball and Ian Holliday (eds.), *Mass Conservatism: The Conservatives and the Public since the 1880s* (London: Frank Cass, 2002), p. 224.
[52] Powell, *Daily Telegraph*, 25 April 1981.

about in Britain. I do not need opinion polls … to tell me that. I have the evidence of my own sense as I go about the country.'[53] Powell was not alone in this view. According to an *Economist* editorial the week before, 'Britain has said something to itself' and produced 'some restoration of the idea that Britain can do things well.' 'Britain had long needed its own sort of cultural revolution,' the article went on, shaking off the 'malaise' of the immediate postwar and Vietnam generation, with its tendency to view 'military values and men as out-of-date jokes.' Now a younger generation could look upon soldiers who were 'men a bit more handsome and heroic than Mr David Bowie.'[54] This gendered understanding of the value of war in society echoes the words of Powell and his supporters, who viewed the 1968 generation as decadent without the experience of war. Anthony Barnett's near-contemporary portrayal of the politics surrounding the Falklands War speaks at length about how memories of the Second World War, when Britain 'knew itself,' worked to legitimate military action.[55] Thatcher's Churchillian rhetoric famously came home, too, when she spoke at a Conservative rally at Cheltenham: 'We have to see that the spirit of the South Atlantic – the real spirit of Britain – is kindled not only by war but can now by fired by peace.' Now it was time, she argued, 'for management to lift its sights and to lead with the professionalism and effectiveness it knows is possible.' Now was the time for the railwayman to stand for 'true solidarity,' not with his union on strike the following day, but by putting 'his family, his comrades, and his country first.'[56] According to Thatcher, it was war, then, which bore Britain's revival: finding that prior, truer self in memories, not of 1945, but of 1940. The speech inhabited the same imaginative world as Powell's 'Enemies Within' speech.

Though Thatcher had shown her mettle in the Falklands, protecting British interests, she tellingly failed to do so when American marines invaded Grenada in October 1983. Friendship with the United States had failed to prevent the Grenada invasion; this confirmed for Powell, as Simon Heffer put it, that 'America's loyalty to her British ally [was] a sham.' This was of particular significance at a time when the United States was about to station nuclear weapons on British soil. Thatcher's commitment to the Anglo-American alliance, her willingness to bind Britain to the nuclear deterrence policy of the United States against

[53] Powell, quoted in 'Sure Signs That Britain Has Returned to Normal,' *The Economist*, 26 July 1982, p. 21.
[54] 'At the End of the Day,' *The Economist*, 19 June 1982, p. 13.
[55] Anthony Barnett, *Iron Britannia* (London: Allison and Busby, 1982).
[56] Margaret Thatcher, 'Speech to Conservative Rally at Cheltenham,' 3 July 1982, MTFW 104989.

Soviet power and her use of the language of 'freedom' and 'Western civilization' against communism were signs, Powell thought, of an 'American view of the world.' This view he described as, 'in the strictest terms, Manichean. It divides the world into two monoliths – the goodies and the baddies, the East and the West, even the free and the enslaved. It is a nightmarish distortion of reality.'[57] It was, in other words, a view of the world without a need to protect the conservative nation. To depend on the United States or the Continent of Europe for British arms was, as he put it in 1989, 'suicide.'[58] Thatcher's political rhetoric was highly patriotic; she often talked of British greatness, but – as Richard Vinen has found – she said very little about English nationalism.[59] Similarly, Thatcher's approach to Europe might read, by her Bruges speech of 1988, as nationalistic, but the underlying argument in that speech remains: 'We have not successfully rolled back the frontiers of the state in Britain, only to see them re-imposed at a European level with a European super-state exercising a new dominance from Brussels.'[60] Through the prism of Powell, it appears to be less sovereignty than the nature of political and economic order that remained Thatcher's concern.

While Powell viewed the Brixton and Liverpool riots of 1981 as the beginnings of an inevitable civil war between those who identified with and those who were alienated from the state, Thatcher's government – after the Scarman Report – turned to support the structures of social authority in Britain's minority communities. Ambalavaner Sivanandan refers to this as the 'culturalism' or 'ethnicism' of the Thatcher period and views it as an attempt to contain Black Power politics. The report's discussion of the black community in Brixton begins by pathologizing family life in the Brixton community.[61] It eschews the charge that the riots were caused by high unemployment or widespread institutionalized racism. It was, rather, the 'racial disadvantage' of certain groups, 'the cure being to pour money into ethnic projects and strengthening ethnic cultures.'[62] The fight against racism was reduced, Sivanandan argues, to 'a fight for culture.' In fact, as David Feldman's recent work on 'Why the English Like Turbans' emphasizes, the formalized recognition of

[57] Heffer, *Like the Roman*, pp. 844, 879.
[58] Enoch Powell, 18 February 1989, in *Enoch Powell on 1992*, ed. Ritchie, p. 50.
[59] Vinen, *Thatcher's Britain*, pp. 225–226.
[60] Margaret Thatcher, 'Speech to the College of Europe,' 20 September 1988, MTFW 107332.
[61] Gilroy, *There Ain't No Black in the Union Jack*, p. 133.
[62] A. Sivanandan, 'Why Muslims Reject British Values,' *The Observer*, 16 October 2005.

ethnic difference as a means of ordering society was in no way a new phenomenon in the history of British governance – particularly in the British Empire.[63] This 'ethnicism' can be seen, too, as a continuation of Thatcher's war for British (middle-class) values. The cohesion of families in Asian communities – and their 'innate conservatism' – increasingly appealed to some Conservative politicians in the 1980s as a possible source of middle-class authority in the inner city. As Cowling put it in 1978, 'If there *is* a class war – and there is – it is important that it should be handled with subtlety and skill.'[64]

The first Thatcher government did not respond to right-wing calls for the 'repatriation' of black Britons nor did it repeal race relations legislation, yet racial antagonisms certainly remained in a wide range of public policy areas throughout the Thatcher years, in urban programmes, policing, youth unemployment, housing and education. Institutionalized racism persisted; black people, particularly black men, would continue to be perceived as a threat to the market order.[65] As Sir Kenneth Newman, the Commissioner of Metropolitan Police, infamously put it in 1982: 'In the Jamaicans, you have a people who are constitutionally disorderly ... It's simply in their make up, they're constitutionally disposed to be anti-authority.'[66] As well as inducing investment in ethnic community centres, the 1981 riots led to a substantial increase in expenditure on crowd-control technologies, such as protective body-armour, armoured vehicles, weaponry and communications devices. Remarkably, this investment would soon be put to use to contain the miners' strike of 1984–1985. As Lord Whitelaw, the former House Secretary, argued, 'If we hadn't had the Toxteth riots, I doubt if we could have dealt with Arthur Scargill [leader of the National Union of Mineworkers].'[67]

In an analysis of the British Nationality Act of 1981, David Dixon has argued that Enoch Powell was the 'immediate progenitor of Thatcherism' and that 'their ideologies of race and nation are fundamentally the same.'[68] But Thatcherism was a changeable entity. The Powellite nature of the British Nationality Act does not give a complete picture of Thatcher's views on race and nationality. The message on the Conservative political campaign poster of 1983 (which was produced to

---

[63] Feldman, 'Why the English Like Turbans.'
[64] Cowling, *Conservative Essays*, p. 1.
[65] See Anna Marie Smith, *New Right Discourse*, p. 177.
[66] As cited in Gilroy, *There Ain't No Black in the Union Jack*, p. 84.
[67] As cited in Anna Marie Smith, *New Right Discourse*, p. 177.
[68] David Dixon, 'Thatcher's People: The British Nationality Act 1981,' *Journal of Law and Society*, 10: 2 (Winter 1983), pp. 161–180 (pp. 171–172).

generate electoral support for the Act) is yet another strategic approach to nationality within Thatcherism. And it certainly breaks with a Powellite vision of the nation. The poster, which came in two varieties, presents a photograph of a black man or an Asian man in a suit, with the line 'Labour says he's Black, Tories say he's British.' For Powell, race in Britain in the 1970s and 1980s produced an insurmountable identity politics. As a solution, this poster promises to wash away history and identity. In Powellite fashion, it argues in fine print against the treatment of a non-white Briton as a 'special case' to fight discrimination. The poster provoked resentment, because 'it misunderstood the wish of many to retain their own identity, to be both British *and* black.'[69] But the poster also nicely reflects on what it means to be British within Thatcherism. Britishness is expressed in their shared suit. The man, as Paul Gilroy has noted, looks ready for a job interview: 'isolated and shorn of the mugger's key icons – a tea-cosy and the dreadlocks of Rastafari – he is redeemed by his suit, the signifier of British civilisation.'[70] Here, the Manichean world, the inside and outside of the nation, seems to be defined by one's orientation towards capital.

In contrast, in February 1981, Powell moved an amendment during the Nationality Bill's Commons committee stage against the provision that nationality could be passed to children by mothers as well as fathers. He argued that nationality in the last resort was 'tested by fighting'; 'primary allegiance' was expressed, therefore, through the male.[71] A man's nation, he argued, was the nation for which he would fight and his nationality was the expression of his ultimate allegiance. The essential difference between man and woman, he maintained, was between fighting (active citizenship) on the one hand and the preservation and creation of life on the other: 'The two sexes are deeply differentiated in accordance with those two functions.'[72] Remarkably, he refused to escape this fundamental vision of citizenship despite the diminishing prospect of mass mobilization around full-scale war. His arguments were, in 1981, lampooned.

To mark the revival of the Conservative Philosophy Group in 2007, John Casey recounted an interaction between Margaret Thatcher and Enoch Powell at a meeting of the group shortly before the Argentinian invasion of the Falkland Islands. It began, Casey remembers, when Edward Norman, then Dean of Peterhouse, attempted to deliver a

---

[69] Ibid.
[70] Gilroy, *There Ain't no Black in the Union Jack*, p. 65.
[71] 'Mr Powell's Views "Will Encourage Thugs,"' *The Times*, 20 February 1981.
[72] 'Powell Attack on Nationality Bill,' *The Times*, 18 February 1981.

Christian argument for nuclear weapons. When the discussion turned to 'Western values,' Thatcher interjected that Norman had effectively proven that nuclear weapons were necessary for 'the defence of our values.' Powell's reply to this assertion, though filtered through the long memory of John Casey, offers a key insight into the ambiguities of a 'nationalist' politics: 'No, we do not fight for values. I would fight for this country even if it had a communist government.' 'Nonsense, Enoch,' Thatcher retorted. 'If I send British troops abroad, it will be to defend our values.' And to this Powell replied, 'No, Prime Minister, values exist in a transcendental realm, beyond space and time. They can neither be fought for, nor destroyed.'[73] Thatcher, apparently, looked on at Powell 'baffled.'[74] If values cannot be 'fought for,' perhaps Powell was no revolutionary. This disagreement, on the eve of the Falklands War, suggests Powell's refusal to become a genuine member of Britain's Thatcherite revolution. Thatcherism did not seek to conserve Powell's 'fragile web of understood relationships' – the 'little platoons' of affection – that make up the conservative nation. There was no alternative; traditional industrial communities and the mediation of local governance could not survive. As one analysis put it: 'Thatcherism enjoyed negative success as the corrosive agent which broke down the certainties of old forms of social life.'[75] If we look to Thatcher's record, we see less a concern with the protection of particular institutions between the state and the individual, and more a sense that certain cultural and social forms enable a healthy market order. In this sense, in the long intellectual battle between Powell and what he regarded as an 'American' vision of the world, Powell lost.

---

[73] John Casey, 'The Revival of Tory Philosophy,' *The Spectator*, 17 March 2007, p. 24.
[74] Ibid.
[75] D. Hayes and A. Hudson, *Basildon: the Mood of a Nation* (London: Demos, 2001), p. 19, cited in Evans, 'Thatcherism and the British People,' p. 237.

Select bibliography

MANUSCRIPTS

ALBERT SLOMAN LIBRARY, UNIVERSITY OF ESSEX, COLCHESTER
University of Essex Collection, Special Collections (UEC)

BIRMINGHAM CITY ARCHIVES, BIRMINGHAM
Archive of the Indian Workers' Association 1959–1998 (IWA)
Charles Parker Archive
Papers of Philip Donnellan (PPD)

BODLEIAN LIBRARY, SPECIAL COLLECTIONS & WESTERN
MANUSCRIPTS, OXFORD
Conservative Party Archive (CPA)

BRITISH LIBRARY, ASIA, PACIFIC AND AFRICA COLLECTIONS, LONDON
Papers of Frank Lugard Brayne (PFLB)

CHURCHILL ARCHIVE CENTRE, CHURCHILL COLLEGE, CAMBRIDGE
Papers of J. Enoch Powell (POLL)
Papers of Winston Churchill (CHUR)
Papers of Margaret Thatcher (THCR)

MACMILLAN ONLINE (www.qa.amdigital.co.uk/collections/Macmillan-
Cabinet-Papers)
Macmillan Cabinet Papers, 1957–1963 (MCP)

MARGARET THATCHER FOUNDATION WEBSITE
(www.margaretthatcher.org)
Papers of Margaret Thatcher (MTFW)

STAFFORDSHIRE RECORD OFFICE, STAFFORD

Papers of J. Enoch Powell, MP (SRO)

OFFICIAL PAPERS

HANSARD

House of Commons Daily Debates (HC)
House of Lords Daily Debates (HL)

HOUSE OF COMMONS PARLIAMENTARY PAPERS ONLINE

Parliamentary Papers (PP)

THE NATIONAL ARCHIVES, KEW

Records of the Cabinet Office (CAB)
Records of the Home Office (HO)
Records of the Foreign Office (FCO)
Records of the Prime Minister's Office (PREM)

TAPED INTERVIEWS

Benn, Tony. Telephone Interview. 20 November 2005.
Joshi, Shirley. Personal Interview. September 2005.
Powell, J. Enoch. Interview with Bill Schwarz. 26 April 1988.
Powell, J. Enoch. Interview with the Imperial War Museum. 1987–1988.

FILM

British Film Institute: National Film Archive Catalogue (NFA)
Canadian Broadcasting Corporation (CBC)

PUBLISHED WRITINGS OF J. ENOCH POWELL

Biography of a Nation: A Short History of Britain with Angus Maude. London: John Baker, 1970.
Change is Our Ally (ed.) with Angus Maude. London: Conservative Political Centre, 1954.
Collected Poems. London: Bellew Publishing, 1990.
Enoch Powell on 1992, ed. Richard Ritchie. London: Anaya Publishers, 1989.
Freedom and Reality, ed. John Wood. London: B. T. Batsford, 1969.
The House of Lords in the Middle Ages: A History of the English House of Lords to 1540 with Keith Wallis. London: Weidenfeld & Nicolson, 1968.
How Big Should Government Be? with Paul H. Douglas. Washington, DC: American Enterprise Institute for Public Policy Research, 1968.
Joseph Chamberlain. London: Thames and Hudson, 1977.
Lexicon of Herodotus. Cambridge University Press, 1938.
A Nation Not Afraid: The Thinking of Enoch Powell, ed. John Wood. London: B. T. Batsford.

A Nation or No Nation?: Six Years in British Politics, ed. Richard Ritchie. London: Batsford, 1978.

No Easy Answers. London: Sheldon Press, 1973.

Reflections of a Statesman: The Writings and Speeches of Enoch Powell, ed. Rex Collings. London: Bellew Publishing, 1991.

Still to Decide. ed. John Wood. Kingswood, Surrey: Elliot Right Way Books, 1972.

Wrestling with the Angel. London: Sheldon Press, 1977.

NEWSPAPERS AND JOURNALS

Africa Today
The Age (AUS)
The Australian (AUS)
Birmingham Post
Christian Science Monitor
The Chronicle
Daily Express
Daily Mail
Daily Telegraph and Morning Post
East Africa and Rhodesia Newspaper
Evening Mail
Evening Standard
Financial Times
Glasgow Herald
The Guardian
The Independent
The Listener
Morning Star
New Statesman
Northern Territory News (AUS)
The Observer
Powellight
The Scotsman
Sikh Review
Spectator
Sunday Express
Sydney Morning Herald (AUS)
Sunday Telegraph
Sunday Times
The Times
Wolverhampton Express and Star

PRIMARY PUBLICATIONS

Benn, Tony. *Office Without Power: Diaries 1968–72.* London: Arrow Books Limited, 1989.

    Years of Hope: Diaries, Papers and Letters 1940–1962. London: Arrow Books Limited, 1995.

Guilty Men. London: Victor Gollancz, 1940.

'Cato.' *A Changing Partnership: A Report by the Young Conservatives on Problems of the Commonwealth*. London: Conservative Political Centre, No. 248, 1962.

Crossman, Richard. *The Backbench Diaries of Richard Crossman*. London: Hamish Hamilton, 1981.

Elton, Baron Godfrey. *The Unarmed Invasion: A Survey of Afro-Asian Immigration*. London: Geoffrey Bles, 1965.

Griffiths, Peter. *A Question of Color?* London: Leslie Frewin Publishers, 1966.

Hatch, John. 'Africa, in Black and White.' *Encounter*, June 1959, pp. 64–65.

Huddleston, Trevor. *Nought for Your Comfort*. London: William Collins, 1956.

Huxley, Elspeth. *Back Streets, New Worlds: A Look at Immigrants in Britain*. Toronto: Chatto and Windus, 1964.

'Is the Commonwealth Farce? An Answer to "A Conservative,"' *The Round Table*, vol. 54: no. 215 (June 1964).

Kaplan, Marion. 'Their Rhodesia,' *Transition*, no. 23, 1965.

Koebner, Richard. *Empire*. New York: Cambridge University Press, 1962.

Melady, Thomas Patrick. *The Revolution of Color*. New York: Hawthorn Books, 1966.

Montgomery, Bernard Law. *The Memoirs of Field-Marshal the Viscount of Montgomery of Alamein*. London: Collins, 1958.

Oakeshott, Michael. *On Human Conduct*. Oxford University Press, 1975.

Orwell, George. *The Lion and the Unicorn: Socialism and English Genius*. London: Secker and Warburg, 1941.

Perham, Margery. *The Colonial Reckoning: The End of Imperial Rule in Africa in the Light of British Experience*. New York: Alfred Knopf, 1962.

(ed.) *The Diaries of Lord Lugard. Vols. I, II, III, IV*. London: Faber and Faber, 1959 and 1963.

Priestley, J. B. *Postscripts*. London: William Heinemann, 1940.

Procter, James (ed.). *Writing Black Britain, 1948–1998*. Manchester University Press, 2000.

Shrapnel, Norman, and Mike Phillips. 'Enoch Powell: An Enigma of Awkward Passions,' *The Guardian*, 9 February 1998.

Thatcher, Margaret. *Let Our Children Grow Tall*. London: Centre for Policy Studies, 1977.

Utley, T. E. 'Toryism at the Cross-roads,' *Daily Telegraph*, 18 February 1960.

Vallely, Paul. 'Established Values: How the Church Nearly Lost its Way over the Death of Enoch Powell,' *The Independent*, 19 February 1998.

'Old Order Mourns Enoch Powell,' *The Independent*,19 February 1998.

Wambu, Onyekachi. *Empire Windrush: Fifty Years of Writing about Black Britain*. London: Phoenix, 1999.

Williams, Robin. 'Commonwealth Reaction,' *Crossbow*, Spring 1960.

Wilson, Sarah. 'Powell Laid to Rest as the Old Soldier He Really Was,' *The Scotsman*, 19 February 1998.

Worsthorne, Peregrine. 'Bonds that Could Become Fetters,' *Daily Telegraph*, 5 March 1960.

'Class and Conflict in British Foreign Policy,' *Foreign Affairs*, 37: 3 (April 1959), pp. 419–431.
'Trouble in the Air: Letter from Ghana,' *Encounter*, May 1958, pp. 3–13.

SECONDARY PUBLICATIONS

Adamthwaite, Anthony. 'The British Government and the Media, 1937–1938,' *Journal of Contemporary History*, 18: 2 (April 1983), pp. 281–297.
Addison, Paul. *Churchill on the Home Front, 1900–1955*. London: Pimlico, 1992.
  Now the War is Over: A Social History of Britain, 1945–51. London: Jonathan Cape, 1985.
  The Road to 1945: British Politics and the Second World War. London: Pimlico, 1975.
Althusser, Louis. *Lenin and Philosophy and Other Essays*. Trans. Ben Brewster. New York: Monthly Review, 2001.
Anderson, Benedict. *Imagined Communities: Reflections on the Origin and Spread of Nationalism*. London: Verso, 1991.
Anderson, David. *Histories of the Hanged: Britain's Dirty War in Kenya and the End of Empire*. London: Weidenfeld & Nicolson, 2005.
Arendt, Hannah. *The Origins of Totalitarianism* (2nd edn). London: Allen and Unwin, 1958.
Bailkin, Jordanna. *The Afterlife of Empire*. Berkeley: University of California Press, 2012.
Bammer, Angelika (ed.). *Displacements: Cultural Identities in Question*. Bloomington: Indiana University Press, 1994.
Barkawi, Tarak, and Mark Laffey. 'The Imperial Peace: Democracy, Force and Globalization,' *European Journal of International Relations* 5: 4 (1999), pp. 403–434.
Barker, Martin, and Anne Beezer (eds.). *Reading into Cultural Studies*. London: Routledge, 1992.
Barnett, Anthony. *Iron Britannia*. London: Allison and Busby, 1982.
Barnett, Correlli. *The Audit of War: The Illusion of Reality of Britain as a Great Nation*. Basingstoke: Macmillan, 1986.
  The Collapse of British Power. New York: William Morrow & Company, 1972.
  The Lost Victory: British Dreams, British Realities, 1945–1950. London: Pan Books, 2001.
Bartram, Graham, Maurice Slawinski and David Steel (eds.). *Reconstructing the Past: Representations of the Fascist Era in Post-war European Culture* (Keele University Press, 1996).
Beer, Samuel. *Essays on Reform, 1967*. Oxford University Press, 1967.
  Modern British Politics: A Study of Parties and Pressure Groups. London: Faber and Faber, 1965.
Beetham, David. *Transport and Turbans: A Comparative Study in Local Politics*. Oxford University Press, 1970.
Benjamin, Walter. *Selected Writings*. Cambridge, MA: Belknap Press, 1996.

Bentley, Michael. *Public and Private Doctrine: Essays in British History presented to Maurice Cowling.* Cambridge University Press, 1993.

Berkeley, Humphry. *The Odyssey of Enoch: A Political Memoir.* London: Hamish Hamilton, 1977.

Bertossi, Christophe. 'French and British Models of Integration: Public Philosophies, Policies and State Institutions.' Working Paper No. 46, ESRC Centre on Migration, Policy and Society. University of Oxford, 2007.

Betts, G. Gordon. *The Twilight of Britain: Cultural Nationalism, Multiculturalism, and the Politics of Toleration.* London: Transaction Publishers, 2002.

Bew, Paul, Peter Gibbon and Henry Patterson. *Northern Ireland, 1921–2001.* London: Serif, 2002.

Bhabha, Homi. *The Location of Culture.* New York: Routledge, 1994.

Black, Lawrence. *Redefining British Politics: Culture, Consumerism and Participation, 1954–70.* Basingstoke: Palgrave Macmillan, 2010.

Blake, Robert. *The Conservative Party from Peel to Thatcher.* London: Fontana Press, 1985.

Boehmer, Elleke. *Colonial and Postcolonial Literatures: Migrant Metaphors.* Oxford University Press, 1995.

Bonhomme, Samuel. *Enoch Powell and the West Indian Immigrants.* London: Villers Publishers, 1971.

Bosworth, R. J. 'Nations Examine Their Past: A Comparative Analysis of the Historiography of the "Long" Second World War,' *The History Teacher*, 29: 4 (August 1996), pp. 499–523.

Brivati, Brian, and Harriet Jones (eds.). *What Difference Did the War Make?* London: Leicester University Press, 1993.

Brocklehurst, Helen, and Robert Phillips (eds.). *History, Nationhood and the Question of Britain.* Basingstoke: Palgrave Macmillan, 2004.

Brooke, Peter. 'India, Post-Imperialism and the Origins of Enoch Powell's "Rivers of Blood" Speech,' *Historical Journal*, 50: 3 (2007), pp. 669–687.

Brown, Andy R. *Political Languages of Race and the Politics of Exclusion.* Aldershot: Ashgate Publishing, 1999.

Calder, Angus. *The Myth of the Blitz.* London: Pimlico, 1991.

The People's War: Britain 1939–1945. London: Panther, 1971.

Cannadine, David. *Class in Britain.* Harmondsworth: Penguin, 1998.

Ornamentalism: How the British Saw Their Empire. Oxford University Press, 2001.

The Rise and Fall of Class in Britain. New York: Columbia University Press, 1999.

Carruthers, Susan L. *Winning Hearts and Minds: British Governments, the Media and Colonial Counter-Insurgency, 1944–1960.* London: Leicester University Press, 1995.

Carter, Dan T. *The Politics of Rage: George Wallace, the Origins of New Conservatism and the Transformation of American Politics.* New York: Simon and Schuster, 1995.

Catterall, Peter, and Sean McDougall. *The Northern Ireland Question in British Politics.* Basingstoke: Macmillan Press, 1996.

Centre for Contemporary Cultural Studies. *The Empire Strikes Back: Race and Racism in 70s Britain*. London: Hutchinson, 1982.

Chalmers, Malcolm. *Paying for Defence: Military Spending and British Decline*. London: Pluto Press, 1985.

Chauncey, George. *Gay New York: Gender, Urban Culture, and the Making of the Gay Male World, 1890–1940*. New York: Basic Books, 1994.

Clarke, Peter. *Hope and Glory: Britain 1900–1990*. London: Penguin, 1997.

Clemens, Gabriele. 'A History of Failure and Miscalculations? Britain's Relationship to the European Communities in the Postwar Era (1945–1973),' *Contemporary European History*, 13: 2 (2004), pp. 223–232.

Cohen, G. Daniel. 'The "Human Rights Revolution" at Work: Displaced Persons in Postwar Europe,' in Stefan-Ludwig Hoffman (ed.), *Human Rights in the Twentieth Century*. Cambridge University Press, 2011, pp. 45–61.

Colley, Linda. 'Britishness and Otherness: An Argument,' *Journal of British Studies*, 31: 4 (October 1992), pp. 309–329.

Britons: Forging the Nation, 1707–1837. New Haven, CT: Yale University Press, 2005.

Conekin, Becky, Frank Mort and Chris Waters (eds.). *Moments of Modernity: Reconstructing Britain 1945–1964*. New York University Press, 1999.

Connelly, Mark. *We Can Take It! Britain and the Memory of the Second World War*. Harlow: Longman, 2004.

Copping, Robert. *The Story of the Monday Club – The First Decade*. Ilford: Current Affairs Information Service, 1972.

Corthorn, Paul. 'Enoch Powell, Ulster Unionism, and the British Nation,' *Journal of British Studies*, 51: 4 (October 2012), pp. 967–997.

Cosgrave, Patrick. *The Lives of Enoch Powell*. London: The Bodley Head, 1989.

Cowling, Maurice (ed.). *Conservative Essays*. London: Cassell, 1978.

Mill and Liberalism. Cambridge University Press, 1990.

Religion and Public Doctrine in Modern England, Vols. I, II, and III. Cambridge University Press, 1980, 1985, 2001.

Cross, J. A. 'Appraising the Commonwealth,' *Political Studies*, 32 (1984), pp. 107–112.

Damousi, Joy. *The Labour of Loss: Mourning, Memory and Wartime Bereavement in Australia*. Cambridge University Press, 1999.

Darwin, John. *After Tamerlane: The Global History of Empire Since 1405*. London: Penguin, 2007.

Britain and Decolonization: The Retreat from Empire in the Post-war World. New York: St Martin's Press, 1988.

'Decolonization and the End of Empire,' in Robin W. Winks (ed.), *The Oxford History of the British Empire, Vol. V: Historiography* (Oxford University Press, 1999).

End of the British Empire: The Historical Debate. London: Wiley-Blackwell, 1991.

Dawson, Graham. *Soldier Heroes: British Adventure, Empire and the Imagining of Masculinities*. London: Routledge, 1994.

Dixon, David. 'Thatcher's People: The British Nationality Act 1981,' *Journal of Law and Society*, 10: 2 (Winter 1983), pp. 161–180.

Dudziak, Mary. 'Brown as a Cold War Case,' *The Journal of American History*, 91: 1 (2004), pp. 32–42.

Eagleton, Terry. *Ideology: An Introduction*. London: Verso, 1991.

Edgerton, David. *Warfare Britain: Britain, 1920–1970*. Cambridge University Press, 2006.

Edkins, Jenny. *Trauma and the Memory of Politics*. New York: Cambridge University Press, 2003.

Eley, Geoff. 'Beneath the Skin. Or: How to Forget about the Empire Without Really Trying,' in Tony Ballantyne (ed.), *From Orientalism to Ornamentalism: Empire and Difference in History*. Special Issue of *Journal of Colonialism and Colonial History*, 3: 1 (Spring 2002).

'Finding the People's War: Film, British Collective Memory, and World War II,' *American Historical Review*, 105 (2001), pp. 818–838.

Elkins, Caroline. *Britain's Gulag: The Brutal End of Empire in Kenya*. Pimlico: London, 2005.

Evans, Brendan. 'Thatcherism and the British People,' in Stuart Ball and Ian Holliday (eds.), *Mass Conservatism: The Conservatives and the Public Since the 1880s* (London: Frank Cass, 2002).

Favell, Adrian. *Philosophies of Integration: Immigration and the Idea of Citizenship in France and Britain*. Basingstoke: Palgrave, 2001.

Feldman, David. 'Why the English Like Turbans: Multicultural Politics in British History,' in David Feldman and Jon Lawrence (eds.), *Structures and Transformations in Modern British History*. Cambridge University Press, 2011.

Ferguson, Niall. *Empire: How Britain Made the Modern World*. London: Allen Lane, 2003.

Fielding, Steven. 'What Did "The People" Want?: The Meaning of the 1945 General Election,' *Historical Journal*, 35 (1992), pp. 623–639.

Fielding, Steven, Peter Thompson and Nick Tiratsoo. *'England Arise!': The Labour Party and Popular Politics in 1940s Britain*. Manchester University Press, 1995.

Foot, Paul. 'Beyond the Powell: Obituary of Enoch Powell,' *Socialist Review*, no. 217 (March 1998).

Immigration and Race in British Politics, Harmondsworth: Penguin Books, 1965.

The Rise of Enoch Powell: An Examination of Enoch Powell's Attitude to Race and Immigration. London, Cornmarket Press, 1969.

Foote, Geoffrey. *The Republican Transformation of Modern British Politics*. Basingstoke: Palgrave Macmillan, 2006.

Francis, Martin. *The Flyer: British Culture and the Royal Air Force, 1939–1945*. Oxford University Press, 2009.

Fraser, Nancy, and Axel Honneth. *Redistribution or Recognition? A Political-Philosophical Exchange*. London: Verso, 2003.

Fussell, Paul. *Wartime: Understanding and Behavior in the Second World War*. New York and Oxford: Oxford University Press, 1989.

Gamble, Andrew. *The Conservative Nation*. London: Routledge, 1974.

Gare, Deborah. 'Britishness in Recent Australian Historiography,' *Historical Journal*, 43: 4 (2000), pp. 1145–1155.

Gaskill, William. *A Sense of Direction*. New York: Limelight Editions, 1990.

Geelhoed, E. Bruce, and Anthony O. Edmonds. *Eisenhower, Macmillan and Allied Unity, 1957–1961*. New York: Palgrave Macmillan, 2003.

Ghosh, Peter. *Public and Private Doctrine: Essays in British History presented to Maurice Cowling*. Cambridge University Press, 1993.

Gilmour, Ian. *The Inside Right: A Study of Conservatism*. London: Hutchinson, 1977.

Gilroy, Paul. *Against Race: Imagining Political Culture Beyond the Color Line*. Cambridge, MA: Harvard University Press, 2000.

Postcolonial Melancholia. New York: Columbia University Press, 2004.

'There Ain't No Black in the Union Jack': The Cultural Politics of Race and Nation. London: Routledge, 2002.

Gordon Walker, Patrick. *The Commonwealth*. London: Secker & Warburg, 1962.

Gorst, Antony, Lewis Johnman and W. Scott Lucas. *Post-war Britain, 1945–64: Themes and Perspectives*. London: Pinter Publishers, 1989.

Goulbourne, Harry. *Ethnicity and Nationalism in Post-Imperial Britain*. Cambridge University Press, 1991.

Graves, Robert, and Alan Hodge. *The Long Week-End: A Social History of Great Britain 1918–1939*. New York and London: W.W. Norton & Company, 1963.

Green, E. H. H. *Ideologies of Conservatism: Conservative Political Ideas in the Twentieth Century*. Oxford University Press, 2002.

Grierson, Edward. *Death of the Imperial Dream: The British Commonwealth and Empire 1775–1969*. Garden City: Doubleday & Company, 1972.

Gunn, Simon, and James Vernon (eds.). *The Peculiarities of Liberal Modernity in Imperial Britain*. Berkeley: University of California Press, 2011.

Hall, Catherine. *Civilising Subjects: Metropole and Colony in the English Imagination, 1830–1867*. Cambridge: Polity, 2002.

(ed.). *Cultures of Empire: Colonizers in Britain and the Empire in the Nineteenth and Twentieth Centuries. A Reader*. New York: Routledge, 2000.

Hall, Catherine, and Sonya Rose. *At Home with the Empire: Metropolitan Society and the Imperial World*. Cambridge University Press, 2006.

Hall, Stuart et al. (eds.). *Culture, Media, Language: Working Papers in Cultural Studies, 1972–79*. London: Routledge, 2002.

Hall, Stuart, Chas Critcher, Tony Jefferson, John Clarke and Brian Roberts. *Policing the Crisis: Mugging, the State and Law and Order*. Basingstoke: Palgrave Macmillan, 1978.

Hall, Stuart, and Martin Jacques (eds.). *The Politics of Thatcherism*. London: Lawrence and Wishart, 1983.

Hall, Stuart, and Tony Jefferson (eds.). *Resistance through Rituals: Youth Subcultures in Post-war Britain*. London: Routledge, 1993.

Hansen, Randall. *Citizenship and Immigration in Post-war Britain*. Oxford University Press, 2000.

'The Kenyan Asians, British Politics, and the Commonwealth Immigrants Act, 1968,' *Historical Journal*, 62: 3 (1999), pp. 809–834.

Harrison, Brian. *Peaceable Kingdom: Stability and Change in Modern Britain.* Oxford University Press, 1982.

Havighurst, Alfred F. *Britain in Transition*. University of Chicago Press, 1985.

Hay, Colin. 'Chronicles of a Death Foretold: The Winter of Discontent and Construction of the Crisis of British Keynesianism,' *Parliamentary Affairs* 63 (2010), 464–466.

Heffer, Simon. *Like the Roman: The Life of Enoch Powell.* London: Weidenfeld & Nicolson, 1998.

Herman, Arthur. *Gandhi and Churchill: The Epic Rivalry That Destroyed an Empire and Forged Our Age.* New York: Random House, 2008.

Hesse, Barnor, and S. Sayyid. 'Narrating the Postcolonial Political and the Immigrant Imaginary,' in N. Ali, V. S. Kalra and S. Sayyid (eds.), *A Postcolonial Britain: South Asians in Britain* (London: Hurst & Company, 2006).

Higonnet, Margaret R. et al. (eds.). *Behind the Lines: Gender and the Two World Wars.* New Haven, CT: Yale University Press, 1989.

Hiro, Dilip. *Black British, White British.* Middlesex: Penguin, 1971.

Hirschman, Albert O. *The Rhetoric of Reaction: Perversity, Futility, Jeopardy.* Cambridge, MA: Belknap Press of Harvard University Press, 1991.

Hodgkin, Katharine, and Susannah Radstone (eds.). *Memory, History, Nation: Contested Pasts.* New Brunswick and London: Transaction Publishers, 2006.

Holland, Robert F. *Britain and the Revolt in Cyprus, 1954–1959.* Oxford University Press, 1998.

Holmes, Richard. 'The Proper Study?,' in Peter France and William St Clair (eds.), *The Uses of Biography.* Oxford University Press, 2002.

Howe, Stephen. 'Internal Decolonization? British Politics since Thatcher as Post-colonial Trauma,' *Twentieth Century British History*, 14: 3 (2003), pp. 286–304.

Hyam, Ronald, and William Roger Lewis (eds.). *The Conservative Government and the End of Empire, 1957–1964: Economics, International Relations and the Commonwealth Pt. 2.* London: The Stationery Office, 2000.

Jackson, Ben, and Robert Saunders (eds.). *Making Thatcher's Britain.* Cambridge University Press, 2012.

Jarvis, Mark. *Conservative Governments, Morality and Social Change in Affluent Britain, 1957–64.* Manchester University Press, 2005.

Jones, Harriet, and Michael Kandiah (eds.). *The Myth of the Consensus: New Views on British History, 1945–64.* New York: St Martin's Press, 1996.

Judt, Tony. *Postwar: A History of Europe Since 1945.* New York: Penguin Press, 2005.

Kavanagh, Dennis. *Thatcherism and British Politics: The End of Consensus?* Oxford University Press, 1987.

King, Anthony. 'The Afghan War and the Making of "Postmodern" Memory: Commemoration and the Dead at Helmand,' *The British Journal of Sociology*, 6: 1 (2010), pp. 1–25.

(ed.). *Why is Britain Becoming Harder to Govern?* London: BBC, 1976.

Kitson, Frank. *Low Intensity Operations: Subversion, Insurgency and Peacekeeping.* London: Faber & Faber, 1971.

Klose, Fabian. "'Source of Embarrassment": Human Rights, State of Emergency, and the Wars of Decolonization,' in Stefan-Ludwig Hoffman (ed.), *Human Rights in the Twentieth Century.* Cambridge University Press, 2011.

Knapman, Claudia. *White Women in Fiji, 1835–1930: The Ruin of Empire?* (London: Allen & Unwin, 1986).

Kundani, Arun. *The End of Tolerance: Racism in 21st-Century Britain.* London and Ann Arbor, MI: Pluto Press, 2007.

Labour Research Department, *Powell and His Allies.* London: Labour Research Department, 1969.

Lavin, Deborah. *From Empire to International Commonwealth: A Biography of Lionel Curtis.* Oxford: Clarendon Press, 1995.

Lawrence, Jon. *Speaking for the People: Party, Language and Popular Politics in England, 1867–1914* (Cambridge University Press, 1998).

Layton-Henry, Zig. *The Politics of Race in Britain.* London: Allen and Unwin, 1984.

Layton-Henry, Zig, and Paul B. Rich (eds.). *Race, Government and Politics in Britain.* Basingstoke: Macmillan, 1986.

Lee, Hermione. *Body Parts: Essays in Life-Writing.* London: Chatto & Windus, 2005.

Lee, J. J. *Ireland, 1912–1985: Politics and Society.* Cambridge University Press, 1990.

Leed, Eric. *No Man's Land: Combat and Identity in World War One.* Cambridge University Press, 1979.

Levine, Philippa, and Susan R. Grayzel (eds.). *Gender, Labour, War and Empire: Essays on Modern Britain.* Basingstoke: Palgrave Macmillan, 2009.

Lewis, Joanna.'Nasty, Brutish and in Shorts? British Colonial Rule, Violence and the Historians of Mau Mau.' *The Round Table*, vol. 96, no. 389 (2007), pp. 201–223.

Loomba, Ania, Suvir Kaul, Matti Bunzl, Antoinette Burton and Jed Esty (eds.). *Postcolonial Studies and Beyond.* Durham, NC and London: Duke University Press, 2005.

Lord Howard of Rising (ed.). *Enoch at 100: A Re-evaluation of the Life, Politics and Philosophy of Enoch Powell.* London: Biteback Publishing, 2012.

Low, D. A. *Eclipse of Empire.* Cambridge University Press, 1993.

Lowe, Rodney. 'The Second World War, Consensus, and the Foundation of the Welfare State,' *Twentieth-Century British History* 1: 2 (1990), pp. 152–182.

Lynn, Martin (ed.). *The British Empire in the 1950s: Retreat or Revival?* Basingstoke: Palgrave Macmillan, 2006.

MacArthur, Brian (ed.). *The Penguin Book of Twentieth-Century Speeches.* London: Viking, 1999.

McClintock, Anne. *Imperial Leather: Race, Gender and Sexuality in the Colonial Contest.* New York: Routledge, 1995.

McIntyre, W. David. *British Decolonization, 1946–1997: When, Why and How did the British Empire Fall?* Basingstoke: Macmillan, 1998.

'Clio and Britannia's Lost Dream: Historians and the British Commonwealth of Nations in the First Half of the 20th Century,' *The Round Table*, vol. 93, no. 376 (September 2004), pp. 517–532.

Mackenzie, John. 'Gender, Labour, War and Empire: Essays on Modern Britain,' *The Journal of Imperial and Commonwealth History*, 38: 4 (2010), pp. 657–658.

McKibbin, Ross. *Class and Cultures: England 1918–1951*. Oxford University Press, 1998.

McKie, David, and Chris Cook (eds.). *The Decade of Disillusion: British Politics and the Sixties*. London and Basingstoke: The Macmillan Press, 1972.

Macmillan, Harold. *At the End of the Day, 1961–1963*. London: Macmillan, 1973.

Mamdani, Mahmood. *Citizen and Subject: Contemporary Africa and the Legacy of Late Colonialism*. Princeton University Press, 1996.

'Historicizing Power and Responses to Power: Indirect Rule and Its Reform,' *Social Research*, 66: 3 (1999), pp. 859–886.

Mamood, Tariq. *Not Easy Being British: Colour, Culture and Citizenship*. London, 1992.

May, Alex (ed.). *Britain, the Commonwealth and Europe: The Commonwealth and Britain's Application to Join the European Community*. Basingstoke: Palgrave Macmillan, 2001.

Messina, Anthony M. *Race and Party Competition in Britain*. New York: Oxford University Press, 1989.

Miller, David (ed.) *Rethinking Northern Ireland: Culture, Ideology and Colonialism*. London: Longman, 1998.

Mohanram, Radhika. *Imperial White: Race, Diaspora and the British Empire*. Minneapolis, MN: University of Minnesota Press, 2007.

Moore-Gilbert, Bart, and John Seed (eds.) *Cultural Revolution? The Challenge of the Arts in the 1960s*. New York: Routledge, 1992.

Morgan, Kenneth O. *The People's Peace: British History 1945–1989*. Oxford University Press, 1990.

Mosse, George L. *Nationalism and Sexuality*. New York: Howard Fertig, 1997.

Mullard, Chris. *Black Britain*. London: George Allen & Unwin, 1973.

Musembi, Musila. *Archives Management: The Kenyan Experience*. Africa Book Services, 1985.

Nairn, Tom. *The Break-Up of Britain: Crisis and Neo-Nationalism*. Altona, Vic.: Common Ground Publishing, 2003.

'Enoch Powell: The New Right,' *New Left Review*, 1/61 (May–June 1970), pp. 3–27.

Pariah: Misfortunes of the British Kingdom. London: Verso, 2002.

Nardocchio-Jones, Gavin. 'From Mau Mau to Middlesex? The Fate of Europeans in Independent Kenya,' *Comparative Studies of South Asia, Africa and the Middle East*, 26: 3 (2006), pp. 491–505.

Nava, Mica, and Alan O'Shea (eds.). *Modern Times: Reflections on a Century of English Modernity*. London: Routledge, 1996.

Noakes, Lucy. *War and the British: Gender, Memory and National Identity*. London: I. B. Tauris, 1998.

Overdale, Ritchie. 'Macmillan and the Wind of Change in Africa, 1957–1960,' *Historical Journal*, 38: 2 (June 1995), pp. 455–477.

Patterson, Sheila. *Immigration and Race Relations in Britain 1960–1967.* London and New York: Oxford University Press, 1969.

Paul, Kathleen. *Whitewashing Britain: Race and Citizenship in the Postwar Era.* Ithaca, NY: Cornell University Press, 1997.

Pedersen, Susan, and Peter Mandler. *After the Victorians: Private Conscience & Public Duty in Modern Britain.* New York: Routledge, 1994.

Pedraza, Howard. *Winston Churchill, Enoch Powell, and the Nation.* London: Cleveland Press, 1986.

Portelli, Alessendro. *Battle of Valle Guilia: Oral History and the Art of Dialogue.* University of Wisconsin Press, 1997.

Porter, Bernard. *The Absent-minded Imperialists: Empire, Society and Culture in Britain.* Oxford University Press, 2004.

'The Empire Strikes Back,' *History Today*, 46: 9 (September 1996), pp. 11–13.

'How Did They Get Away with It?,' *London Review of Books*, 27: 5 (3 March 2005), pp. 3–6.

Procter, James. *Stuart Hall.* London: Routledge, 2004.

Pugh, Martin. *The Making of Modern British Politics, 1867–1939.* London: Wiley-Blackwell, 2002.

Rajan, M. S. *The Post-War Transformation of the Commonwealth.* London: Asia Publishing House, 1963.

Reese, Trevor R. 'Keeping Calm About the Commonwealth,' *International Affairs*, 41: 3 (July 1965), pp. 451–462.

Reynolds, David. *Britannia Overruled: British Policy and World Power in the Twentieth Century.* Harlow: Pearson Education, 2000.

In Command of History: Fighting and Writing the Second World War. London: Allen Lane, 2004.

Rich, Paul. 'Black People in Britain: Response and Reaction, 1945–62,' *History Today*, 36: 1 (January 1986).

Race and Empire in British Politics. Cambridge University Press, 1986.

Riera, Monica, and Gavin Schaffer (eds.). *The Lasting War: Society and Identity in Britain, France and Germany after 1945.* New York: Macmillan, 2008.

Ritschel, Daniel. *The Politics of Planning: The Debate on Economic Planning in Britain in the 1930s.* Oxford University Press, 1997.

Ritscherle, Alice. 'Opting out of Utopia: Race and Working-Class Political Culture in Britain during the Age of Decolonization, 1948–68.' PhD dissertation, University of Michigan, Ann Arbor, 2005.

Roberts, Andrew. *Eminent Churchillians.* London: Weidenfeld & Nicolson, 1994.

Rose, E. J. B. *Colour and Citizenship: A Report on British Race Relations.* London: Oxford University Press, 1969.

Rose, Peter. *How the Troubles Came to Northern Ireland.* Basingstoke: Macmillan Press, 2000.

Rose, Sonya O. *Which People's War? National Identity and Citizenship in Britain, 1939–1945.* Oxford University Press, 2003.

Ross, Kristin. *May '68 and its Afterlives*. Chicago University Press, 2002.

Roth, Andrew. *Enoch Powell: Tory Tribune*. London: McDonald & Co., 1970.

Rush, Anne Spry. *Bonds of Empire: West Indians and Britishness from Victoria to Decolonization*. Oxford University Press, 2011.

Rutherford, Jonathan. *Forever England: Reflections on Race, Masculinity and Empire*. London: Lawrence and Wishart, 1997.

Saggar, Shamit. 'The Politics of "Race Policy" in Britain,' *Critical Social Policy*, 13: 37 (July 1993), pp. 32–51.

Samuel, Raphael (ed.). *Patriotism: The Making and Unmaking of British National Identity. Volume 2: Minorities and Outsiders*. London: Routledge, 1989.

Särlvik, Bo, and Ivor Crewe. *Decade of Dealignment: The Conservative Victory of 1979 and Electoral Trends in the 1970s*. Cambridge University Press, 2010.

Sartre, Jean-Paul. 'Preface,' in *The Wretched of the Earth*. New York: Grove Press, 1963.

Savage, Mike. *Identities and Social Change in Britain Since 1940: The Politics of Method* (Oxford University Press, 2010).

Schaffer, Gavin. 'Fighting Racism: Black Soldiers and Workers in Britain during the Second World War,' *Immigrants & Minorities*, 28 (July/November 2010), pp. 246–265.

Schoen, Douglas E. *Enoch Powell and the Powellites*. Basingstoke: Palgrave Macmillan, 1977.

Schwarz, Bill. 'Actually Existing Postcolonialism,' *Radical Philosophy* (November–December, 2000).

'"Claudia Jones and the *West Indian Gazette*": Reflections on the Emergence of Post-colonial Britain,' *Twentieth Century British History*, 14: 3 (2003), pp. 264–285.

'"The Only White Man In There": The Re-Racialisation of England, 1956–1968,' *Race and Class*, 38: 1 (July 1996), pp. 65–78.

'Reveries of Race: The Closing of the Imperial Moment,' in Becky Conekin, Frank Mort and Chris Waters (eds.), *Moments of Modernity: Reconstructing Britain, 1945–1964*. New York University Press, 1999, pp. 189–207.

The White Man's World (*Memories of Empire*, vol. 1). Oxford University Press, 2011.

(ed.). *The Expansion of England: Race, Ethnicity and Cultural History*. New York: Routledge, 1996.

Scott, David. *Refashioning Futures: Criticism after Postcoloniality*. Princeton University Press, 1999.

Seldon, Anthony, and Stuart Ball (eds.). *Conservative Century: The Conservative Party since 1900*. Oxford University Press, 1994.

Shepherd, Robert. *Enoch Powell: A Biography*. London: Hutchinson, 1996.

Sherwood, Marika. *Many Struggles: West Indian Workers and Service Personnel in Britain, 1939–1945*. London: Karia, 1985.

Shukra, Kalbir. *The Changing Pattern of Black Politics in Britain*. London: Pluto Press, 1998.

Simpson, Brian A. W. *Human Rights and the End of Empire: Britain and the Genesis of the European Convention*. Oxford University Press, 2001.

Sivanandan, Ambalavaner. 'From Resistance to Rebellion: Asian and Afro-Caribbean Struggles in Britain,' *Race and Class*, 23 (1981), pp. 111–152.

'Race, Terror and Civil Society,' *Race and Class*, 47 (January 2006), pp. 1–8.

Skidelsky, Robert (ed.). *Thatcherism*. London: Chatto and Windus, 1988.

Smith, Anna Marie. *New Right Discourse on Race and Sexuality: Britain, 1968–1990*. Cambridge University Press, 1994.

Smith, Harold (ed.). *War and Social Change: British Society in the Second World War*. Manchester University Press, 1986.

Smith, Malcolm. *Britain and 1940: History, Myth and Popular Memory*. London: Routledge, 2000.

Smithies, Bill, and Peter Fiddick. *Enoch Powell on Immigration*. London: Sphere, 1969.

Soyinka, Wole. *Ibadan: The Penkelemes Years, A Memoir, 1946–1965*. London: Methuen, 1994.

'Twice Bitten: The Fate of Africa's Culture Producers,' *Proceedings of the Modern Language Association* (January 1990), pp. 110–120.

Soysal, Yasemin Nuhoğlu. *Limits of Citizenship: Migrants and Postnational Membership in Europe*. University of Chicago Press, 1994.

Spiering, Menno, and Michael Wintle (eds.). *European Identity and the Second World War*. London: Palgrave Macmillan, 2011.

Srinivasan, Krishnan. 'Nobody's Commonwealth? The Commonwealth in Britain's Post-imperial Adjustment,' *Commonwealth and Comparative Politics*, 44: 2 (July 2006), pp. 257–269.

Steel, David. *No Entry: The Background and Implications of the Commonwealth Immigrants Act, 1968*. London: C. Huret, 1969.

Strobel, Margaret. *European Women and the Second British Empire* (Bloomington, IN: Indiana University Press, 1991).

Summerfield, Penny. *Reconstructing Women's Wartime Lives: Discourse and Subjectivity in Oral Histories of the Second World War*. Manchester University Press, 1998.

Tabili, Laura. 'The Construction of Racial Difference in Twentieth Century Britain: The Special Restriction (Coloured Alien Seamen) Order, 1925,' *Journal of British Studies*, 33, 1 (January 1994).

'We Ask for British Justice': Workers and Racial Difference in Late Imperial Britain*. Ithaca, NY: Cornell University Press, 1994.

Tanner, Duncan, Pat Thane and Nick Tiratsoo (eds.). *Labour's First Century*. Cambridge University Press, 2000.

Taylor, A. J. P. *The Origins of the Second World War*. London: Penguin, 1991.

Taylor, Don. *The Years of Challenge: The Commonwealth and the British Empire 1945–1958*. New York: Frederick A. Praeger Publishers, 1959.

Teitelbaum, Michael S., and Jay M. Winter. *A Question of Numbers: High Migration, Low Fertility, and the Politics of National Identity*. New York: Hill & Wang, 1998.

Thornton, A. P. *The Habit of Authority: Paternalism in British History*. London: George Allen & Unwin, 1966.

The Imperial Idea and Its Enemies: A Study in British Power. New York: St Martin's Press, 1959.

Tiratsoo, Nick (ed.). *The Attlee Years*. London: Continuum International Pub. Group, 1991.

Tudor, Henry. *Political Myth*. London: Pall Mall, 1972.

University of Birmingham, Centre for Contemporary Cultural Studies. *On Ideology*. London: Hutchinson & Co. (Publishers), 1978.

Utley, T. E. *Enoch Powell: The Man and His Thinking*. London: William Kimber, 1968.

Varble, Derek. *The Suez Crisis 1956*. London: Osprey, 2003.

Vinen, Richard. *Thatcher's Britain: The Politics and Social Upheaval of the 1980s*. London: Simon & Schuster, 2009.

Von Eschen, Penny M. *Black Americans and Anticolonialism, 1937–1957*. Ithaca and London: Cornell University Press, 1997.

Wainwright, A. Martin. *Inheritance of Empire: Britain, India, and the Balance of Power*, Westport, CT: Praeger Publishers, 1994.

Ward, Stuart. 'The End of Empire and the Fate of Britishness,' *History, Nationhood and the Question of Britain* (2004), p. 251.

(ed.). *British Culture and the End of Empire*. Manchester University Press, 2001.

Waters, Chris. '"Dark Strangers" in Our Midst: Discourses of Race and Nation in Britain, 1947–1963,' *Journal of British Studies*, 36: 2 (April 1997), pp. 207–238.

Webster, Wendy. *Englishness and Empire 1939–1965*. Oxford University Press, 2005.

Imagining Home: Gender, 'Race' and National Identity, 1945–64. London: UCL Press, 1998.

'"There'll Always be an England": Representations of Colonial Wars and Immigration, 1948–68,' *Journal of British Studies*, 40 (October 2001), pp. 557–584.

Wee, C. J. W.-L. *Culture, Empire, and the Question of Being Modern*. Lanham, MD: Lexington Books, 2003.

Weight, Richard, and Abigail Beach (eds.). *The Right to Belong: Citizenship and National Identity in Britain, 1930–1960*. London and New York: I. B. Tauris, 1998.

Weintraub, Stanley. *Disraeli: A Biography*. New York: Tuman Talley Books/ Dutton, 1993.

Whipple, Amy. 'Revisiting the "Rivers of Blood" Controversy: Letters to Enoch Powell,' *Journal of British Studies*, 46: 3 (July 2009), pp. 717–735.

Williams, Raymond. *The Long Revolution*. New York: Columbia University Press, 1961.

Wilson, A. N. *Our Times*. London: Hutchinson, 2008.

Winant, Howard. *The World is a Ghetto: Race and Democracy since World War II* (New York: Basic Books, 2001).

Winter, Jay. *Dreams of Peace and Freedom: Utopian Moments in the 20th Century*. New Haven, CT: Yale University Press, 2006.

Remembering War: The Great War between Memory and History in the Twentieth Century. New Haven, CT: Yale University Press, 2006.

Wood, John (ed.). *Powell and the 1970 Election*. Surrey: Elliot Right Way Books, 1970.

Woollacott, Angela. *Gender and Empire*. Basingstoke: Palgrave Macmillan, 2006.

Yergin, Daniel. *The Prize: The Epic Quest for Oil, Money, and Power*. New York: Simon & Schuster, 1991.

Young, Hugo. *This Blessed Plot: Britain and Europe from Churchill to Blair*. Basingstoke: Macmillan, 1998.

Young, John W. 'International Factors and the 1964 Election,' *Contemporary British History*, 21: 3 (2007), pp. 351–371.

Zizek, Slavoj. *The Fragile Absolute, Or, Why the Christian Heritage is Worth Fighting For*. London: Verso, 2000.

Zweiniger-Bargielowska, Ina (ed.), *Women in Twentieth-Century Britain: Economic, Social and Cultural Change*. London: Longman, 2001.

Index

Printed in Great Britain
by Amazon

24616354R00216